NUCLEAR WARRIORS

WITHDRAWN

NUCLEAR WARRIORS

Soldiers, Combat and Glasnost

Richard Holmes

JONATHAN CAPE
LONDON

First published 1991
© Richard Holmes 1991
Jonathan Cape, 20 Vauxhall Bridge Road, London SW1V 2SA

Richard Holmes has asserted his right
under the Copyright, Designs and Patents Act 1988
to be identified as the author of this work

A CIP catalogue record for this book
is available from the British Library

ISBN 0–224–02536–8

Typeset by Selectmove Ltd, London
Printed in Great Britain by Butler & Tanner Ltd, Frome and London

Contents

Introduction: The Warrior State   1

1 Occupation Gone?   11

2 The Nature of War   54

3 Field of Battle   98

4 The Real Weapon   143

5 The Nation's Mirror   190

6 Man under Authority   239

7 The Seeds of Time   286

Notes   295

Select Bibliography   325

Acknowledgments   329

Index   331

Illustrations

PLATES

between pages 120 and 121
1 German infantry and cavalry on manoeuvres, 1913
2 Exercise *Lionheart*, West Germany, 1984
3 Machine-gunners on Passchendaele Ridge, 1917
4 French soldiers in Indo-China, 1954
5 The Mi-24 *Gorbach*
6 The US Army's AH-64 *Apache*
7 Pershing II battlefield support missile, with a range of 1,300km
8 German 15cm howitzer, 1916

between pages 152 and 153
9 Spandau on the Western Front, 1915
10 US Army M-60 during Operation *Whitewing*
11 Fifteenth-century 'Gothic' armour for man and horse
12 The *Abrams* main battle tank
13 Training Chief Dingiswayo's Zulu regiment
14 Men of the Sheffield City Battalion drilling in 1914
15 Soviet army T-55 crews mount up
16 US Army helicopters touch down in Vietnam

between pages 200 and 201
17 Studying a large-scale model of Messines Ridge, 1917
18 BTR–60s of a Soviet Motor Rifle Division advance
19 Primitive anti-gas goggles and mouthpads, 1915
20 An American soldier in full protective outfit
21 *Boy's Own Paper*, 1918
22 Mass in the field, Indo-China
23 The part-legendary exploits of Agostina
24 A Soviet night fighter pilot

The author and publishers gratefully acknowledge the following picture sources – General Dynamics Land Systems Division: 12; Robert Hunt Library: 8, 9; Imperial War Museum: 3, 14, 17, 19; The Mansell Collection: 23; Charles Messenger: 2; Bruce Myles: 24; Novosti Press Agency: 15, 18; Popperfoto: 10; The Board of Trustees of the Royal Armouries: 11; SABC/Emil Wessels: 13; US Army: 6, 7, 20; US Marine Corps: 16.

Every effort has been made to obtain the necessary permissions with reference to copyright material, both illustrative and quoted; should there be any omissions in this respect we apologise and shall be pleased to make the appropriate acknowledgments in any future edition.

INTRODUCTION

The Warrior State

The long and malevolent shadow of war falls starkly across the
twentieth century. Looking back from our present vantage point
we might term it the age of the warrior state, a generalisation which
could stand alongside other historical shorthand like Renaissance,
Reformation, Enlightened Despotism and Industrial Revolution.
The anatomy of the warrior state seems alarmingly familiar. Its
armoured limbs swing across our television screens, its breath
scorches humanity from Beirut to Baghdad, and from Port Stanley
to the Panchir Valley. Its brain is dominated by a corporate logic
which subordinates the individual to the collective, and its appetite
seems insatiable. We are fascinated by its recent history: only the fact
that this book took longer than expected prevented me from firing
my own contribution to the stunning barrage of books marking the
fiftieth anniversary of the Second World War.

The maintenance of armed forces and the conduct of military
operations have been a dominant preoccupation of twentieth-century
governments. The two world wars gulped material resources at a
literally unprecedented rate. Since 1945 the armed equipoise which
has passed for peace has been scarcely less rapacious. In 1955 the
United States spent 10.5 per cent of its Gross Domestic Product
on defence. This figure had fallen to an average of 5.8 per cent
over the period 1971–9, but rose to 6.6 per cent in 1987. In 1987
Britain spent 4.7 per cent of its GDP on defence: £18.6 billion,
about a billion less than on health and education, respectively. These
figures pale into insignificance before the 17 per cent of Soviet Gross
National Product allocated to military use in 1987, and we should
not surprised that the fragile Soviet economy bent beneath such a
staggering burden.[1] Neither raw figures nor overall percentages are
much help to us as we struggle with the more mundane sums on
grocery bills or payslips, and, as we shall see later, there is in any

I

case a dispute over the real damage done to economies by military expenditure. For the moment, though, it will be enough simply to note the warrior state's predilection for swallowing treasure: it is no accident that Soviet defence industries earned the sobriquet 'metal eaters'.

Mere figures, too, do little justice to the human cost of war. Although the world's population has increased some 3.6 times since the beginning of the nineteenth century, war-related deaths in the same period have been multiplied by 22.4. Over 80 million human beings have died as a result of war this century.[2] The Gulf War between Iran and Iraq claimed at least a million Iranian and 400,000 Iraqi lives. It is easy for an Englishman to become misty-eyed about the effects of the First World War on British demography (indeed, I shall do so shortly), and to let distance and political antipathy help him ignore the analogous impact of war on the populations of Iran and Iraq, yet this bloodletting, with its contemporary Sommes and Passchendaeles, has gone on while we have lived our lives in the brisk world of the 1980s. Counting the dead simply shades in the tip of the iceberg, for to asess the impact of war on human beings we must include physical wounds – some transient, others disabling – and the psychological scars borne by combatants and civilians alike.

Just as the medieval knight – that individual embodiment of the warrior state – drew sustenance from the social and economic fabric of feudalism, so the warrior state itself embodies a complex and interventionist administrative, fiscal and economic apparatus. National experiences inevitably differ, but the pattern of growing state intervention promoted by the demands of war is a familiar one. In the British case, Kathleen Burk concludes that:

> The First World War caused striking changes in the organization and procedures of British government . . . However, the extensive system of government controls was very rapidly dismantled after the war. Yet the precedent had been set. The interventionist ministries were consciously chosen as models when controls were once more needed in the Second World War, and that time, the controls survived the war for a much longer period.[3]

The commonplace example underlines the general point. Opening hours of public houses, sharply restricted by the Defence of the Realm Act in 1915 in order to prevent munitions workers from spending longer at the bar than at the workbench, were not widely liberalised till 1988.

Of course the warrior state did not spring into being, fully armed, as the last seconds of the nineteenth century ticked away. Its genealogy stretches deep into history, with the influence of seventeenth-century Europe, Frederician Prussia and Revolutionary France, to name but three of its most prominent ancestors, still visible. The destruction wrought in parts of Europe during the Thirty Years War of 1618–48 merits comparison with the worst excesses of our own age. The impact on French society of the *levée en masse* of 1793 stands alongside that of conscription – military and industrial – on Britain, Germany and Russia in the Second World War. And if the sheer numbers involved in twentieth-century battles lend mournful length to their casualty lists, in terms of the proportion of participants killed or wounded few can equal the bloodbaths of Lake Trasimene (217 BC), Malplaquet (1709) or Antietam (1862).

If most of the twentieth-century warrior state's grim features can be seen on the faces of its ancestors, it still displays distinctive traits of its own. It is a widespread, almost universal, phenomenon: every continent is speckled with examples, from the military regimes of South America to the democracies of Europe and North America. As the century has gone on, it has marched as steadily through apparent peace as through actual war; and its towering size, sustained by its enormous appetite, sets it apart from its progenitors: in absolute terms, history has seen nothing to equal the size of twentieth-century armies; the quantity of weaponry at their disposal, and their destructive power – applied or latent. Finally, as the very term warrior state implies, the twentieth century has witnessed the large-scale blurring of distinctions between the civilian and the military, between the soldier who fights in battle and the worker who equips him, between defence industry *per se* and aerospace or computer research. Civilians have found themselves 'legitimate' targets in interstate war, as strategic bombing has scoured their homelands, and the inverted logic that enables the terrorist to see himself as a victim of 'state terrorism' encourages the use of car-bomb and bullet against civilian targets.

Our relationship with the warrior state is, to say the least, uneasy. We are eager to condemn its activities when they increase our tax-bill, impel our children into uniform, and splash film of ravaged townscapes or huddled refugees into our living-rooms. We applaud them when they protect us from invasion, enable us to suppress malignant political regimes, and help safeguard our societies from violent minorities within them. Although the military instrument has frequently been used in circumstances where greater honesty or industry (or simply better communications) could have resolved a dispute peacefully, there have been times – the Second World War prominent among them – when there was little alternative to military action and no substitute for victory. As we lambast the rapacity of defence budgets and the introspective preoccupations of armed forces, it is worth remembering that force of arms – with all its attendant horrors and injustices – stood between Europe and the long night of National Socialism.

The tribal machismo that leads, even in peacetime, to bloody noses, smashed windows and rampant sexuality, fuels our suspicion of the young men at the cutting edge of the warrior state. We retain all the ambivalence Rudyard Kipling described in 'Tommy':

> Yes, makin' mock o' uniforms that guard you while you sleep
> Is cheaper than them uniforms, an' they're starvation cheap
> An' hustlin' drunken soldiers when they're goin' large a bit
> Is five times better business than paradin' in full kit.
>   Then it's Tommy this, and Tommy that, an' 'Tommy, ow's yer soul?'
>   But it's 'Thin red line of 'eroes' when the drums begin to roll . . .

The refrain is a familiar one. There must, no doubt, be a barracks somewhere – but not, please God, near me. And if soldiers have to train, they should somehow contrive to do so in a way that will not mar beauty-spots, blow shell-holes in moorland, or leave ugly tank tracks across the heath.

Nuclear weapons have sharpened our ambivalence: we may approve of the fact that they have helped to deter war between the superpowers, but can only be horrified by the threat they pose to the fabric of our world. Where a previous generation sought a choice between Verdun and Auschwitz – between costly resistance and catastrophic capitulation – we have had to tread the path between Armageddon and Utopia. Thus far we have picked our way safely along the ledge, albeit at a heavy cost, both material and emotional. There is no guarantee that we shall continue to be as fortunate.

Marked changes in the climate of superpower relations in the late 1980s have already begun to unbuckle some of the warrior state's armour, and, barring accidents, we shall continue to see reductions in nuclear and conventional arms, as well as shrinking military budgets, in both the major alliances. But far from divorcing us from the warrior state, the political events of the 1980s have complicated our relationship. On the one hand, developments in the Soviet Union and Eastern Europe have been hailed as the dawn of a new era, when the world will be a safer place and armed forces will become increasingly irrelevant: an age when the warrior state will be a topic of historical reflection rather than present concern. On the other, realists or cynics, depending on one's viewpoint, urge caution. They warn that an economically robust Soviet Union might prove a more dangerous adversary than the present limping giant; point to fundamental strains within the Soviet state which may arrest or even reverse the move towards *perestroika*, and cite the bloody evidence of Tiananmen Square as evidence of the mutability of political affairs. Moreover, as Robert O'Neill warns us: 'It would be shallow thinking to attribute the essential causation of what we have come to call limited wars to superpower rivalry and the existence of nuclear weapons.[4] There are hard-tempered mainsprings of war in the Middle East and Africa; the Gulf Crisis, unresolved as this book went to press, proves the point all too well. The proliferation of guerrilla conflicts, many of which exist quite independently of superpower friction, suggests that even a successful East-West *rapprochement* will solve only one of the many serious problems facing humanity.

Armed forces, the Nuclear Warriors of this book's title, thus find themselves in an extraordinarily difficult position, arguably more difficult than at any time this century. Most, with their natural conservatism and tendency to think in terms of the worst possible case, have taken a cautious view of events. In his 1990 'Options for Change' study, the British Secretary of State for Defence sketched out relatively conservative proposals for halving the size of the British Army of the Rhine and making small reductions in the Royal Navy and the Royal Air Force. It is clear that there are more radical thinkers – in uniform as well as out of it – who seek a more profound functional reorganisation based on matching force structures more precisely to the political objectives which they might support, and who recognise that only a reassessment as fundamental as Haldane's great reform of 1906–8 will meet the changing demands

5

of the 1990s. American blueprints for change seem altogether more comprehensive, with plans for a reduction of about 500,000 in active-duty military personnel and restructuring of military forces into four components, an Atlantic force, a Pacific force, a contingency force capable of rapid deployment, and a long-range strategic nuclear force.

Despite the Gulf crisis, it will be impossible for defence ministries to remain deaf to loud demands for a 'peace dividend'. Defence spending, in East and West alike, has been threat-related for too long for the diminution of that threat not to have a rapid effect. Like it or not, armed forces will be compelled to adjust to changing circumstances, and their continued emphasis on the uncertainty of international politics will simply fuel accusations that self-interest or bureaucratic inertia lie at the heart of their resistance to change. There exists the very real possibility that armed forces, on both sides of what used to be the iron curtain, will be subject to unstructured disarmament – to the haphazard cancellation of procurement programmes here, and the reduction of force levels there, without profound and thoroughgoing review of the purposes for which those forces exist. Hardly a quality newspaper – on either side of the Atlantic – has shirked from entering the fray with serious reflection on the future shape of armed forces. Popular journalism, on screen and in print, has had a field day, and the redeployment of money currently spent on defence has become little less than an article of faith.

The dilapidation of alliances as the cement of threat looses its adhesion will complicate the process. In NATO's case, Germany's preparedness to act as the garrison-town for the land forces of the alliance – with all that it means in terms of armoured regiments in beet-fields, low-flying aircraft, and lager-filled young men 'goin' large a bit' in Paderborn on a Saturday night – is fast evaporating. And green politics – which will colour the first decades of the twenty-first century just as the warrior state dominated the majority of the twentieth – will also create difficulties. Even if the utopian desire of the extreme Greens for general disarmament does not commend itself widely to electorates, the fact that most major European political parties will be encouraged to stitch threads of green into their programmes in an effort to hijack the environmentalist vote will encourage high-profile but unstructured tinkering with armed forces. All this may gratify those who see the warrior state as a universal bogey-man, responsible for many of the world's ills, but it will

6

neither represent a logical response to an evolving political situation, nor, in itself, make for a safer world.

The warrior state would have problems enough even if its motive power had not begun to falter. Shortage of manpower, the result partly of the demographic downturn into which much of the northern hemisphere is descending, and partly of dissatisfaction with terms and conditions of military service, threatens to impose unstructured disarmament of its own by spontaneous cuts in force levels. Indeed, we may expect to see a marriage of convenience between the diminution of the threat and manpower shortages, as governments announce reductions which conveniently match their failure to recruit soldiers.

There is also widespread concern over the way that armies go about their business, inspired by the fear that they have become excessively bureaucratic, infatuated with expensive (and often unreliable) technology, and filled with officers whose principal aim is to get promoted. Although elements of this concern can be perceived in almost every major army, the dispute is at its fiercest in the United States, where the 'military reform debate' looks set to run and run. As Samuel P. Huntington, one of the founding fathers of military sociology, has observed, 'the reformers almost totally eschew any discussion of nuclear strategy and nuclear weapons'.[5] In contrast, the European defence debate has centred upon the possession and use of nuclear weapons. The misfortunes of Britain's *Trident* programme are front-page news, while the fact that British military doctrine has been comprehensively overhauled has attracted infinitely less attention.

The relationship between firepower-heavy attritional operational doctrine and fast-moving manoeuvre doctrine forms another facet of the military reform debate. The proliferation of firepower and the continuing vulnerability of flesh and psyche alike on the late twentieth-century battlefield has nerved yet another assault on the warrior state. Battle, runs this argument, can reach such a pitch of intensity as to become intolerable to its participants. There is therefore little point in maintaining a military apparatus largely devoted to fighting high-intensity battle as this is a type of warfare that simply cannot be fought. The fact that a perceived need to be prepared to fight high-intensity battle encourages the stockpiling of costly and complex weapons systems, many of which have a poor track-record even in the piping times of peace, casts further doubt upon its usefulness: indeed, the rapidly increasing costs of military equipment would raise serious doubts about the viability of technology-hungry armies even if military budgets increased – which they will not.

This book is about soldiers and combat in a time of change and challenge. One of the problems facing students of the defence debate is that many of the works on it are written (by accident or design) in armour-plated prose, impenetrable to outsiders. To help the reader find his way through this book, I have erected as many signposts as possible, and, at this early stage, a map of the way ahead might make the journey less perplexing.

In general the book starts with large issues and gradually concentrates on smaller ones. Chapter 1 tells the reader something about my own approach to the subject, for my opinions are filtered through background and experience, and it would be wrong to claim an objectivity which the emotional luggage of twenty years as a professional historian and occasional soldier may so easily have bent. The chapter goes on to address the central nuclear balance, concluding that a good deal of thorny underbrush has grown up around the hard logic of nuclear deterrence, and that if we cannot disinvent the nuclear weapon, we should reduce our reliance on it to the absolute minimum.

It is attractive, but unwise, to discuss nuclear weapons in purely practical terms, quite apart from moral considerations: the third section of the chapter reviews the morality of armed conflict, for without a robust moral framework armies cannot expect to meet the present challenge with any confidence. Finally, the chapter considers the causes of war, concluding that while the accession of an apparently benevolent Russian leader may have weakened the mainspring for one sort of conflict others, no less powerful, remain.

Chapter 2 opens by examining the nature of modern armed conflict, with its wide scales of activity and intensity. It then reflects on the levels of military action – the strategic, operational and tactical – and the function of battle. Like many military historians I am preoccupied with battle, but acknowledge the warnings, most recently expressed in Victor Davis Hanson's *The Western Way of War*, that such emphasis can prove delusive.[6] Indeed, losing battles – or even losing wars – may be less decisive than we care to imagine, and it is worth asking whether changes in the meaning of victory are not among the profoundest to affect war over the past two centuries. A visitor from another planet, asked to compare the prosperous elegance of Munich or Stuttgart with the squalid urban neglect in parts of Britain or North America, might feel inclined to wonder just who surrendered on Luneburg Heath in 1945. The chapter concludes with an assessment of the part played by technology in war, its conclusions – in favour of simple, robust 'gothic' weapon systems rather than elaborate and costly 'baroque' ones – lending weight to the accusation that I am a military Luddite:

Lu'ddite *n.* & *a.* (Member) of bands of English artisans (1811–16) who raised riots for the destruction of machinery; (person) similarly engaged in seeking to obstruct progress. [perh. f. Ned *Lud*, insane person who destroyed two stocking-frames about 1779 . . .][7]

The focus of Chapter 3 is narrower, and it considers the problems of assessing the shape of future war and producing doctrine to fight it. This has never been an easy task, and the dilution of yesterday's aggressive certainties make it even harder as the century spins to its close. Chapter 4 has an even narrower concern, with the soldiers at the coal face of military action, who manipulate the technology, fight, suffer and die. It examines ways in which the changing nature of battle and developments in Western society have combined to influence combat performance. The relationship between armies and the societies they spring from and defend is the subject of Chapter 5. Command in peace and war is the topic of Chapter 6, and the impact of the information revolution – the quietest but most profound revolution of the century – upon military command looms especially large. It is fruitless to expect a sharp division of neat subjects into concept-tight chapters. Technology, for instance, is considered at length in Chapter 2, but bubbles up elsewhere – for example in Chapter 6, which must of necessity compare the roles of brain cell and microchip. After all, the real world shuns narrow definitions, and attempting to impose them on a subject as varied as this would do violence to the whole.

Some matters of interest have been excluded. Arms reduction negotiations, alliance politics, and the detailed structure of high commands are not considered in detail, although all, in their way, are relevant to the subject. The first two are more properly the concern of the political scientist than the military historian, though the evidence of history suggests that alliances will indeed become less cohesive as their *raison d'être* fades. The latter omission reflects my limited ability to tolerate endless wiring diagrams of defence ministries: we may hope, however, that the political and economic constraints of the 1990s will encourage more functionalism and fewer creaking single-service empires.

My concerns are unashamedly with the English-speaking world, and with armies in particular rather than armed forces in general – though my examples come from every continent and from two thousand years of history. There are admittedly dangers in seeking universal parallels: it is difficult enough to compare the world's two greatest English-speaking armies which seem superficially so similar but are in fact so different. Some will doubt whether contemporary events are a proper field for the historian, and will question the academic rigour of discussing German defensive doctrine in 1917 and the role of the armed helicopter in the same book. I leave them to the dozens of respectable monographs, thickly garnished with footnotes, which bore deeply into every aspect of the subject, and hope that they emerge wiser. Why write the book now? Why not wait until the situation has become clearer? Because it is precisely now that armies, and the societies which employ them, must set their agendas. The situation may clear less rapidly than we hope, and in the meantime hard decisions – specifically in terms of recruitment and equipment procurement – must be taken. Carrying on with the illusion of business as usual simply increases the risk of unstructured disarmament, of salami slicing which will bring no favours to armies or states. And history? Why, that began this morning, and without knowing where we have come from it is hard to see where we might be going: and that, as the warrior state takes what might be its last faltering strides, is more important now than ever.

I

Occupation Gone?

Farewell the plumed troop and the big wars
That make ambition virtue! O, farewell!
Farewell the neighing steed and the shrill trump,
The spirit-stirring drum, the ear-piercing fife,
The royal banner, and all quality,
Pride, pomp and circumstance of glorious war!
And, O you mortal engines, whose rude throats
The immortal Jove's dread clamours counterfeit,
Farewell! Othello's occupation's gone!

Shakespeare, *Othello*

I am a child of the nuclear age in the most literal sense, conceived within days of the explosion of the first atomic bomb over Hiroshima on 6 August 1945. The evidence of war was never far distant as I grew up in English Midlands scarred by the attentions of the *Luftwaffe*, and marked as deeply if less visibly by memories of an earlier war, when the local Territorial battalion had slogged on with the 46th Division from disaster at Gommecourt in 1916 to triumph at Riqueval two years later. There had been few professional soldiers in my family, but enough relatives and friends had been swept into uniform for talk of Alamein and Caen to arouse a boy's already ambivalent interest in war. It was soon clear that those who had most to remember often had least to say: as John Guilmartin reminds us: 'Them that know ain't talking, and them that are talking don't know.'[1] My father rarely spoke of the blitz, and became uncharacteristically sharp when pressed to do so: a great-uncle kept his memories of Mons and the Ancre to himself, but once scandalised a convivial family gathering at Christmas by singing:

We don't give a bugger for old von Kluck
and all his bloomin' Mausers . . .

It was some years before I read the text of the song and realised that, port or no, he had spared us the full majesty of the rhyme.

The state of the world in the 1950s gave war a different dimension. We listened to news of the Korean War on the radio, though a household stiffened by the bad news of 1940–2 could take even the destruction of a British battalion on the Imjin River in its stride. In any case, the Gloucesters' last stand fitted comfortably into the familiar iconography of Victorian prints in the hall, with the 24th Regiment swamped by the Zulu tide at Isandalwana or the last survivors clustered round the colours of the 66th at Maiwand.

But there was something more sinister abroad as the chill of future war settled on to my landscape: when I discovered Tolkien I knew what 'the drums in the deep' below the mines of Moria sounded like. First they were 'atomic bombs', then 'nuclear weapons', and no amount of centrefold drawings in my *Eagle* comic could remove a disturbing sense of threat. When, at the time of the Cuban missile crisis in 1962, I came home for the weekend from boarding school to discover that the cupboard below the stable stairs had been converted into an air-raid shelter, I was really shaken to find that my pipe-smoking, phlegmatic, infinitely wise father took it so seriously. Uncle Ernest's stories of his air-sea rescue launch, or the village policeman's musings on Shermans in the *bocage* were one thing: this was quite another.

The same ambivalence characterised my schoolmasters' reflections on their military service. Although some had enjoyed a 'good war', there were levels of recollection to which small boys were not party. Despite (or maybe because of) this reticence I showed an early interest in military history, only to be checked abruptly by a master who suggested that one should not study what one had not experienced: for him this aspect of the past was emphatically another country whose frontiers were not easily crossed. Undeterred by his warning, I pressed on, through a first degree at Cambridge and research at Northern Illinois, to spend five years working on the French Army of the Second Empire. There, too, there were inconsistencies: however clinically I argued that there was good and sufficient reason for examining the French military background to the Franco-Prussian

War, I was impelled by concerns as emotional as academic. Perhaps the blood of my Huguenot ancestors was thicker than I knew; perhaps an early glimpse of those dusty *cuirassiers* in the then unmodernised *Musée de l'Armée* in Paris had struck a resonant chord, or perhaps Philip Guedalla's haunting prose in *The Two Marshals* had inspired a nostalgic affection for that army of red trousers and wasted gallantry and for that unlovely part of Lorraine 'between the spires of Metz and the bare uplands of Gravelotte'.

My own approach to the study of military history has always been inconsistent, pulled one way by the appeal of the most passionate drama of all, and another by utter horror of what goes on at the sharp end of war.

Early interest in deeds of derring-do and subsequent concern for operational narrative or military organisation increasingly failed to veil my concern for the human face of war. The business of being a military historian brings one into almost daily contact with harrowing reading, and my professional armour has never been strong enough to protect me from its darts. Looking back, I suspect that this uneasiness was always more pronounced than I recognised at the time. When weighing my earliest memories in the process of writing this book, I was surprised to discover that I could remember the names of the two officers who headed the list of a dozen men from the village I grew up in who had perished in the First World War. I have not been in the church that houses their memorial for thirty years, but when I tested recollection against *Officers Died in the Great War*, I found not only that the imprint was as clear as I thought, but that the example makes my point perfectly.

Lieutenant St George Swaine Showers was a Special Reserve officer (giving an immediate pull of affection to a reservist like myself) who earned two mentions in his Regimental History. The first was when he 'organised the battalion front line for resistance to a possible counter-attack' at Roeux, near Arras, in May 1917. His last appearance was in September that year when 2nd Battalion The Essex Regiment mounted a raid with the familiar purpose of killing and capturing as many Germans as possible 'with a view to identifying enemy formations' and, history adds more sourly, giving offensive support to operations further north, where the fighting below Passchendaele gasped on in the mud. All seven officers involved were killed or wounded, though we shall never know whether it was machine-gun or trench mortar – or, less probably, bomb, bayonet or rifle-butt – that did for young Showers.

Second-Lieutenant Gerald Wellesley Piggott, heir to Blackmoor Hall, had followed his father into the army from Wellington College and the Royal Military Academy. He transferred from his county regiment to the Royal Field Artillery, and it was on 127th Battery's gun-line near Brielen that German shrapnel found him during the Second Battle of Ypres in 1915: he died of wounds in a field hospital. His battery commander, in a classic lament for a dead subaltern, wrote: '. . . he was very keen and had plenty of pluck'.[2]

This one memorial illuminates so many of the points made by J.M. Winter in his study of the lost generation: the 'staggering burden' of loss borne by men under thirty, the disproportionate distribution of casualties between officers and men, and the slaughter of social elites.[3] It goes much further should we chart the spread of T.E. Lawrence's 'rings of sorrow' across this one small English village, its blighted cottages with husbands or sons gone and a big house with the life blown out of it.

Almost any village war memorial delivers its own silent shock, although a few underline the capricious nature of war by celebrating safe returns: every one of the twenty-five men from Coln Rogers in Gloucestershire who went to the war was spared – and so, adds their commemorative plaque, was Doris Barton of the Voluntary Aid Detachment. Such mercy is rare. Many families have the melancholy distinction of earning several mentions. At one social extreme, the Lees, father and son, died in the same unit on the same day on the Somme, one as a sergeant and the other as a corporal, and lie buried in the same cemetery. At the other, the fate of the Cawleys of Berrington Hall in Herefordshire is almost as sombre. A photograph shows Lord Cawley and his four sons in front of the Hall's handsome red sandstone portico before a day out with the North Herefordshire hunt in 1908. Three of the young men were dead ten years later. Stephen, a regular major in the 20th Hussars, died among the cornstooks at Néry in 1914 when L Battery Royal Horse Artillery made its enduring mark on British military history. Harold's seat in the House of Commons did not dissuade him from joining a New Army Battalion of the Manchester Regiment: he was killed as a captain at Gallipoli. Oswald, a Member of Parliament like his brother, clattered off with the Shropshire Yeomanry, and died at Merville, near Armentières, in the last year of the war. The eldest son survived to inherit the house and the barony, but *his* third son was killed serving with the King's Shropshire Light Infantry in Tunisia in 1943.

Multiply the grief ten thousandfold for England alone, with 723,000 war deaths. Spread it to the Beauce and Burgundy (1,327,000 French dead), to Lower Saxony and Pomerania (2,037,000 Germans) to the Ukraine and Byelorussia (1,811,000 Russians), from the Adige (578,000 Italians) to Anatolia (804,000 Turks), and across the Atlantic to New Brunswick and Manitoba (61,000 Canadians), New Jersey and Arkansas (114,000 Americans) and we begin to count the cost of a single war: 9,450,000 combatants died, and to this must be added thousands killed by war-related illness.[4] Western readers, so often brought up with the notion of the First World War as *the* killer, may care to reflect on Russian casualties in the Second World War. Some twenty million Russians perished, about one in four of the population, compared with about one in 150 in the United States and 1 in 50 in Britain. Leningrad alone lost perhaps 1,300,000 of its citizens, about as many as were killed by atomic bombs dropped on Hiroshima and Nagasaki.[5]

The act of commemoration is important, helping bereaved and survivors alike to put loss and suffering into context. On a greater scale, memorials and cemeteries form 'the symbolic tomb of an ideal' or perhaps act as focus for national reconciliation and understanding, like the Vietnam memorial in Washington.[6] They also emphasise the fact that death is no respecter of persons: Patton lies among 6,000 men of his 3rd Army in the American Military Cemetery at Hamm, next to Pfc John Hrzywarn of Detroit; Lieutenant-General R.G. Broadwood, killed commanding a British division in 1917, left instructions that he was to be buried between a subaltern and a private soldier.[7] Yet just as statistics blunt the edge of human suffering, so names graven in stone lend sharp-edged dignity to death in battle. Paul Fussell wrote of the 'almost unendurably ironic peacefulness' of First World War cemeteries, while William Manchester regretted that such things were 'essentially counterfeit . . . they are usually beautiful and in good taste, whereas combat is neither'.[8]

It is easy to step from mawkish sentimentality to ghoulish realism when considering death in battle, but consider it we must, for it is what converts the young men in sepia portraits to lists on stone above Omaha beach, on the Menin Gate or the soaring arch at Thiepval. We must imagine them as George Hennell saw them in the breach at Badajoz in April 1812:

15

There they lay, one upon the other, two or three deep, many in the ditch half in and half out of the water. In coming out you were obliged to tread on many. I went two or three times to the town, the last time the smell was horrible. You were continually treading upon feet or heads.[9]

Or as a Belgian artillery officer saw them near Liège in 1914:

On both sides of the winding road bodies lay in the ditch. A little chasseur, quite a child, not yet twenty, was among them, almost kneeling on the bank with his head hanging down, so that he looked as if he was sobbing. Opposite him lay a man of the reserve class, with grey hair and clutching hands. All along it was the same spectacle. Bodies; still more bodies. On their backs, their arms crossed, mouths open, their skulls smashed, their wounds bleeding.[10]

Or as Lieutenant John Glubb found them near Armentières in 1915:

the troops suffered heavily and were too tired to bury their dead. Many of them were merely trampled into the floor of the trench, where they were soon lost in mud and water. We have been digging out a lot of these trenches again, and we are constantly coming upon corpses. They are pretty well decomposed, but a pickaxe brings up chips of bone and rags of clothing. The rest is putrid grey matter.[11]

Numbers submerge personality. Michael Herr found an essential truth by writing of 'the total impersonality of group death', and we must look harder at the individuals who make up war's jetsam.[12] Homer's descriptions of death in close-quarter battle would have been familiar to combat veterans right up to the seventeenth century, when firearms began to replaced edged weapons as the main casualty-producer, and 'villainous saltpetre', not human muscle, drove death home.

Adamas tried to save himself by retiring among his men. But Meriones followed him as he withdrew and caught him with his lance half-way between the navel and the privy parts, the most painful spot in which a wretched soldier can be struck. There the weapon went home, and Adamas collapsing writhed around it, as a bull twists about when the herdsmen have caught and roped him in the hills and bring him in against his will. Thus the stricken warrior writhed, but not for long – only till the lord Meriones came up and pulled the spear out of his flesh. Then night descended on his eyes.[13]

The musket brought a different sort of death, although technical limitations, linear tactics and frenzied excitement among combatants meant that, if combat was generally impersonal as men fired into the smoke-shrouded ranks opposing them, death often came from very close range:

a bayonet went through between my side and clothes, to my knapsack, which stopped its progress. The Frenchman to whom the bayonet belonged fell, pierced by a musket ball from my rear-rank man. While freeing myself from the bayonet, a ball took off part of my right shoulder wing and killed my rear-rank man, who fell upon me.[14]

Sometimes the greater precision of the rifle converted life to death in the twinkling of an eye, as it did to Major Billy Congreve, near Longueval on the Somme in 1916. This brave and inspiring young staff officer was talking to a sergeant in a front-line trench, congratulating him on the progress of work: 'Just as he said the word "work" he was hit. He stood for half a second and then collapsed. He never moved or spoke, and he was dead in a few seconds.'[15] On other occasions the bullet was crueller. Guy Sajer, an Alsatian serving with the Germans on the Eastern front, saw his close friend Ernst Neubach fatally wounded:

He must have been hit in the lower jaw. His teeth were mixed with fragments of bone, and through the gore I could see the muscles of his face contracting, moving what was left of his features.[16]

With the murderously effective artillery of the twentieth century came the most capricious and dehumanising death of all, the limb-severing, body-smashing death delivered by the shell.

17

Sergeant Sobczynski had lost both legs, high up, close to the crotch. We got belts and tried to put tourniquets around the stumps. I was working on one, the CO was trying to get a belt round the other one, but it kept slipping off . . . I lit one [cigarette] and put it in his mouth. He forced himself up on both elbows and looked down. He could see both legs were gone. He said. 'Bad, ain't it, doc?' He died real quick. [17]

Nor should we forget the murdered environment in which men fight. Squalor – from excrement where men paused in urgent need, trampled grass and crops, smashed fences, burned farm-buildings and slaughtered beasts – was a feature of the pre-industrial battlefield, even before we consider the dead, often half-stripped and bootless, and the litter of discarded and broken weapons, personal effects and paper – letters, news-sheets, orders. The addition of artillery, with the products of the teeming factories of the industrial age ploughed into the earth through the intermediary of the gun, pressed home the assault upon nature and artifice alike. Captain J.E. Crombie of the Gordon Highlanders passed through Arras in March 1917, and found:

the long narrow ribbon of street utterly silent, and the walls, with nothing but ruin behind them, aslant and tottering, till it seemed that a push with your hand would overset them . . . It is these ghastly, sightless, purposeless walls that catch you, and the silence. [18]

Military history might have provided me with a refuge had I been able to insulate myself from what I chronicled, almost as a medical historian might describe an operation before the invention of anaesthetic, secure in the knowledge that the pattern of events could never recur. But the repetitious character of war inspired no such confidence. Perhaps one gains some comfort from mumbling the ritual lament for a humanity which has put itself at the same old fence so often, adding the fervent hope that it will not happen again, and I do it often enough. Here again the theory of the reading-room meets the reality of daily life. I spent much of my career at Sandhurst, teaching military history to officer cadets and young officers whose professional careers were likely to contain events similar to those we discussed. The risks they ran grew increasingly apparent as Oman,

Northern Ireland and then the Falklands imposed their burden of casualties: it was almost as if I was teaching Showers and Piggott.

Finally, there was my own military persona. I enlisted into the Territorial Army at the age of eighteen. A varied career has taken me from private soldier to colonel, and has included command of an infantry battalion full-time for two and a half years. While I would not wish to make too much of this, there is no doubt that the experience has helped shape my own practice of military history. It has given me a deep and lasting affection for soldiers, and there is scarcely a day when it does not help remind me of the truth of Clausewitz's assertion that:

> If no one had the right to give his views on military operations except when he is frozen, or faint from heat and thirst, or depressed from privation and fatigue, objective and accurate views would be even rarer than they are. But they would at least be subjectively valid, for the speaker's experience would precisely determine his judgement.[19]

Three years ago I was plodding across the Welsh mountains with my battalion, its soldiers proving that an infantryman is best defined as something to hang things on. Bent like a beggar under my pack, with the rain in my face and the muscled shoulder of Crychan Forest mocking me on the horizon, knowledge of how near I was to my own physical limits reminded me forcibly of Clausewitz's stricture. Just as a similar experience almost a decade before had induced me to examine the power and mechanism of the individual soldier across history, so this combined with a bout of intense study on the operational level of modern war to make me ask myself just how we would cope with the sort of conflict to which the miscalculations of statesmen, pressures of nationalism, or thirst for resouces might consign us.

Or might they not? Even then, long before the avalanche of change had swept across Eastern Europe, burying the old dogmas beneath it, it seemed probable that familiar bets were no longer safe. Were Soviet motor riflemen, clearly visible beneath the veneer of 'Orange Forces' in the exercise instruction, really our most likely adversaries? Indeed, were there any real adversaries at all, or were we simply picking out the steps of a ritual dance, a dance of death for Showers and Piggott, but perhaps little more than an antiquarian survival for Holmes? Given that I had many other useful (and largely dry) things to do with my time, I needed to think through the rationale of my own contribution to the Warrior State.

I had all the buzzwords, understood the acronyms, and was so immersed in the professional literature that the appearance of another *Military Affairs* article on Operational Art filled me with a profound sense of *déjà vu*. If I deferred to my regular comrades' ability to hurl armoured brigades about the North German Plain, I was less prepared to accept that they knew their soldiers any better than I knew mine, and certain they could not love them more. Many of my regular friends, for all their brisk exteriors, were no less ambivalent about the nature of war than I was. We were all, to a greater or lesser degree, servants of war in the nuclear age, with doubts, fears, ambitions, affections and values that sometimes sat uneasily beneath its shadows. In our youths we may have sought the opportunity to prove something to ourselves by hazarding our persons, and entertained secret fantasies about winning decorations and saving wounded comrades. By the time we had reached the plateau of our middle years it was overwhelmingly clear, even if it had not been so before, that war was squalid, wasteful, and seldom the best way of attaining a political objective. But it was equally clear that something ugly hung over the land to the east of Brunswick, and that, doubts or uncertainties apart, democracy was worth preserving by treasure at best and blood at worst. Moreover, it seemed that there was a close-coupled relationship between the two, as my father's generation was rarely slow to point out, for in 1940–1 it had paid the human price of underfunded defence.

Fashionable sterotypes cast professional soldiers in simply defined roles. There is often the easy assumption that they believe war is a good thing, seek to maintain high levels of defence expenditure regardless of their social cost, and resist reductions in the defence establishment primarily because their own promotion prospects would suffer. In short, that they will resolutely oppose the radical reductions in force levels which the developing political situation seems likely to demand. Yet in reality there is much uncertainty here, just as there is about the nature of war. 'Oh Lord,' quipped one good friend, 'give us agreement in the CFE [Conventional Forces in Europe] negotiations, but don't give it until I've made brigadier.' The ambivalence stems in part from a genuine (and, as we shall see, well-founded) suspicion that all sorts of war have not suddenly become impossible simply because of the momentous events in the Soviet

Union and Eastern Europe. It also arises from the fear that armies will be used as political footballs, kicked about for short-term gain by politicians who may fail to define long-term strategies to which their armed forces should be shaped. Both pressures tend to produce more collective conservatism than individual officers would recognise as wise, but without a clear agenda, which can only be agreed upon by the honest interaction of soldiers and civilians, this conservatism will prove hard to shake.

In *Firing Line* I looked back at the behaviour of the soldier on the battlefields of history. This book looks forward, to examine the Nuclear Warriors, the men who will fight on the battlefields of the next quarter-century, and will form the armies of an age indelibly coloured by the ramifications of *glasnost*. It would be impertinent to suggest that it can set the agenda for any particular army, still less to do so for all those in the northern hemisphere. But it does attempt to list the items which must form part of the military agenda for the nineties.

Rummaging about in the banalities of my own life is neither mere self-indulgence nor an attempt to persuade the reader I am endowed with unique insight. It is an early admission that – like any historian, no matter how objective he strives to be – I am a creature of preconceptions and prejudices, experience and affections.

And history is important. Bernard Brodie wrote, in his introduction to Michael Howard and Peter Paret's edition of Clausewitz's *On War*, that:

> Our own generation is unique, but sadly so, in producing a school of thinkers who are allegedly experts in military strategy and who are certainly specialists in military studies but who know virtually nothing of military history . . . Yet the only empirical data we have about how people conduct war and behave under its stresses is our experience with it in the past, however much we have to make adjustments for subsequent changes in conditions.[20]

Or, as Clausewitz himself tells us: 'Historical examples clarify everything and also provide the best kind of proof in the empirical sciences. This is particularly true of the art of war.'[21] Those who doubt the application of Clausewitz, a creature of the horse and musket age, to the era of the armed helicopter and the anti-tank guided missile, would profit from reading Martin van Creveld's 'The Eternal

Clausewitz'; they might also note the paucity of modern thinkers who have addressed war with Clausewitz's breadth and penetration.[22]

There must be more to a study of men in future battle than simply stretching battlefield history forwards. Armies have mainlined on the hard drug of technology too avidly for it not to loom large in this book. We cannot follow the 'military specialists' of the generation that drew up the blueprints for the First World War by ignoring the political dimension; nor should we don the blinkers that prevent us from looking at the moral issues that military men, and the societies which employ them, should confront resolutely. Even before we consider performance in battle, we must put that battle into context, discuss the doctrines and equipment that influence its character, and go on to consider the nature of the armies that may fight it and the leaders responsible for its conduct.

All this, of course, may make me few friends at either political extreme. My concern for difficult moral issues, and suggestion that armies must become smaller and less technology-hungry will not please some, who will detect limp-wristed liberalism. My conviction that the military instrument retains utility into the twenty-first century, *glasnost* notwithstanding, will alarm others, who will ascribe to me sinister, militaristic values. The fact that I see the flak curling in from both flanks as I write gives me a perverse satisfaction: after all, I am a Nuclear Warrior myself.

The New Theology

As Lawrence Freedman points out, 'the quest for a nuclear strategy that can serve definite political objectives without triggering a holocaust has occupied some of the best minds of our time.'[23] Nuclear strategy is to the late twentieth century what theology was to the Middle Ages. It has exercised the brains of many capable and honourable men (and as many who are less clever and less objective), and spawned orthodoxies and heresies as complex as those that engaged Aquinas or Duns Scotus, Arminius or Gomarus. It is as much about belief as about quantifiable fact, and death by fire is the price of error. Passionate conviction denies opponents the moral authority to speak, and a contradictory viewpoint marks its holder as a sinner. Much literature is unintelligible to all but a few acolytes, and an academic obsession with minutiae (precise balances of forces, the capabilities of different hardware, and how many angels can sit on the head of a pin) makes understanding no easier. Some new prophets arise to castigate the original sin of the existing world-order or offer appealing mantras which guarantee salvation: Protest and Survive, Freeze the Arms Race. Others pursue a place – a chair here, a research contract there – with a zeal unequalled since eighteenth-century Anglican churchmen sought bishops' mitres and canons' stalls. The gap between academic theologian and parish priest is immense, as General Sir John Hackett recognised when complaining about the growth of strategic analysis. 'These military metaphysicians', he declared, 'shy like the Devil from holy water at being introduced to a practitioner . . . they don't like talking to people who have to do it, because sometimes their feet are invited back to earth and that's a very uncomfortable position for a military metaphysician.'[24]

For the past quarter-century we have felt ourselves to be living on the eve of Armageddon, just as our medieval ancestors believed that the second coming was at hand: the flash of the nuclear explosion has replaced the flames of hell in our imagination. In May 1980 a National Opinion Poll in Britain found that 65 per cent of those interviewed expected nuclear war in their lifetime, and a year later 65 per cent thought that the prospects for world peace were worse than a year before. An American Gallup poll in September 1981 established that 68 per cent of interviewees believed that an all-out nuclear war between the United States and Russia was possible – their replies ranged from 'almost certain' to 'some chance'. A staggering 90 per cent believed that their own chances of survival were at best 'just 50–50'.[25] Small wonder that the East German novelist Christa Wolff called our time *der Vorkrieg*, the prelude to war, and the word *Kriegsstimmung,* war-mood, perfectly captured the feeling of the age.

The issue of nuclear war forced its way into almost every aspect of our life. Modern music was affected: A *Times* article described the 'almost Tallis-like, polyphony [which] conjures the image of a derelict landscape after the holocaust', and added that Stockhausen has said that he is 'composing music for the apocaplypse'. Film and literature too are pervasively irradiated, with a 'Technological Manichaeanism' of polarised images in the cosmic romance.[26] The vision of a post-apocalypse world, with survivors living in a blasted cityscape with endemic gang warfare or the new feudalism of the remote countryside, has become commonplace. So commonplace, perhaps, that it has lost part of its ability to shock. 'The danger is that the more we read and learn about war, particularly nuclear war,' wrote James Adams, 'the idea becomes, if not acceptable, certainly imbued with a sense of inevitability.'[27]

Some of the products of the genre are powerfully convincing: *Threads* and *The Day After*, *The Fate of the Earth* and *When The Wind Blows* have, in their different ways, contributed to a rising tide of revulsion against nuclear weapons. Martin Amis's collection of short stories, *Einstein's Monsters*, combines marvellous writing and the irrefutable logic of desire to avert a nuclear war with sheer demonology and unprovable assertions: we are back among the stakes and firewood of the *auto-da-fé*. The other side of the house is scarcely more tolerant. Opposing nuclear weapons weakens their deterrent value, runs the argument, because the credibility of their owner's will-power is undermined: opposition to nuclear weapons may paradoxically make nuclear war more likely. This not unreasonable claim slips easily into an attack on the immaturity (at best) or treason (at worst) of the bomb's opponents. At the very end of the spectrum, End Time theology closes the loop by looking at the bomb as part of God's plan for Armageddon, and Survivalists prepare themselves for the challenge of 'the culling'.[28]

Now, with all the suddenness of Paul's conversion on the road to Damascus, salvation seems at hand: perhaps the flames of hell do not await us. The partial success of nuclear arms reduction talks, coupled with the dramatic reduction in East-West tension as a result of the initiatives of Mikhail Gorbachev, has sustantially reduced the level of fear, and the Armenian earthquake has fostered ties of sympathy. A new, hopeful spirit is abroad, and in late 1988 polls of West German public opinion suggested that belief in the likelihood of war had been swamped by confidence in its disappearance. But just as earlier fears may have been liars, so our new hopes may be dupes. The greatly reduced possibility of war between the superpowers must be influenced by the successful continuation of Gorbachev's internal reforms, and the immense difficulties facing him may inspire more empathy than confidence. The dangers of nuclear accident and nuclear proliferation remain profoundly disturbing, all the more so because nuclear weapons now exist in areas where deep-seated conflicts already exist and circumstances do not always encourage mature reflection.

The very existence of nuclear weapons raises important questions about the nature and probability of war, and thus of the shape of the battlefield and the frequency of combat. Central to the issue is the question of whether nuclear weapons are really weapons in the usual sense of the word, or simply instruments whose use means that the purpose of their existence has failed. Supporters of nuclear deterrence point out that there has been no war between the superpowers despite periods of high tension, and attribute this to the existence of nuclear weapons, which make the risks of war too great to be worth any possible gains. This is an attractive but ultimately unprovable case, for we cannot be sure that there would indeed have been a major war had it not been for nuclear weapons: even the role played by American 'atomic diplomacy' in bringing about an armistice in Korea remains disputed. One authority suggests that, at the most, 'signals of a nuclear possibility were a reinforcement to Chinese preferences already established before those signals were conveyed', while another believes that 'covert but quite explicit' threats of nuclear escalation broke the deadlock.[29]

What is more certain is that a major power which does not possess nuclear weapons when its principal rival does is running the risk of nuclear blackmail, and that a total disinvention of nuclear arms is unrealistic. It is less easy to see logic in the vertical proliferation of nuclear weapons to the point where each superpower has the ability to destroy its rival's population several times over. 'And one of the questions we have to ask ourselves as a country', demanded Henry Kissinger in 1974, 'is what in the name of God is strategic superiority? What is the significance of it, politically, militarily, operationally, at these levels of numbers? What do you do with it?'[30] There are several answers to this rhetorical question. Advocates of a graduated ladder of escalation, with Herman Kahn as their doyen, argued that there were numerous thresholds before and beyond the use of nuclear weapons, and that a range of nuclear capabilities enabled policy-makers to control the ascent towards final 'spasm war'.[31] Developments in weapon technology also encouraged proliferation as each side sought to capitalise on technical advances of its own or to close a window of opportunity (real or imagined) opened by its opponent. There was more than a little plain medieval spear-counting in the belief that a bigger arsenal was a better one, and, finally, arms control negotiations helped define the hierarchy of nuclear weapons as a framework for discussion, and thus reinforced the notion of graduated deterrence.

History demonstrates that men do not generally behave rationally and reasonably in war, and, therefore, assumptions we might make

25

about their decision-making in nuclear war (for which there is no historical evidence) must be risky indeed. Kahn's intellect was too acute to ignore the problem of rationality, but his pattern of escalation none the less called for the recognition of crucial thresholds at a time when turbulent emotions and parlous communications made it difficult. Thomas Schelling was less sanguine about the process of escalation. 'Violence, especially in war,' he wrote:

> is a confused and uncertain activity, highly unpredictable, depending on decisions taken by fallible human beings organized into imperfect governments depending on fallible communications and warning systems and on the untested performance of people and equipment. It is furthermore a hot-headed activity, in which commitments and reputations can develop a momentum of their own.[32]

Schelling advocated the 'shared risk' of 'the threat which leaves something to chance', and drew his strength precisely from that element of irrationality which had been the most serious flaw in Kahn's argument.

Given the propensity of military men for thinking in terms of the worst possible case, and the preference of strategists for theories which diminish the role of chance, it is not surprising that United States nuclear policy came to favour the Kahn model and pursued escalation dominance, defined by Lawrence Freedman as 'an attempt to prevail in a conflict by dominating at any particular level of escalation and putting the onus on the other side to move to a higher and more dangerous level'.[33] With the appointment of Robert S. McNamara as Secretary of Defense in 1961, and the shift of the United States from massive retaliation (a doctrine attractive to America's allies because it guaranteed an American nuclear response to Soviet aggression, but undermined by the development of Soviet nuclear capability) towards flexible response, the defence intellectuals came into their own at the Pentagon, and America set about acquiring the weapons for escalation dominance. Russia viewed these developments with alarm, fearing that America was striving to achieve the ability to deliver an overwhelming first strike. One of Khrushchev's replies, the deployment of nuclear missiles in Cuba in 1962, resulted in American warnings of a 'full retaliatory stroke' that owed more to massive retaliation than to graduated deterrence.

McNamara, for all his public espousal of graduated deterrence, grew concerned that once the nuclear threshold had been crossed, war would become uncontrollable. Russian assertion that no limits would be recognised once nuclear weapons had been used, and that 'an immediate retaliatory strike of enormous destructive power' was inevitable, cannot have encouraged confidence in neatly runged ladders of escalation.[34] European leaders feared that McNamara's concern with stopping short of the nuclear threshold implied a weakening of the American nuclear guarantee to Europe: diminishing the risk of nuclear war might make a conventional attack more likely. The Strategic Arms Limitations Talks between the superpowers (SALT 1 of 1972 and SALT 2, signed in 1980 but not ratified by the US Senate) also disturbed some Europeans, leading to fears that freezing the nuclear balance might leave Europe outside the shelter of the American nuclear umbrella.

However, in the early 1970s détente made major conflict appear unlikely, and nuclear policy which left much to chance and relied upon the deterrent effect of mutual assured destruction (with the appropriate acronym MAD) seemed satisfactory. But as the decade went on, the deterioration of relations between the superpowers and evidence of a sustained Soviet military build-up encouraged a return to escalation dominance, and from 1974 onwards the Americans looked into selective nuclear options that would reduce reliance on assured destruction and introduce the possibility of fighting a protracted nuclear war. This change of course brought with it a new concern for the survival of American land-based ICBMs, initiating the long and bizarre debate over the deployment of the MX missile.[35] At the same time development of the medium-range Soviet SS20 missile led to the decision, in 1979, to deploy Cruise and Pershing II missiles to Europe, and the first of the cruise missiles arrived in England in December 1983.

The facts that this theatre nuclear force modernisation programme was a response to European pressure; that cruise was a highly unsuitable weapon for use in a first strike, and that the decision to deploy the new weapons was matched by withdrawal of 1,000 old battlefield nuclear systems did not prevent an element of the European public from accusing America of planning to fight a nuclear war in Europe. European peace movements, in decline for many years and revived by the neutron bomb controversy in 1977–8, grew rapidly in strength. Though the deployment of Cruise and Pershing II was an impressive sign of the Alliance's political resolve, one official involved in the decision admitted to journalist Jon Connell that: 'If it had come down to a choice between having Cruise and Pershing and having no peace movements, I think I'd have chosen no peace movements.'[36] In retrospect, NATO's 'dual track' decision – to deploy Cruise and Pershing while at the same time offering to negotiate arms control – seems to have been proved correct by the fact that successful negotiations have indeed taken place. But, as is so often the case with nuclear theology, it is difficult to be certain of precise cause and effect.

A longer vista of uncertainty was opened by President Reagan's speech of 23 March 1983 which initiated the Strategic Defence Initiative. 'Star Wars', as it soon became known, offered the enticing prospect of using technology for defence rather than pre-emptive attack or post-strike revenge. In principle, the concept is simple: incoming missiles are shot down before they reach their targets. In practice, the difficulties are enormous. The successful interception of a dummy warhead over the Pacific in June 1984 was indeed 'a staggering technical triumph', but it gave no real indication that a system could be developed to deal with thousands of warheads and even more decoys when missing a handful would result in the devastation of scores of American cities and the deaths of hundreds of thousands of their citizens. The desirabilty of hitting an enemy missile during the early 'boost phase' of its flight means that many of the defensive missiles must be mounted on satellites, and the cost of lifting hundreds of satellites into orbit is prodigious, up to $500 million apiece at 1986 estimates. Kinetic energy weapons, chemical and x-ray lasers, and particle beam weapons all have their advocates, and all present formidable technical problems.

The need for the defence to possess at least a degree of automation raises the question of the sophistication and reliability of computers required. Even if a system could be built to work as well as its enthusiasts believe, it would still be vulnerable to technological sidestepping – the proliferation of warheads, the development of sophisticated decoys, rockets with a minimal boost phase, sub-orbital weapon systems, and so on. There is also the risk that deployment would prove destabilising rather than the reverse, with the possibility of a Star Wars race or, in an extreme case, a pre-emptive strike before the system is deployed. Yuri Andropov was not unreasonable when he complained that an initiative designed to make Russia 'incapable of dealing a retaliatory blow is a bid to disarm the Soviet Union in the face of the United States nuclear threat'.[37]

Star Wars and the arms control negotiations share, albeit in very different ways, the common aim of reducing the possibility of nuclear weapons being used. There is wide agreement that of all the rungs in the escalatory ladder that which involves the use of nuclear weapons is the most momentous. However, it is dangerously naive to suppose that because nuclear war is utterly terrible, conventional war is somehow tolerable. The destructive power of modern conventional armaments has blurred the distinction between small nuclear weapons and large conventional ones. Moreover, there is a high probability that certain sorts of conventional war will bring nuclear war in their wake. There is much truth in Neville Brown's assertion that:

> the sharpest and most negative threshold of conflict escalation is not that between non-nuclear and nuclear or non-chemical and chemical. It is that between armed peace and any kind of European war.[38]

Nevertheless, the possibility of war occurring, not necessarily between the superpowers, suggests that at least as much effort must go into the control of escalation as into the prevention of armed conflict. But as Richard Smoke points out, there is a danger here of 'reverse psychology': discussion of escalation control may create the illusion that war is more controllable that it actually is.[39] Although escalation is sometimes deliberate, it often stems from the character of war and the stress imposed on decision-makers.

In the summer of 1914 the growing pressure on leading actors in the drama – many of them elderly men whose physical and psychological tolerance of stress was poor – led to the sharp reduction of alternatives, concentration on threats posed by potential opponents, and a desire to preserve cognitive consistency by eliminating information which conflicted with preconceptions. The basis of Moltke's passionate assertion that it was impossible to vary the mobilisation plan so as to attack Russia rather than France was contradicted, after the war, by the head of his railway department, who argued that a radical change in deployment was possible. Moltke himself was unwilling to deviate from the plan, and the Kaiser, torn between martial ardour and fear of European catastrophe, was unable to give him consistent direction. John G. Stoessinger wrote of 'the overwhelming mediocrity of the personalities involved' in 1914, and we may hope that modern leaders might not display such a fatal mixture of arrogance, stupidity and weakness. But we would be rash to assume that they will necessarily handle crises a great deal better, and, at least in the military context, the information revolution may not improve matters, as we shall see in Chapter 6.[40]

The risk that the release of any nuclear weapon, even for a demonstrative strike over trackless forest or arctic tundra, would be followed by unpredictable and rapid escalation to all-out nuclear exchange has persuaded many commentators that nuclear weapons have no practical utility. McGeorge Bundy, President Kennedy's special assistant for national security affairs, wrote of the gulf between the calculations of strategists and the realities of nuclear war.

> Think Tank analysts can set levels of 'acceptable' damage well up in the tens of millions of lives. They can assume that the loss of dozens of great cities is somehow a real choice for some men. In the real world of real political leaders – whether here or in the Soviet Union – a decision that would bring even one hydrogen bomb on one city of one's own country would be recognised in advance as a catastrophic blunder; ten bombs on ten cities would be a disaster beyond history; and a hundred bombs on a hundred cities are unthinkable.[41]

Admiral Noel Gaylor, a commander-in-chief of US forces in the Pacific in 1972–6, affirmed that:

> It is my view that there is no suitable military use for nuclear weapons, whether 'strategic' weapons, 'tactical' weapons, 'theater' weapons, weapons at sea or weapons in space . . . We could not possibly gain an advantage by the initiative use (first use) of nuclear weapons to defend Europe against a conventional attack . . . I personally do not believe that a President of the United States would be likely to release tactical nuclear weapons to stop a conventional attack.[42]

General Sir John Hackett, in his important study of the profession of arms, points to 'the dangerous and probably suicidal folly' of believing that a nuclear war can be won, or even survived 'in any acceptable sense of the term', and elsewhere he warns of 'a very high probability of early and steep escalation into the strategic all-out exchange that nobody wants'.[43] Powerful support comes from McNamara himself who, writing in 1983, maintained that 'nuclear weapons serve no useful purpose whatsoever. They are totally useless – except only to deter one's opponent from using them. This is my view. It was my view in the early 1960s.'[44]

The paradox that possession of nuclear weapons serves a purpose while their use does not is widely supported. A churlish critic might make more of Michael MccGwire's observation that large numbers of officers or officials have turned alarmist only after their retirement, and Neville Brown points to the apparent mismatch between McNamara's words in 1983 and his deeds while in office.[45] Nevertheless, toleration of the principle of deterrence, if only as a step towards nuclear disarmament, has a wide constituency which includes both the Archbishop of Canterbury and the Cardinal-Archbishop of Westminster, Basil Hume. The Roman Catholic bishops of America were less sympathetic: their pastoral letter of May 1983, 'The Challenge of Peace', attacked the role of nuclear deterrence as the basis of Western defence policy. The Church of England, however, supports the paradox entirely: its essentially unilateralist report *The Church and the Bomb* was voted down in the General Synod of February 1983, but the same synod promptly declared itself against first use of nuclear weapons.[46]

The issue of nuclear first use has come to loom large in the debate, with many (not simply an extreme fringe) pressing NATO governments to sign a 'no first use' declaration, and the Soviet Union offering to reciprocate. The chief objection to such a declaration is starkly outlined by General Sir Anthony Farrar-Hockley. Writing with the authority of a former commander-in-chief of Allied Forces Northern Europe, he states that:

> capacity to sustain a conventional defence which is limited to a matter of days is not an exaggeration of weakness; it is probable that in a completely conventional war NATO would run out of weapons platforms, munitions, and certain essential items of equipment before it altogether ran out of fighting men.[47]

Estimates of the amount of time that NATO could sustain conventional war in the Central Region vary, but WINTEX 83, the NATO annual command and staff exercise conducted early in 1983, saw Warsaw Pact forces cross the Inner German Border on 3 March. Nuclear release was requested on 8 March, and the first nuclear strike was delivered on the 9th.

A week, give or take a day or two, is as long as most authorities expect conventional war to last unless NATO's war-fighting capacity is dramatically improved, and General Bernard Rogers, the former Supreme Commander Allied Forces Europe, took much trouble to emphasise that conventional weakness lowered the nuclear threshold. But we must not assume simply increasing conventional forces will solve the problem: moreover, some analysts argue that the conventional balance is in any case not as bad as official figures often suggest. Even conventional war in Europe would have awesome consequences, and there is no guarantee that successful NATO conventional defence would not push the Russians towards nuclear release. Indeed, the Soviet General Rair Simonyan believes that 'no side will accept defeat before it uses all the weapons it has'.48

Recent events diminish confidence in the survivability of nuclear war. Civil Defence is an emotive issue, for while governments argue that it gives at least a proportion of the population a chance of survival, anti-nuclear campaigners maintain that it makes nuclear war more psychologically acceptable by providing an illusion of survivability, and wastes money into the bargain. Soviet emphasis on Civil Defence has been seen by some analysts as evidence that the Soviet leadership believed that the casualties resulting from nuclear war might be acceptable.49 Christopher Donnelly wrote that 'we are seeing a very gradual development of effective civil defence within a limited budget', but stressed that its functions are limited, that it is an adjunct to the military, designed to be employed in time of war and, like so much else in the Soviet Union, it suffers from poor command and control at local level. It did not perform well in the Chernobyl disaster (for which it was neither structured nor prepared), and its derisory achievements in the Armenian earthquake led the Soviet health minister to complain of the system's 'bankruptcy'. Much as one might acknowledge that Armenia would feature no more prominently in Soviet Civil Defence plans than, say, southern Alaska might in a United States equivalent, the inability of a power which allegedly takes Civil Defence seriously to cope with a moderate natural disaster inspires little confidence. Even the hurricane which struck southern England in October 1987, a tiny event by comparison, gave a chastening demonstration of the fragility of our environmental fabric.[50]

The 'Nuclear Winter' theory raised grave concern over the long-term ecological effects of nuclear war. First expounded in the TTAPS study (named after its contributors, Turco, Toon, Ackerman, Pollach and Sagan), it has since been developed further, notably by Paul R. Ehrlich and Carl Sagan. Ehrlich observed that the 1944 Hamburg firestorm, caused by conventional bombing, sent flames 15,000 feet into the air, destroyed six square miles of the city, and made underground shelters so hot that the corpses in them burst into flames when doors were opened and oxygen entered. Nuclear firestorms could be infinitely greater, and the smoke, dust and debris thrown up by them would blot out the sun. A nuclear war involving only part of the nuclear arsenal of the superpowers could:

> change the climate of the entire Northern Hemisphere, shifting it abruptly from its present seasonal state to a long, sunless, frozen night. This will be followed after some months by a settling of nuclear soot and dust, and then by a new, malignant kind of sunlight with much of its ultraviolet band, potentially capable of blinding many terrestrial animals. The ozone in the atmosphere, which normally shields the Earth from dangerous ultraviolet radiation, would be substantially depleted by nuclear war.[51]

This would be 'a mortal or near-mortal blow' to the ecosystem of the earth.[52] Critics of the theory point to the unprovability of its assumptions (we are back in the realms of belief and disbelief). There is certainly no unanimity among its supporters as to the level of nuclear exchange that could, *in extremis*, be ecologically tolerable: Sagan suggested that perhaps 100 megatons in all, delivered by 1,000 weapons of 100 kilotons each, might just not produce catastrophe. Even if we allow for a fair margin of error in the calculations of the Nuclear Winter lobby, its warnings should be taken seriously.

An exchange which, improbably, stopped short of that required to produce a nuclear winter would nevertheless cause casualties on a massive scale. In 1979 a United States study suggested that a 1 megaton airbust over a city of 4 million inhabitants, say Detroit, would kill 500,000 and seriously injure 600,000, destroy buildings over an area of 300 square kilometres, and inflict burn injuries on several hundred thousand people.[53] A German assessment of the consequences of a theatre nuclear war, with a total yield of 23.5 megatons, reckoned on 6 to 7 million civilian and 400,000 military casualties.[54] A more recent World Health Organisation report put the casualties resulting from the use of 20 megatons in the Central Region at 9 million killed and another 9 million seriously injured.[55] And a war involving 20 megatons would be a modest one, for as early as Exercise SPEARPOINT in October 1961 three NATO corps alone planned to deliver 20–25 megatons in 500–1000 strikes.[56] Casualties on this scale swamp our comprehension. As Nicholas Humphrey pointed out in his Bronowski Memorial Lecture in 1981:

> We . . . react selectively to man-sized threats. It is not giant dangers or giant tragedies, but the plight of single human beings which troubles us. In a week when 3,000 people are killed in an earthquake in Iran, a lone boy falls down a well-shaft in Italy – and the whole world grieves. Six million Jews are put to death in Hitler's Germany, and it is Ann Frank, trembling in her garret, who remains stamped into our memory.[57]

There were 60,000 Allied casualties at Second Ypres, but the vision of young Gerald Piggott, kicking on the ground between his 18-pounders, stays with me.

To regard nuclear weapons as usable in any normal sense is to fly in the face of a growing weight of evidence which points to their gigantic casualty-producing potential, the risk of irrational escalation entailed in the use of battlefield nuclear weapons, and the immense – perhaps terminal – environmental damage done by a nuclear exchange. Retaining the most basic strategic deterrent is one thing: planning to use smaller nuclear weapons to buttress a failing conventional defence is quite another. Depending less on nuclear weapons may be neither inexpensive nor easy: the reduction of theatre and battlefield nuclear forces must be matched by an increase in conventional capability or a marked scaling-down of the threat. There are no cheap indulgences, no easy ways to paradise, but reducing our reliance on nuclear weapons would at least start us on the path to salvation, a route more obscured than illuminated by forty-five years of nuclear theology.

One can argue that, since we have so far avoided nuclear war and our chances of continuing to do so look increasingly good, the nuclear theologians have done us no real harm. This is to overlook the distortive effect of nuclear theory on the defence debate generally. Analysts frequently consider the peaceful purposes to which the money expended on nuclear weapons might be put, and almost as often fail to consider the enhancements in conventional defence that would be possible if nuclear weapons were scrapped. The latter, incidentally, are relatively disappointing. In the British case, abolition of the submarine-launched deterrent might permit the army, for instance, to add a handful of extra armoured regiments to its strength: a useful increase, to be sure, but scarcely a war-winner.

We tend not to consider alternative uses for the brain-power and teaching time which nuclear theory has consumed. In the early 1980s a Sandhurst cadet could cheerfully differentiate between theatre, intermediate-range and strategic nuclear missiles and with some confidence discuss the relative throw-weights of the superpower nuclear arsenals. He might well never have heard of S.L.A. Marshall who (considerable warts and all) remains one of the most important and original writers on small-unit action, and the library's only copy of *Men Against Fire* was taken out a dozen times in a decade. The State Department has attracted deskfuls of analysts with well-polished MAs in strategic studies, more familiar with the complexities of nuclear arms control than with the sordid realities of low-intensity operations. Part of the problem faced by the West in conducting negotiations on conventional force reductions and then redefining its military posture stems from sheer lack of familiarity with the subjects under discussion.

The debate on nuclear theory has been a gigantic free-for-all, with academics, politicians, journalists and the military (serving and retired) all striving to lay hands on the ball. Conventional forces, in contrast, have attracted far less serious attention: John J. Mearsheimer's *Conventional Deterrence* is one of the few books in the same league as the major works of nuclear theology. Armed forces have generally not helped promote discussion. The meeting point between those who wear uniform and those who do not is often uncomfortable; many conventional issues are concerned with hard technology which tends to baffle the outsider, and, most notably in Britain, the concerns (sometimes legitimate, sometimes obsessive) of official secrecy make it difficult to obtain information on a whole range of conventional military activities.

The evolving climate of superpower relations will inevitably force change. Watch the subtle shifts in emphasis as universities which offered dazzling graduate programmes on nuclear theory and defence economics suddenly discover low-intensity operations and intervention forces. This is no help to us when we need it most. For it is now that we must look most penetratingly, not at those weapons which there has rarely been much chance of using, but at those we might employ, those which might be of some practical value in furthering national interests. We need fewer academic theologians, preoccupied with the labyrinthine nuclear debate, and more parish priests, able to argue, with soldiers, politicians and financiers alike, the benefits of a rotor-borne intervention division here or an amphibious brigade there. In a hundred years' time much of the nuclear debate will seem as relevant as the heresies which tore the Christian church a thousand years ago, and their intellectual intricacies and flashes of intolerance will mystify and alarm; but conventional armies will still be with us, and it is to their structure and use that we should bend our minds.

Killing No Murder?

It is not merely the human cost of war – nuclear or conventional – that stuns the imagination. Military expenditure also spawns figures which are impossible to grasp. In 1982, the last year in which the Stockholm Institute of Peace Research felt able to hazard a guess at overall military expenditure, military spending world-wide totalled about $720 billion – an array of noughts which means little. To make it more comprehensible, we might reflect that the total abolition of defence spending in Britain would enable the government, if it so desired, almost to double the amount spent on health or education – although in practice the need to do something about unemployed ex-servicemen and redundant defence industry workers would reduce its room for manoeuvre. Peering harder into the opaque noughts, we see that one *Challenger I* Main Battle Tank, at around £1.5 million, costs roughly the same as 176 kidney dialysis machines at £8,500 each. *The Pacifist* magazine, its stance on such matters evident from its title, points out that the cost of one aircraft carrier of the *Nimitz* class could give 20 million Americans one solid meal a day for six months while, at the other end of the scale, a 9mm automatic pistol would buy a year's supply of Vitamin A capsules for 1,000 pre-school children. These comparisons are emotive: deliberately so, for I use them to illustrate just how hard-pressed defence budgets will become if the assumptions underlying their existence are seriously questioned.

The assault is already well under way, and those who oppose it are accused of narrow-minded conservatism, self-interest, or both. A critical survey of defence expenditure suggests that 'the strength of the armament institutions and the pervasiveness of military and patriotic values in the state apparatus will provide strong economic and ideological bases for continuing the present pattern.'[58] The military-industrial complex has been heavily attacked, and even those disinclined to share the political assumptions upon which some of this criticism is based can scarcely gain comfort from the 1985 admission that the US Navy had paid $659 apiece for seven ashtrays for its E-2C Early Warning planes. Comparisons are increasingly drawn between the costs of hi-tech military hardware and the funding of hospitals, famine relief or research into the ozone layer. In August 1988 a *Times* correspondent fired one of the first shots in what has since become a sustained barrage, asking: 'In these days of *glasnost* and disarmament, surely part of the resources devoted to military security could be diverted to international studies of problems threatening all nations on our planet.'[59] As Paul Kennedy's persuasive study of empires unbalanced by the cost of their armies and fleets reveals, looking back is no more comfortable than looking forwards.[60]

Revulsion is not enough. Nor is Dwight MacDonald's injunction that we must get the modern national state before it gets us.[61] Dismembering a world-order composed of nation states or imposing discipline on them through a supra-national organisation may be laudable long-term goals, but the obstacles that stand between us and such objectives are immense. Moreover, even if the nation-state is, as some would argue, only a transient form of human organisation, there is no certainty that what follows will be more pacific: smaller states in loose organisations may actually be more bellicose. In the meantime, the self-interest of individual states, competition for finite resources in an overcrowded world, heady waves of ideology, and misunderstanding – not always accidental – of the motives of others, all put barriers in our path. Thus the balance between aircraft carriers and millions of meals, 9mm pistols and vitamins, will always be difficult to strike. It is not a simple matter of 'either – or', for one cannot quantify security, measure freedom or trace the path of a deflected threat. Given the choice between a tank and 176 kidney dialysis machines, we might well – in the circumstances which prevail in 1990 – choose the latter. Our decision might have been different in 1940.

We cannot ignore the problem of evil. Because nuclear war is awful, and conventional conflict may be better only by a matter of degree, we can easily shy away from admitting that some things in this world are so wrong, some regimes or activities so evil, that they must, in the last analysis, be opposed by force if need be. I would be ashamed to live in a society where a pacifist's rights were not acknowledged, and believe that, in Britain in the First World War, it required as much moral courage not to bear arms as it did physical courage to face the shock of battle. Yet in the century of Josef Stalin, Adolf Hitler and Pol Pot, I find it impossible to accept the full-bodied pacifist position. I agree with Nicholas Fotion and Gerard Elfstrom that: 'Going without any means of armed defence is roughly equivalent to walking unarmed through Central Park in New York City in the middle of the night', and concur in 'the general wisdom of having a rule that outside aggression will be met by an armed response'.[62]

Like many general principles, this is robust and easy to explain by familiar analogy, but it is infinitely more difficult to apply in practice, and emerges only painfully from two thousand years of debate. Let us first consider the broader aspect of the question, *jus ad bellum*, the principles governing the pursuit of war itself. War was accepted as a matter of routine by the authors of the Old Testament, and the Commandment 'Thou Shalt Not Kill' does not refer to killing in battle. The word used for kill is *ratsach*, and in its other appearances the context demands a translation of 'murder', that is the wilful killing of one civilian by another. For killing in war the words *harag* (slay), *carath* (cut down) or a form of *macah* (strike or smite) are appropriate. Killing in battle was taken for granted, and Psalm 35.5 refers to an enemy as 'chaff before the wind', demonstrating that those outside the community were victims of the cultural pseudospeciation, the dehumanising of the enemy which has been a grim feature of war in our own century. In his brilliant *A Time For War: A Study of Warfare in the Old Testament*, T.R. Hobbs points to the folly of using the text

'Thou Shalt Not Kill' 'simply as a prop for one's own disposition and attitude . . .'[63]

Christ said little about war, and though his emphasis on forgiveness and peacemaking inspired many of his followers to religious pacifism, there were some Christian soldiers in the Roman army even before the Emperor Constantine's conversion to Christianity in AD 312. This brought about a major change of attitude, with the notion of a Christian empire and its Christian army as bulwarks of civilisation, and Michael Howard has observed that for a thousand years Christianity was 'one of the great warrior religions of mankind'.[64] It was in this context that St Augustine of Hippo drew a distinction between just and unjust wars, a concept elaborated by St Thomas Aquinas in *Summa Theologiae*:

> In order that a war may be just, three things are necessary. In the first place, the authority of the prince; for it does not belong to a private individual to make war, because, in order to obtain justice he can have recourse to the judgment of his superior . . .
> In the second place, there must be a just cause; that is to say, those attacked must, by a fault, deserve to be attacked . . .
> In the third place, it is necessary that the intention of those who fight should be right; that is to say, that they propose themselves a good to be effected or an evil to be avoided . . . those who wage wars justly have peace as the object of their intention.[65]

Aquinas's justification contains a serious weakness, for a medieval churchman's judgment of justice and evil is an uncertain guide in a more subjective age, when colonial wars, wars of national liberation, and, no less pertinently, class wars, may all be deemed just in the eyes of those that fight them. In December 1984 the Ayatollah Khomeini painted his own vivid picture of just war.

> War is a blessing for the world and for all nations. The Koran says: 'Fight until all corruption and rebellion have ceased.' The wars the prophet led against the infidels were a blessing for all humanity. Imagine that we soon win the war (against Iraq). That will not be enough, for corruption and resistance to Islam will still exist. The Koran says: 'War, war until victory' . . . Thanks to God, our young people are now, to the limits of their means, putting God's commandments into action.

39

They know that to kill unbelievers is one of man's greatest missions.[66]

Some authorities maintain that a framework established in the era of the broadsword goes too far in the age of the ICBM. 'Today the just war justifies Armageddon if our hearts be pure,' argued Donald Wells, 'and this is to justify too much.'[67]

The seventeenth-century Jesuit Francisco Suarez linked the right to make war to natural law, and his analogy between the corporate and the domestic – that defence of life, property and aid to a third party unjustly attacked justify violence – has a ready appeal. Hugo Grotius was a Protestant, but concepts of just and unjust wars, framed though they were by a jurist rather than a theologian, owed much to his Catholic predecessors. The balanced views of Grotius and his disciples Pufendorff, Wolff and Vattel were drowned by the turbulence of war in the age of the nation-state, and Francis Lieber, who did so much to codify laws of war in the regulations he drafted for the Union army, frankly acknowledged that war had 'come to be acknowledged not to be its own end, but the means to obtain great ends of state'. Even the 'Commission on Responsibilities', appointed by the victors to investigate responsibility for the First World War, concluded that 'a war of aggression may not be considered an act contrary to positive law, or one which can successfully be brought before a tribunal'.[68]

The First World War inspired, in the League of Nations, a supra-national institution whose covenant included mechanisms for the non-violent resolution of disputes between members and provided for the use of force against a member who resorted to war in defiance of the League's decision. The Kellogg-Briand Pact of 1928 went even further, formally condemning recourse to war as an instrument of national policy. The League was doomed to failure because it lacked ability to enforce its will, and the Pact was relevant only to the forty-four nations that signed it: neither could prevent the onward rampage of Germany, Italy or Japan. Towards the close of the Second World War there was a high-level political decision to punish German and Japanese aggression by trying those responsible, but, as Telford Taylor, chief counsel for the prosecution at Nuremberg, wrote: 'the inclusion of the aggressive war charge was bound to enmesh the Nuremberg proceedings in lasting controversy, although in the upshot no man suffered death and few any lesser penalty on that basis.'⁶⁹

Nuremberg may not have resolved the salient issue of *jus ad bellum*, the criminality of aggressive war, but war crimes trials at the end of the Second World War did underline the existence of rules which applied in the conduct of war – *jus in bello*. Rules on morality *in* war had been developed alongside the debate on the morality *of* war, with the Church's attempt to regulate war through the Peace of God (998) and Truce of God (1095) as milestones. (These sought to protect churchmen, peasants, and the helpless, and to prohibit warfare during planting and harvest, with excommunication as the penalty for transgression.) Francis Lieber's statement of 1863 is of fundamental importance, and underlies much subsequent legislation: 'men who take up arms against one another in public war do not cease on this account to be moral human beings, responsible to one another and to God'.⁷⁰ Such rules found expression both in international agreements, like the Geneva Convention of 1864 and the Hague Conventions of 1899 and 1907, and in military regulations. The 1914 edition of the British *Manual of Military Law* devoted 130 of its 800 pages of text to 'The Laws and Usages of Wars on Land' and acknowledged 'customary rules, which have grown up in practice, and . . . written rules . . . purposely agreed by the Powers in international treaties'.⁷¹ The 1956 edition of the US Army's Field Manual 27–10, *The Law of Land Warfare*, contains provisions so similar as to show a common descent, and both manuals emphasise that expediency cannot justify departure from the rules.

Numerous judgments at the end of the Second World War punished German and Japanese combatants for personal commission of war crimes, and went further, pointing to a commander's ultimate responsibility for the acts of his subordinates. Lieutenant-General Tomokjuki Yamashita, 'Tiger of Malaya', was hanged for having 'unlawfully disregarded and failed to discharge his duty as commander to control the operations of members of his command, permitting them to commit brutal atrocities and other high crimes'.⁷²

Once again practice raises difficulties even when principles are clear. A mass of evidence from both world wars and subsequent conflicts shows violations of the most generally accepted laws of war, often by the victors. Occasional disclosures reveal Allied actions which might have resulted in a war crimes trial had their perpetrators been German or Japanese: the destruction of an Indonesian supply ship by the crew of a British submarine off Borneo in 1944, with the deaths of 50 women and children, is a recent case in point.[73] During the Vietnam War and in its immediate aftermath there was much anguished breast-beating in the United States as evidence of war crimes by US military personnel came to light, with the My Lai massacre as the *cause célèbre*: it is not too much to speak of a literary school of ritual self-humiliation. For all this, it is clear that expediency had played a part in definition and recognition of illegal acts and punishment of offenders.

The advance of technology has made matters no easier. The development of weapons that kill at a distance helps us to dissociate ourselves from causing death. Man is not a 'professional' carnivore with lethal teeth or claws, and it is his development and use of weapons that distinguishes him from killers in the animal world. Plying sword or spear in the mêlée left a man in no doubt as to the effects of his acts. Pulling a trigger, jerking a lanyard and pressing a button increasingly distance us from the act of killing. Using language to depersonalise the enemy – Krauts, Japs, gooks, dinks, slants, slopes – and applying the obliquespeak of technology to weapons – 'combat unit at the air-sea interface' – and their effects – 'servicing the target array' – contributes to the same process. The growing dependence of a nation's war-fighting ability upon its industrial power-base encouraged attacks on industrial targets, and the haphazard effects of bombing meant that many of those killed were combatants only in the sense of being citizens of the nation under attack. We might reflect on the justice of trying a frightened and exhausted private soldier for violating rules of engagement in terror or frustration while a bomber pilot who does infinitely more damage by, for instance, jettisoning his bombs short of a heavily defended target, escapes unscathed.

This is no aimless foray into a murky wood best avoided by military professionals and the societies whose clients they are. War in the late twentieth century is hedged about with complex moral issues, and the paradox of deterrence is especially obdurate. Yet we should not attempt to deny the problems, or to hope that others will solve them. Society, whether nation-state or world government, ultimately requires some coercive power. Pascal declared that 'justice without force is a myth' and Cardinal de Retz warned that 'Laws unsupported by force soon fall into contempt.'[74] The fate of the League of Nations reinforces the point.

The decision to go to war, and decisions relating to the means used to pursue that war's end, involve moral choices. Some are immense, made by men whose intellect, experience and education, great through they may be, may not match the scale of consequence before them. After all, democratic politicians are elected for reasons that usually have little to do with their ability to manage crises, and the techniques demanded for climbing the greasy pole of power in an authoritarian state, and staying at the top when there, may not make for deft handling of external relations. The evidence, from this century alone, of leaders with judgment impaired by physical or psychological flaws gives pause for thought. Moreover, it is deceptively easy for the good of the state – or the benefit of a party within it – to become an end that justifies disproportionate means and blinds men to the possible consequences of their action. The Falklands War is a recent example. The Argentinian junta believed that invasion would strengthen its own internal position, and finished, not undeservedly, with the worst of both worlds: humiliating military defeat, and an irresistible wave of popular opposition.

Other choices, though still matters of life and death, have narrower consequences, and are taken in the hot-blooded realm of combat when time for choice is short and death snaps his fingers in the air. Shakespeare's John Bates, the night before Agincourt, thought that: 'we know enough if we know we are the king's subjects. If his cause be wrong, our obedience to the king wipes the crime of it out of us.' This blunt utilitarianism has long comforted soldiers whose practical alternative to facing the bullets of the enemy might be to face those of their comrades. In any case the tight little loyalties of the combat group provide moral justifications of their own, and good men can fight hard for a bad cause. Even here, though, judgment must be illuminated by informed conscience and guided by regulation.

The Historical Perspective

It would help if we took a longer view of history. Our eyes are fixed on a snapshot of our own age, with its urgent issues and passions. We imagine that these are more important than the reasons that drew men to fight in the Crusades, the Thirty Years War or the Napoleonic

43

Wars, and we arrogate to the isms of our own age an importance we deny to the mainsprings of past war. We find it amazing that the events immediately following the assassination of an Austrian archduke could produce such an immensity of suffering. Standing atop the pitted carapace of Fort Douaumont at Verdun, where losses were measured in tens of thousands, regret for wasted French and German manhood, much of it immured in the nearby *ossuaire*, is all the more poignant because the issues men died for there seem so unimportant to us. This is not to say that our own beliefs have no value, but rather that we should weigh our action in a balance that does not pivot on an ideological conflict which has lasted barely minutes of the world's long day. We are shackled by what George Orwell called 'the smelly little orthodoxies of our time'. Blow the world apart because the Russians want to take Antwerp? It is a proposition which might amuse if it did not horrify.

Part of the blame for our predicament lies with technology. As Jacques Elleul declared, it is an illusion to think that because we have broken through the prohibitions and taboos of primitive society we have become free:

> We are conditioned by something new: technological civilisation . . . the sharp knife of specialisation has passed like a razor into the living flesh. It has cut the umbilical cord which linked men with each other and with nature.[75]

Forty years ago, with the world accelerating down the sharp rifling of technology, C.S. Lewis argued that we were producing a generation to whom courage, faith, justice and mercy were intellectual abstractions, and recommended a return to the study of literature as a means of building character. A recent *Military Review* article makes the point brilliantly, arguing that literature 'brings moral depth to leaders' characters, gives an appreciation for what James Schall calls "the infinity of particular life"; and . . . inspires them to great visions and efforts.'[76] I cannot speak for American military colleges, with which my contact has been confined to slightly breathless lecture tours, though I fear that a few of my former pupils at Sandhurst might have thought that Thackeray was sergeant-major of Old College and de Vigny kept the wine bar just opposite the Staff College gate.

In 1982 Michael Howard warned us to stop being frightened, and trying to frighten each other, with visions of Soviet windows of opportunity or the prospect of inevitable nuclear war. He concluded that defence would continue to be a necessity in a world of sovereign states, and that nuclear war will remain a terrible possibility. But its probability is fast reducing. As *glasnost* thaws relations between the superpowers there is less fear in the air. There s also a feeling abroad that things have changed in some profound and lasting way. In 1989 the mood of the moment was caught by an article on 'The End of History' written by Francis Fukuyama, a junior official at the State Department. He argued, not that there would be no more history in the sense of merely cataloguing events, but that history in the Hegelian sense, the history of ideology, had come to an end. The world had emerged from a long detour down the Marxist cul-de-sac, and a potent mixture of liberal democracy and capitalism was indisputably triumphant. Fukuyama's message was echoed by several Western political leaders, who announced not merely that the Cold War was over, but that the West had won it. There was no counter-claim from a Kremlin under siege.

The Fukuyama thesis attracted critics as well as supporters, and despite its immense appeal, it is, in a sense, unhistorical. The events of the late 1980s may indeed rank alongside those of 1789 in terms of their impact on human affairs, but we can no more assume that the frame of history is frozen today than an observer in 1815 could guarantee a quiet monarchical Europe. History gives one confidence only in the mutability of human affairs. Our vision may easily swivel, in Orwellian fashion, from an East-West bipolar world to one dominated by tension between a developed North and a hungry South. The ideological component of war is, as we shall see, difficult to quantify: many past conflicts have had nothing to do with ideology, and the collapse of one particular ideology, in this case Communism, cannot predicate the end of ideology in general. Nor can we ignore the effect of religion, for if one of the striking facts of the 1980s was the diminishing strength of extreme ideologies – from Prague to Pretoria – another was the growing militancy of Islam.

In any case, the results of the collapse of Communism will not, of necessity, be peaceful. Loosening the central control which was a characteristic of even pre-Revolutionary Russia has encouraged the inherent centrifugal tendencies of the Soviet Union. The national identities of the Baltic states of Latvia, Lithuania and Estonia have triumphantly re-emerged, tension between Armenia and Azerbaijan grows, with bloody and well-publicised clashes which the Soviet army has found it impossible to prevent. The wave of Islamic fundamentalism coursing through the Middle East finds answering ripples among the growing number of Muslims living in the Soviet Union. The Soviet presence is unwelcome in Eastern Europe, and the news that Soviet troops will have withdrawn from Czechoslovakia by the end of 1990 is likely to increase already powerful pressures for withdrawal from the rest of Eastern Europe.

The balance of power in Europe since 1945 has pivoted on a strong, unified Russia committed to providing 'fraternal assistance' to her client states. However unattractive this has seemed to the West, there is no guarantee that the partial dismemberment of the Soviet Empire will produce a more stable situation. The great empires of the past were not only dangerous when in a predatory and expansionist mood: as they shrank they created uncertainties and tensions, as events in the Balkans in the years before the First World War so amply demonstrate. Advocates of the conspiracy theory of Soviet policy would pursue the argument further, suggesting that successful reforms resulting in an efficient economy will put the Soviet Union in a better position to pursue a forward foreign policy, and that Gorbachev's fair words have done far more damage to Western resolve than the sabre-rattling of some of his predecessors.

Yet to a world which has lived so long on the edge of the nuclear abyss, *glasnost* seems to offer the prospect of imminent salvation. It comes at a time when the Western military's demands upon manpower and economic resources alike cause public concern. The tendency to justify defence expenditure by pointing to (or even exaggerating) the threat means the moderation of that threat has already produced demands for changes in policy, some of them radical. In December 1988 Admiral Elmar Schmahling, head of the West German Office for Studies and Exercises, advocated the abolition of NATO and the Warsaw Pact, and the removal of nuclear weapons and Allied troops from German soil.[77] Low flying by military aircraft has already become a major political issue, and the rules governing '443 areas' over which troops can exercise with little constraint have been redrafted.

The speed with which post-*glasnost* euphoria has spread is a measure of the level of fear that existed before it. It is still too early to judge the impact or durability of Gorbachev's policy, either within the Soviet Union or outside it. There are, however, few grounds for optimism. Even if the Soviet Union does not simply unravel from within (and as I write there seems every prospect of its doing just that) the economic and political problems facing its leaders are immense. In January 1990 a leading foreign affairs expert, writing under the pseudonym of Z, predicted a long and painful retreat from Communism, with a military reaction as one possible response to destabilising reform.[78]

Nor is the disintegration of the Soviet Empire the only potential cause of instability in Europe. The unification of Germany is now an established fact. Questions of the relationship of a united Germany to NATO and the Warsaw Pact properly lie outside the compass of this book, though unification may indeed be the catalyst that converts NATO from a primarily military alliance to a principally political association. Professor Norman Stone, speaking with his customary vigour on the BBC on 2 March 1990, argued that a united democratic Germany, bereft of those qualities which had made it such a menace between 1870 and 1945, could only be welcomed. Others are not so sure, among them the novelist Günter Grass, who observed:

> In the course of barely 75 years as a unified nation we have filled the history books with suffering, rubble, defeat, millions of refugees, millions of dead, and crimes that can never be undone.[79]

The prospect of a united Germany certainly alarmed Grass, and generated a lively debate in the British press. Some look nervously at Germany's eastern border, that traditional *casus belli:* others, perhaps more realistically, predict economic imperialism, with the mark of the 1990s achieving more than the panzer division of the 1940s. There are those with even closer concerns. When I visited Moscow in early 1990 my Russian military hosts spoke gloomily about the threat posed by Islamic fundamentalism and the danger, as they saw it, of a strong, united Germany. The latter is a fear too deeply etched into the Russian historical experience to be easily allayed.

Whether we are dealing with the threats of today or the uncertainties of tomorrow, we still need Professor Howard's four requirements – 'clear heads, moral courage, human compassion, and above all, a sense of proportion', and we will obtain these only by raising our head above the parapet of our own time to look more widely about us.

Rumours of Wars

Like it or not, we must look harder at war itself, and not avoid the subject because it appals us, or hope that by ignoring it we may persuade it to go away. 'The fact that slaughter is a horrifying spectacle', warned Clausewitz, 'must make us take war more seriously . . .'[80] The banality 'If you wish for peace prepare for war' is used effectively by Edward Luttwak to demonstrate the paradoxical logic of strategy.[81] Liddell Hart's extension, 'if you want peace, *understand* war' takes us on the next leg of our journey. We might note here that politicians have often failed to understand war: in the British case neither Asquith before the First World War nor Chamberlain before the Second had devoted much thought to a subject which alarmed them. This lack of understanding has not necessarily made politicians more reluctant to employ the military instrument. An unfashionable paradox suggests that soldiers, who know most about war, often recognise its risks more than their political masters: as Machiavelli asked, 'who ought to be fonder of peace than the soldier whose life is placed in jeopardy by war?'

In his examination of the causes of war, Michael Howard noted how the subject has been tackled by 'mathematicians, meteorologists, sociologists, anthropologists, geographers, physicists, political scientists, philosophers, theologians and lawyers' – to name only the most obvious.[82] For us, the issue is a crucial one, for an analysis of the causes of past wars throws light on to the potential causes of future conflicts, and is thus central to our inquiry.

An influential psychological explanation of war explores the transformation of hostility from its immediate causes within the repressive agencies of family or state to a more distant target; the displacement of familial loves and hatreds to the greater entity of creed or state; and the projection of individual unrecognised dark impulses to third parties. The modern nation-state serves as the agent for release, because aggressive impulses manifest themselves in group form and the state is the group organisation of our age.[83] This is only one of a number of explanations offered by psychologists whose views on the human psyche seem almost as varied as personality itself. Ethologists, who study the behaviour patterns of animals, and anthropologists, who study the society and customs of mankind, veer as sharply between attributing innately aggressive motives to man, and blaming the corrupting influence of society upon a creature who started as a gentle herbivore.[84]

If the sheer variety of psychological, ethological and anthropological interpretation does not daze us, we can identify the unsatisfactory as well as the helpful aspects of the analysis. Psychologists tell us much about individual behaviour, but falter when they apply judgments on the individual to the actions of groups, and it is difficult to disagree with Emile Durkheim's conclusion that: 'The psychological factor is too general to predetermine the course of social phenomena. Since it does not explain one social form rather than another, it cannot explain any of them.'[85] Although the ethologists are sometimes illuminating, especially with their studies of inter- and intra-specific aggression and the territorial imperative, it is not always helpful to compare humans with animals, especially as the business of war has no real equivalent in the animal world. The anthropologists' distinction between various forms of fighting, and their suggestion that war is a comparatively recent creation, are useful, though broad generalisations on the causes of wars and affection for what T.C.W. Blanning aptly castigates as 'a conspiracy theory of historical causation' are less so.[86] Social scientists who have studied groups, from George Homans's *The Human Group* to John Hockey's *Squaddies: Portrait of a Subculture*, tell us much about group identity and group values, though they are more helpful for telling us why groups of men fight than why wars start.

Quantitative examinations, focusing on the frequency and character of past struggles to detect the phenomena of 'war contagion' or 'periodicity in war', have enjoyed much recent popularity as well they might in an age fascinated by things that can be caught and counted. They often interpose a sloping glacis plate of terminology which makes them impenetrable to those not equipped with jargon-piercing devices to break through laminated equations or case-hardened prose. Follow me into this:

if events are generated randomly, the number of periods in which x events occur is given by

$$Ne^{-\lambda}\lambda^k/k!$$

where N is the total number of observations (for example, 96 five-year periods) and λ is the average number of events per period (119 wars/96 periods = 1.24). The actual number of periods characterised by k wars (where k = 0, 1, 2, . . .)

can be computed from the data. The observed and theoretical distributions can then be compared by a chi-square goodness-of-fit test.[87]

I have spent all my professional career studying the subject under discussion, but this little masterpiece puts me back in the infant class. Categorising and quantifying so diverse a subject as war is not easy, and the compressions resorted to in some studies do not make encouraging reading. Quincy Wright's huge *Study of War* and David Singer and Melvin Small's *The Wages of War*, to name but two, help add to our data base, but most of the quantitive studies get us no closer to the causes of war than an analysis of the number of times Beethoven used F sharp tells us about the appeal of his Ninth Symphony.

Historians are no more unanimous about the causes of war than scholars in other fields. The sheer scale of the First World War encouraged many historians to discover 'causes of peculiar complexity and profundity, from the neuroses of nations, from the widening class struggle, from a crisis in industrial society'. Michael Howard, having argued to this effect against A.J.P. Taylor, later wondered if he had not in fact been wrong, and whether the causes of the First World War had actually been no more profound than those to which Thucydides attributed the Peloponnesian war: 'What made war inevitable was the growth of Athenian power and the fear this caused in Sparta.'[88] Marc Bloch warned us against a 'graduated classification of causes' of wars, observing how: 'Reality offers us a nearly infinite number of lines of force which all converge together upon the same phenomenon', and Bernard Brodie suspected that any general theory that was not inherently eclectic was bound to be wrong.[89]

Despite these warnings, the temptation to construct complex hierarchies of cause seems irresistible. These should not, however, overgrow foundations laid by Clausewitz and built on by both Geoffrey Blainey and Quincy Wright. Men may fight because of individual aggression, young-blood machismo, group loyalty and comradely honour, but wars are rooted in conflicts of power between states, conflicts that may have less to do with specific issues than with status and function in the international system. They require a rational calculation that the gains of going to war exceed the benefits of remaining at peace, and the abundant evidence of the risk of war,

Clausewitz's 'realm of chance', rarely makes this an easy decision. For this reason, argued Professor Howard, the abolition of nuclear weapons would not be 'an unmixed blessing', for: 'Nothing that makes it easier for statesmen to regard war as a feasible instrument of state policy, one from which they stand to gain rather than lose, is likely to contribute to a lasting peace.'[90] The frequency of botched cost-gain analysis is emphasised when we consider how few twentieth-century wars have actually profited the aggressor: of the century's five largest conflicts, in four – the two world wars, the Korean War and the Gulf War – aggressors fired the starting pistol for a race they failed to win.

Causes of conflict exist in areas untouched by *glasnost*. Geopolitical realities cannot be ignored, whether on the small scale (can Israel ever afford to relinquish the Golan Heights?) or the larger (physical proximity gives events in Central America an interest to the United States which Europeans frequently fail to grasp). The quest for strategic resources has often taken nations to war in the past, from Frederick's smash and grab for the rich province of Silesia in 1740 to the Japanese search for oil before the Second World War. The spectre of a Soviet descent upon the oilfields of the Gulf may have been exorcised, at least for the moment, but Western concern for the area will remain. Irredentist demands for the return of national territory have similarly led to conflict, most recently when long-standing claims to the Falklands provided the Argentinian military with a delusive opportunity to foster national unity and recover 'lost' territory at the same time. The question of the eastern border of a united Germany looms large. Some of the inhabitants of Polish Silesia still consider themselves German, as a demonstration in Wroclaw in November 1989 showed. 'Helmut, you are our Chancellor too', read a banner held up at a mass meeting attended by Chancellor Kohl and Prime Minister Mazowiecki. It is small wonder that a poll conducted by the *Gazeta Wyborcza*, Poland's first independent newspaper, found that only 7 per cent of those questioned were in favour of German unification.[91]

The prospects of war being abolished from above by the submergence of nation-states or the advent of world government are remote, although improvements in relations between the superpowers have greatly reduced the danger of a head-on clash between the United States and Russia. What, then, about the prospects of it being abolished from below, by the unwillingness of its actors to play the parts assigned them? Two distinct lines of debate meet here. One, brilliantly argued by John Keegan in *The Face of Battle*, suggests that the changing conditions of war have made it intolerable to participants. This case has been reinforced by Frank Barnaby who declares that 'humans, at least in the developed countries are, or are becoming, too fragile to participate directly in modern war', and by Richard Gabriel, who argues that 'war has become an activity that has surpassed the ability of human beings to endure it'.[92] The other line argues that changing social attitudes to war, in which the anti-nuclear movement has played a large part, have reduced men's willingness to fight. Both arguments are considered at length later, and neither can be easily or totally dismissed. In the meantime, we should note Jacques Elleul's verdict on predictions of the internal collapse of war:

> At the beginning of 1914, a short war was predicted; the morale of the troops, it was said, could not endure a long one. The same prophecy was made in 1941, at the beginning of the all-out bombing of Germany; human beings, it was said, could not endure such a pounding. In 1917 it was assumed that the misery attendant on the Russian Revolution would soon bring about the collapse of Communism. None of these predictions came true; morale, and morale alone, sustained human stability.[93]

We might also observe that several wars have existed alongside these dire predictions, suggesting that at the most the 'abolition from below' arguments applies to specific types of war fought by particular adversaries, and certainly not to war in general.

There is now less chance of a deliberate nuclear exchange between the superpowers than at any time in the past quarter-century, and obituaries of the Cold War are probably not premature. However, other arenas of conflict have not been warmed by the improving climate of superpower relations, and potent and destabilising issues – resources, refugees and drugs prominent among them – pose political problems whose solutions may have a military component. And the history of the twentieth century points emphatically to the certainty of uncertainty. It was eminently reasonable, in view of the state to which the Treaty of Versailles had reduced Germany, to doubt whether she would ever again pose a serious military threat to Britain and France; and yet she did so, most effectively, in twenty years, and lack of a flexible military instrument west of the Rhine played its own faltering role in making German aggression feasible. Of recent conflicts, neither the Soviet invasion of Afghanistan nor the British recapture of the Falklands conformed to the strategic presumptions of the major participants. The motor riflemen who went to Afghanistan in the early stages of the invasion were trained and equipped for a different kind of war, while the need to recapture the Falklands came as an unpleasant shock to a defence establishment thinking hard about other things. The real problem facing military establishments beyond the 1990s is to assess how best they can contribute to national interests which will demand economy and agility rather than high cost and fixation on a single dominant threat. Othello's occupation has not gone, but the manner in which it will be exercised has unquestionably changed.

2

The Nature of War

For Warr, consisteth not in Battel onely, or the act of fighting; but in a tract of time, wherein the will to contend by Battel is sufficiently known; and therefore the notion of Time, is to be considered in the nature of Warre; as it is in the nature of Weather. For as the nature of Foule weather, lyeth not in a showre or two of rain; but in an inclination thereto of many days together: So the nature of Warre, consisteth not in actuall fighting; but in the known disposition thereto, during all the time there is no assurance to the contrary. All other time is Peace.

Thomas Hobbes, *Leviathan*

Armed conflict exists in two spectrums, a horizontal span of scale, and a vertical range of intensity. At one end of the horizontal spectrum lies general war, major conflict between large states or power blocs, fought without limitations: all-out nuclear war would be the modern example. In practice, the two world wars are the closest recent history brings us to this end of the spectrum, although limitations can be discerned even in them. Chemical weapons were not used in the Second World War (although they were available to both sides), and in the First, despite some lapses (Turkish treatment of prisoners captured at Kut-al-Amara is a disgraceful example), participants sought to make the conduct of fighting troops conform to generally accepted standards. The Canadian Corps' order for the attack on Vimy Ridge in 1917, for instance, specified that enemy wounded 'will be treated exactly the same as our own wounded'.

Although, in an important sense, it is true to see the twentieth century as the age of total war, it is no less true that wars resulting in the total destruction of the adversary have become less, not more, frequent. Rome's victory over Carthage in 146 BC saw the demolition of the city and the massacre or enslavement of its citizens. The Mongols remorselessly laid waste huge tracts of Central Asia and subjugated the divided principalities of Russia: Otto Hoetzsch argued that their 'cruel, deceitful and degrading behaviour' had profound and lasting effects upon Russia.[1] Turkish victory at Mohacs in 1526 led to the destruction of the kingdom of Hungary and the degradation of its nobility. In eleventh-century England, insurrection against the Normans, with Scottish and Danish support, led to the Harrying of the North. The chronicler Oderic Vitalis, an eyewitness, believed that 100,000 people perished, and Richard Muir suggested that 'the rural landscape of the North of England was moulded by the atrocities of war, and one can argue that it has still not recovered from the horrors of 1069–71'.[2] In contrast, Allied victory in both world wars was followed by settlements whose relative moderation contrasted sharply with the means used to prosecute the war.

General war in our own century does not necessarily produce results commensurate with the blood and treasure it consumes. John G. Stoessinger observed that unless the vanquished is totally destroyed, the victor's peace is seldom lasting. Negotiated peace settlements have a greater chance of success than settlements imposed by force of arms: the Treaty of Versailles – in effect a twenty years' truce in a European civil war – underlines the point.[3] The losing side's decision to prolong the war beyond the point where defeat is obvious produces no useful result for either side (witness the case of Germany and Japan in the Second World War) and, if the losing side has access to nuclear weapons, may well produce the least useful result of all. We may confidently expect an orchestra of experts to thunder out that *glasnost* means general war is now a thing of the past. Barring accidents they are almost certainly right, but it is scarcely a novel notion: general war in the twentieth century has such a dismal track-record that, *glasnost* or not, it can no longer appeal to a state whose political culture is even approaching maturity unless the alternative is demonstrably more dire.

Limited war envisages a more precise use of the military instrument to further policy. The most crucial limitation is that of the war's objective, for it is unrealistic to expect a state to accept substantial limitations if it is contending for an objective of prime national interest. The objectives of combatants need not be symmetrical: in

55

Vietnam, United States policy objectives implied a greater degree of limitation than the North Vietnamese recognised, and rendered certain sorts of military activity, such as the use of nuclear weapons, inappropriate. The war's objective is likely to influence the means used in its prosecution, although there is no simple correlation between the two. Both the nature of weapons employed, and the targets against which they are directed, are subject to limitation, and it is possible to vary means in order to increase the pressure imposed on an opponent: the bombing of North Vietnam in 1972 is an example. Limiting the geographical area of the war has the dual effect of reducing the risk of casualties being suffered by non-participants and preventing the deepening of conflict. The British government's declaration that an exclusion zone of 200 nautical miles from the centre of the Falklands existed from 12 April 1982 was a precise definition of geographical limitation, and its modification on 23 April to include 'any approach on the part of Argentine warships . . . which could amount to a threat . . . ' was carefully phrased so as not to betoken a general widening of the war.4

Time is an important limiting factor. For centuries the practical problems of carrying on the war outside the summer months made for annual campaigns (with some exceptions, like the White Mountain operation of 1620), and the limited obligations of feudal hosts hauled together by the *arrière-ban* also made short campaigns imperative. In our own age, the fundamental need for popular support for war, and the way this may be eroded by a lengthy conflict with mounting casualties and no sign of victory, may make a long war an unattractive option. The chances of United Nations involvement or the intervention of other powers (not to mention the damage done to a nation's social and economic fabric by a long war) also make a short war attractive. A Western power engaged against an Asian opponent may find itself at a serious disadvantage, for its own short-war imperatives are likely to match badly with the protracted war which Maoist doctrine advocates and Eastern culture makes tolerable. American recognition, early in the Vietnam War, that the North Vietnamese were employing what seemed to be 'a no-win strategy' should have underlined the danger of fighting an enemy less bound by time constraints.

At the opposite end of the spectrum from general war lies low-intensity conflict. Although a widely used expression, this is something of a misnomer, for it usually includes revolutionary wars, which may themselves contain a range of activities from subversion and terrorism to conventional military operations. These have been a major feature of twentieth-century conflict. In some cases they have been primarily concerned with the replacement of one regime by another, while in others they have focused upon the ejection of a colonial or occupying power: often the two have been blurred as a left-wing movement contends for national liberation, intent not merely on ejecting the occupier but also on assuming his authority. Although such wars are not necessarily low-intensity throughout their duration, they usually commence with low-intensity activities which impose particular demands upon armies, calling for early recognition of the importance of political and economic facets of the response. Terrorism, an element of low-intensity operations, which can be used as a tactic in a revolutionary or liberation war, may be the only effective weapon at the disposal of a dissident political or nationalist group, or may be sponsored by a state that wishes to avoid a direct conventional clash.

Our perception of the utility of war at various points in this spectrum is inevitably subjective. Because general war between nuclear-armed powers carries with it the very high risk of nuclear release, it is not a useful way of furthering state policy save in utterly exceptional circumstances, and this has tended to make other options preferable. But for much of history war was regarded as a natural state of affairs: indeed, it was the prime *raison d'être* of warrior aristocracies, the justification for their existence and the basis of their moral authority to rule. It was only in the eighteenth century, as public men and jurists confronted the evidence of the immensely destructive Thirty Years War, that the legitimacy of war was first seriously questioned: there is much truth in the aphorism that war is as old as history but peace is a modern invention.

The vertical range of conflict deals with intensity rather than with scale. Its lower end comprises the low-intensity operations we have discussed, as well as the small-scale operations – patrolling and so on – which may continue during an operational pause in a more intense campaign. It extends through the mid-intensity operations which, for instance because of the means employed in them, often form part of limited war, and ends in high-intensity battle, with the use of nuclear and chemical weapons at the very end of the scale.

A diagrammatic representation of the vertical and horizontal spectra cannot be more than a crude generalisation to which there are evident exceptions. Nevertheless, such a diagram does furnish a rough and ready guide. Most military operations are likely to occur along the diagonal line between scale and intensity, with the risks of general war and the difficulties of fighting high-intensity battle suggesting that most military activity will take place at or below the limited war/medium intensity intersection. If we were to place a dot on this graph to mark each armed conflict which has taken place since 1945 (there were 162 in the period 1951–85 alone) we should discover a thick cluster down at the bottom left-hand corner of the graph, with a mere spatter in the centre, a spot or two towards the top right and nothing where general war and high intensity intersect. We might observe that this is yet another paradox, for much military activity (and certainly the great majority of military expenditure) is devoted towards fighting wars in precisely that area where our graph suggests that they are least frequent.

No less central to our grasp of the dimensions of conflict is an understanding of the three levels of war. First of these is strategy, which may subdivided into grand strategy (the application of national

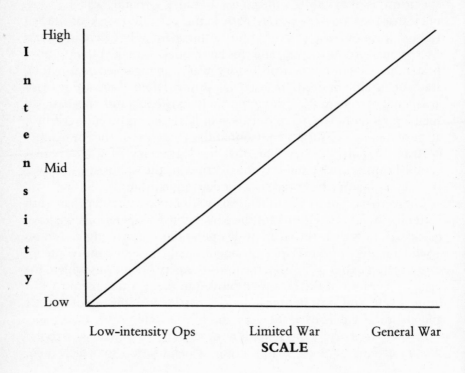

resources, economic, psychological, diplomatic and military to achieve the policy objective of a state or alliance) and military strategy (the use of military measures to attain these goals). The operational level of war is concerned with the use of military forces to achieve the aim of military strategy, and operational art translates strategy into operational or tactical action. Tactics is the art of employing units in engagements and battles to achieve operational objectives. Strategic theory may be broad enough to contain eternal truths: indeed, the elements of Clausewitz which show their age the most are those in which he descends from the higher plane to address nuts-and-bolts issues. Operational art evolves more quickly, while tactics, being heavily weapon-dependent and terrain-sensitive, change more rapidly still.

It is deceptive to allocate precise responsibilities within the hierarchy of military command for these levels, for much depends on the context in which forces are employed. In the context of NATO's Central Region the four-star commander of Allied Forces Central Europe is the crucial commander at the operational level, while in the Falklands it was the two-star commanders of the Task Force and Landing Force who were operational-level commanders. It is noteworthy that the 1982 edition of Field Manual 100–5 Operations, the US Army's 'keystone' manual, specifically associated operations with large formations, while the 1986 edition, written after the Grenada operation, implicitly recognises that small forces can have operational significance.[5] Moreover, it is possible for an apparently tactical act to have immense operational, even strategic, importance. In 1982 the loss of either British aircraft carrier would have ended the war at a stroke, and the sinking of the cruiser *General Belgrano*, in the words of Admiral Sir John Fieldhouse, 'cut the heart out of the Argentinian Navy and we only had their Air Force to deal with then'.[6]

This three-tier definition might have caused concern to an English-speaking military officer or commentator as little as ten years ago, for, as Edward Luttwak observed in an article which marked the start of a period of sustained interest in the operational level of war:

It is a peculiarity of Anglo-Saxon military terminology that it knows of *tactics* (unit, branch and mixed) and of *theater strategy* as well as *grand strategy*, but includes no adequate term for the *operational* level of warfare – precisely the level that is most salient in the modern tradition of military thought in continental Europe.[7]

Christopher Donnelly suggested that the adjective 'operational', long applied by the Russians to the level of war linking the strategic to the tactical, tended to cause confusion in translation because its basic meaning in British and American military doctrine simply indicates the ability to operate.[8] The new *British Military Doctrine* tackles the confusion of terminology head-on by pointing out that 'operational' has two meanings, one 'concerned with operations' (as in 'operational level', 'operational commander' or 'operational concept'), and the other 'fit to engage in operations' (as in 'non-operational', because of breakdown, casualties, etc.).[9]

We are still not out of the semantic minefield. It was once adequate to use 'strategy' to describe the conduct of war in general and to apply 'tactics' to what actually happened on the battlefield, and much of what was written on strategy in the eighteenth and nineteenth centuries comprehends what we now see as the operational level. Recognition that what went on when armies were in presence, but not actually in battle, in a theatre of war differed from tactics at one extreme and strategy at the other encouraged nineteenth-century theorists to develop the term 'grand tactics'. The term *operativ* in the context of military art or level of war was first used by the Germans in the First World War and passed from Germany to Russia as *operativnyi* in 1922. The lack of an Anglo-Saxon or French equivalent was no accident, but bore witness to pronounced differences in national military development and, particularly in the French case, to the importance attributed to battle.[10]

Luttwak maintained that the gap in Anglo-Saxon military terminology reflected a neglect of the operational level of war: officers neither used the term operational, nor practised war in operational terms except 'in vague or ephemeral ways'. He blamed this on British and American experience of twentieth-century war. In the First World War the Americans were employed late, and then under French direction, while the British failed to transcend their colonial experience. The latter point is especially relevant, for the regimental system, which makes such a powerful contribution to the low-level cohesion of the British army, was ideally suited to colonial campaigning, but adapted less well to the demands of general war. Indeed, it was one of the obstacles in the way of effective inter-arm co-operation, lack of which, as Shelford Bidwell and Dominick Graham have argued, is a long-term source of British weakness.[11] In addition, examples of capable operational generalship (by MacArthur and Patton among the Americans and O'Connor among the British) did not become organic to the national tradition of warfare. In the British case, the long series of campaigns associated with the withdrawal from Empire tended to encourage emphasis on the tactical skills which were relevant in Malaya, Aden or Borneo at the expense of operational doctrine geared to a European conflict, reinforcing the colonial rather than the continental tradition. Given that there has only been one postwar year (1968) when the British army has not lost a soldier killed on operations, there was a natural tendency for it to concentrate on what was happening on an almost daily basis rather than on a more conjectural campaign in the Central Region. A scholar looking back at the period 1945–88 might find it difficult to discern a consistent British operational doctrine for medium- or high-intensity war: but he could certainly find (most notably in Frank Kitson's *Low Intensity Operations*) a substantive corpus of work on war in the minor key.

For the Americans, campaigns in Korea and Vietnam did little for operational art, with Inchon as 'the single brilliant exception'. American ground forces went on to absorb new generations of weapons, mobility in and between theatres was improved, and much attention was devoted to the management of resources at all levels. 'Nevertheless,' Luttwak observed trenchantly, 'the entire organism continues to function only at the lowest and the highest military levels, while the operational level in between remains undeveloped.'[12] Evidence of neglect of the operational level of war was to be found in the military doctrine then current in the US Army, Active Defense, which sought to use firepower to erode an attacker's inventory in an attritional battle in which it was hoped that victory would go not to the big battalions but to the most abundant killing-power.[13]

Luttwak's point was well made, and he is scarcely to be blamed if there is danger in armies, where fashions have a seductive appeal, that the operational level of war has become something of a shibboleth whose recitation may be a substitute for deep understanding. Such an understanding is, however, fundamental if we are to grasp the character of late-twentieth-century war. First, activities at the operational level must contribute to the strategic aim. This may seem as obvious a point as the Clausewitzian insistence, one level

61

up, that 'war is the continuation of policy by other means', but history suggests that, just as military strategy can lose sight of its political purpose, so too can tactical achievements fail to contribute towards the strategic aim. It implies that commanders at the operational level must have a clear concept of the strategic purpose of their operations. Not least among the title-deeds of chaos in the Anglo-French Suez operation of 1956 was the confusion over the political point of military activity: General André Beaufre, commander of the French land forces engaged, wrote that 'people thought to solve a highly involved political problem by launching a military operation'.[14] On 12 March 1951 Brigadier A.K. Ferguson, British military attaché in Korea, summed up the practical problems caused by weak links between a war's strategic purpose and its tactical instruments.

> I foresee difficulties in maintaining morale indefinitely in present circumstances, in view of the ill-defined task set for the United Nations forces. You have no doubt heard of General MacArthur's remark of some months ago, when he said he was fighting 'in a political vacuum'. It seems to me that the reputed objective of UN forces in Korea, which is 'to repel aggression and bring peace and security to the area' is much too vague under present circumstances to give the Supreme Commander in the field a military objective, the attainment of which would bring hostilities to a close.[15]

Second, the operational level must comprehend war in the third dimension, and the American expression AirLand Battle is particularly appropriate. Inter-service rivalries, with squabbles over who flies which to do what, sharpened by the growing cost of helicopters and fixed-wing aircraft alike, together with genuine failure to understand the difficulties faced by practitioners in a different dimension, makes thorough-going co-operation hard to achieve. The Soviet practice of subordinating the majority of air assets to commanders at the Front (equivalent to a Western army group) or TVD (theatre of military operations) level has much to commend it, though it can scarcely appeal to Western air force officers who fear the submersion of their own service.

It would be rash to predict the imminent demise of independent air forces, although the logic for their existence has grown weaker. Much of the argument in their favour turned on the fact that they alone could carry out the function of strategic bombing. Air arms in the period 1920–50 were doctrine-led in a way which ground forces rarely are. There were times when theory ran far ahead of practice: Guilio Douhet wrote in 1921 about an air war which, at the time, far eclipsed the means at hand with which to wage it.[16] The advent of the ICBM eclipsed the strategic function of the bomber, though it did not make long-range bombers irrelevant, as the use of B-52s against North Vietnam demonstrated. We may expect that air forces will resist being tied to the coat-tails of ground operations, and will continue to emphasise that flexibility and range makes air power an asset which requires specialist management. It would be surprising if the issue of reach did not loom large in air doctrine and procurement alike, not merely because it is the quintessential advantage enjoyed by air power, but also because operations which enable air forces to make the best use of long reach are precisely those in which they may justly claim a measure of independence.

The operational level implies substantial scale of space and time. Operation *Overlord* was over a year in gestation, and used 5,000 vessels to put 326,000 men ashore in Europe in its first week. On the Eastern Front the Vistula-Oder operation of 1944 was launched on a front of 500km to a depth of 600km, took nearly three months to plan and lasted for two weeks. In an operation of such scale, which may assume the proportions of a campaign, the commander will be concerned with the management of tactical battles within an overall concept of operations, in which deception is likely to feature and inescapable logistic problems will require solution. Operation *Urgent Fury*, the liberation of Grenada by US forces in October 1983, was on a smaller scale by comparison, with 13 ships and 15,000 men directly involved, but the fact that it proceeded with some difficulty serves only to highlight the importance of proper understanding of the operational level, not least between the three services.[17]

The Function of Battle

Battle is the most striking component of war, and stands squarely at the centre of military history. The American combat analyst S.L.A. Marshall saw it as 'the epitome of war'.[18] General Henri Jomini, officer in the Napoleonic French and Russian armies and theorist of long-lasting importance, if pedantic bent, wrote that: 'Battles are the definitive clash of two armies which dispute great questions of politics and strategy.' His rival Clausewitz for once agreed, seeing combat as 'the central military art; all other activities merely support it'.[19] Colonel Charles Ardant du Picq, whose *Etudes sur le combat* (*Battle Studies*) was the first truly modern examination of the performance of men in battle, was of the same opinion, declaring that 'Battle is the final objective of armies . . .'[20] Finally, John Keegan, baring the face of battle with consummate success, maintained: 'Military history, we may infer, must in the last resort be about battle.'[21]

For all this, the eminence of battle is easily exaggerated. This tendency stems in part from the selective process of human memory and the part this plays in historiography. Asked to recall the events of 1916, a British veteran might be more likely to focus upon the battle of the Somme than upon months of less dangerous and less memorable routine in the trenches, in reserve or on the move from one sector to another. In a diary kept at the time, however, other events might loom as large. Ernest Shephard, an acutely observant company sergeant-major in the Dorsets, kept a meticulous diary during his time at the front, and although he recognised that 1 July, the first day of the battle, was the culmination of much effort and a time of acute peril, the space accorded it is by no means disproportionate, vying with descriptions of a big parade, the syllabus of the GHQ Cadet School, or a 'ramsammy' in the sergeants' mess. And he found time to record a memorable feature of 1 July 1916: 'A lovely day, intensely hot.'[22]

Military historians are, of course, busily concerned with making order out of chaos, although in doing so they risk imposing upon events a coherence and logic which participants may not have recognised at the time. Over-simplification of hugely complex events conspires to infect all but the most objective writing, and deliberate falsification has characterised some 'official' history: Napoleon's attempt to re-order the events of Marengo so as to show him in a better light is a glaring example.

Some of the best-known clichés of battle historiography are demonstrably false. Take, for instance, the *Times* correspondent W.H. Russell's account of the stand of the 93rd Highlanders at Balaklava on 25 October 1854. He described how Russian cavalry approached, and 'in one grand line charged in towards Balaklava. The ground flew beneath their horses' feet; gathering speed at every stride, they dashed towards that thin red streak tipped with steel'. The Highlanders stood their ground and fired, driving the Russians off and saving the British base of Balaklava.

It soon becomes clear that this was scarcely an engagement and certainly no battle. There is some difficulty in reconciling Russell's account with the paucity of Russian casualties. The 93rd's surgeon put Russian dead at 'not more than twelve', and a suggestion that many mortally wounded Russians clung to their saddles long enough to slump to the ground just out of sight is unconvincing. An officer of the 93rd told a comrade: 'the cavalry were never within eight hundred yards of our line and between us there was a ravine deep enough to swallow up the whole of them if they charged; we fired a volley at them and a fellow was seen to fall off a grey horse, but we couldn't tell if he were hit by us or not.' None the less, Russell's account (with the 'thin red streak' soon turned into the 'thin red line' of popular mythology) was rapidly confirmed by Robert Gibb's painting (with an officer falling from a grey almost on to the Highlander's newly whitened spats): fiction had become truth.[23]

The British Official History of the First World War has been attacked for a lack of objectivity: here it is perhaps kindest to agree with Tim Travers that it 'tended to avoid specific criticisms and tell the story as a straightforward narrative'.[24] Yet the work of the Battles Nomenclature Committee reveals just how difficult it was even to decide what to call a First World War battle, and set time-limits to it. The process of dividing war up into periods marked by battles, and splitting those battles into clearly defined phases is probably as inevitable as our hunt for a hierachy of causes for a war, but it can be just as distortive. Artists lend momentum to the process, with battle-pieces – from Uccello's stylised *The Rout of San Romano*, through countless groaning canvases of Austerlitz and Wagram, Salamanca and Waterloo, to Terence Cuneo's realistic *Goose Green* – setting the seal on it.

Our fascination with battle can also exaggerate its frequency. For much of history pitched battle was a relatively uncommon event, made so because the process of deploying an army on suitable terrain meant that battle was a matter of seduction, difficult to accomplish without both participants' consent. Sir Charles Oman observed of the Middle Ages that:

Great battles were, on the whole, infrequent, a fact which appears strange when the long-continued wars of the period are taken into consideration . . . Even when two forces were actually in presence, it sometimes required more skill than the commanders owned to bring on a battle. Bela IV of Hungary and Ottokar II of Bohemia were in arms in 1260 and both were equally bent on fighting, but when they sighted each other it was only to find that the River March was between them.[25]

Lack of maps did not help, and much laborious manoeuvring might be involved before even seventeenth- or eighteenth-century armies could get to grips. On the morning of Kolin in 1757, when Frederick the Great was giving out his orders in the inn of Slati Slunce on the Kaiserstrasse east of Prague, he announced: 'Gentlemen, many of you must still remember this neighbourhood from the time we stood here in 1742. I am certain I have the plan somewhere, but Major von Griese cannot find it.' In the event, the Austrian position was wider than expected and the Prussian attack went awry.[26] A shortage of accurate timepieces had similar effects, and numerous battles were ruined because signal guns were misunderstood or simply not heard: well might Lewis Mumford argue that the clock is the most important machine of our culture.[27]

Sometimes the scarcity of battle was no accident. Sun Tsu, who wrote in China in about 500 BC, became accessible in the West after his translation into French in the eighteenth century, and there were even four Russian translations current by the time that a good English-language version appeared in 1963. His suggestion that war might be more about the avoidance than the fighting of battle is an important one: 'to fight and conquer in all your battles is not supreme excellence: supreme excellence consists in breaking the enemy's resistance without fighting'.[28] This was a difficult philosophy to apply in the Middle Ages, when knightly machismo demanded battle at all costs and honour forbade the refusal of a challenge. Nevertheless, it was only after the French adopted the policy of refusing battle except on terms that suited them that the English position in France became untenable. In 1373 the Earl of Lancaster marched the length and breadth of France but could not provoke a battle in which his archers might have repeated the success of Poitiers, Crécy and Auray. Instead, the French, under Bertrand du Guesclin, shunned major battle but sapped English strength by skirmishes, ambushes and sieges, fighting exactly that sort of war which the English, at the very periphery of their power, found most taxing.

Avoidance of battle was also feasible enough in eighteenth-century Europe, when a commander might be manoeuvred into a position in which he would prefer an honourable capitulation to a last-ditch defence, especially if many of his soldiers, in Barry Lyndon's words, did not much care whether the eagle they marched under had one head or two. Moreover, the campaign might have well-defined geographical objectives – a province, a river or fortress-line to 'improve' the frontier – which could be secured by manoeuvre. The strength of fortresses was a brake on offensive operations, for ponderous siege trains and provision convoys did not make for lightning war.

The growth of national armies together with improvements in armaments and training made battle increasingly bloody. Marlborough lost 33 per cent of the soldiers he committed at Malplaquet in 1709, and at Zorndorf in 1758 the Prussians lost 38 per cent and the Russians 50 per cent of those engaged.[29] Soldiers were expensive to train and equip, and battle killed or wounded them in numbers not easily replaced from a Europe whose population growth had not matched the increasing size of armies. Battle was notoriously uncertain, a fact illustrated by Frederick's own track-record. Maurice de Saxe was overstating the case when he affirmed that 'a skilful general could make war all his life without being forced into one', but knowledge that a morning of bad luck (or, more appositely, a half-remembered piece of ground) could undo the work of months gave even Frederick pause for thought, despite his assertion that: 'It is battle that decides the fate of a state.' The military historian Hans Delbrück earned much criticism from his countrymen when he questioned whether Frederick was always anxious for battle. Why, he asked, did Frederick, after his great victory at Hohenfriedberg in 1741, decline to use his two-to-one superiority to finish off his opponents, but resort again to a war of manoeuvre?[30]

There was also evidence that battle, risky and costly though it was, often decided very little: Marlborough's brilliant victory at Blenheim in 1704 did not prevent the War of Spanish Succession lurching on, through increasingly unsatisfactory actions at Ramillies, Oudenarde and Malplaquet, to a compromise peace. We should not overestimate the importance of humanitarian restraints or doubts about the utility of battle during the eighteenth century, though both made some contribution to the limited war which most historians see as characteristic of the period.

The French Convention's *levée en masse* decree of August 1793 had profound implications for the utility of battle and much else besides. Although views of its effectiveness in producing soldiers vary – an estimate of one million men under arms by August 1794 is probably optimistic – neither casualties nor a high desertion rate could alter the Revolutionary armies' ability to spend manpower in a fashion that the tight monarchical armies could not equal. Much of it was at best part-trained, but the fact that many of the *ancien régime*'s gunner officers had not emigrated, unlike so many of their comrades in the cavalry and infantry; that the rapid promotion of experienced and ambitious sergeants provided a nucleus of competent leadership; and that tactics based on swarms of tirailleurs were both well-suited to the men swept into the army in the 1790s and profoundly galling to pipeclayed lines of conventional infantry, all combined to enable the Revolutionary armies to use battle as a bludgeon against which the armies of old Europe lost their edge. Lazare Carnot, a former engineer officer who headed the Committee of Public Safety's war section, ordered his armies to: 'act in mass formation and take the offensive. Join action with the bayonet on every occasion. Give battle on a large scale and pursue the enemy till he is utterly destroyed.'[31] Carnot's aggressive vigour had economic and political as well as military motives, for by carrying the war on to foreign territory it could be made to pay for itself by requisitions or plain looting, and the revolutionary gospel could be spread to an 'enslaved and reactionary' Europe.

Discovering Napoleon's views on battle is made no easier by the fact that he never formulated a precise system of warfare on paper, and his massive *Correspondance* can, like Hegel's philosophy or the Old Testament, be construed in numerous ways. Nevertheless, his approach to battle was consistent in both theory and practice. 'I see only one thing,' he wrote in 1797, 'namely the enemy's main body. I try to crush it, confident that secondary matters will then settle themselves.'[32] 'It is upon the field of battle', he declared, 'that the fate of fortresses and empires is decided.'[33] He recognised that chance played a large part in war, and strove to minimise the damage inflicted by bad luck and to capitalise upon the least hint of good. By ensuring the security of his own army, using a variety of stratagems to deceive the enemy ('Napoleon has *humbugged* me, by God,' acknowledged Wellington before Waterloo), and moving with his *corps d'armée* within concentrating distance, Napoleon tried to unite to face his opponents on ground of his own choosing.

Often he succeeded by using *manoeuvre sur les derrières*, pinning the enemy to his position by a feint attack and marching on his flank or rear, cutting lines of communication and forcing him to fight in unfavourable circumstances or to surrender. It was above all by mobility, leading to the concentration of force at the decisive point, that Napoleon operated when at his best, and he sometimes used this mobility to strike an alliance at its natural point of cleavage. The technique, when it worked, could indeed produce decisive results, with the utter overthrow of Prussia as a result of Jena in 1806 as the classic case.

Yet there were difficulties even with the Napoleonic battle. Few produced the results of Jena. Austerlitz, another master-stroke, inflicted far less damage on the Russians, with their remarkable recuperative powers, than Napoleon believed, and the Austrians had recovered sufficiently to fight him to a standstill at Aspern-Essling four years later. And when manoeuvre was impossible (or simply, because of Napoleon's health or state of mind, unacceptable) he embarked upon straightforward slogging matches. Borodino, where the French and Russian armies between them sufferered 100,000 casualties – 30 per cent of the combatants – is an example of frontal bludgeon-work which few other military reputations would have survived. We may attribute this, in part, to the influence of Napoleon's military education. The Comte de Guibert had warned of the indecisive combat of armies which states could neither recruit nor pay, and Frederick had advocated 'short and lively wars'. Napoleon's capricious disregard for casualties also helped. 'You cannot stop me,' he warned the Austrian diplomat Metternich: 'I can spend 30,000 men a month.' This analogy, linking war with commerce, has become a familiar one. It was a thread that Engels drew from Clausewitz, as he wrote to Marx in 1857: 'Fighting is to war what cash payment is to trade, for however rarely it may be necessary for it actually to occur, everything is to be directed towards it, and eventually it must take place all the same and must be decisive.'[34] In Napoleon's case it was as much the routine daily expenditure of a campaign (he was losing five to six thousand a day on his advance to Moscow in 1812) as the exorbitant cost of battles like Borodino that eventually bankrupted him.

Napoleon's ultimate downfall had important economic and political aspects, but it is ironic that it was failure in battle (the very medium in which he had once excelled) that destroyed him. Forsaking manoeuvre might work well enough, though at a price, when numbers were on his side: when they were not (at Leipzig in October 1813 he was outnumbered nearly two to one) he traded resources he could not replace for those his opponents could. He remained reluctant to delegate, and when he did so he was often disappointed, because many of his senior subordinates were unsuited to independent command and because of an over-centralised staff system in which even the great Berthier, his chief of staff, was firmly directed by his master's will.35

As the glare of Napoleon's comet sunk over the horizon towards Saint Helena, his interpreters attempted to establish the principles which had brought him success. Jomini declared that strategy was the key to warfare, that it was controlled by scientific principles, and that these principles prescribed offensive action as a means of massing superior forces at the decisive point.36 The influence of the eighteenth century, as much spiritual as intellectual, made Jomini hanker after the order, precision, and smaller armies, of 'the good old times' when the fate of provinces, rather than the survival of nations, was at stake. Although he agreed with Napoleon that the prime object of strategy was the destruction of the enemy army, he argued that by skilful selection of the correct line of operations (and here the geometricity of the eighteenth century loomed large) a general could force his opponent to fall back.

We should not make more of the clash between Jomini and Clausewitz than the evidence warrants, for the former certainly did not ignore the question of morale, but he did oversimplify the events of 1796–1815, bending them to fit his pattern and conveniently overlooking those which could not be persuaded to conform. Jomini was a good publicist (like some subsequent analysts he made a point of telling his audience what it wanted to hear) and his enormous influence spread through Europe to the United States, where 'Old Brains' Halleck, Lincoln's military adviser for much of the American Civil War, worked on his translation of Jomini's *Vie de Napoléon* while in the field.

Sir Edward Hamley, the first professor of military history at the British army's Staff College, whose *Operations of War* drew heavily, if uncritically, on Jomini, recognised that Napoleon had been most successful in short campaigns, and suggested that the object of a war should be limited to what could be accomplished in one. Just as Jomini had shied away from the mass armies of the Napoleonic wars, so Hamley declined to draw the logical conclusion from the American Civil War – that economic strength and numbers of men under arms would grind down even an enemy who showed himself superior in manoeuvre. He also doubted the value of battles – which were merely 'incidents in a campaign' – and saw armies as being so constrained by logistics that their operations had strict limitations.

Clausewitz enjoyed far less influence than Jomini during his life. His chief work, *Vom Kriege* (*On War*), was published after his death in an unrevised form, and its inconsistencies and repetitions blurred the intellectual strength of its argument. Furthermore, its emphasis on the unpredictable and uncertain nature of war was far less appealing to many readers than Jomini's geometrical certainties: the best prescription for victory that Clausewitz could offer was to be strong in general but above all at the decisive point. Clausewitz sought to reach the essence of absolute war by means of logical analysis, so as to enable his readers to understand war in the form that it actually takes. Analysis was constantly tried against the touchstone of war to test the validity of theory. War is 'an act of force, and there is no logical limit to the application of that force'.[37] But absolute war is circumscribed. First, because it is a 'political instrument, the continuation of political activity by other means'.[38] Second, neither side is fully in control of events because of the activities of its opponent. Without the opponent there is no war but bloodless occupation or untrammelled massacre: this notion of mutuality is an important one. Third, war is impeded by the element of friction that constantly intrudes itself between the real and the ideal, making even the simplest things difficult.

The destruction of the enemy's forces, argued Clausewitz, was the most significant military objective of war, and this could best be achieved by battle. 'Since the essence of war is fighting', he wrote, 'and since the battle is the fight of the main force, the battle must always be considered as the centre of gravity of the war.'[39] Manoeuvre was not, in some gentlemanly eighteenth-century way, a means of threatening lines of communication: it was the way of bringing about battle, 'a struggle for real victory, waged with all available strength'.[40] Clausewitz pushed the point home with typical vigour: 'We are not interested in generals who win victories without bloodshed. The fact that slaughter is a horrifying spectacle must make us take war more seriously, but not provide an excuse for gradually blunting our swords in the name of humanity. Sooner or later someone will come along with a sharp sword and hack off our arms.'[41]

It is typical of the tensions within *On War* that this emphasis on seeking battle is counterbalanced by belief that defence is the stronger form of war. Clausewitz recognised the moral value of the offensive, but saw the momentum of the attack gradually exhausting itself. The offensive proceeds with diminishing power until 'the culminating point of victory' is reached, when the attacker is himself vulnerable to 'the flashing sword of vengeance' in the counter-attack.[42] Clausewitz's personal experience of the 1812 campaign, when he fought as a colonel in Russian service, undoubtedly lent emphasis to this view. Finally, we should note his identification of the 'remarkable trinity' of which war is composed. Violence and passion concern the *people*; chance and uncertainty are the medium in which the *army* must operate, and political purpose and effect is the business of the *government*.

Although Clausewitz's errors and omissions were numerous – neglect of seapower, scant attention to surprise, disregard for logistics – it was the form in which his views appeared and, above all, his refusal to offer pat solutions to immense problems that lessened his impact on his own age. In this century the lack of a satisfactory English translation until Michael Howard and Peter Paret's edition of *On War* appeared in 1976, coupled with a tendency to blame the events of the First World War upon 'The Mahdi of Mass', as Liddell Hart called him, combined to impede understanding.

The prophet had only a measure of honour in his own country. The elder von Moltke, architect of Prussian victory in the Austro-Prussian war of 1866 and the Franco-Prussian war of 1870–1, was much influenced by him, especially in his realistic acceptance that friction meant: 'No plan of operations can look with any certainty beyond the first meeting with the forces of the enemy.'[43] Unlike Clausewitz, who never held important command in the field, Moltke was 'essentially a grammarian of war who indulged in little abstract speculation'.[44] He was sceptical about the function of politics, arguing that political considerations could be taken into account only as long as they did not make improper military demands. And if he accepted the Clausewitzian imperative of battle, he rejected the notion of defensive war except as a temporary expedient to be adopted in the event of a sudden enemy offensive.[45] In both 1866 and 1870 the rapidity of Moltke's strategic *aufmarsch* gave him an initial advantage, and the flexibility of his armies enabled him to capitalise on errors of his opponents.

Moltke and his subordinates made their own mistakes, and in 1870 General von Steinmetz, commanding the First Army, displayed pig-headedness which almost any army would have found embarrassing. Some of the difficulties subsequently experienced by the Germans were rooted in a misreading of the events of 1866 and 1870. Moltke's opponents showed a poor grasp of the strategic and operational levels, and though they sometimes out-performed the Prussians tactically (the achievements of the Austrian artillery at Sadowa and the French infantry at Gravelotte deserve recognition) their inability to produce cohesive operational plans cost them dear.

Moltke's general staff played a key role in victory, acting as the central nervous system of a mass army, striving to keep headstrong or overcautious commanders on course, providing a fund of professional advice, and linking the army's individual formations to the directing brain of Moltke himself. The Germans could no more patent the general staff than they could strategic deployment by railway, and many of the advantages they enjoyed in 1870 had vanished a generation later. Worse, for all the alleged objectivity of the general staff, it was not above burnishing the official account to remove flaws, and the swirling uncertainties of August 1870 vanished in well-polished prose.[46] It was easy, and not altogether misleading, to attribute success to a system which enabled the Germans to be strong on the battlefield by marching to the sound of the guns, using this strength to outflank the enemy and thus compensate for the tactical advantage conferred on the defender by breech-loading rifles. It was similarly easy for the war's battles to assume immense significance, even though Sedan (which resulted in the destruction of an entire French army and the capture of Napoleon III) was fought on 1 September, and the war dragged on till 28 January 1871.

The chief emphasis of the war's literature lay upon its first six weeks and major battles rather than upon the fighting in the provinces which taxed German skill far more than the flailing blows of the Imperial armies. However, even in this, the second of Moltke's dramatically successful wars, we see constraints upon the decisiveness of battle. No longer were major actions one-day affairs as a rule: Rezonville-Gravelotte consisted of two full days of fighting divided by one of redeployment, just as Gettysburg, seven years before, had burned on for three days. The mobilisation of mass armies supported by the resources of burgeoning industry also militated against decisiveness, and the relative simplicity of the breech-loading rifle helped even sketchily trained irregulars operate with effect against the flank and rear of armies which would have swept them away in open field.

The legacy of 1870 did more than sour Franco-German relations, effectively ensuring a future clash. It fostered the militarisation of German society and encouraged the military's tendency, already visible in friction between Moltke and Bismarck during the war, to see its activities as being independent of politics. Count Alfred von Schlieffen, Moltke's successor as chief of the general staff and the archetypical ascetic professional soldier, grappled with the problems of fighting a war on two fronts (a result of the Franco-Russian treaty of 1894) and controlling the huge armies brought into being by conscription. Schlieffen was well aware of the destructive potential of modern weapons, and convinced that 'ordinary victories' were no use to him. Desire to avoid frontal assault and fascination with the flank attack – 'the essential substance of the whole history of war' – led to a focus on the battle of annihilation, exemplified for him, after reading Hans Delbrück's study of the battle, by Hannibal's great victory of Cannae.[47]

Delbrück had greater influence than Clausewitz upon Schlieffen's planning, underlining the at best patchy impact of Clausewitz upon German military thought. Schlieffen proposed to turn Germany's central position to his advantage by acting strategically on interior lines (in the event, concentrating in the west and holding in the east) but moving operationally on exterior lines to produce the encirclement he craved. Instead of concentrating prior to battle, which would be likely to result in a head-on conflict as the enemy followed suit, he sought to concentrate during it, by gathering momentum on the wheeling flank so as create a centre of gravity (*Schwerpunktbildung*). The ensuing battle would be decisive, ending the war in the west with a single mighty blow.

One acute commentator on Schlieffen has observed that his apolitical, purely practical approach 'turned war into a trade and the commander into a mechanic . . .'[48] His was certainly a heady cocktail of Clausewitzian emphasis on decisive battle and Jominian regard for geometry, and his preoccupation with the maintenance of an unbroken advancing line was almost like eighteenth-century tactics

74

writ large – not surprisingly, perhaps, for until 1909 Schlieffen's model was Frederick's victory of Leuthen. Schlieffen's plan failed, in part for reasons of which Clausewitz had already warned: the advancing troops and their commanders were ground down by the friction of war, and the will of the commander (the younger Moltke, nephew of the old Field Marshal) crumbled at the crucial moment.[49] There is also doubt as to whether Schlieffen's decisive battle was logistically sustainable. The younger Moltke has had a bad press, but he took logistics far more seriously than Schlieffen had: even his concern may not have guaranteed food, fodder and above all ammunition at the decisive point.

The French sought a decisive battle just as much as their opponents. Clausewitz had at least a supporting role to play, for the French had studied him eagerly after the Franco-Prussian war. It was study as selective as that which went on across the Rhine, as the French fell upon those passages in which Clausewitz wrote of the supremacy of moral forces. Here Clausewitz melded encouragingly with Ardant du Picq to depict battle as, above all, a clash of will, and both the popular philosophy of Henri Bergson and the 'Nationalist Revival' movement fostered l'élan vital, that furia francese which alone could check the rising menace of Germany. For the French the decisive battle was a national imperative, a means of expunging the stain of 1870 and an affirmation of the strength of French manhood.[50] It was a belief bolstered by a narrow view of history, for emphasis on the decisive battles of the Napoleonic period discouraged interpretation of the Wars of the Revolution and Empire as a long struggle in which the weight of resources wore France down.

The quest for battle in the years leading up to 1914 was also, by yet another paradox, a response to the very growth of firepower which would make battle less productive and more costly. Determination was, so it was argued, an answer to firepower. This was nothing new. In 1863, as cavalry sought to find a role on a battlefield made increasingly complex by the multiplication of fire, a French cavalry officer had claimed that:

> weapons so deadly and dangerous from a distance can never replace the action of cavalry on the battlefield, nor even diminish or hinder it . . . we will prove to our detractors and our enemies that *the impossible can be asked of the reserve cavalry*.[51]

75

The evidence of the Boer War, when men armed with magazine rifles using smokeless powder stopped British attacks in their tracks, persuaded both French and British armies to recast their infantry regulations in recognition that close-order attacks would be impossible on battlefields dominated by fire.

There was a reaction against what a French officer called 'acute transvaalitis' even before the Russo-Japanese War. The evidence of this war – when brave and bloody attacks had brought the Japanese victory at Port Arthur and Mukden – was widely misinterpreted by the many military attachés who assembled it. There was much emphasis on its being a special case – the terrain was atypical and the Japanese showed a disregard for casualties which European armies could not be expected to share. It was used to justify an increased emphasis on the offensive and a return, in the French army's 1913 Regulations, of shoulder to shoulder formations. In Russia there was a lengthy debate between the 'academics' like Colonel A.A. Neznamov, who argued that 'fire decides battle' and the 'nationalists', who were influenced not merely by General Dragomirov's 1906 assertion that the complementary realationship between bullet and bayonet would remain, regardless of improvements in firearms, but also by old Suvorov's maxim that the bullet is a fool but the bayonet knows what it is about. In Britain, even Lieutenant-General Sir Ian Hamilton, an officer with a reputation for intellect, wrote how:

> Blindness to moral forces and worship of material forces inevitably leads in war to destruction . . . all that trash written by M. Bloch [Polish author of the prescient *Is War now Impossible?*] about zones of fire across which no living being could pass, heralded nothing but disaster. War is essentially the triumph, not of a chassepot over a needle gun, not of a line of men entrenched behind wire entanglements and fireswept zones over men exposing themselves in the open, but of one will over another weaker will.[52]

The fact that there was a skein of truth in comments like this (after all, it is hard to disagree with Hamilton's first sentence) only made their effect more pronounced as European armies prepared themselves physically and psychologically for the battle from which only cowards hung back and in which great sacrifices had to be accepted.

The short-war philosophy that held sway on both sides of the Rhine before 1914 was reinforced by belief that a long war would impose immense economic and social strain, and that the offensive, with all its moral strength, would produce a decisive result quickly. The first years of the First World War did little to justify such widespread confidence in the utility of battle. The great battle of encirclement eluded the Germans in the west, and victory in the east at Tannenberg produced little immediate effect despite its impressive scale. For the British and French a series of offensive battles failed to reap any reward commensurate with the losses suffered. The German offensive at Verdun in 1916, planned by Falkenhayn, Moltke's successor, as a giant suction-pump through which French life-blood would be drained, proved as damaging to the Germans as it did to the French. Part of the German difficulty lay in Falkenhayn's disguising of his real intentions not only from his superior, the Kaiser, but also from the Crown Prince who, as commander of the German 5th Army, was the operational commander and should therefore have been in Falkenhayn's mind. If Falkenhayn hoped for an attritional battle brought on by the French need to defend Verdun, then it was not in his interests to take it, but the Crown Prince certainly thought in terms of capturing the city.[53]

The arrival of Hindenburg and Ludendorff at supreme headquarters brought with it a change of emphasis. A more objective view was taken of Germany's military position, with attempts to harness all Germany's resources to the war on the one hand and a realistic shortening of the front by the withdrawal to the Hindenburg Line on the other. However, American entry into the war meant that a policy of waiting on the defensive on the Western Front (despite the skilful development of defensive techniques in 1916–17) was no longer tolerable. The German plan for the spring offensive of 1918 emphasised tactics before strategy. The attack was directed against those points where tactical success was most likely: Ludendorff, writing after the war, admitted that 'I was influenced by time and by tactical considerations.'[54] There was no clear operational link between the tactical battle and a strategic goal, and the offensives of March–May 1918, despite impressive success, were ultimately purposeless. Worse still, Ludendorff's decision to hold the salient hammered into Allied lines invited counter-attacks and brought on exactly that sort of fighting which Germany, at the end of her resources, could least afford.

The Allies were no more successful in appealing to the arbitrament of battle. In his final dispatch, Sir Douglas Haig declared that:

> if the operations of the past 4½ years are regarded as a single continuous campaign, there can be recognised in them the same general features and the same necessary stages which between forces of approximately equal strength have marked all the conclusive battles of history . . . If the whole operations of the present war are regarded in the correct perspective, the victories of the summer and autumn of 1918 will be seen to be as directly dependent upon the two years of stubborn fighting that preceded them.[55]

There is conflict between historians over the extent to which Haig's dispatch embodied his view of the war as he fought it or whether it was simply an *ex post facto* rationalisation of what had actually happened.[56] As far as my argument is concerned, however, this debate is irrelevant. What matters is that battle, in a climactic sense, had been less important than an attritional struggle in which manpower, popular support and economic strength had proved decisive.

Questions of the function and utility of battle lay at the heart of the inter-war military debate. The French believed that another European war would take the same attritional form as the First World War, and the Maginot Line was an attempt to deter aggression by making it appear utterly unprofitable or, if Germany did attack, to interpose a barrier behind which France could mobilise reserves and industry. It was a policy which relegated battle to a subordinate role and, if we see the whole of the Second World War in Europe as the sustained attrition of Germany, it may have had more to recommend it than its tactical and operational failure suggest. Some theorists, notably J.F.C Fuller and Basil Liddell Hart in England, Charles de Gaulle in France, and Heinz Guderian in Germany, saw mobility as a means of reintroducing decisiveness into war. In his short book *Paris, or the Future of War*, Liddell Hart argued, in a phrase that may not unfairly typify the views of the tank pioneers, that tanks should be:

> concentrated and used in as large masses as possible for a decisive blow against the Achilles' heel of the enemy army, the communications and command centres which form its nerve system. Then not only may we see the rescue of mobility from the toils of

trench-warfare, but with it the revival of generalship and the art of war, in contrast to its mere mechanics.[57]

Fuller (who disagreed with Liddell Hart in certain important respects) nevertheless saw battles, in a striking phrase, as 'works of art and not merely daubs of blood'.[58]

The debate has been capably explored elsewhere, but we should recognise that it was more complex than is often supposed, and was not simply a case of far-sighted reformers colliding with the bone-headed conservatism of the military establishment.[59] It ended with a French army which retained its traditional basis of conscript infantry with a leavening of armoured formations, a motorised British Expeditionary Force, and a German army in which the undigested ingredients of the debate were most clearly visible. The mechanisation of the Germany army had been, and was to remain, selective. Behind the panzer divisions trailed foot-mobile infantry with horse transport: an infantry division in 1940 had 942 motor vehicles but 5,375 horses. Diversity ruled where quantity did not: the German army had over 1,000 types of wheeled vehicle on its inventory. Even at the peak reached in mid-1943 less than twelve per cent of panzergrenadier battalions were equipped with armoured vehicles, and on one day early that year Army Groups North and Centre could muster just three battleworthy tanks between them. This was undoubtedly an exception, but the panzer division with an effective fighting strength of thirty tanks was not.[60]

The Russian army, too, had been through a debate on mechanisation, complicated, in the most bloody way, by the intervention of Stalin. V.K. Triandifillov's book *Basic Character of Operations of Modern Armies* discussed the concept of 'deep battle', and Marshal M.N. Tuchachevskii elaborated it in the 1920s and 30s. Tuchachevskii pressed ahead with the creation of a mechanised force quite independent of the mechanisation of the main army. This, in a fashion similar to that described by Fuller and Liddell Hart, but tracing its ancestry certainly to Peter the Great's *corps volant*, and perhaps as far back as the Mongol *tumans*, would thrust into the enemy's deep rear. In the words of Brigadier Richard Simpkin:

Tuchachevskii saw these 'fast forces' as working at operational level, well beyond the scope of the main forces. Rather they would co-operate with airborne forces, especially *mechanised* airborne forces, in extremely wide and deep sweeps against the enemy's soft underbelly.[61]

The development of the Red Army along the lines suggested by Tuchachevskii and his allies came to a bloody halt in the 1930s when Stalin purged the army: between a quarter and a half of the officer corps perished, and Tuchachevskii himself was shot in July 1937.[62]

For all Tuchachevskii's emphasis on deep offensive operations, he was less confident in offensive strategy, and feared that a war leading to the annexation of territory would result in the army's morale being sapped by the task of occupation, a view mirrored in later Soviet concern for the 'unusability' of armed force and no doubt given weight by recent experience in Afghanistan and, even more tellingly, in the Soviet Union's southern republics.[63] And, despite his emphasis upon the military elements of conflict, he believed that the means of waging war stemmed from the organisation of the industrial base and the sustenance of the working population, echoing the conviction of Marx and Engels that war has a fourfold nature – diplomatic, economic, psychological and only as a last resort military.[64]

In 1941 the immense damage done to the Red Army by the purges made the task of the invading Germans infinitely easier. In 1940 their concentrated armour had unravelled the Allied armies in France and Belgium in a campaign more reminiscent of Moltke's great victory in the 'Six Weeks War' of 1866 than the stalemate of 1915–17. This victory encouraged Hitler to press on with his deep-seated desire to overthrow the Bolshevik order and obtain *Lebensraum* in the east, and the plan for Operation *Barbarossa* spoke of 'daring operations led by deeply penetrating armoured spearheads'. In the first few weeks the Germans snapped up hundreds of thousands of Russians in great battles of encirclement – Minsk, Smolensk, Kiev, Vyazma-Bryansk – but Soviet political will held, new factories were set up east of the Urals to replace those swamped by the tide of invasion, and German behaviour in occupied areas alienated national groups who might have preferred German to Soviet rule.

It is fundamentally misleading to search for a decisive battle on the Eastern Front, balancing Stalingrad against Kursk as the most likely alternatives. We should instead consider the war as a sustained campaign of attrition, with German manpower and machinery being exchanged for Soviet resources at a rate that the Germans, with their poorly developed industrial power-base, could not afford. True,

Stalingrad was psychologically significant in that it was Germany's first substantial defeat (Alamein cannot begin to compare with it in scale), and Kursk was materially important in that it wrote off Germany's last armoured reserve, condemning her commanders in the east to a strategy of stop-gaps thereafter.

After the war it suited British and Americans alike to discuss the war with German generals so as to gain a better idea of how to fight the Russians. Some of this discussion was counter-productive, for the Germans, understandably enough, emphasised their own tactical excellence and the clumsiness of their opponents. More attention might have been paid to Soviet achievements at the operational level, but it was not until the appearance of John Erickson's magisterial studies of the conflict, *The Road to Stalingrad* and *The Road to Berlin*, that the war was properly explored, in English, from the Soviet viewpoint. Western interest in small-group cohesion as a means – even the prime means – of promoting battlefield performance also helped veil the very real importance of ideology in the fighting in the east, and the way in which what Omer Bartov calls 'the barbarisation of warfare' produced a struggle more nearly approaching totality than any other modern conflict.[65]

Two major developments overshadowed the utility of battle in the postwar world. The first was the development of the nuclear weapon which, as we have seen, has made direct armed conflict between the superpowers a high-risk venture. Indeed, Stoessinger has argued convincingly that, as war between the superpowers is suicidal and wars between smaller powers with powerful friends are likely to be inconclusive and interminable, decisive war has become the privilege of the impotent. The Falklands may not bear him out, but the Iran–Iraq war sustains his case powerfully. The Arab–Israeli wars are most usefully considered as a long campaign with periods of 'peace' interspersed by sharp bursts of mid- or high-intensity operations. They too suggest that battle may have limited use, and it is significant that Israel's security seems more assured on her south-western border, where the frontier was the result of negotiation, rather than to the east, where it was imposed by military success. One could scarcely wish for a more impressive victory than that achieved by Israel in the Beka'a valley in June 1982, with the Syrian air force driven from the sky and the way to Beirut opened by Israeli ground forces. Far from being decisive, however, this battle led the Israeli army into fighting in the streets of Beirut in circumstances where neither tactical flair nor technical superiority were of much use. Worse, the fighting in Beirut accelerated the process (grimly continued by the *intifada* on the West Bank) of turning the David of 1948 into the Goliath of 1988 with all that implies in terms of world public opinion and international support. However, caution is appropriate. Israel did not obtain lasting peace through military victory in 1967 or 1973, but there is every probabilty that her defeat in either war would indeed have been conclusive: she may not have gained security by victory but she could ill afford the penalty of defeat.

The second crucial development of the postwar years has been the rise of guerrilla warfare. This, of course, is not a new phenomenon: Clausewitz had made penetrating observations on what he called 'peoples' war' as a result of the Spanish experience in 1808–14. He saw popular forces as auxiliaries to regular armies, not substitutes for them, and thought in terms of war between states rather than internal revolution. Just as conventional soldiers were preoccupied with decisive battles, so many nineteenth-century revolutionaries believed that insurrection would be short and sharp, and the success of Parisian revolutionaries in the 'June Days' of 1848 gave them some comfort. Nevertheless, colonial wars provided evidence of long-running campaigns with no natural culminating point, and in the Boer War the British defeated the Boer regular armies in six months but took two painful years to overcome commandos whose flexibility and mastery of the veld caused serious problems to a numerically superior British force. T. E. Lawrence, accompanying the Arab forces in their revolt against the Turks during the First World War, emphasised the same point when he wrote: 'Granted mobility, security, time and doctrine, victory will rest with the insurgents.'[66]

Mao Tse-tung reached different conclusions. He believed that guerrillas were fundamentally important, and that their bands were 'the university of war' for the population upon which they, in turn, depended for support. But in order to triumph, the insurgents had to move through the guerrilla phase, establishing base areas (Lawrence's imperative of security), to engage in open battle with their opponents. His three-phase concept of protracted war (elaborated by Truong Chinh), rising from contention through equilibrium to the general counter-offensive – placed no time-limits on the struggle, and it was possible to revert from open operations to guerrilla warfare if things went wrong. When the Viet Minh took on the French in strength in the Red River Delta in 1951 they were roughly handled, but reduced the scale of their operations. This encouraged optimism among the French, who occupied a position at Dien Bien Phu, at the outer limit of their own logistic reach and, so they wrongly assumed, too far away from Viet Minh bases on the Chinese border for them to operate effectively. There was fuzzy thinking in the French high command as to the real function of Dien Bien Phu, but an underlying belief in the superiority of Western firepower in a pitched battle sustained commanders and garrison alike.

The battle misfired. When they attacked in March 1954 the Viet Minh produced artillery whose bombardment knocked the defenders' bunkers to pieces about their ears, and a combination of human wave assaults and dogged trench-digging enabled their infantry to overwhelm French positions. Although Dien Bien Phu was a substantial reverse, it need not have proved fatal to a state which still had considerable armed strength at its disposal. However, the war was bitterly unpopular in France, and the battle profoundly influenced the negotiations which began in Geneva on the very day the last of Dien Bien Phu's positions fell. The battle was indeed decisive, but its real effect was psychological – on public opinion in Indo-China, in France and in the wider world – rather than purely military.[67]

American experience in the second Indo-China war bore out the lessons learnt by the French. In this case the Americans did not suffer defeat on anything approaching the scale of Dien Bien Phu – pitched battles in the Ia Drang and A Shau valleys in 1965–7 and at Khe Sanh in 1968 were American victories, and the United States cannot be said to have been defeated in strictly military terms. Reliance on firepower (a classic ingredient of a military culture which emphasises decision by battle) and lack of resolve to continue the war ultimately proved fatal to the Americans. The dimension of their failure is epitomised by a conversation between an American colonel and a North Vietnamese colonel in Hanoi in April 1975. 'You know you never defeated us on the battlefield,' said the American. 'That may be so,' replied the Vietnamese. 'But it is also irrelevant.'[68]

The British response to insurgency, which rejected the quest for decisive battle in favour of patience, good intelligence and sharply-honed low-level skills, proved much more successful, with the Malayan campaign of 1948–60 as its paradigm. It is essential to note that the scale of operations in Vietnam was much wider than in Malaya (the Americans had to contend with substantial main force units in large-scale conventional operations), and that the British had the immense advantage of being both the military and civil authority in Malaya while the Americans were supporting a corrupt and inefficient government in South Vietnam. Yet if no direct read-across is possible, the exploits of Australian and New Zealand troops in Vietnam suggest that the British approach had much to commend it. Nevertheless, it is arguable that even a complete transformation of United States tactics would not have altered the result of the war for, like the first Indo-China war, it was decided on the political and psychological front, not among the paddy-fields and rubber trees of the theatre of war.[69]

The theorists of urban guerrilla warfare sought to confront their enemy not in jungle or sierra, where firepower could be fully employed and the effect of operations on the media (and thus on public opinion) might be remote, but in the city. In the aftermath of fighting in Bolivia in 1966–7 South American theorists wrote of Ché Guevara's failure to foment revolution by creating a *foco* which would create revolutionary consciousness, achieving a sudden insurgency – a decisive battle of popular morale. The government would have ample power close at hand, but if it responded to the insurgents with the full range of weapons at its disposal it would alienate opinion and so bring insurgent victory closer. In practice urban guerrillas enjoyed no decisive success, in part because South American governments were prepared to use authoritarian measures which made supporting the insurgents a dangerous business, and in part because frustrated or misguided insurgents carried out acts of terrorism which impaired their own standing in the eyes of the community far more than they hurt the government. Provided that a government retained its resolve, and either demanded public support by coercion, or inspired it by skilful propaganda, it was likely to win.

The concept of the decisive battle will be of limited value in the 1990s and beyond. The risks of escalation will continue to make general war between nuclear powers an unreliable political instrument, forcing much military activity down into the low-intensity zone, precisely that in which both scale and intensity make battle itself least relevant. Popular resolve will remain crucial, for without it states will neither be able to maintain effective military establishments in peacetime nor use them effectively in war.

Yet battle is not obsolete. It remains an effective tool in limited war: the actions in the Falklands may have an old-fashioned ring to them, but they decided the campaign: with the loss of the islands went the junta's popular support, and with that went the war. The loss of the initial battle in general war might well have the same effect, persuading the public on the losing side that a compromise peace would be preferable to escalation: thus even in conventional war military operations are in part the 'armed propaganda' beloved of urban guerrillas. Battle also imposes strains on alliances, a fact of particular significance in the 1990s. In both 1914 and 1940 the Anglo-French alliance was weakened by military defeat. In 1914 Sir John French, alarmed at the losses that the BEF had suffered and deeply disillusioned by what he saw as the unreliable behaviour of his ally, proposed to withdraw his force from the line altogether, and was dissuaded only by the forceful personal intervention of Lord Kitchener, secretary of state for war.[70] In 1940 Lord Gort decided unilaterally upon evacuation through Dunkirk, a decision which had military logic to commend it but left an enduring scar on Anglo-French relations.

In the 1990s winning battles may not guarantee victory, but sustaining early defeats will sap popular resolve to continue the war. There is a mismatch here between the sustainability of war in different parts of the world. In the West, with its multiparty democracies, hyperactive media and well-developed tradition of liberal dissent, battle will spread powerful and unsettling ripples. British fatal casualties – military and civilian – in the Falklands equalled those sustained by any one of several hard-hit battalions on the first day of the Somme in 1916 – and were exceeded by those incurred by a single American regiment (the 107th Infantry of the 27th Division) in its attack on the Hindenburg Line in September 1918. During the Falklands War popular journalism tightened its focus on to individual casualties and their families, and it is likely that sustained heavy losses would have blunted national resolve. Totalitarian states, with controlled (or undeveloped) media and no legitimate tradition of dissent find it easier to sustain lost battles and long butcher's bills: the Gulf War is a chilling case in point.

It would be dangerous to claim that pitched battle has lost its utility, for there may yet be circumstances when the national interest demands that armies submit to its iron arbitrament. But the risk of escalation, the effect of casualties upon public opinion, and the uneven track-record of battle as a means of settling disputes will all promote caution. This reticence will be more marked in the northern hemisphere than the southern, and the armies and populations of Africa and Asia are likely to learn still more of the painful lessons so abundantly commemorated in stone across northern France and Belgium.

The conclusions which our Nuclear Warriors should draw from this are scarcely elusive. They should recognise that the exceedingly remote risk of general war demands a latent capability for sustained large-scale military action, but that such action will be so dependent on popular support that it will occur only when fuelled by the total and willing mobilisation of economy and society. While regular forces will leaven the armies which might fight such a war, the bulk of the combatants will be mobilised reservists or conscripts. The issues generating the popular support without which such an effort is impossible will be few, and we have more chance of seeing them in the southern hemisphere or the Islamic crescent than we do in the northern hemisphere.

It is far more likely that armies will find themselves used to project a nation's power far beyond its borders, on a limited scale and with limited objectives: the intervention operation was a characteristic of the 1980s, and it seems set fair to characterise the 1990s too. But the evidence of this section sketches in narrow parameters for such operations. They are anything but a guaranteed 'quick fix': for every military officer or civilian official warmly recommending intervention, there are a dozen, five years later, debating how best to ensure an honourable withdrawal. Particular care must be taken to ensure that there is not a potentially fatal mismatch between the surgical action imperatives of the interventionist – in, fix, out – and his opponent's ability to sustain low-intensity operations. The international risks of unilateral military action also suggest that intervention forces will rarely operate on a single-nation basis. Given that intervention is difficult enough even when conducted by the armed forces of one nation, a lesson driven home by Grenada and underlined, if less vigorously, by Panama, the command and control problems facing a multi-national intervention force are considerable.

Finally, to reiterate Clausewitz, war is a mutual activity. Intervening militarily against an opponent who declines (or is simply unable) to respond with conventional military force, but resists at the level of lowest possible intensity, places the most severe strain on the intervening army and makes its arraignment before the bar of world opinion almost certain. An army which faces stone-throwing youths with armoured personnel carriers could easily win the battle – if such a clash could meaningfully be termed battle – but it would eventually lose the war, as much in the hearts and minds of its own soldiers as in the columns of the press, domestic and foreign. For the intervention to be successful, therefore, it must embody the highest degree of flexibility, whose ability to give conventional battle may actually be less important than its ability to sustain low-level operations where the skills of the soldier mesh with those of the policeman, the diplomat – and even the agronomist and the doctor. Battle is but one instrument in the case: the sharpest, perhaps, but not necessarily the most useful.

Tools of the Trade

Writing in 1979, Michael Howard constructed a new framework for strategy, considering it in four dimensions, operational, social, logistic and technological.[71] The importance of the operational and social emerges clearly from the previous section, and emphasis on the need for economic strength points the way towards the logistic and technical. The former was widely ignored until the publication of Martin van Creveld's masterly *Supplying War: Logistics from Wallenstein to Patton*. Logisticians were 'the Cinderellas of war' for a variety of reasons. The 'gentlemen' of the combat arms tended to disdain the 'players' of the supporting services, as demonstrated by the late militarisation of the latter and their officers' painful ascent to proper commissioned rank: the Royal Indian Army Service Corps' initials RIASC were snobbishly alleged to stand for Really I Am So Common. There is also a more basic friction between those whose primary trade is combat and those who keep them supplied: witness unflattering nicknames from the *Ettappenschweine* of the First World War to the REMF (Rear Echelon Mother-Fuckers) of Vietnam. Moreover, military historiography's emphasis on battle helps to push logisticians into the shadows of military history.

We may consider logistics – 'the practical art of moving armies and keeping them supplied' – to have two aspects, the first concerning the manufacture or procurement of logistic resources and the second their supply to forces in the field. By the mid-nineteenth century the former, nerved by the teeming factories of the Industrial Revolution, had become more important than most professional soldiers were inclined to recognise. The American Civil War makes the point perfectly. In 1860 the states that were to make up the Union had 110,274 industrial establishments with $949,335,000 of capital investment: the states of the Confederacy 18,026 and $100,665,000 respectively. The North's arsenals produced 2,500,000 small arms during the war. The South imported 600,000 and captured thousands more, but its industry, old-fashioned and short of resources, could not begin to compete with the North's. A single anecdote is telling: when Union raiders killed John Jones, an expert barrel-straightener at Richmond Armory, production dropped by 369 rifles per month and it took several months to train a replacement.[72] The Confederacy's considerable achievements in the tactical and operational spheres were blunted by the North's growing industrial strength. Once Grant applied the operational logic of using 'all parts of the army together, and somewhat towards a common centre', with the Army of the Potomac elbowing its way from the Rapidan to Petersburg and Sherman gnawing from Atlanta to Savannah and up into the Carolinas, no tactical brilliance could save the Confederacy.

The relative simplicity of rifle and artillery ammunition in the American Civil War and the slow rates of fire of the muzzle-loading weapons most widely used enabled ammunition production to keep pace with expenditure. In the opening months of the First World War, however, magazine rifles and quick-firing artillery gobbled ammunition in unprecedented quantities. In 1914 British gunners fired a million rounds, four times as as many as they had in the whole of the Boer War. Pre-war ammunition scales, reflecting the prevailing notion of short, intense battles with high expenditure, proved unable to meet the unrelenting demands of trench warfare. The British began the war with 1,500 rounds in stock per 18-pounder gun: on the Somme in 1916 each had 1,000 rounds actually on the gun position. The 'Christmas pause' of 1914 arose partly because all combatants were short of ammunition, and immense efforts – with enduring social and economic consequences – were needed to enable industry to sate the hungry guns. In Britain, the Ministry of Munitions, set up as a response to a much-publicised munitions crisis in the spring of 1915, 'left a lasting impression on people's thinking', and in the Second World War Lord Beaverbrook consciously modelled the way he ran the Ministry of Aircraft Production on David Lloyd George's conduct of the Ministry of Munitions.[73]

The Second World War became a *Materialschlacht* in which Germany and Japan were utterly outbuilt by their opponents, and the importance of America as 'the arsenal of democracy' can scarcely be overstated. American war production was truly prodigious: 100,000 aircraft in 1944 alone, 84,000 tanks, over 2 million trucks, 6 million miles of barbed wire, and 2,500 Liberty ships. Russia's war production, too, clawed its way back up after the disasters of 1941–2: from 1943 about 30,000 tanks a year rolled off her production lines. German manufacture of armoured vehicles peaked at 19,000 in 1944.[74] The quest for essential resources had been one motive for Japanese expansion, and the combined effects of American island-hopping, naval blockade and air bombardment had so limited her raw materials and lacerated her industrial infrastructure that many historians endorse Lisle Rose's insistence that 'she simply could not have continued the war beyond mid-autumn' even if atomic bombs had not been dropped.[75]

Industrial weight is of little use unless it can be brought to bear, and the improvement of armies' logistic services helped shift food, fuel and ammunition from processing plants, factories and refineries to the troops that needed them. The adaption of the railway to military use in the nineteenth century was of immense importance, enabling troops and supplies to be delivered rapidly to forward railheads, and the wars of 1866 and 1870–1 showed the intimate relationship between large conscript armies and the railways that moved them to their concentration areas and kept them supplied thereafter. August 1914 saw 'war by timetable' puff and rattle its way across Europe as the combatants swept their armies to the frontiers by rail. The weak link remained the gap between railheads and advancing armies, and, as we have seen, it remains doubtful whether the decisive battle in Champagne, Schlieffen's objective, could have been sustained.

In the Second World War, neither the proliferation of trucks nor the use of transport aircraft should obscure the continuing importance of the railway. However, aircraft could, at times, be decisive: they supplied the British bastions of Kohima and Imphal on the borders of Burma in 1944 and were indispensable for the 14th Army generally, while on the Eastern Front they sustained the German pockets at Kholm and Demyansk. In the latter case their achievement was misleading, for the *Luftwaffe*'s success at

Demyansk encouraged the Germans to expect too much of it at Stalingrad.

A first glance might suggest that logistics since 1945 has become more simple. High-mobility load carriers, palletised loads and integral cranes have made land transport more efficient. Every dimension of air transport has been transformed. Huge long-range aircraft like the *Galaxy* speed intercontinental resupply; medium-range aircraft, with the *Hercules* as their exemplary workhorse, have had an immense impact, while the helicopter, in a variety of guises from *Skycrane* and *Chinook* to the versatile UH-1B *Huey* confer unprecedented versatility on armies that can afford to deploy them in significant numbers. We have already explored one aspect of American failure in Vietnam, but must not ignore the contribution made by the helicopter to the considerable tactical success achieved by the Americans. Nor should popular mythology overemphasise the helicopter's vulnerability (in logistic and combat missions) in that war. Although the Americans did indeed lose more than 8,000, over 5,000 of them to enemy action, the loss rate was only 1 to 7,000 sorties flown, a better performance than the fixed-wing aircraft loss of 1 per 2,000 sorties, and well below the aircraft loss rate of the Second World War.[76] The maintenance of many sophisticated items has become easier as 'black boxes' are replaced, to be discarded or repaired, and 'go/no go' systems allow simple users to test complex equipment. Finally, the large-scale use of automatic data processing makes stock management more efficient.

This is, however, only one side of the coin. On the other, the sophistication of logistics has been outstripped by armies' appetite for technology and by the spread of accurate long-range weapons systems. Between them these developments make logistics at once more exigent and more vulnerable. Many of the items jostling their way up the line of communications require special storing or handling – refrigeration here, a dust-free environment there; and the sheer variety of items required has accelerated uncontrollably. Let us first consider the needs of that most basic of building blocks, the infantry battalion. At the close of the Second World War the battalion, British or American, was essentially a body of rifle-carrying infantrymen: a light machine-gun gave the squad or section its firepower, mortars and anti-tank guns provided some integral support, and radio communications did not go below platoon level. Now every soldier has an automatic rifle and each fire-team its light machine-gun. The range and sophistication of mortars has increased to the point where they are close to becoming anti-armour weapons in their own right. Anti-armour weapons have more than doubled in number, and in many tactical circumstances they no longer support the infantry: the infantry supports them. Radios have quadrupled. Battalions that ride to battle in Mechanised Infantry Combat Vehicles like *Bradley, Marder* or *Warrior* fight from vehicles whose sophistication exceeds that of Second World War tanks. The battalion's demand for ammunition (in both quantity and variety) has grown, and so too has its appetite for spares and repair facilities.

Ascend the level of sophistication, through tank units, with their more than 6,000 separate maintenance items per tank and greedy demands for fuel, artillery units, which need shells (constantly growing in calibre) and rounds for multi-launch rocket systems (220–227mm in calibre and 3 metres long), to air assault units whose helicopters require in the order of ten hours' maintenance for each hour in the air, and the real size of the problem begins to manifest itself. The dumping of ammunition, in some respects a useful practice, has always had the disadvantage of ensuring that a good deal of it is never actually fired (an earnest thesis could be written on the subject of the shells that have been dumped and captured or simply dumped and lost). Many types of modern ammunition cannot be left at the mercy of the weather for an indefinite period, and some sorts are in such short supply that dumping is unacceptable.

The thorny question of demography and its effect on recruitment will be explored more fully later, but in passing we should note the already large size of logistic corps (in the British army, for example, the Royal Electrical and Mechanical Engineers have almost as many officers and men as the Royal Artillery) and the fact that they are attempting to recruit exactly those young men who are increasingly attractive to civilian employers as high-quality labour becomes more scarce. In conclusion, it is hard not to agree with Chris Bellamy that modern weaponry and its support requirements:

far from reducing the gap between the mobility of armies (as determined by the nature of their means of transport) and the ability of their supply apparatus to keep up, will widen the gap still further.[77]

Discussion of modern weapon systems has already forced us to confront that god at whose shrine most modern armies worship: technology. That it has transformed war is beyond question. The technological developments of the nineteenth and early twentieth centuries – rifled, breech-loading artillery and infantry weapons; ironclad, turreted steamships; submarines; telephone, telegraph, and radio; internal combustion engine and aircraft – had profound effects on the conduct of war. Technology produced the locked front of the First World War, though the absence of adequate tactical communications was as much to blame as the excessive presence of firepower for much of what went on on the Western Front. It made possible the powerful cocktail of blitzkrieg, opened the way to unrestricted submarine warfare and strategic bombing and, ultimately, conceived the nuclear weapon and a bulging quiverful of delivery systems. It helped the huge armies spawned by conscription to move, live and fight. In the process it changed the style of military command, as we shall see in Chapter 6; played a powerful role in modernisation (though economic historians emerge with bruised knuckles from this debate); gave impetus to competition between nation-states in the form of the arms race, and increased the cost of war and the armed equipoise that passes for peace.[78]

For all this, military technology is imperfectly understood by users and critics alike. First, the arms races that have accompanied the explosion of military technology are neither primarily about arms nor inevitably destabilising. They are indices of social and economic efficiency, though sometimes their evidence (rather than the mere fact of their existence) helps precipitate conflict by pointing to a shift in power. It may be too early to pass substantive judgments on recent reductions in the Russian defence budget, but it is likely that the arms race has ultimately carried out its traditional function of measuring relative economic strength, and that the Russian is lying exhausted on the track. The Soviet Union may be a military superpower but it is an economic cripple: and the mismatch between the two cannot be tolerated indefinitely, and it is only by reducing the weight of military demands that the economy can be reformed. Full tank parks have existed at the expense of empty supermarket shelves, and it is impossible to see Gorbachev or, indeed, almost any potential successor, opting for guns rather than butter in determining Russia's future economic priorities.

Second, the existence of large and growing arsenals does not necessarily imply increasing enthusiasm for their use. The gap between the weapons available to most armies and their senior officers' genuine comprehension of their capabilities has widened. Michael Howard painted a convincing picture of military specialists who regard the possibility of war with constant dread. 'There have been exceptions,' he writes: 'Douglas MacArthur was one, and there may be others in some armies at or around the rank of colonel, but they are mavericks, men born out of their age, working against the grain of their time.'[79] Third, as the earlier part of this chapter has shown, there are a large number of circumstances in which a large amount of a combatant's technology is of little practical use in war, and may have limited persuasive functions even in peace.

Finally, despite conventional wisdom which emphasises the giddy speed of technological change, it is easy to exaggerate the rapidity of its impact upon societies in general and armies in particular. In 1960 the Parisian weekly *L'Express* published a series of texts by Russian and American scientists giving their view of society in the year 2000. We still have a decade or so to run, but already may suggest that their predictions overshot the mark. Voyages to the moon would be commonplace; all food would be synthetic; world population would have quadrupled but stabilised; disease and famine would have been eliminated; knowledge would be stored in electronic banks and transmitted directly to the human nevous system, and natural reproduction would be forbidden.[80]

In military terms there has often been a gap between what is technologically feasible and what is actually in service. There was a time-lag between the impact of the industrial revolution on, say, the textile industry (with the key developments of the spinning jenny, frame, carding machine and mule in 1760–80) and its effect on armies. The infantry of the Napoleonic wars fought mainly with smoothbore flintlock muskets although both the rifle and the percussion cap had been invented. This gap is widening, and falling defence budgets will widen it still further: for all the pace of change, military hardware is surprisingly long-lasting, and cannot be jettisoned merely because something better is available. Equipment which is flexible enough to be modified in service probably represents better value than the state of the art crystallised for a brief moment. A quest for the latter may lengthen the procurement process as technological advances constantly outpace the development of a particular item, leading to a never-ending round of trial and modification. Stretchability, the ability to receive frequent in-service improvement, will feature prominently in the list of essential characteristics for military equipment in the 1990s and beyond.

Modern technology creates tensions even within the armed forces that acquire it. Its ever increasing cost is prohibitive, especially within the context of defence budgets which grow far less rapidly than the cost of the equipment they finance, if, in an age of decreasing perceived military threat and increasing environmental concern, they grow at all. At 1985 prices, the *Abrams* main battle tank cost $2.7 million, over fifty times the cost (in real terms) of its Second World War ancestor. A modern fighter aircraft, the F-16 *Falcon*, at over $21 million, cost sixteen times as much as its 1945 predecessor, and a destroyer of the DDG-51 *Arleigh Burke* class, at more than $1.3 billion, was a staggering 150 times the cost of a Second World War vessel.[81] If equipment costs continue to grow at this rate, and defence budgets retain approximately their present shape (and they will not), by the second decade of the twenty-first century we will be approaching single-ship navies and one-plane air forces.

Enhanced performance is one ingredient of growing cost. Mary Kaldor saw 'baroque' technological change consisting largely of improvements to a given set of 'performance characteristics', and the advent of 'gross, elaborate and very expensive hardware'.[82] At least two flaws defaced the towering baroque edifice. First, that in many circumstances numbers or specific tactical skills may be more important than technological sophistication. In aerial combat, for instance, if one gets within an enemy missile envelope, life expectancy is poor even if one's aircraft enjoys a substantial technological edge. In the Falklands the Argentine forces actually enjoyed technical (as well as numerical) superiority in several important areas, night vision devices and infantry weapons among them, but could not cope with a rough old war.

The second major difficulty concerns maintainability. In 1980 the RH-53D helicopter, in its minesweeping role, required 40 hours of maintenance for one hour of flight, and 53 per cent of the fleet was incapable of action at any given time. A spring 1980 report revealed that two-thirds of F-111D bombers were grounded at any one time, and the F-14A was not serviceable nearly half the time: both required 98 hours of maintenance for an hour's flight. In its operational testing, the XM-1 *Abrams* tank had 104.3 mean miles between failures compared with the testing goal of 272. It is hard to dissent from Mary Kaldor's conclusion that: 'In the end, the budget can never keep up with the demands of baroque technology.'[83]

Things would be simpler if there was a clear relationship between cost, doctrine and equipment. In an ideal world an army's tasks would be defined for it by its political masters; soldiers (and, of necessity, airmen and often sailors alongside them) would elaborate the doctrine best suited to fulfil this mission and procure the equipment with which to implement it, having proper regard to the need to recruit and retain the men (and women) who will operate it. In practice this smooth chain of cause and effect is tangled, duplicated or even broken. The Soviet system, which uses 'military science' to identify the 'laws of war' and to proceed thence to what Christopher Donnelly calls 'military development' – the organisation, training and equipment of armed forces – establishes a robust doctrinal mould into which equipment is poured. Even so, difficulties occur as the political leadership fails to define future tasks accurately, the conservatism of senior officers opposes radical thought, and inter-arm pressures (for instance, friction between the tank and the artillery lobby) hamper objectivity.

In the Soviet system procurement is driven by doctrine, and the subordination of Soviet defence industry to the overall plan means that the Russians are not subjected to the pressures created by an independent defence industry clamouring to sell its wares, with a measure of partisan support from politicians and the military, serving and retired. Sometimes the independent process does work well. There may be a perceived need which technology is harnessed to meet. On occasions the outcome is fortunate, as the case of the British army's *Wheelbarrow* device for investigating Improvised Explosive Devices demonstrates. On other occasions the outcome is less satisfactory. The US Army's *Sergeant York* air-defence gun was the child of uncertain procurement aims and changing requirements, though in view of the growing Soviet helicopter threat there was certainly a need for some sort of low-level air defence system. The result was a weapon system which 'died of embarrassment' after dismal performance in tests.[84]

Jon Connell's obituary on *Sergeant York* perceptively suggests that better results could have been achieved if the army had thought more about tactics and less about technology. This highlights a continuing difficulty with the application of technology. Most armies tend to apply new technology within existing organisational and tactical patterns, with the interests of individual services and arms (often fuelled by their control over slices of the defence budget) militating against radical thought. Thus the tank was seen, even by many of its supporters, as fitting within the existing military framework: light tanks carried out the traditional cavalry role of scouting and reconnaissance, medium tanks exploited a breakthough, and heavy tanks provided the infantry with fire support almost as if they were mobile pill-boxes. The Germans were initially no less shackled by convention, and their first tank, the A7V, was manned by soldiers from several branches of the service, each exercising his own technical speciality: drivers, machine-gunners, artillery gunners and signallers, more like a very small battle group than a rather large vehicle crew.[85]

The concept of an armoured corps (*Panzertruppen*), with its tanks supported by in-house infantry was a significant break with tradition. A similar organisational breakthrough might have been achieved in England had the decision been taken to expand the Royal Tank Regiment as an armoured corps in its own right, rather than to mechanise cavalry regiments which, for all sorts of excellent reasons, saw a direct descent from the well-bred horse to the 'brazen chariot'. *Blitzkrieg* owed much to harnessing the tank and the dive-bomber to new tactical doctrine, rather than compressing them within existing boundaries. The debate over the employment of *Bradley* and *Warrior* reveals familiar tensions, and in the discussion surrounding the future role of the helicopter in the British army we see the battles of the 1920s and 1930s being re-fought: this time rotors are to tracks what tracks were to boots (and hooves).

It is unfair to mock inherent military conservatism: the military are not necessarily more conservative than other professional groups, and they are uncomfortably aware of what might happen if they get things wrong. Nor can we brush technology aside, and demand a return to simple virtues and simple weapons: being significantly outclassed in a particular technological area can bring catastrophe – ask a Syrian air-defence gunner about the Beka'a in 1982. However, it is essential to recognise that technology is no panacea. As the distinguished American defence analyst Steven Canby observed: 'Technology may indeed offset poor military practice and organization. But it is cheaper, simpler and more logical to remove the malpractices first.'[86] What we can do is to recognise that in many – though by no means all – situations, robust 'gothic' weapon systems, procured to meet a specific doctrine, are likely to fare better than the florid output of the baroque arsenals. We can also try (against the pull of much institutional deadweight) to make doctrine drive procurement, and to strive for compromise between the old loyalties to arm-of-service tribal markings and enthusiasm for new weapon systems which may alter familiar functions and organisations. None of this is easy, though we in the West may gain some comfort from the fact that internal pressures in the Soviet Union – social and political as well as economic – will make it less easy for the Russians to operate as they have in the past, and will encourage agreements (explicit or implicit) which reduce areas of technological competition. It is the tiredest of clichés to say that technology is a good servant but a bad master, yet its exponential proliferation points to the need to remember exactly that.

Our diagram of the scale and intensity of war will retain its validity into the next century, and, barring accidents or unforeseen political developments, armed conflict will continue to occur principally in the low-intensity quadrant. Western armies need to retain a capability for escalation in scale and intensity, and their approach to force reduction should bear in mind the deterrent effect that conventional forces exercise. None the less, they would do well to emphasise – in doctrine, procurement and training – ability to act at that level where conflict is most frequent. Power to destroy the world three times over, or to marshal formidable armoured strength on the North German Plain, will have less relevance than the ability to employ the military instrument selectively in a complex hostage situation or the war against drugs – no less a part of a nation's strategy, surely, than defence against foreign aggression. War, even when Hobbes discussed it in the seventeenth century, did not consist of battle alone, and at the close of the twentieth century the role of battle has shrunk still further. Large-scale high-intensity battle between massed armies is increasingly improbable: it is by armed combat in smaller scale and lower intensity that military power will primarily be applied in future.

3

Field of Battle

Everything Pierre saw was so indefinite, that in no part of the scene before him could he find anything fully corresponding to his preconceptions. There was nowhere a field of battle such as he had expected to see, nothing but fields, dells, woods, troops, woods, camp-fires, villages, mounds, streams. With all Pierre's efforts, he could not discover in the living landscape a military position. He could not even distinguish between our troops and the enemy's.

'I must ask someone who understands it,' he thought . . .

Leo Tolstoy, *War and Peace*

Peering into a misty future to glimpse the shape of future combat has fascinated many, from practical soldiers to cerebral theorists: the predictive works of I.S. Bloch and Sir John Hackett bracket our own century. Future war has long fascinated novelists, from H.G. Wells in *The War of the Worlds* to Tom Clancy in *The Hunt for Red October* and *Red Storm Rising*. When I was a boy, Wells's account of the torpedo-ram *Thunder Child* rushing to take on the Martian fighting-machine gripped me: now I am deprived of a night's sleep by the need to follow Clancy's USS *Chicago* under the polar icecap. Every generation has produced its prophets, and a succession of wars has proved that many of their carefully thought-out (and often noisily publicised) theories are simply wrong.

There is no shortage of answers as to why this is so. The 'bloody fools' school of historiography maintains that armies, with their formalised hierarchies in which like promotes like, preoccupation with the worst possible case, and inter-arm compartments which obstruct creative thought, have generally been bad at prediction.

It points to armies' fondness for fighting the next war on the evidence of the last, and fastens upon the writings of genuinely prescient commentators to demonstrate how easy it would have been to get it right if only a little thought had been devoted to the matter. Thus all combatants are blamed for failing to recognise what barbed wire and the machine-gun would do to war in 1914: had they only taken I.S. Bloch more seriously a generation's misery might have been averted.

Military conservatism undoubtedly has much to answer for, but it is not a satisfactory all-embracing explanation of the apparent failure of so many armies to foresee the character of future combat. The case of 1914 is anything but straightforward, and even before exploring it more fully we should note that the popular stereotype of trenchlock applies most strongly to the Western Front: there was wide movement on the Eastern Front, in the Balkans and Mesopotamia, and even on the Western Front before October 1914 and after March 1918.

In any event, the prospect of tactical stalemate on a battlefield dominated by fire was widely discussed before the war. A memorandum of 1905 warned:

> All along the line the corps will try, as in siege warfare, to come to grips with the enemy from position to position, day and night, advancing, digging in, advancing again, digging in again, etc., using every means of modern science to dislodge the enemy behind his cover.[1]

Its author was neither a military radical nor a perceptive outsider: it was Schlieffen himself, chief of the Great General Staff and author of the German army's war plan. In 1909 a British General Staff conference was assured that it was 'impossible to take a position which is well defended by machine-guns until these guns have been put out of action'. The speaker was no maverick but the future General Sir Aylmer Haldane, and in his regard for the efficacy of fire he was by no means unusual in the pre-war armies.[2]

The principal difficulty in 1914, as so often before and since, lay in reconciling technological developments, whose effect on battle had not been demonstrated in analogous circumstances, with military doctrine. We have seen some of the effects of armies' bittersweet love affair with technology, and must now go further, first by accepting the probability that much military technology will be incomprehensible to the men who control it. They will not merely be unable to understand how it works, which is neither surprising, nor in itself a great disadvantage, for we may doubt Caesar's awareness of the technicalities of forging the heads of *pila*, or Wellington's of the proportion of sulphur in the gunpowder used by his infantry. Their real problem lies in assessing the impact of new technology on battle. In an era when technology accelerates sharply, a long career will encompass momentous change. When he deliverd the Roskill memorial lecture in 1986, Michael Howard began by considering the career of Captain Stephen Roskill. Roskill had been taught at Dartmouth by instructors who had been trained on full-rigged men of war and who thought of gunnery in terms of point-blank exchanges, and almost his last official act before retirement was to act as British observer at the Bikini atomic bomb tests in 1946.[3] Field Marshal Sir William Robertson, Chief of the Imperial General Staff in 1915–18, had started his career as a trooper in the 17th Lancers, armed with bamboo lance and muzzle-loading pistol: he ended it in the era of machine-gun and flame-thrower, poison gas and Zeppelins.

The changes facing today's senior officers are no less momentous. Most major armies are headed by men whose experience was formed by the Second World War. They are likely to have been too young to have actually served in it (although there are still senior Soviet officers quilted with medal ribbons from the Great Patriotic War), but when they were trained at Sandhurst, West Point, Warminister or Fort Benning in the 1950s, their instructors were Second World War veterans, and the armies they joined were branded by that war. This is nowhere better illustrated than in the war's effect on British tank design. Until the late 1960s the Royal Armoured Corps was dominated by men influenced by Normandy, men for whom the memory of being outclassed by German armour had a lasting effect. No more thin armour and pea-shooters: British affection for the heavy-gun tank, which coloured a generation of tank design, was hardened in the flames of burning Shermans around Villers-Bocage and Hubert-Folie.

At the simplest level, changes in infantry weapons have had a tactical effect which needs to be constantly remembered by those brought up on heavy-calibre bolt action or semi-automatic rifles. The proliferation of firepower within the infantry section or squad made some time-honoured battle drills no more than tactical rituals.

It is significant that the experience of the Falklands provoked a major rethink in British low-level infantry tactics, and one may argue that it is only now that the infantryman's most serious problem, the last few hundred metres of the assault, has been addressed in a logical and comprehensive manner. In July 1916 a British officer wrote that:

> too much thought appears to have been given to facilities *after* occupation of enemy lines and too little to the means of getting infantry across 200 yards of good fields for machine gunfire.[4]

His comment would scarcely have been less relevant sixty years later, but it is not easy for even the most agile of brains, brought up on the flanking Bren gun and linear assault of the section attack, to adjust to fire teams crawling forward, sluicing the enemy position with automatic fire before 'posting' grenades into trenches. The more technology involved, the greater the problem of adjustment. Bending attitudes forged among the Centurions and M-48s of the 1950s to accommodate the Precision Guided Munitions and Multi-Launch Rocket Systems of the 1980s is no easy matter.

Not all experience is delusive, nor do all military minds harden, like arteries, with age. Nevertheless, it remains difficult to judge what past experience – individual and collective – has future relevance. Any modern conflict spawns a shoal of books, their merit often in inverse proportion to the speed of their appearance. Most strive to draw conclusions, judgments which are accepted by some and rejected by others on the grounds that the war in question is a 'special case' whose circumstances are unlikely to be repeated.

Once again the first few years of this century are instructive. The British army, lamentably unprepared for the Boer War, learnt many useful lessons from that conflict – and almost as many dangerous ones. Without R.B. Haldane's comprehensive recasting of the army it is hard to see how Britain could have played any useful part in the First World War on land, and the formidable performance of her infantry and gunners at Mons and Le Cateau in 1914 bore tribute to skills honed in the aftermath of South Africa. Less useful was the 'lesson' that field artillery needed shrapnel rather than high explosive: August and September 1914 showed that projectiles which had worked well enough against Boer riflemen in open country were less use against an enemy who quickly turned villages into fortresses and laced farmland with trench-lines. Questionable, too, was the 'lesson' of Klip Drift, that charging cavalry could find a place on a battlefield dominated by the breech-loading rifle.[5] Finally, the Boer War reinforced British preoccupation with the tactical at the expense of the operational. The flying columns that scoured the veld in pursuit of elusive commandos were badly coordinated, and in the inability of Kitchener, his staff and senior subordinates to recognise the operational dimension, we see early symptoms of the disease that was was to infect GHQ in 1914.[6]

The Boer War and the Russo-Japanese War which followed it attracted scrutiny matched in our own day by the interest accorded to the Arab-Israeli wars. The Six Day War of 1966 persuaded many (not least the Israelis themselves) that blitzkrieg was alive and well. One commentator found the campaign: 'strongly reminiscent of Blitzkrieg, World War Two style . . . the techniques used seem to have been lifted bodily from the German campaigns of the 1939–1941 period . . .'[7] Observers were less prepared to recognise that Israeli success hinged upon the same transient factors which made possible German victory in 1939–41: total air superiority, unrestricted space in which to manoeuvre, and an enemy whose linear mind-set was paralysed by encirclement.

The Yom Kippur War of 1973 was the child of the 1967 war. The Egyptian strategic aim of drawing the regional problem to the world's attention and showing Israel that her neighbours could not be ignored found expression in an operational plan for a limited offensive across the Suez canal. This was designed, on the evidence of 1967 and subsequent fighting in 'The War of Attrition', to deny Israel the opportunity to employ the manoeuvre warfare at which she excelled. When Egypt allowed herself to be drawn forward into Sinai, things went wrong. Conversely, the Israelis sought to re-fight the 1967 war, and their unsupported armoured counter-attacks against Egyptian positions east of the canal failed in the face of a blizzard of *Sagger* wire-guided missiles.

It was only when the Israelis had adjusted their tactics, learning new lessons and re-learning old ones, that they gained the upper hand. The Israeli Air Force, after losing 14 per cent of its first-line strength in the first 48 hours, changed its attack profile, going in low among the 'ground clutter' on gun and missile radars and using 'chaff' and Electronic Counter Measures to confuse air defences. Ground forces redeveloped combined arms tactics, with infantry in M113 APCs moving with tanks to pour suppressive fire on to any position that might shelter a *Sagger* operator. The new tactics, together with the timely arrival of US-supplied TOW missiles and significant command errors on the part of both the Egyptians and the Syrians enabled the Israelis to cross the canal themselves, imperil an Egyptian army, and roll the Syrians back across the Golan.

The Yom Kippur War printed a ream of 'lessons' of its own. Commentators were at first inclined to emphasise the importance of the *Sagger* missile and its ground-to-air cousin, the man-portable SAM–7, leading some to suggest that the tank was obsolete, and the war certainly struck a note of caution in a Soviet army which placed such emphasis on the tank.[8] Subsequent analysis suggested that the kill rate of *Sagger* had been far poorer than first believed. Most tanks had been knocked out by other tanks, and the Israelis believed that only 25 per cent of tanks damaged had been hit by missiles, further suggesting that only 25 per cent of missiles fired had actually hit their targets. Given the low kill rate of *Sagger* even when it hits, the war emphasises the effect of weapon density, and the density achieved on the Suez front was exceptional. Similarly, the much-vaunted SAM–7 was credited with only three confirmed kills, as opposed to the 31 of the ZSU–23/4 anti-aircraft gun.[9]

The 'lessons' of the war were held by some to justify the continued existence of the tank, and by others to prove its obsolescence. The war showed both the vulnerability of the aircraft, and the ability of tactical and technical countermeasures to enable it to operate effectively. It emphasised the weaknesses of fortifications (much of the Bar-Lev Line), and their strength (the Budapest strongpoint on the canal and the *telal* positions on the Golan). In short, it suggested all things to all men, and its evidence could be construed in a number of ways even by those who were neither stupid nor ill-informed. Like their counterparts before 1914 they were engaged in a difficult business, and we should not be surprised that some of them fared as badly as economists or weather forecasters. Samuel Johnson believed that war and medicine were alike because both were bloody and conjectural: doctors, however, have to cope with fewer imponderables than soldiers.

The Drive of Doctrine: Attrition and Manoeuvre

Military doctrine should be the flywheel which powers research, development, procurement, training and tactics. In fact the relationship between theory and practice is never so cosy, and is often decidedly uneasy as weapons already in service are used in a doctrine for which they were not procured. This is not unreasonable, for weapons and equipment may have a longer life-cycle than doctrine as strategic priorities change or operational concepts evolve. Few planners are able to start with a clean sheet of paper, but will not only bring with them the mental baggage of experience but also inherit an organization with its hierarchy, rivalries, equipment and training apparatus. Persuading such a cumbersome whale to alter course is often time-consuming, given the built-in ability of many of its major organs to impede the passage of instructions along the central nervous system. Indeed, most armies, despite their apparently hierarchical structures, display an administrative equivalent of the Clausewitzian notion of friction. Everything that might be very simple is very difficult because of the need to consult staff papers, redraft projects, and run ideas along a labyrinthine wiring diagram.

It is harder to achieve doctrinal change in peace than in war. In war radical solutions are easier to apply, for relevant evidence is available, bureaucratic constrictions are less tight, and dominant personalities find it easier to hold sway. The result need not be benevolent. The French General Robert Nivelle made his reputation by recapturing Fort Douaumont in October 1916, using a shattering artillery preparation, followed by swift infantry assault behind a creeping barrage. This had proved brilliantly successful as a tactical ploy of limited scale. It was over-sold as an operational doctrine aimed at producing a war-winning breakthough by 'violence' and 'brutality'. An army and government desperate for the philosopher's stone bought the doctrine without looking at it too closely. Nivelle was pushed on, as powerful men often are, by intimates who enjoyed his confidence, and the mortally ill Colonel d'Alenson, desperate to see the war won before he died, played his own part in the tragedy. Nivelle's offensive collapsed in ruins along the Chemin des Dames in April 1917. German withdrawal to the Hindenburg Line had already lamed it, inadequate artillery support and robust defences crippled it, and waiting German counter-attack divisions administered the killing blow.[10]

An instance of successful doctrinal change was that which paved the way for the German offensive of spring 1918. The fighting of 1917, costly though it had proved to the Allies, had persuaded the German high command that it could not tolerate a continuation of the battle of attrition, especially in view of America's entry into the war. Just as the Germans had rapidly distilled the lessons of the Somme fighting in 1916 into the pamphlet *Experience of the First Army in the Somme Battles* and thence into doctrine, so they blended the evidence of their opponents' attacks, the writings of a perceptive French officer, Captain André Laffargue, and their own experience on the Eastern Front to produce a doctrine for the offensive. Surprise, forfeited by ponderous preparatory bombardments, would be maintained by use of a short but paralysing lightning barrage. Storm troops would rapidly infiltrate a defence already knocked off balance, pressing on where they found gaps and following no rigid plan. Battle-groups moving behind them mopped up resistance. This doctrine was brilliantly successful at the tactical level, but Ludendorff was unable to forge an operational plan which harnessed it to a strategic purpose. This failure should not be allowed to obscure the importance of the example, and the German army of 1917–18 deserves our attention for its doctrinal adaptability.[11]

We are currently witnessing two interesting examples of doctrinal shift. The first comes as the Soviet army responds to President Gorbachev's *rapprochement* to the West. Its traditional structure, with emphasis on massed tanks and artillery, is well-suited to offensive operations, and so it should be, for it was created precisely for such a purpose,[12] but, as Western proponents of non-provocative defence have been quick to point out, the existence of large forces with manifest offensive capability arouses fear which in turn provokes a military response. By reducing the offensive component of the Soviet panoply Gorbachev will not only take some of the crippling strain off the economy: he will also reduce the level of tension by appearing less threatening. His initiative has already begun to cause massive structural changes within the Soviet army and to initiate a profound reappraisal of military doctrine.

Among the world's major armies, the Soviet has long been uniquely fitted for matching doctrine and force structure to strategic purpose, but it remains to be seen how well it can cope with the changes currently being demanded of it. It is in a period of yawning uncertainty, where there are no comfortable patterns to follow. Reform of the resource-hungry defence industries and thoroughgoing cuts in the defence establishment are central to Gorbachev's programme, and the early signs suggest that this has made him few friends among the military, with its conservatism, vested interest in maintaining the status quo and – let us never underemphasise it – weighty cultural baggage of the Great Patriotic War. About 10,000 senior officer posts have already disappeared from an officer corps some 250,000 strong, small comfort for those who hoped for more splendid epaulettes and fringe benefits to match.

Yet the need to retain military support must rank high on Gorbachev's agenda, for with it he has at least some prospect of checking a reform process which threatens to run totally out of control. Many of the Soviet army's senior officers are relatively young and new in post. Something approaching a purge of the army's upper echelons has taken place and, while the officer corps as a whole may have suspicions about Gorbachev, the men at its head recognise that Russia cannot continue to build strong armed forces on a fractured economic foundation. Nor should we ignore the importance of the Soviet army as a binding agent within the state and a source of stability when so much of the political structure is creaking ominously.

What Soviet soldiers would call the 'socio-political' guidelines have already been sketched out. In October 1985 Gorbachev referred to the need to achieve only 'reasonable sufficiency' in the composition of Soviet armed forces, and to formulate a doctrine which was genuinely defensive. Reducing reliance on nuclear weapons reflected acknowledgment of the fact that these were the only weapons which could pose a real threat to the existence of the Soviet state: shrinking the USSR's nuclear arsenal would not only encourage the West to follow suit, but would also reduce the West's perception of Soviet threat, thereby easing Russian access to Western technology and industrial expertise.

The 'military-technical' elements of policy are currently being evolved. As one might expect from an organisation which sets much store by the analysis of historical experience, Soviet operational research has ransacked the evidence of the past, and seems to have concluded that Khalkin-Gol (Zhukov's victory over the Japanese in Manchuria in 1939) and Kursk (the defeat of the last major German offensive, in 1943) are the most appropriate defensive models.

These models have a tripartite structure. First, the erosion of the enemy's offensive strength in fortified forward areas; second, counter-attacks against the weakened foe, and finally, a counter-offensive which converts tactical gains to operational success and strategic victory. Such a plan offers good prospects for success provided that mobilisation time is available, and that the mobilisation process produces sufficient well-trained, properly equipped forces. To ensure that the military instrument meets the new demands imposed upon it the Soviet General Staff will continue the force-restructuring whose origins predate glasnost, creating tank and motor rifle divisions which place less reliance on armour and embody better-balanced combat units. The removal of air assault and bridging assets from divisional command and their concentration at a higher level will increase the defensive appearance of Soviet forces, and give greater flexibility to those elements deployed in depth.

The restructured forces will probably form two main groups. One, composed chiefly of motor rifle divisions, will be deployed in partially prepared defensive belts, to cover the frontier and check any enemy advance. In an ideal world the non-Soviet Warsaw Pact would have provided an outpost line for this position, but the radical nature of political change in Eastern Europe must diminish confidence that such a line can now be held. Behind this deep defensive framework, manned by units at or near combat strength in peacetime, tank armies, containing a high proportion of mobilised reservists, will deal with deep penetrations and carry out large-scale counter-offensives.

Such a structure demands thorough tactical revision, and the Soviet military press shows every sign of moving rapidly through many of the arguments on positional versus mobile defence which characterised their Western equivalents a decade or so ago. It also demands reorganisations, not simply of combat formations, but also of the military districts of the Soviet Union, to enable them to plan properly for defence and deal with the training and mobilisation requirements of the revised force structure.

All the signs suggest that even more profound changes are in the wind. One of the the characteristics of the Gorbachev era has been the increased importance of civilian defence intellectuals, many of them English-speaking, and it is them, rather than jutting-jawed colonel-generals, who tend to speak at conferences in the West. They are not popular with senior officers, who resent their influence upon what was once demonstrably military policy. Among their suggestions has been one which may fit snugly into the throughgoing restructuring which cannot be far away: the ending of conscription. This would enable the Soviet army to recruit fewer, better-trained and better-motivated soldiers, and would at least partly defuse nationalist hostility to military service.

The objections of senior officers are based on both military and social grounds. Regulars would be much more expensive, and the size of the army would be sharply reduced. Moreover, it the citizen's duty to serve the state, and the introduction of a regular army would strike a heavy blow at this time-honoured principle. Since the army is set to become smaller in any case, the former objection loses much of its validity. And the evidence of Afghanistan, and of more recent internal security operations within the Soviet Union itself, underlines the importance of cohesive, well-trained units which are not prey to nationalist internal tensions. Not for nothing did the Russians deploy parachute units – with a high proportion of regulars and a fiercely selective recruitment system even for their conscripts – against nationalist rioters in Tbilisi in 1989. We may expect that – for all the dismissive articles in the military press – the ending of conscription in the Soviet Union is a very real possibility.

It is likely that the Soviet General Staff will pursue a two-tier policy. At one level it will do its best to meet the political requirement by restructuring to reduce tension and cost. At another, its duty of planning to win a war if one starts remains unchanged, and it will seek to accomplish this by using the reductions to improve efficiency. The uninspiring performance of army and KGB alike in recent counter-insurgency highlights the fact that the Soviet army, like many others, has centred its training and procurement on a form of conflict which has a diminishing chance of occurring. The restructuring process may well create an army more flexible than the armour-plated titan of the 1980s. Yet the sheer scale of the task facing the general staff would be daunting even if its army was impermeable to the acid of nationalism which is currently eating at the Soviet Union from within. If the staff enjoys even a chance of success it is because the linkage between strategy, operational art and tactics, and the relationship of all three to procurement and force structure, is well understood. However, it remains to be seen whether even the sternest military logic can triumph over medium-term political instability and chronic economic weakness.[13]

The second army in the process of major doctrinal change is the British. Largely as a result of the initiative of Field Marshal Sir Nigel Bagnall, whose tenure of key senior appointments culminated in his tour as Chief of the General Staff in 1985–8, the British army has abandoned its long-standing affection for meeting a Soviet offensive primarily by means of firepower delivered from static positions in favour of a more dynamic doctrine. As Field Marshal Bagnall put it:

> We have . . . got to be prepared to fight a more mobile battle so that we can achieve a concentration of force at critical points, and when I talk about a concentration of force, of course I include air power . . . We have then got to break out of the defensive mentality. Of course, the risks are high in a battle of manoeuvre, but so is the pay-off high if successful, whereas a static concept, resulting as it does in a battle of attrition, can only end in ultimate if not early disaster.[14]

Bagnall was in the fortunate position of combining reforming zeal with the authority and personality which helped him to impose his will.

What remains to be seen is the durability of the concept he has left behind him. It would be surprising, given the army's pattern of promotion, if its upper echelons did not contain a majority of officers in important command appointments who share his views. The establishment of the Higher Command and Staff Course, which prepares selected officers (most students are colonels) for senior appointments and emphasises the operational level of war will also help ensure that the new doctrinal thrust retains momentum. Nevertheless, the battle is certainly not won. Deep-seated British suspicion of doctrine *per se* continues to shake its hoary locks, and policy which was initially heavily dependent on personalities may lose momentum as they move through, and ultimately out of, the army. Past evidence is not encouraging, for the last twenty years have been littered with tactical ploys (it would be misleading to call them doctrine in any meaningful sense) which have scarcely survived the service careers of their creators.

The doctrinal debate within the British army is of particular interest because it concerns a shift from a firepower-dominated attritional style to a movement-dominated manoeuvre style, and in so doing epitomises the emphasis on manoeuvre warfare which has accompanied Anglo-American interest in the operational level. It is most useful to see attrition and manoeuvre as opposites on the operational/tactical spectrum. Attrition reflects the Clausewitzian logic of applying the full weight of resources, human and material, to the enemy's main body. It is attractive to an army whose numerical superiority rests on a powerful industrial base. Grant's campaign in Northern Viriginia in May–October 1864 was attritional in concept, with the bludgeon of the Army of the Potomac shivering the rapier of the Army of Northern Virginia. Grant refused to allow tactical defeat in the Wilderness to turn him from his purpose: 'I intend to fight it out on this front if it takes all summer,' he declared. American military policy in both world wars was heavily attritional, its emphasis on pounding the enemy to fragments with the pile-driver powered by military and industrial mobilisation. America became the quintessential war arsenal. Major-General Brehon B. Somervell's 1942 pronouncement was characteristic: 'when Hitler put his war on wheels he ran it straight down our alley. When he hitched his chariot to an internal combustion engine, he opened up a new battle front – a front that we know well. It's called Detroit.'[15]

At the tactical level, the attritional battle has four elements. First, the attacker manoeuvres to seize suitable terrain. This 'shaping of the battlefield' is important for attacker and defender alike, and in the age of air power both sides will use their air forces to assist the process by 'freezing off' the crucial sector. Second, he weakens the enemy by wearing-down attacks while building up his own reserves. He mounts his decisive attack by massing all his resources against the vital sector, and finally exploits his success to convert the enemy's defeat into rout. Possible ingredients of the attritional style may be rehearsal (not training in the abstract, but practice of the specific); rigid, centralised command to assist the efficient application of mass, and the liberal use of firepower to the point where fire leads and manoeuvre follows. The First World War axiom 'artillery conquers, infantry occupies' was the perfect expression of an attritional concept. Cases inevitably differ. Equal importance will not be attached to each phase, and such is the nature of an attritional battle that the attacker may himself be so exhausted that exploitation is limited.

Nevertheless, the pattern emerges, with variations, from numerous attritional battles. At Borodino, for instance, Napoleon spent 5 September 1812 clearing the Russians from their outlying positions (including the powerful Schevardino redoubt), and on 6 September he concentrated his own forces. He attacked on the 7th, with a full-scale frontal assault and diversionary operations against the Russian flanks. After a bloody struggle the Great Redoubt, key to the Russian position, was captured, but Napoleon refused to commit the Guard, his only intact reserve, and the Russians withdrew in good order. Alamein was consciously attritional, and not without reason, for Montgomery had the recent evidence of the Gazala battles of mid-1942, when a numerically superior 8th Army had been beaten in dribs and drabs, without applying its full weight. He laid great emphasis on shaping the battlefield and the men who were to fight on it, and envisaged a battle whose three phases corresponded neatly with the attritional pattern – break in, 'dogfight' and break out.

Manoeuvre lies at the opposite extreme. Sun Tsu's comments are telling: they contain the first use of the terms direct and indirect in this context, and the notion of the indirect approach of manoeuvre as opposed to the direct approach of attrition is central to the debate. 'In all fighting,' he wrote,

> the direct method may be used for joining battle, but indirect methods will be needed in order to secure victory . . . Military tactics are like unto water; for water in its natural course runs away from high places and hastens downwards. So in war, the way to avoid what is strong is to strike what is weak.[16]

Attacking the weak elements in the enemy's array might cause his collapse far more efficiently than by defeating his strength by brute force, and Sun Tsu argued that 'supreme excellence consists in breaking the enemy's resistance without fighting'.[17] For Basil Liddell Hart the indirect approach was essential to victory:

> throughout the ages, effective results in war have rarely been attained unless the approach has had such indirectness as to ensure the opponent's unreadiness to meet it. This indirectness has usually been physical, and always psychological.[18]

His metaphor was similar to Sun Tsu's, as he likened the manoeuvre attack to flowing water, which beats upon an earthern dam and finds a small crack through which it bursts to rush out in an expanding torrent.

If the direct method was in use long before Clausewitz codifed it, the indirect method also enjoys a long history. The Thebans' great victory over Sparta at Leuctra in 371 BC has been hailed as its first recorded example. Outnumbered by almost two to one, the Theban general Epaminondas realised that pushing head-on at the Spartan phalanx could have only one result. Accordingly, he concentrated his best troops in a great block on his left, turning the Spartans' right flank, and then pressing in from the enemy's shieldless side to crumple their phalanx. At Leuthen in 1757 Frederick shunned the obvious frontal approach, but feinted to pin the Austrians to their position before hooking into their left flank in an oblique attack which showed the king and his army at the very height of their powers. Subsequent examples of manoeuvre warfare include Grant's attack on Vicksburg and Stonewall Jackson's campaign in the Shenandoah Valley in the American Civil War; the German spring offensive of 1918, and Ariel Sharon's jab across the Suez canal at Chinese Farm in 1973.[19]

Manoeuvre is especially useful to the defender. Although the purely attritional defence has a superficial attraction, often heightened by the cutting edge given it by much weapon technology, a defender who hopes to defeat a numerically superior enemy by attrition alone is courting disaster. He may hope to use tactics and technology to exact such a penalty that his opponent will either have his will broken by heavy casualties or will eventually be so eroded by losses that he lacks the resources to persist, but he risks sharing the fate of Osman Pasha, Turkish defender of Plevna against the Russians in 1877. Although Osman's men inflicted terrible casualties on the attackers – taking the Omar Tabrija redoubt alone cost the Russians 6,000 men – Russian will held, and fresh troops arrived to replace casualties. The Turks achieved the unusual distinction of inflicting more casualties than they actually had soldiers, but it availed them nothing. Osman eventually tried to break out, but was pummelled back into Plevna, where he capitulated. Tactically, the Turks had made excellent use of counter-attacks, and in the early stage of the fighting they cheaply recaptured positions which the Russians had taken at great cost. At the operational level they had no answer to the big battalions: writing them down by firepower bought time and headlines, not victory.

Manoeuvre, whether in attack or defence, relies on more than simple movement. The units that move must contain effective combat power: just as steam is latent heat so manoeuvre is latent firepower. It aims, as Liddell Hart observed, at psychological dislocation as much as – or even more than – physical destruction. This dislocation is obtained partly by surprise, at the strategic, operational, or tactical level, partly by the application of prepared strength to unprepared weakness, and, no less essentially, by the tempo of operations. The concept of tempo is fundamental to successful manoeuvre warfare, for it is by maintaining a high tempo that a manoeuvre force imposes its will on its opponent.

In his instructive study of manoeuvre warfare William Lind wrote that 'combat can be seen as time-competitive observation-orientation-decision-action-cycles'. A combatant observes the situation, makes an appreciation and formulates a course of action, takes the action, and then sets out to begin the process again.[20] At the lower tactical level this 'OODA loop' may be short, as an infantryman identifies and engages targets with his rifle or a tank driver negotiates a series of obstacles. In a large headquarters it is likely to be longer, and may be partly institutionalised into a regular pattern of daily activity as reconnaissance reports are received, plans are made, orders sent out and a new set of reports arrive.

The importance of tempo as a means of turning inside the opponent's OODA loop was demonstrated by retired USAF colonel John Boyd. Boyd started from a study of American aviators in air-to-air combat in the Korean War. They achieved a 10:1 kill ratio, despite the general superiority of the principal Communist fighter, the MiG-15, to the American F-86: it was only in observation through the F-86's bubble canopy and in his ability to pass from one manoeuvre to another because of his aircraft's exceptionally effective hydraulic controls that the American pilot enjoyed real advantage. Boyd maintained that these advantages proved decisive, because they enabled American pilots to force their opponents into a series of actions, assessing how the situation changed with each and steadily gaining a time advantage until a firing opportunity was offered. Sometimes the enemy pilot realised what was happening and panicked, making his downfall all the more certain. Colonel Boyd expanded the evidence of the air war over Korea to form the Boyd Theory, in which consistently moving through the OODA loop quicker than an opponent confers a decisive advantage. Each time the slower side acts, the faster one has already embarked upon a new course of action which renders the slower side's action inappropriate. With each sequence the faster side's time advantage is magnified until the slower side can no longer act effectively.

This tempo is not produced simply by moving fast. Rapid decision-making is crucial, and it is often impracticable for decisions to be referred up the chain of command. Even though modern communications make this theoretically possible, untidy practical obstacles interpose themselves. Radio sets break or are jammed, and the ponderous nature of many headquarters does not encourage the swift transmission of information or decisions. Since it is unlikely that commanders can be efficiently *told* what to do in changed circumstances, they should *understand* what their superior's aim is, the better to shape their own activities, in a purposeful way, to this end. The *Befehlstaktik* of meticulous orders, so beloved of devotees of the direct method, suits manoeuvre warfare less well than *Auftragstaktik* or directive control.

If a receptive and decentralised system of command assists rapid decision-taking, well-understood drills and common operating procedures speed action. Drills are widely misunderstood by many Western armies, who chuckle at the prospect of the Soviet soldier being schooled in tactical drills and mock Soviet officers as mere managers of drills. In fact Soviet emphasis on drills has much to commend it. In a fast-moving battle, specific rehearsal of an operation is clearly impossible, and if a commander strives to tell his subordinates exactly how they are to carry out their task he will waste scarce time. Yet often one hears commanders trundling laboriously through an orders process that includes 'grouping – normal', or the stern injunction that a hot meal will be served on the objective. It is far better that the components of battle should be ready-made, to be slotted together to meet the requirement of the moment, and that an operating commonality – of tactics, battle administration and the orders process – forms a shorthand which obviates the need for the elegant copperplate for which there may simply be no time.

If drills play a large part in tactical manoeuvre, it is unwise to apply them strictly to the operational level. Yet that is precisely what much military doctrine, and many commanders across history, have attempted to do. After all, the reduction of uncertainty in the minds of his subordinates is one of the commander's goals, just as a doctrine which has the merit of offering infallible victory to he who applies it wholeheartedly has concerned so many theorists of a Jominian bent. In truth, there are no certainties in war. Flawless plans go wrong; reliable commanders have bad days; dependable units panic. Clausewitz trickles his sand into all parts of the military machine. A scheme which worked well one day works badly another, because it is not applied with the same vigour, because the enemy has grown accustomed to it, or simply because it is raining. An operational plan which is not dynamic, which follows a set pattern (even if that pattern worked very well very recently) risks being predictable, and with prediction comes disaster as the enemy tightens his turn into the OODA loop.

Manoeuvre warfare proved immensely appealing in the late 1980s, so much so that it is in as much danger of being misunderstood as attrition warfare ever was. We should perhaps recall the notion of the spectrum with attrition at one extreme and manoeuvre at the other. There are times when manoeuvre is inappropriate, and a commander may have to slide the operational cursor towards attrition. Why, if manoeuvre has so much in its favour, should this be so? First, because manoeuvre demands space – the expression 'room for manoeuvre' has it perfectly – and both geography and troop density reduce this. The trenchlock of the Western Front in 1915–17 was the quintessence of attrition, and it occurred not primarily because Schlieffen had planned an attritional battle: as we have seen, he was trying to recreate Cannae, a shining example of manoeuvre warfare. There came a time, though, when tactical manoeuvre was difficult as troop density enabled a continuous front to be established from Switzerland to the North Sea. Attempts to sidestep the Western Front either failed because the same tactical circumstances replicated themselves, as they did at Gallipoli, or because success was strategically irrelevant to the war's central points of issue, as it was in both Palestine and Mesopotamia. Room can be created by using attrition to create space (by smashing a hole in a defensive line, for instance) or in using vertical manoeuvre by helicopter to exploit the space in the enemy's rear. Neither method is infallible, not least because of the possibility that the enemy's army will be not only dense but deep.

Reductions in force levels add to the attractiveness of manoeuvre. On the one hand they permit the channelling of resources into smaller, more flexible units: witness current Soviet structural changes which are producing well-balanced combat units with a potent mix of armour, motor rifle troops and artillery. On the other they significantly reduce the force to space ratio, creating room for manoeuvre where none might have existed with the big battalions of yesteryear.

Geography presents a two-fold problem. In the first instance, there are geopolitical realities which no amount of operational slickness can manoeuvre away. A generation of senior NATO commanders bewailed the demands of the government of the Federal Republic of Germany for forward defence. Forward defence brought with it several military difficulties: some formations were drawn forward on to ground that was ill-suited to defence, too much was put in the shop window and not enough in reserve, and so on. It is possible that there was room for compromise over points of detail, which may have resulted in NATO forces being tugged forward less far than was militarily wise. However, it was unrealistic to expect the most benign German government to accept what might have seemed to I (British) Corps the operational logic of starting its main defensive battle on the line of the River Weser. Moreover, the addiction of manoeuvre *aficionados* to Field Marshal Erich von Manstein's masterful counterstroke at Kharkov in 1943 conceals the fact that there is simply not depth enough in Western Europe for manoeuvre defence on this scale to be carried out. Swinging back over the Dutch border to defeat the Soviet first tactical echelon is an operational ploy which would have received muted applause from Bonn.[21]

Some terrain has value that is primarily political or economic. Other ground is of military value, and even though manoeuvre warfare seeks to focus on the enemy, not the ground, it cannot avoid this fact. Logistic depots and airfields must form fixed points which manoeuvre cannot ignore, and if other facilities may be more easily moved they nevertheless make the terrain they are sited on of at least transient value. Terrain also affects the speed and manner in which it is crossed, and this tends to restrict manoeuvre. Waterways present only a limited obstacle to late-twentieth-century armies. Soviet tanks can snorkel across a river less than 5.5 metres deep. Tracked bridge-layers can quickly lay single-span or scissors bridges across gaps up to about 22 metres, while longer gaps can be crossed by girder bridges, pontoon bridges like the Soviet PMP, or ferries like the GSP. One of the striking features of the Yom Kippur War was the efficiency with which the Egyptians crossed the Suez canal and kept their bridges operating despite air attack. For all this, the effect of waterways cannot be ignored. Bridges are vulnerable to precision-guided munitions, and the need for good approaches and firm banks limits the choice of temporary crossing sites. In short, although watercourses are not impassable barriers, they will impose delay, however brief, and cause bunching which will consume time and offer attractive targets.

Other natural features – hills, mountains and woods – also restrict manoeuvre, canalising movement along roads or tracks and thus magnifying the effects of blocking actions, vehicle breakdowns and navigation errors to enhance overall friction. There is little terrain that is literally impenetrable, although extremes like jungle or high mountain will demand specialised training and equipment, and may impose so much friction that operations are of strictly limited scale. When writing about guerrilla warfare, Clausewitz identified five essential conditions for its success: one was the warlike nature of the people who fought it, and another was the 'broken and difficult' character of the countryside. Both were dominant characteristics of the Soviet war in Afghanistan, and we should not underestimate the effects of terrain in eroding Soviet ability to prosecute the war effectively.

Attacking through an area that has seemed impassable to large-scale military movement has been an attractive option in the past. Wolfe's men took Quebec after scaling cliffs, the natural obstacles facing MacArthur at Inchon were so immense that he undertook the landing against the weight of professional advice, and German choice of the 'impenetrable' Ardennes for their advance in 1940 contributed to the psychological dislocation of the French high command. Well might FM 100–5 emphasise that: 'The most promising approaches are often those which appear most unlikely.'[22] In any case, armies do not all take the same view of terrain. Christopher Donnelly observes that:

> How a NATO officer and a Soviet officer interpret the term 'road' shows an interesting cultural, or environmental, bias. What to a NATO officer is a dirt track, a forest ride, a narrow path through a forest is, to a Russian, almost as much of a 'road' as is an *autobahn*, and therefore just as much a candidate for the regimental main axis or rear supply route.[23]

In their Ardennes counter-offensive in the winter of 1944 the Germans pushed formations along tiny roads in atrocious weather. Even the Americans, despite their allegedly road-bound mentality, could use routes that modern forces might regard as hopelessly inadequate: 5th Infantry Division crossed the Moselle at Arnaville, south of Metz, in September 1944, approaching along narrow lanes which tax my peacetime map-reading. In one important respect mobility has not necessarily improved with time. If a present-day American armoured force attempted to re-create Patton's relief of Bastogne in December 1944 it would find that the weight of its tanks meant that only one of the routes used at the time, the main Arlon–Bastogne highway, would be tankable by the M-1 *Abrams*.

Discussion of operations in the winter of 1944 naturally leads to consideration of the impact of weather. Extremes of temperature affect manoeuvre, both intense heat and cold requiring the troops that fight in them to be specially trained and equipped. Yet even the less extreme weather of north-west Europe has its own limiting effects. On 21 March 1918 the Germans attacked the British in a thick fog which blinded the interlocking arcs of fire upon which the defenders' redoubt system depended. Both sides claimed that the fog had hampered them. The British blamed it for the rapid collapse of the Fifth Army's Battle Zone, while the Germans argued that it had 'prevented our superior training and leadership from reaping its true reward'.[24]

Some modern weapons have sights which peer through night and fog, but many do not, and most aircraft are affected by poor visibility. Heavy rain reduces off-road mobility, and the passage of large numbers of vehicles grinds wet soil to mud. We may think of mud as being characteristic of the Western Front during the First World War, but mud is the inescapable product of rain, farmland and soldiers: the first French charges up the slope in front of Wellington's position at Waterloo left the ground 'in places so churned to mud that no squadron could keep its alignment'.[25] The addition of shellfire and tracked vehicles deepens the quagmire. Chris Bellamy points out that the heavy rain which fell on Lower Saxony before the British exercise *Lionheart* in 1984 created seas of mud, and the British were forced to spend all the £8 million earmarked for compensation.[26]

Man-made features also influence manoeuvre. Accelerating urbanisation has created massive towns whose suburbs sometimes link to form huge agglomerations. The Ruhr, with its built-up wedge running from Dortmund to Duisburg and down towards Bonn, is a labyrinthine example of the urban belt that has become common not only in Europe but also in America, North and South, and Asia. Types and density of housing naturally vary, from the middle-class suburbs and workers' flats of Europe and North America to the 'misery belts' of *favelas* around the cities of Latin America. Fighting in towns and villages imposes a regimen of its own. Drastic reduction of engagement ranges, modification of weapon effects, difficulties with command and control, and high consumption of troops and ammunition alike are characteristics of fighting in cities. Firepower may increase the attacker's problems, for, as the evidence of Stalingrad, Caen, Hue, Beirut and Khorramshahr shows, resolute defenders can turn rubble and gutted buildings to their advantage. Moreover, urban operations impose moral and presentational strains on the armies that fight them. The image of Israeli 155mm guns battering Beirut echoed far beyond the blast of their shells, and the human consequences of street-fighting in a populated city shocked many Israeli soldiers.

Finally, technology nudges the cursor between attrition and manoeuvre. Several military commentators have divided history up into periods marked by the dominant characteristics of the weapons employed. Major-General J.F.C. Fuller called them 'shock cycles' and 'projectile cycles', while Tom Wintringham prefered 'armoured and unarmoured periods' with the qualities of 'mobility, hitting-power and protection' as the 'keys of victory' within them.[27] This cyclical view, with tactics swinging along the sine curve of weapon development, undoubtedly oversimplifies, but it does establish helpful patterns. For much of the Middle Ages the armoured knight rode supreme across Europe, his charge the basis of a Fuller 'shock cycle' or Wintringham's 'Second Armoured Period, 744 to 1346'. His decline was not as rapid or complete as Wintringham's selection of the battle of Crécy for the period's terminal date suggests. As Ferdinand Lot has observed, it took English knights to capitalise upon the damage done by archers' firepower at Crécy, and the armoured horseman lurched on into the sixteenth century despite his declining utility, outlasting even his old enemy the bowman.[28] The knight is also a good example of the 'master weapon' which dominates tactics for a period, developing in response to threats against it (in the knight's case gaining ever-heavier armour in an effort to keep out missiles). This development usually proceeds to the point of overspecialisation, at which the weapon loses its utility: the tank's critics prophesy that it will eventually lumber into extinction as the knight did.

At some point in the late Middle Ages firepower, delivered by crossbow, longbow or handgun, wrested the ascendancy from the horseman. At the same time the castle, long the refuge of the refractory vassal, became vulnerable to the new technology. When Franz von Sickengen, leader of the rebellious Rhineland knights, was put to the ban of the Empire in 1523, he retired to stand siege in his castle at Landstuhl. A generation before he might have held out until the besiegers melted away, but not so in the age of gunpowder: the Emperor's gunners knocked down his walls and killed him.

Between the beginning of the sixteenth century and the second decade of the twentieth, firepower grew. It did so irregularly, with a great leap (the perfection of the flintlock musket and socket bayonet) in the late seventeenth and early eighteenth centuries, through slow growth in the late eighteenth and early nineteenth centuries to further rapid acceleration in the second half of the nineteenth century with rifled breech-loaders, smokeless powder, the magazine rifle and the machine-gun. Throughout this period Fuller's 'constant tactical factor' (the tendency to produce weapons that killed at ever-increasing range) applied, and both the volume of fire, and the distance to which it could be applied, grew beyond measure. It did not significantly increase the distance between the forward elements of contending armies. The bulk of infantry combats in the 1980s have taken place at well inside the effective range of the small-arms used, and the infantrymen killed one another at distances which would not have seemed surprising to their fathers or grandfathers. Moreover, the constraints of terrain and climate help restrict the engagement ranges of all direct-fire weapons. In typical West German terrain a moving tank is visible at 500 metres for only 40 per cent of the time, and at above 1,000 metres it may be seen for only 34 per cent of the time.[29]

Although increased firepower did not lengthen the range at which all combatants fought, it did increase the depth of the battlefield. A soldier at Waterloo was comparatively safe a few hundred metres from the forward lines of infantry: he might be hit by a stray cannon-ball or caught in an eddy of cavalrymen (the Scots Greys got among unfortunate French artillery-drivers), but would be unlucky in either case. A century later artillery reached out into the deep rear. The town of Bapaume was about twenty kilometres from the main British gun-line on the Somme, but heavy pieces hit it with such regularity that the headquarters of XIV Reserve Corps sought safer quarters elsewhere. Aircraft gave twentieth-century firepower a longer lethal reach than that provided by even the heaviest guns: the front line, back areas, choke points on the lines of communication and, through the agency of strategic bombing, the industry and population of homeland itself, all were at the mercy of air power.

The growing number of 'razors in the air' helped create that unnerving phenomenon, the empty battlefield. For troops to expose themselves to the weight of fire that could be brought to bear on them produced disaster for little benefit: this was a lesson taught

Ritualised Combat

1   German infantry and cavalry on manoeuvres in Silesia, 1913.

2   A British Carl Gustav team takes on a US M1 *Abrams*. Exercise *Lionheart*, West Germany, 1984.

Real War

3 Mud, Blood: Canadian machine-gunners on Passchendaele Ridge, autumn 1917.

4 . . . and Waiting: French soldiers in Indo-China, 1954.

Rotorborne Firepower

5 The Mi-24 *Gorbach*, usually known by its NATO name *Hind-D*, carries a 12.7mm Gatling-type gun in a chin turret, twin rocket pods and *Falanga* missile racks under its wings.

6 The US Army's AH-64 *Apache*. A 30mm cannon is just visible between the landing gear, and eight Hellfire anti-tank missiles cluster beneath the winglets.

Death from Afar

7   US Army *Pershing II* battlefield support missile, with a range of up to 1,300km, 1980s.

8   German 15cm howitzer, with a range of 10km, 1916.

the Prussian Guard by the *Chassepots* of the French 6 Corps at Saint-Privat in 1870, and it has been painfully relearned on countless battlefields from the Somme to Majnoon. To avoid fire, they took cover, and temporary shelter was soon converted into trench-lines and strongpoints. The huge size of conscript armies made possible continuous fronts with a high weapon density, and where this occurred firepower extinguished manoeuvre. Chris Bellamy has pointed to the paradox that twentieth-century battlefields tend to be both empty, with few signs of life, and crowded, with masses of troops in concealment in the front line and more exposed in the deep rear.

The same logic which led the ancients to armour man and horse against sword, spear and missile inspired the development of armoured vehicles during and after the First World War. The tank was initially a means of overcoming barbed wire and the machine-gun: conceptual thinking was required to combine technology with doctrine to produce a new style of warfare. The infiltration techniques used by German stormtroops in 1918 pointed the way ahead, and the combination of the armoured vehicle and ground attack aircraft in the operational doctrine of blitzkrieg swung the pendulum in favour of manoeuvre, making possible the German invasion of Poland in 1939, of France and the Low Countries in 1940, and of Russia in 1941.

The pendulum had begun to swing back even before the Second World War ended. Shaped-charge anti-armour weapons, fired by PIAT, bazooka or *Panzerfaust*, reduced armour's ability to ride roughshod over infantry, especially in close country or towns. Belts of mines and anti-tank strongpoints, like the Russians used at Kursk, could soak up an armoured punch, leaving it vulnerable to counter-attack. Much of the impact of blitzkrieg was psychological, and was reduced once armies and their commanders knew what to expect.

The war's evidence was selective, however. The Western Allies were engaged in several radically different theatres of war – Pacific islands, Burmese jungle, North African desert and Italian ridges as well as Norman *bocage*. Defeat of German land forces was only one of a number of concerns, and neither technical research nor operational doctrine reflected single-minded preoccupation with it. Britain herself was seriously menaced only in 1940–1, and the continental United States was never threatened. The Soviet Union, on the other hand, was constantly engaged against the main forces of Germany in a costly and exhausting struggle for its very existence. The Russians learnt hard lessons in a rough school. Their operational art improved enormously during the war, and by its end they had perfected a technique based upon the synthesis of manoeuvre and firepower.

At the heart of the Red Army's effectiveness was its ability to make mobility the handmaiden of firepower, enabling it to administer concentrated shock at selected points. It was adept at massing forces to achieve an overwhelming local superiority, and supporting tank and infantry units in key sectors with ferociously heavy artillery bombardments. At the tactical level it was often outclassed by the Germans (as late as April 1945 a single *Panther* of *Das Reich* destroyed 14 T-34s in a day while covering the evacuation of the Vienna bridgehead), but at the operational level it excelled.[30]

Colonel T.N.Dupuy and Martin van Creveld are among the distinguished scholars who have drawn our attention to the remarkable achievements of the German army: its consistent ability to outfight Allied formations of similar size; its efficient generation of fighting power, and its remarkable recuperative powers all demand our admiration. We may attribute many (but by no means all) German errors at the strategic level to the personality of Hitler and his domination of the high command, and his interference at the operational level produced baneful influences there too. Nevertheless, applause for German performance at the tactical level and recognition that the strategic waters were muddied by Hitler and his entourage should not deflect us from the conclusion that the Germans were soundly beaten at the operational level in the East. That this was partly the result of inexpert political intervention in military matters points up a moral of its own.

Just as the war had produced evidence which was construed in different ways, so the postwar years confirmed no universal truths. America's initial nuclear monopoly, followed by her (increasingly challenged) nuclear supremacy, led to the de-emphasis of conventional forces which the lacklustre performance of many US units in Korea underlined. Despite her immense economic power and technical resources, America had fallen behind Russia in tank design: Congressman Philbin's subcommittee found what it called a 'deplorable situation' in US tank production. Neither the M-47, rushed into production as a result of Korea, nor its successor the M-48 were an accurate reflection of the state of the art, and even the M-60 (with its many modifications and long service life) did not enjoy the technical lead over its potential opponents which America's industrial position might have implied.

Strategic Air Command had gorged itself on the military budget in the 1950s and 1960s, and the war in Vietnam (in which much equipment and doctrine forged for Western Europe was largely irrelevant) cast its long shadow over the late 1960s and early 1970s. It was only in the 1980s that the US Army's conventional war-fighting ability at last matched America's status as a world power, and it is no coincidence that the period witnessed its intellectual and spiritual renaissance as the ghost of Vietnam was laid and new doctrines were forged. The M-1 *Abrams* is the first US postwar main battle tank which genuinely reflects the industrial power-base that produces it, though even in its case teething troubles have been painful, and concerns remain about the beast's prodigious thirst.

British experience was different yet again. As a result of his time in the desert, Montgomery had pressed for the development of a 'capital tank' which would carry out the roles of both 'infantry' and 'cruiser' tanks. The eventual result was the *Centurion*, which entered service just too late to see action during the war, but remained the mainstay of the Royal Armoured Corps until its replacement by the *Chieftain* in the 1960s. British design priorities, in great measure as a result of Second World War experience, emphasised firepower and protection at the expense of mobility, and early marks of *Chieftain* were seriously under-powered. In the 1980s the purchase of tanks destined for the deposed Shah of Iran enabled the British to partly re-equip their tank fleet with the *Challenger*, and a decision taken in early 1989 will lead to the development of a new tank by Vickers, although the upgraded *Abrams* was seen as a better prospect by many senior officers.

Tank design in both Britain and America was influenced by strategic considerations which inhibited single-minded concentration on a Soviet threat to Europe and by the lack of a clear link between doctrine and procurement. The Russians, on the other hand, were in no doubt of the importance of powerful land forces in which the tank played the leading role, and in their case the coupling between doctrine and procurement was close and robust. The current state of the Soviet economy bears eloquent witness to the demands imposed upon it by the 'metal eaters' of the arms industries, but the results of this endeavour sit squatly on tank-parks from the Oder to the Ussuri Rivers. Emphasis on cheap, simple and reliable weapons, easily used by conscripts, permeates the Soviet system. Tanks have tended to be fast and well-armoured with a low silhouette, and if the quality of their gunnery has lagged behind that of Western tanks, quantity, as Lenin is alleged to have said, has a quality all of its own.

The West Germans, initially dependent on American equipment, developed their own *Leopard* after the failure of a joint attempt to agree on a co-operative venture, MBT-70, with the Americans, and *Leopard II* has followed it. The Israelis, too, at first relied on imports, and *Super Shermans*, M-48s and *Centurions* all played their part in the Israeli re-run of blitzkrieg in 1967. The 1973 war demonstrated the political dangers of dependence on external support and lent momentum to Israeli-built products, notably the *Merkava* tank, which received its baptism of fire in the Lebanon in 1982. *Merkava* was designed with crew protection as its first priority. The engine is at the front, behind a sloping glacis plate of composite armour. Halon gas is automatically injected into the crew and engine compartments when a fire is detected, and is swiftly evacuated before it harms the crew. The 105mm gun mounted on *Merkava* is smaller than the 120mm or 125mm which is standard elsewhere, but on the evidence of 1982 it had no problem disposing of the Soviet-supplied T-62 tank, even at very long ranges.

Tank development was not going on in a vacuum. As tanks became heavier and mounted larger guns, anti-tank guns grew in an effort to keep pace. Kinetic energy weapons, relying upon the velocity of their shot for penetration, could not grow large enough to match developments in tank armour and still remain easily usable on a ground mount. Chemical energy weapons, which penetrated armour by means of explosive effect (like the jet of hot metal created by the shaped charge of the High-Explosive Anti-Tank round) became attractive alternatives, fired from recoilless guns (whose vicious backblast and high trajectory were substantial tactical limitations), and providing the warheads in Anti-Tank Guided Weapons.

Artillery grew in range and weight of shell as the 105mm, which had formed the mainstay of field artillery, began to be replaced by the 155mm. New technologies extend range still further, with rocket-assisted projectiles, Extended Range Sub Calibre and Extended Range Full Bore munitions. Mechanical loaders and rammers on some equipment give a burst-fire capability, and such developments make the robot gun a probability within a decade or so. Multi-Launch Rocket Systems with crushing area effects and a variety of Terminally-Guided Sub-Munitions have greatly enhanced the effectiveness of artillery, and developments in fire-control computing and position-finding have increased accuracy and speed of response. Surveillance and Target Acquisition Systems make it difficult for enemy units to remain undetected even as they move far in the rear, and the combination of sophisticated surveillance and long-range weapon systems make deep attack at least technically feasible. Remotely delivered mines impede movement, and an effective robotic mine, able to seek out and attack a nearby target, lies not far in the future.

Modern mines are extremely difficult to detect, and anti-tank mines can be fitted with double-impulse and tilt fuses which increase the hazards of trying to clear them with mine-rollers and mine-ploughs. Fuel Air Explosives are at least part of the answer. These may be delivered by aircraft bomb or tactical missile, and consist of fuel which mixes with the air and is then detonated to an explosion within the aerosol cloud to produce high over-pressures across a wide area. They are more efficient than conventional explosives, and their blast effects are comparable with small nuclear weapons. They are likely to be extremely effective against dug-in infantry: troops outside the immediate fireball are killed by the effects of over-pressure on the lungs. Defences that might protect against bullets, splinters or fragments are no use against Fuel Air Explosives: the American analyst Ken Brower suggests that 'the effects of the blast cannot be defeated unless all around protection is provided, i.e., personnel have to be located in a pressure tight cocoon'.[31]

Fuel Air Explosives are still some way from becoming a 'master-weapon'. They are seriously affected by weather conditions, and need to be large (500 pounds or more) in order to be fully effective, so they are better suited for attacks on strongpoints than for dealing with widely dispersed infantry. They are exceptionally useful for clearing mines: in the late 1970s the US FAESHED (Fuel Air Explosives Helicopter Delivered) performed extraodinarily well against a variety of mines.[32]

The armed helicopter, its missiles equipped with increasingly automated guidance systems, the growing number of all-weather aircraft and the lethality of the weapons they carry, have increased the potential impact of air upon the land battle. Here, as elsewhere, the case is anything but clear, for the proliferation of air-defence systems can result in very high attrition rates, as the Israelis discovered in the early days of the Yom Kippur War. However, in the fighting in the

Beka'a valley in the Lebanon in June 1982 the Israelis used slickly planned Electronic Warfare to confuse Syrian missile radars before attacking missile sites and lacerating the Syrian air force.33

The supreme difficulty lies in ascertaining where these developments have left the balance between attrition and manoeuvre. The evidence of the Yom Kippur War was initially believed by many to reveal the weakness of the tank when faced with belts of anti-tank guided weapons: one reading of the evidence of 1973 suggested that the pendulum had swung back to the point where fire dominated manoeuvre much as it had on the Western Front in 1915–17. The Russians, with huge armour-heavy ground forces, found the results of the war disturbing, and considered three main methods of maintaining a high rate of advance despite the challenge of the missile. One option was to employ massive pre-emptive nuclear strikes, which would open up gaps through which they could move. This raised serious political questions, and the high risk of nuclear escalation made it increasingly unlikely.34 Another was to increase the effectiveness of artillery, enabling it to saturate an anti-tank guided weapon defence, and increasing emphasis on self-propelled artillery in the Soviet army followed the war.

The third possibility, the manoeuvre option, envisaged a pre-emptive conventional attack which would result in the attackers arriving before the defenders had completed their deployment. Many Western commentators argued that it would be as difficult for the Russians to fight a 'come as you are' war as it would for their opponents, but the importance attached to surprise in Soviet military theory suggests that the manoeuvre option had many attractions, especially if NATO was in disarray or had had its resolve undermined by the sort of on/off mobilisations which had paved the way for the Arab attack on Israel in 1973.35

In purely technical terms the manoeuvre option became more attractive in the 1980s. The development, first of ceramic compound armours, and then of Explosive Reactive Armour has grave implications for the effectiveness of a predominantly missile-armed defence. This new armour, consisting of appliqué explosive plates which disrupt an incoming chemical energy warhead, was first used by the Israelis in the late 1970s, and an Israeli M-60 equipped with reactive armour fell into Russian hands in 1982. It is likely that the Russians had already been working on such armour, for it was quickly deployed and is currently found on about half the Soviet T-64B, T-72 and T-80 fleet. Although some success has been achieved with 'tandem' warheads (one warhead triggers the appliqué explosive and the other goes on to attack the main armour) the effectiveness of chemical energy weapons is very much restricted by the combination of ceramic armour and explosive plates. The pendulum still swings. The development of the electrothermal gun is well under way, and within a decade or so the electromagnetic gun will be in service. Both accelerate a projectile to such speeds that no armour can withstand them. The advent of the new guns will, no doubt, lead to mutterings that the day of the tank is over. But these weapons rely upon cumbersome power sources, and so will need mounting on a heavy vehicle, with a cross-country capability and armoured protection: they may simply lead to a revamped tank.

There will still be targets against which chemical energy rounds are effective. About 75 per cent of infantry casualties in conventional war are caused by the blast or fragments of artillery shells or mortar bombs. Putting infantry into Armoured Personnel Carriers, a process which began in the Second World War, protected them against fire and also made it easier for them to keep pace with armour. The carrier and tank enjoy differential protection: only those wartime carriers which were based on tank hulls (like the British *Kangaroo*) offered the same protection as the tank. The Yom Kippur War showed that even the more sophisticated Mechanised Infantry Combat Vehicle, for all that it mounted a cannon-armed turret and ports through which its occupants could fire, was several times more vulnerable than the tank. The Russians had developed their main infantry combat vehicle, the BMP, at a time when they thought in terms of the early use of nuclear weapons, and it is well suited to operating in a nuclear environment against a shocked and disorganised enemy. Its limitations were revealed in 1973 and, significantly, the Russians have not replaced all their personnel carriers with infantry combat vehicles, keeping carrier-mounted units for attack on prepared positions and BMP units for exploitation, possibly as part of an Operational Manoeuvre Group.

Western armies have been attracted by the infantry combat vehicle, partly because of the apparent virtues of the BMP. The Germans were first in the field with their *Marder*, and now both British *Warrior* and US *Bradley* are deployed. All have far less protection than the tanks they will accompany which gives rise to concern, and this fact alone will tend to separate armour from infantry. Moreover, the insatiable demands of machinery reduce the amount of infantrymen actually available for dismounted duties. Major-General Richard Scholtes notes that the 17,000-man American armoured division can dismount a strength of only 960 infantrymen.[36]

Manoeuvre warfare will be the dominant military fashion of the 1990s. It will gain strength from force reductions which make room for manoeuvre and encourage the creation of flexible all-arms combat units, but it will lack universal appeal. While it may be the most appropriate garb for the armies of the northern hemisphere, subject as they are to the radically wielded shears of financial restraint, manpower shortages and public opinion, it will be less attractive to armies of the southern hemisphere, whose modest technical sophistication and abundant manpower may make attrition not merely acceptable but unavoidable. The most manoeuvre-minded army cannot totally shun attrition, for the extreme (but, as we have seen, the least probable) case may demand total national defence even with attrition as its price.

A force structure for the nineties should, therefore, embody manoeuvre as well as attritional elements. The former, high-cost and high-mobility units composed of regulars, could project power beyond the national border to intervene or reinforce: the latter, low-cost reserve or conscript forces, would be usable only in indisputable national emergency, where the full weight of public opinion nerves the war effort. The sword of manoeuvre, lighter and sharper as it will become as the nineties wear on, will rarely need the spiked shield of attrition: but it will be dangerously fragile without it.

Blueprints for Battle

Soviet military doctrine is in a state of flux. Having already sketched out the framework of the new policy, we must now consider the doctrine which is being dismantled as this book goes to press, for it has formed the model which opposing doctrines have sought to counter and, if glasnost falters, it may so easily be the groove into which the Soviet military machine once more slides. Indeed, the US Army's leading Sovietologist, Colonel David Glantz, has warned that another operational model should be considered alongside the Khalkin Gol and Kursk paradigms: it is the Manchurian model, where a defensive posture was covertly transformed into an offensive one. Thus we cannot ignore the past half-century of Soviet military thought because it seems to have lost some of its relevance: it stands like a rock in the mainstream of military history, and we ignore it at our peril.

The emphasis placed by Soviet strategists on the initial period of any future war, given their desire to avoid both nuclear use and a long struggle in which the West's economic strength would tell, suggests that any war they intitiated would be screened by elaborate deception, both political and military. Each major sphere of interest – the Far East, the whole of Western Europe, and the Middle East – would form a Theatre of War (TV). It would be subdivided into a number of TVDs (variously interpreted as Theatre of Military Operations or Theatre of Strategic Military Action). The Western TV appears to have three TVDs, North-Western, Western and South-Western. Bellamy suggests that the Western TVD is probably divided into three 'strategic directions', running toward Denmark, Britain via the Low Countries, and across France to the Iberian Peninsula.[37]

Within a TVD an offensive would take the form of massively concentrated thrusts along key axes, with high Soviet weapon density in these areas giving the best possible chance that the defence, whatever the individual effectiveness of its weapons, will simply be overwhelmed. One Soviet estimate suggests that doubling the density of anti-tank weapons more than doubles the effectiveness of the defence: conversely, the stronger the attacker the smaller his losses.[38]

Attacking units and formations are stacked in two or occasionally three waves (echelons) so as to place sustained pressure on the chosen point of impact. A battalion might have two companies in its first echelon and a company in its second; a division two regiments in its first and two in its second echelon. In addition, each unit or formation maintains a small reserve. Once a hole is made in the enemy defence, a force is pushed through in order to penetrate deep into the defensive system, disrupting its cohesion. This task may be entrusted to a second echelon, but is more likely to be the responsibility of an Operational Manoeuvre Group. The Soviets fit their pattern of echelons to the structure of the defence to be attacked. Thus a defence which consists of a single echelon would probably be attacked by one echelon, its reserve, and OMGs to exploit a breakthough. Not only does the echelon system facilitate concentration, but it also aids regrouping, the shifting of forces from axis to axis to reinforce success or increase force ratios at the crucial point.

Although this is not a book on the nuts and bolts of operational art, Soviet concepts have profound implications for the nature of battle in the next quarter-century, and so we must tease more detail from them. This is because the Soviet operational style has at least partly inspired a series of different operational responses from the US AirLand Battle, through to various models of non-provocative defence.

The concept of deep battle pervades Soviet operational thinking. By immediately extending battle throughout NATO's operational depth the Russians would most effectively destroy NATO nuclear assets and disrupt command and control systems, get their forces so enmeshed with NATO formations and centres of population as to make nuclear first use hazardous. The concept of deep battle is not new, but the evolving means at the disposal of Soviet commanders, especially in terms of air assets, fixed- and rotary-wing alike, with airmobile and air-assault brigades, have lent sharper teeth to it. Similarly, the OMG, discerned by some as a new and sinister development, was a logical development of the Second World War mobile group and has foundations deep in Imperial Russia.39 We should guard against the crisp vision of an OMG straining at the leash, poised behind the chosen sector, waiting for a breakthough. It is more likely that that it would coalesce late, by concentration on the battlefield in a manner which Napoleon, Moltke, or Schlieffen with his *Schwerpunktbildung* would have understood. The term second echelon also merits consideration, since 'second echelon attrition' has an irresistible appeal to many NATO theorists. The idea that there will be a unified second echelon, clearly identifiable from the first, hanging about in the Warsaw Pact rear, is misleading. If the Russians believe that they are facing a defence thin enough to be attacked by one echelon, this, and concern about the damage that Follow-On Forces Attack (FOFA) may do to units out of contact, will induce them to push as many of their assets as far forward as possible. The realities of road-space mean that some echeloning is inevitable: a motor rifle division takes up nearly 250km of road in tactical march column, and moving along two routes takes about four hours to pass a given point.

In sum, Soviet operational concepts are comprehensively thought through, and it is twenty years out of date to envisage a clumsy steamroller composed of robust but old-fashioned equipment. We must constantly bear in mind that the risks of war against NATO have long been so great as to make it a high-risk venture, and that the whole thrust of political direction under Gorbachev has been aimed at the reduction of tension, the avoidance of provocation and the ending of the arms race. If political intentions changed, Russia's military capabilities remain impressive despite the doctrinal upheaval discussed earlier. The machine would, no doubt, not work perfectly. Several aspects cause continual difficulties in training and are much discussed in the Soviet military press, for instance the problem of co-ordinating artillery fire and managing infantry and armour on the objective. The Soviet Air Force and Air Defence Command have been going through a painful period, and Herr Rust's unscripted appearance on Red Square did not materially enhance the latter's status. There is wide disaffection among aircrew and a shortage of training equipment.[40] In general, however, Soviet doctrine is firmly based on relevant historical evidence, amplified by searching analysis, and is backed by a procurement system which has produced several first-rate pieces of equipment (and others which are far less good). While some Western doctrine has tended to slide from high-attrition to high-manoeuvre, the Soviet synthesis of manoeuvre and attrition, weighted by mass and transmitted through the depth of the enemy's deployment has much logic to commend it. The evolving defensive doctrine, as we have seen, embodies the same elements, with strongly posted covering forces extracting an attritional penalty from an attacker, before deeply based mobile forces unhinge him by manoeuvre.

Traditional United States military doctrine was influenced by Napoleon, through the medium of Jomini, and by the technogical surge of the Industrial Revolution, heightened by the fact that engineering was the dominant academic bias at West Point. Although there were American commanders who were masters of manoeuvre war – Lee, Jackson and Patton among them – attrition, applied through powerful industry and abundant manpower, was her preferred strategic, operational and tactical *modus operandi,* as we saw earlier in this chapter. In the wake of Vietnam US Army doctrine was redefined in the July 1976 edition of FM 100–5 *Operations,* a work which emphasised the value of new weapons to 'Active Defense', and recognised the need to win the first battle of any war – appropriately enough, in view of discussion of a 'come as you are' war in the wake of 1973.

In the debate which followed the appearance of this manual, Steven Canby pointed out that lateral concentration to focus all available assets on the head of a Soviet armoured thrust dealt with only one possible Soviet ploy, and was vulnerable to a more subtle 'reconnaissance pulled' attack which avoided American strength and sought American weakness in the classic 1918/1940 pattern. There was wider concern over the fact that even if active defence defeated the leading Soviet elements it could not cope with the jarring impact of successive echelons. Finally, there were suggestions that the doctrine was essentially attritional and might result in a forward-leaning linear defence.[41]

The new doctrine was not universally popular even with senior officers. General Donn A. Starry, who took over Training and Doctrine Command in 1977, and General Edward C. Meyer, who became Chief of Staff of the Army in 1979, had misgivings of their own, the latter because active defence was applicable only in the context of a European war which he believed to be less likely than conflict elsewhere. Several other threads – including the artillery's interest in interdiction, integration of nuclear weapons into attacks on the second echelon, General Starry's notion of 'the extended battlefield', and increasing need to defend US vital interests outside Europe – were knitted together in a 1981 operational concept for the AirLand Battle. This took as its basis the Clausewitzian view of war as a continuation of policy by other means, and declared that 'the purpose of military operations cannot be simply to avert defeat – but rather it must be to win'.[42] It dealt with battle against well-equipped armoured forces – not necessarily in Europe – and emphasised attack on the enemy second echelon.

In early 1980 work began on a new FM 100–5, with the active participation of USAF's Tactical Air Command, and the finished version was published in 1982. The pamphlet embodied a clear statement of the value of manoeuvre:

> The AirLand Battle will be dominated by the force that retains the initiative and, with deep attack and decisive maneuver, destroys its opponent's abilities to fight and to organize in depth.[43]

The concept of Follow-On Forces Attack painted a vivid picture of a non-linear battlefield, with distinctions between forward and rear areas blurred. Its components were the deep battle against enemy follow-on forces, the main battle, and rear operations against special forces and air assault elements. Nuclear and chemical attack must be expected, and the lethality of such attacks, together with the disruptive effects of Electronic Counter-Measures, placed a premium on the initiative of junior commanders.

The new doctrine did not please everyone. Some saw it as evidence of American desire to fight a war in Europe – rather than to win one if it broke out: the West German Greens complained of 'lateral escalation'. Other West Germans suspected that it was incompatible with the forward defence of the Inner German Border. In 1984 Manfred Worner, then Minister of Defence, warned that although he was prepared to accept FOFA as a concept:

> there must not be the slightest doubt that stopping the first echelon has the highest priority for the FRG and the Alliance as a whole, because it would make little sense to fight the second echelon once the first one has reached the Rhine.[44]

Because nuclear planning was firmly integrated, some argued that the doctrine could actually lower the nuclear threshold, and might encourage the Russians to believe that approaching conventional missiles were nuclear. Others, however, believed that FOFA might weaken deterrence by strengthening conventional forces and thus indicating to the Soviet leadership that NATO would not escalate to nuclear weapons. Expense was also a key issue. The Germans argued that killing deep was more expensive than killing close, and complained that the diversion of resources to FOFA and the deep battle might weaken NATO's ability to fight the contact battle. Discussion of FOFA coincided with a continuing debate on burden-sharing within NATO, which only served to complicate matters.[45]

Unlike the Warsaw Pact, which had an ostensible commonality of military thinking, the member states of NATO must subscribe to a joint doctrine which, of necessity, forms the basis for action but does not impose the rigid constraints which a Soviet theorist might regard as essential. The current doctrine is embodied in Allied Tactical Publication 35(A), a thoroughgoing 1982 revision of a 1976 document. Although it embodies the views of a disparate alliance, the document sensibly addresses fundamental issues, noting that manoeuvre is a key element of defence and stressing that the defensive battle should be fought with as much aggressive spirit as possible. It does not embody FOFA, but in 1983 FOFA was agreed as an Allied Command Europe 'subconcept of operations', and a November 1984 decision approved a Long Term Planning Guideline for FOFA, giving political endorsement to the concept.[46]

Although the United States has confirmed that AirLand Battle doctrine will apply in Europe only inasmuch as it is compatible with NATO doctrine, there is concern over how the 150-kilometre deep counter-attacks envisaged in the former can co-exist with the forward defence emphasis of the latter. The allocation of air resources for deep strike missions requires careful consideration, given that such missions will be directed against targets outide the interest of individual national corps. The role of the US Joint Surveillance Target Attack Radar System in crisis management also merits great thought. At present the relationship between reconnaissance and strike is insufficiently intimate, and more work needs to be done on the timely engagement of identified targets.

Two substantial doubts overhang FOFA. Some thought that by diverting resources away from the contact battle it might encourage Soviet planners to hope for a favourable ratio of forces in the contact battle, encouraging what Lieutenant-Colonel John E. Peters calls 'standing-start blitzkrieg' – the 'come as you are' war.[47] More damaging is the reliance placed on emerging technology. The Joint Surveillance Target Attack Radar System plays a crucial role in target acquisition, and a family of long-range weapon systems delivers 'smart' munitions on to targets in the deep rear. Some of the system's critics warn that there may not be a second echelon as such to attack, although simple considerations of terrain and deployment suggest that there will certainly be some targets of operational significance within range. Air Vice Marshal John Walker emphasised the ability of air interdiction to cause 'aggravated muddle', and his realistic description of the target array makes the point that whatever we say about first and second echelons, as things stand there is simply too much ironmongery to fit in the available real estate.

His divisions have 3,000 or more vehicles of all types. If they were advancing on four lines of communication each line would have four separate columns, each of those 25km long . . . The books tell us that we face about 90 divisions, front to back. Can you imagine it when the bridges start to fall and the choke points start to fill with lucrative targets? And what is the effect on the front when the replacement for an exhausted division is not yet ready to take its place?[48]

Whether the weaponry of deep strike can destroy them is another matter. A 1987 Congressional assessment concluded that command, control and communication (C3) and weapon systems are unequal to the task at present, and Air Vice Marshal Walker rightly acknowledges the weaponeering difficulties of attacking modern bridges. Moreover, attack systems will be operating at the end of their technological reach, and are vulnerable to an assortment of countermeasures, many of which, not least the deception of heat-seeking warheads by spoof heat sources, are both cheap and effective.[49] There may be doubt over the long-term continuation of funding for these expensive systems, especially in an era when the threat seems to be diminishing and political pressure within the USA demands reconsideration of the American commitment to Europe. Another American survey warned that:

we may become too enchanted with the *potential* of emerging technology. First, this may make us fail to continue procurement of proven weapons systems and C3 upgrades to carry through any war in the meantime. And second, we may build current strategy, plans, and tactics as though the potential capability already exists. We must commit to the new systems today, but only in terms of funds for development and procurement setup. We must not commit *away* from our old systems until the new systems are truly proven capable and reliable, and are fully deployed to all using agencies.[50]

Follow-On Forces Attack in general and the AirLand Battle in particular are the result of serious thinking which cannot be brushed aside lightly. At present, however, they overstretch the available technology, and risk being technologically sidestepped, just as new armour has sidestepped the anti-tank missile. Nevertheless, they do highlight two inescapable truths. The first is that Soviet resources, even taking into account the reductions under way when this book went to press in early 1991, are at present too great to be dealt with in a contact battle, however capable the defence. The second is that air assets have a vital role in reaching deep into the rear to disrupt, delay and destroy. Whether these air assets should consist of manned aircraft or Remotely Piloted Vehicles is not central to the debate, though it lends edge to it.[51] We would be wise not to seek a 'master doctrine' using 'master weapons', but to recognise that balance in doctrine and procurement is essential. General Hans-Henning von Sandrart, NATO's Commander-in-Chief Central Europe, takes a level-headed view, noting that 'the battle in depth must be regarded as an integral part of the NATO operational planning and conduct of operations', but concluding that 'considerable efforts, plus much thinking about the concept, are needed, and not only by the German Army'.[52]

German operational thinking is dominated by the need to provide forward defence, defined as 'cohesive defence near the border with the object of preventing any loss of ground and preventing damage'.[53] It is laid down in Army Regulation 100/100 of 1973, which discusses the conduct of armoured operations close to the border. Much emphasis is placed upon the ability of forward brigades to block attacks within their allocated areas, hold key terrain and counter-attack when the enemy thrust flags. Doctrine and procurement are attuned, because the German *Leopard* tanks and *Marder* MICV are well-suited to this shadow-boxing, and the absence of unarmoured infantry means that armoured forces are not shackled by the limited mobility of foot-soldiers.[54] The *Bundeswehr* has a well-deserved reputation for operational slickness, although it is hard to resist the conclusion that it would be matching rapier against broadsword. Moreover, the impact of improvements in East-West relations, the effects of the 'demographic downturn', and most strikingly, German unification, are certain to cause instability.

We have already seen how British doctrine has evolved consider-ably in recent years, reflecting a new grasp of the operational level of war. Britain currently has three armoured divisions in West Germany in peacetime, and these would be joined in war by the 2nd Infantry Division, a largely Territorial Army formation which would assume responsibility for ground west of the River Weser. This deployment already has an old-fashioned feel to it, and it is hard to see it being maintained at even the 50 per cent of current strength envisaged in 'Options for Change'.

For the past twenty years the armoured divisions planned to fight a series of positional defensive actions, essentially attritional in character, forcing an attacker to buy space with time and lives but ultimately offering no solution save nuclear release. Dangerous thrusts might be blocked by counter-penetration, or vital ground recaptured by counter-attack, but both were essentially reactive. Cynical German observers were inclined to say that the main operational objective of 1 (British) Corps was maintaining its own integrity rather than defending the territory of the Federal Republic of Germany, to which pained British officers replied that there was little merit in being drawn forward to face early defeat. The latter were right inasmuch as the ground in the corps sector offered the uncomfortable prospect of a Soviet attack breaking through the Belgian corps front, immediately to its south, and then pressing on up the finger valleys which run south-east to north-west, imperilling forces deployed forward.[55]

British doctrine in the 1970s and early 1980s was also best suited to take advantage of *Chieftain*, with its impressive gun but (at least initially) less impressive engine, and by the large amount of non-mechanised infantry in the corps. The arrival of *Challenger* and *Warrior*, and, even more crucially, changes in attitude to emphasise manoeuvre rather than attrition, have inspired a more 'Germanic' style, characterised by mobility, quick reaction and an offensive spirit. 1 (British) Corps could no more shake itself free of geographical or logistic reality in 1988 than it could in 1978 – whatever it did, features like the 'gaps' at Sibesse, Springe and Coppenbrugge, and dominating terrain like the Vorholtz, could not be ignored; but it added counterstroke – 'an operation designed to destroy an enemy who is either on the move, or temporarily halted . . . a fully offensive operation designed to seize the initiative and to win' – to its vocabulary.[56] The intellectual mainspring of counterstroke is the same as that which drove American thought on the AirLand Battle: the belief, justified by much military history, that numbers alone are not the chief determinant of victory in war. Thus it is not the act of counterstroke which should concern us but the mental qualities and physical assets which make it possible.

Nowhere are issues of mental qualities and physical assets more relevant than in airmobile operations. The chief virtues of airmobile formations are their speed and flexibility, both essential attributes given Soviet emphasis on high-tempo operations. They can move faster than ground forces to deal with breakthroughs or *desant* operations, and, using terrain to achieve a measure of protection, can concentrate rapidly to administer fire and shock. 'Armed and transport helicopters bear the same relation to airmobile formations', considers a team at the British Army's Staff College at Camberley, 'as tanks and armoured personnel carriers do to armoured formations.'[57] Unfortunately, the high cost of helicopters makes airmobile forces increasingly expensive as one moves along the spectrum of air-mobility towards the helicopter-rich US Combat Aviation Brigades, and this, added to the helicopter's vulnerability in the European environment (a matter of much conjecture), inspires deeper concern over its employment than mere conservatism might imply.

Nevertheless, an airmobile element unquestionably forms part of any balanced force. In the European context an airmobile division, composed, say, of the British 24th Airmobile Brigade, the German 27th *Luftlandebrigade*, with Dutch recce helicopters, the Belgian Para Commando Regiment and some US Apaches, would provide Northern Army Group with a much needed operational reserve. The case for concentrating airmobile assets at a high level is a strong one. An airmobile brigade here or there will make little difference, and using airmobile forces as if they were simply ground-based forces that can fly is to miss the point. Moving an airmobile unit into a static counter-penetration task is like putting a small rock in front of a steamroller. It is far better to throw it, very hard indeed, at the side of the driver's head.[58] Perhaps the strongest argument in favour of airmobile forces lies in their strategic flexibility. A tank division in Europe is of little rapid utility elsewhere – witness the laborious move of the British 7th Armoured Brigade from Germany to the Gulf in 1990. It is unlikely either to deter an adversary in, say, the Middle East, or to be of any use in opposing him militarily for some considerable time. An airmobile formation is infinitely more flexible, although rotors need no less logistic support than tracks, and an airmobile force opposing an enemy strong in armour needs to have good anti-tank weaponry of its own.

The trend towards manoeuvre, clearly visible in the evolution of both United States and British operational doctrine, does not merely attract criticism from those who have an instinctive preference for attrition, or fear that one cannot manoeuvre effectively with limited space in the face of so much mass. It is hotly assailed by several authorities who maintain that it is illogical to have a posture which is defensive in strategic intent but aggressive in operational application. Armoured and airmobile forces have threatening implications: their intent may be defensive, but their capability and publicly discussed application may be offensive. The advocates of non-provocative defence argue that a manoeuvre-heavy force structure alarms a potential adversary. There is unquestionably some truth in this. After all, NATO has long perceived Soviet capability for offensive action as threatening, despite declarations of defensive intent. No military man, brought up to think in terms of the worst possible case, would be justified in thinking otherwise. Nuclear weapons further threaten and provoke an adversary and, in addition, threaten stability by offering valuable targets best dealt with in a pre-emptive strike.

There are various models of non-provocative defence. Horst Afheldt elaborated a plan for 'chessboard' defence, with West Germany divided into areas of 10–15 square kilometres, each containing a squad of lightly armed infantry who live nearby. Attacking armour is dealt with by the squad's anti-armour weapons, or by indirect fire produced by another squad. Norbert Hannig planned to place a 'fire barrier', heavily mined, covered by a variety of rocket launchers with precision-guided munitions along the Inner German Border. Locally based anti-armour squads operate just behind the fire barrier, and further to the rear surface-to-air and surface-to-surface missiles guard against airborne assault. Another scheme (and there are many), put forward by the Study Group on Alternative Security Policy (SAS), envisages a three-tier defence. A static containment force of decentralised infantry covers the IGB. Mechanised troops with a limited degree of operational mobility are stationed just behind, forming a rapid commitment force. The rear protection force consists of light infantry to deal with airborne assaults, and light armoured forces to deal with penetrations.[59]

Non-provocative defence has attracted increasing interest in Germany over the past decade, enjoys a measure of support within the *Bundeswehr*, and in the prevailing political and economic circumstances will gain more momentum. It cannot be dismissed as the utopian ravings of Green cranks: the SAS scheme in particular has much to recommend it. Nor does support for non-provocative defence necessarily imply rejection of nuclear weapons: indeed, some of its advocates argue that it places nuclear weapons in a properly deterrent rather than a war-fighting role.

With a Soviet doctrine emphasising offensive operations, the disadvantages of non-provocative defence are substantial. At the strategic level it may deter attack less than a defence which implies punishment. Operationally, it presents the classic symptoms of semi-static defence, and is vulnerable to attritional breakthrough followed by exploitative manoeuvre. Tactically there are two serious problems. The first concerns the real effectiveness of the weapons used by the infantry upon which so many of the schemes place great reliance. The kill probability of missiles against the current range of Soviet armour is so poor (and will be poorer still against the Future Soviet Tank) that a defensive fabric without a proportion of kinetic energy projectiles will find itself in trouble: by denying itself 'provocative' weapons, non-provocative defence deprives itself of a balanced force structure. The second problem concerns issues of human sustainability. The persuasive Lutz Unterseher argues that he does not expect his infantry to be heroes and fight on to the end, but he is less clear on how they will survive under the flailing hooves of the attack.[60]

If, however, the current trends in Soviet defence policy continue, then the arguments against non-provocative defence lose much of their cogency. With the threat of a Soviet attack substantially scaled down, NATO could defend itself with far fewer in-place forces than it possesses at the moment. A fortified buffer zone manned by regulars backed by large reserves and mobile counter-attack forces, in essence mirroring the evolving Soviet deployment, would confer acceptable security at reduced cost.

All this doctrine will help shape the character of combat in the next quarter-century. It will continue to evolve. A steady reduction in the Soviet threat will encourage non-provocative defence. The AirLand Battle will continue to attract critics, but periodic rewrites of FM 100–5 will keep US doctrine abreast of strategic and technical realities, and the underlying logic of the AirLand Battle is robust enough to survive for many years. However, a steady thawing of the political climate between the superpowers, coupled with the tensions in US-European discussions over defence manning and expenditure, will magnify American interest in areas other than Europe, and we should not be surprised to see this reflected in doctrine, procurement and force structure. Negotiations on conventional force reductions, and changes in German political and popular attitudes will also play their part, and there will inevitably be substantial cuts in conventional forces, with both budgetary constaints and manpower shortages lending weight to the process.

Technological trends point down no smooth and easy path. Much equipment procurement over the next two decades is circumscribed by decisions already taken, although we will inevitably see increasing interest in unmanned systems, and major advances in artificial intelligence will bring the partly robotic battlefield closer. Micro-electronics will continue to exert a profound influence, giving systems increased power, smaller size and greater flexibility. Refinements in surveillance devices will bring 'the transparent battlefield' ever closer. The pendulum will continue to swing between fire and manoeuvre, and there will inevitably be moments when it seems to confer an advantage on one or the other. At present ceramic and explosive reactive armour give the edge to armoured manoeuvre. In a decade's time the electromagnetic gun will enhance firepower, but no doubt further advances, perhaps in rotary-winged aviation, will once again encourage manoeuvre.

It is hard to resist the suspicion that the rival plans for the European land battle are losing much of their relevance, and a historian looking back from the vantage-point of another hundred years may compare them with articles on the cavalry charge written in the 1930s, or the logic which inspired the construction of the *Iowa*, *Kongo* or *King George V* class battleships: in short, they are ideas whose time is already past. Yet their underlying doctrines still command serious attention. Growing recognition of the importance of manoeuvre is fully in accord with the uncertain strategic priorities confronting soldiers in East and West alike, for the mental flexibility and tactical mobility which are inherent in manoeuvre warfare will be important in projecting military power outside the rusting confines of the Cold War. The diminishing utility of high-intensity battle, which will gulp blood and treasure whatever its doctrinal thrust, will encourage increasing emphasis on manoeuvre. Not, perhaps, armoured blitzkrieg on the North German Plain, but the use of home-based intervention forces to support national policy or buttress an alliance by rapid deployment, with combat more in the minor key than in the crashing chords of the full orchestra of battle.

Neither doctrine nor available technology has yet successfully challenged the centrality of man as a decision-maker in peace or as a combatant in war – though some would argue that such a challenge cannot be long delayed. What we must now do is to shift our gaze from lofty considerations of textbooks and hardware, and to focus more sharply upon the soldier, squinting into his weapon sight, jammed shoulder to shoulder in a helicopter as it whumps across the nap of the earth, or cowering in his foxhole as the ripples of rocket-fire crease the landscape. Without him, neither doctrine nor technology will be much use.

4

The Real Weapon

The effect of physical and psychological factors form an organic whole which, unlike a metal alloy, is inseparable by chemical process. In formulating any rule concerning physical factors, the theorist must bear in mind the part that moral factors may play in it . . . One might say that the physical seem little more than the wooden hilt, while the moral factors are the precious metal, the real weapon, the finely-honed blade.

Clausewitz, *On War*

Quantification is the curse of our age. We are obsessed by counting and costing. Nowhere is this anxiety more prevalent than in defence. With the old mask of espionage under the fresh paint of satellite photography, armies strive to compile the orders of battle of potential opponents, amassing evidence as much to encourage internal support for defence as to meet external threat. Such work is not the preserve of intelligence staffs: groaning shelves of open sources – books, journals, annuals – tell the inquisitive reader about the Soviet 25 152mm self-propelled gun, the Mi-28 *Havoc* attack helicopter, the BM-27 220mm multi-launch rocket system, and much else besides. We know that among its tanks the Yemen Arab Republic has 45 T-62 and 64 M-60AI; that Singapore's 155mm guns include 38 Soltam M-71 and 16 M-114AI; and that the Greek army still fields 120 M-3 half-tracks.[1]

This interest has several dimensions. One is the concern of what we might best call the military enthusiast, that bane of picture captioners. He may well have missed military service himself (psychologists mutter darkly about compensation), and his areas of interest may

143

inspire a curling of the toes: one day I shall write *Boots of the Third Reich* and retire to live in comfort. We should be cautious about deploying academic disdain too soon, for the factual knowledge displayed by the military enthusiast testifies to industry which shames many students. Nevertheless, his horizons are usually narrow, and his concern with uniform, equipment and weapons fits comfortably into the material-dominated ethos of our time.

Many professional officers and defence officials are scarcely less preoccupied with quantifiable fact, whether it be the throw-weight of the superpowers' nuclear arsenal, the proportion of motor riflemen to tanks in the Soviet division, or the hit probability of the MILAN missile. In a sense this concern is perfectly proper, for we would rightly feel uneasy about a defence establishment which was ignorant of the capabilities of the weapons and equipment used by itself, its allies or its potential opponents. Yet in no less important a sense it is at best disturbing and at worse delusive. Disturbing, because it seeps into everything from military education to strategic planning; delusive, because it encourages a Jominian view of a battle in which slide-rule and calculator reign supreme.

If we were to assess the ingredients of victory in war then combat power, a mixture of manpower, equipment, logistics and training, would undoubtedly loom large.[2] Indeed, we might be forgiven for taking some time to get much beyond combat power, especially in an age when equipment is seen to be so important. Military history demonstrates, though, that combat power is no accurate guide to military performance. It is barely true to say that the side with the most combat power generally wins. Of the actions examined by Major-General J.F.C. Fuller in the first edition of *Decisive Battles: Their Influence upon History and Civilisation*, thirteen went the way that the balance of combat power would have suggested. But in ten cases the result of the battle was not that which would have been predicted by a comparison of combat power.[3] Moreover, the first group includes some examples where the balance of combat power was so immensely uneven that no other result could reasonably have been expected: the defeat of 100,000 exhausted Frenchmen in an untenable position by 250,000 Germans at Sedan in 1870, and the mauling of a primitive Ethiopian force by an Italian army with tanks and aircraft at Mai Chio in 1936 are cases in point. Of the eleven actions examined in *America's First Battles*, five went against the logic of combat power.[4] We may thus conclude that combat power is not, in itself, decisive. Outnumbered armies have very often won in the past and, no doubt, will do so in the future.

Two considerations flow naturally from this. The first is that there does come a point when combat power will be likely to prove conclusive. In other words, that the balance of forces is so utterly uneven that the outcome is reasonably predictable. Clausewitz believed that numbers were important, but even he warned that: 'Superior numbers, far from contributing everything, or even a substantial part, to victory, may actually be contributing very little, depending on the circumstances.' It was only when numbers reached such superiority as 'to counterbalance all other contributing circumstances' that they became decisive.[5] Yet even here we must use comparisons of combat power with care, for what is reasonably predictable is never absolutely certain. The forces at the Battle of Goose Green, won by 2nd Battalion The Parachute Regiment in 1982, were so ill-balanced that British victory flew in the face of the weight of conventional wisdom. Similarly, when Marshal Soult attacked Marshal Beresford at Albuhera in 1811 he manoeuvred so as to focus his combat power on to the ridge on the allied right, achieving a local superiority which should have won him the battle. He claimed afterwards that he had been deprived of victory only by the unreasonable behaviour of his opponents. 'There is no beating these troops,' he announced. 'They were completely beaten, the day was mine, but they did not know it and would not run.'[6]

The Goose Greens and Albuheras, battles won against all the logic of the calculator, are admitted exceptions. In most cases there comes a time when crushing superiority of combat power, if properly applied, tells. The Soviet army has developed norms – operational, tactical, and logistic – to ensure a common approach to planning. For example, by careful use of historical data and modern analysis, norms have been produced to enable a commander to ascertain the fire required to deal with a particular target at a given range, the time for which the defence will be suppressed by bombardment of specified weight and duration, and so on.[7] When these norms are applied (and all Soviet regulations have the force of law), they ensure that an adequate ratio of combat power exists to produce victory, always provided that the data was correct in the first place.

Second, we must consider those factors which have enabled armies outmatched in combat power to win. The new *British Military Doctrine* adds both a conceptual and a moral component to combat power to produce an overall analysis of fighting power, and the evidence of history suggests that it is right to do so.[8] The conceptual component comprises the thought process behind the ability to fight – application of the principles of war, military doctrine itself, and the development of an innovative approach which prevents stagnation. While the conceptual component cannot be considered in isolation, for there is often a close association between successful doctrine and good morale, it none the less makes a frequent contribution to victory against the run of mere numbers.

The case of France and Belgium 1940 is among the most compelling. Although the Germans were marginally inferior to the Allies in both manpower and numbers of armoured vehicles (they enjoyed a clear superiority in aircraft), they achieved a stunning victory by use of blitzkrieg doctrine. Even when Allied formations might have compressed combat power to their advantage, defective doctrine inhibited them. General Jean Flavigny's XXI Corps, which arrived behind the pierced Meuse front on 14 May, contained two good divisions, 3rd Armoured and 3rd Motorised Infantry, which in combat power alone were easily a match for the *Grossdeutschland* Regiment immediately in front of them. Given the superiority of 3rd Armoured's Hotchkiss H-39s over the panzers Mk I and II, it had every chance of breaking right through 10th Panzer Division to reach the Meuse. But Flavigny strove, in obedience to doctrine, to contain the breakthrough before he counter-attacked, and 3rd Armoured was first split up in penny packets on a twelve-mile front. When Flavigny did launch his counter-move, it too was doctrinally 'sound': the tanks supported the infantry, and the latter's commander led the operation. We should not be surprised that it foundered.[9]

Getting doctrine right is only part of the problem. Armies often have two levels of doctrine, one official and one (or, indeed, more) unofficial. This may be part of an attempt to mislead an opponent, but it is more likely to result from change sprinkled on the surface not penetrating to the roots. By the spring of 1918 the British army's defensive structure superficially resembled the 'deep defence' used by the Germans. A GHQ instruction on defence of 14 December 1917 introduced a three-tier system of Forward Zone, Battle Zone and Rear Zone, each based on a network of defended localities with reserves for counter-attacks. This document was imperfectly understood at all levels. Army commanders, intent on offering a robust defence as far forward as possible, pushed too many men into the Forward Zone, where the opening bombardment would be most damaging. The strongly garrisoned Battle Zone was also in range of the mass of German artillery, while the Rear Zone was, in places, only marked out on the ground. While the Germans kept about two-thirds of their troops available for counter-attack, the British had only one-third uncommitted. At the lowest level, the concept of elastic defence was unpopular. 'The British army fights in line', complained one seasoned NCO, 'and won't do any good in these bird-cages.' Added to this was the fact that the British had been attacking repeatedly and proposed to continue doing so: preparing a deep defensive position did not meet the strategic imperative of expelling the Germans from France.[10]

A similar doctrinal confusion existed in the French army of the Second Empire. In Italy in 1859 French infantry achieved impressive results by moving rapidly forward in columns behind a screen of tirailleurs while their artillery engaged the enemy infantry. This combination of fire and shock proved decisive at Magenta and Solferino, so much so that the Austrians, whose deliberate defensive fire was no match for it, recast their infantry tactics as *Stosstaktik* after the war.[11] Introduction of the *Chassepot* rifle into the French service in 1866 led to much discussion of infantry tactics in the military press, and two committees reported on the matter. Two advisory *Observations* on infantry tactics appeared in 1868, and a new infantry drillbook in 1869. When the Franco-Prussian war broke out some officers and men remained convinced of the merits of the old-style tactics of tirailleurs, columns and assault with the bayonet which had worked so well in 1859. Others, influenced by pre-war emphasis on the superiority of fire, favoured a less dense deployment, a higher proportion of tirailleurs and the use of solid defensive positions from which the *Chassepot* would give a good account of itself. In 1870 the lure of *belles positions* competed with the stirring rattle of the *pas de charge*, and inconsistency triumphed.[12]

The tale of the tactical debate within the French army in the 1860s undoubtedly has a sad ending, but it does demonstrate the importance of doctrinal development. Many French officers had recognised that the tactics which had won Magenta and Solferino required re-examination in view of improvements in weapons, and the work of the two committees was impressively thorough. The opinions of senior officers were canvased, and units were invited to consider tactics at regimental study days. That this development ultimately proved incomplete must be blamed on a suspicion of radical change in the face of a recent victorious war, the stifling tightness of the bonds of experience, and, above all, the absence of a directing nerve-centre within a Ministry of War split into arms directorates competing for funds and status.

For an example of more successful doctrinal development we must look to the Soviet Union. Survival in the Great Patriotic War was made possible only by rapid development which, as early as December 1941, contributed to a counter-attack which pushed the Germans back from the gates of Moscow, and in 1944–5 produced operational expertise on a literally unprecedented scale. Postwar military thought was profoundly influenced by the war, and military-historical analysis continues to contribute, with modern operational analysis, to the formulation of doctrine and identification of ideal force structure. For instance, emphasis on artillery – which has doubled in tank divisions and grown by 40 per cent in motor rifle divisions since 1971 – is not only in accord with the importance historically attached to the artillery arm in Russia, but reflects the value of indirect fire against a defence which makes substantial use of anti-tank missiles.[13] The war in Afghanistan may not be one of the brightest jewels in the Soviet military crown, and it is still too early to draw definitive conclusions. Nevertheless, the evidence points to considerable development in tactics and force structure: even at the most superficial level, the army which withdrew in good order across the Oxus in 1989 looked – with its practical, fur-collared field jackets and combat caps – very different from the force which had entered Afghanistan eight years before.

An essential ingredient of doctrinal development in the Soviet army is its general staff, which has much in common with the old Prussian general staff, and well it might, given Russian fondness for borrowing good ideas from the West. A combination of study at military academies and service with troops gives a good mixture of practical experience and serious study, and advancement through the general staff inhibits (if it cannot entirely prevent) the growth of arm-of-service trade-unionism which helps make changes in doctrine or procurement so difficult in many other armies.

British and American readers may wonder why their own staff systems are not really general staffs in the German or Soviet sense of the word. In the British case, the reasons lie largely in the staff's origins. The powerful Esher Committee of 1903–4 had favoured a 'blue ribbon' general staff on the German pattern, but many influential officers opposed it, and there was a lengthy and damaging battle over the appointment of Major Algy Lawson (who was not staff trained) to the post of Brigade Major 1st Cavalry Brigade. The argument was eventually decided in Lawson's favour by the forceful personal intervention of his corps commander with the Secretary of State for War. The Hutchinson Committee of 1905 produced a pale compromise. There was to be neither a separate General Staff Corps (which is what the 'blue ribbon' arguments favoured) nor accelerated promotion for selected staff officers, and officers on various staffs were to be regarded as interchangeable. The cohesion of the staff was not improved when the first three incumbents of the post of Chief of the Imperial General Staff were scarcely first-rate staff brains. The experience of the First World War conspired to push the staff even further away from the blue ribbon concept. During the war all staff officers, regardless of rank, wore collar-patches of the appropriate colour (red for general staff, dull cherry for medical, yellow for pay, and so on). In order to reduce the profile of the 'gilded staff', collar patches disappeared from uniforms of officers below full colonel after 1918, at the same time as the abolition of the rank of brigadier-general. The latter was briefly replaced by the hybrid colonel-commandant, and then by brigadier.[14]

Elihu Root, who founded the US War Department General Staff in 1903, was even more influenced than his English counterparts by the German system, but his general staff found itself pulled in the two directions suggested by its title, and the General Staff Act neither gave the general staff real power over the bureaux of the War Department nor guaranteed the Chief of the General Staff's supremacy over the Adjutant General. Graduates of the Command and General Staff School at Fort Leavenworth served in staff appointments throughout the army, while the War College at Carlisle Barracks prepared more senior officers for general staff service proper. The latter's curriculum was heavily weighted in favour of international relations and similar subjects, good grounding for administrators in the War Department, but less useful for senior staff officers at formation headquarters. In 1917 the American Expeditionary Force found itself woefully short of operational staff officers, and Pershing was reduced to training them himself. A similar crash programme began in 1940.[15]

In both Britain and the United States mistrust of strong centralised authority (within the army as outside it), together with a geographical position which tended to permit military mistakes to be made without catastrophic consequences, and a suspicion of professional elitism, obstructed the development of a strong general staff. Exactly the contrary conditions applied in Prussia, with its tradition of what Hans Rosenberg terms 'bureaucratic absolutism', which nineteenth-century Englishmen and Americans would have found abhorrent, together with a geo-strategic position which made military miscalculation potentially fatal, as the Jena campaign of 1806 so amply demonstrates.[16] Generalisations about the value accorded to education in Germany, Britain and the United Sates are less easy, but we can observe a sharp contrast between professional and technical education in Germany and Britain throughout the period in question. Even in America, where military education has long been more serious and prestigious than in Britain, there was nothing to equal the *Kriegsakademie*, that fiercely selective cradle of the General Staff. Passing its three-year course and completing a one- to two-year probationary period were essential precursors to obtaining the distinctive carmine trouser stripes of the General Staff. In terms of professional military education there was simply nothing to match it.

We have already seen the importance of the General Staff within the German military system, and it was inevitable that it should have been one of the targets of the Treaty of Versailles. Although abolished as such, it flourished covertly as the *Truppenamt* of the War Ministry until it was able to throw off this thin disguise in 1935. During the Second World War the General Staff was damaged by political interference in operational matters, but this should not conceal the *Truppenamt*'s valuable contribution to military regeneration in the inter-war years. Martin van Creveld accurately assesses the General Staff as:

> an exclusive club, an elite within an elite; their prestige in the eyes of the people was unrivalled, their influence on national life, out of all proportion to their numbers. Their impact on the army's fighting power cannot be overestimated.[17]

The German General Staff was, to a very great extent, the product of specific social and political circumstances and so defies replication, although Russia has certainly profited from its gleanings from the German experience. Blue ribbon staffs may not be in the Western tradition: but without them the production and development of doctrine are difficult in the extreme.

The skill of the commander is undoubtedly one ingredient of fighting power. Those who see command primarily as a matter of science would choose to include it within the conceptual component, while those who see it as an art would place it in the moral component. In fact it bridges the two, for while one dimension of command is chiefly intellectual, another is mainly spiritual, and the really successful commander will show not merely a technical mastery of his craft, but will understand the need for emotional contact with his men in the most passionate drama of all. The relative quality of leadership is another of the reasons for combat power not invariably proving conclusive. When small forces defeat large ones it is often because of the commander's personal contribution. Alexander at the Granicus, Issus and Arbela; Napoleon in Italy in 1796; Jackson in the Shenandoah Valley in 1862 and Rommel at Gazala in 1942, all show the impact of quick decision, military skill and personal example. It is no accident that these generals were all leading practitioners of manoeuvre warfare, for it is in manoeuvre that the quality of senior leadership (rather than the quality of weaponry) is most crucial. Nor should the importance of speed of decision be overlooked, for it is this which often enabled small, sharp armies to Boyd cycle their larger, less responsive opponents.

Surprise is an integral part of the process of cutting inside an enemy's turning circle. It is as much neglected as misunderstood. Neglected, because, as Brigadier Jeremy Mackenzie observed, it is something upon which the Soviets place an emphasis in no way matched by NATO.[18] Misunderstood, because of frequent suggestions that modern intelligence gathering is so sophisticated that surprise can no longer be effective. This overlooks the surprise achieved, despite firm intelligence indicators, by the Japanese in 1941, by the Germans at the start of their Ardennes offensive in 1944, and by the Arabs in 1973, and, more generally, that surprise does not just consist of attacking unawares but has technical and doctrinal components as well. Historically, intelligence operatives have often been aware of the impending attack, but have been unable to convince their superiors, especially if a military response to their warning would have destabilising political consequences. In 1973 the fact that Israel had mobilised in response to previous warnings, which had proved false alarms, reduced the likelihood of mobilisation to meet the genuine threat in October. The 'stop-go' scenario has long been seen as particularly unsettling to an alliance like NATO, whose political cohesion might be strained by frequent fluctuations in the imminence of attack.

In order to understand surprise we must appreciate its full implications. In order to be surprised one does not simply have to be taken totally unawares by an attack. Discovering that attack is imminent but having insufficient time or resources to take steps to meet it is scarcely less surprising. In March 1918 British GHQ was well aware that attack was likely, the commanders of the Third and Fifth Armies had received specific warning that their sectors were threatened, and forward units were well aware of the 'dreadful note of preparation' opposite them. Yet when the opening barrage hammered and roared its way across the British position on the morning of 21 March many units were effectively suprised because there was no effective counter-action that they could take as the iron flail scourged them. In this context the use of artillery to project surprise and dislocation into the British rear is especially noteworthy. Lieutenant Arthur Behrend, in a heavy battery in Third Army's rear, awoke:

> with a tremendous start conscious of noise, incessant and almost musical, so intense that it seemed as if a hundred devils were dancing in my brain. Everything seemed to be vibrating – the ground, the dug-out, my bed . . . It was still dark.[19]

Despite all the warning and preparation, the attack generated what one luckless infantry brigadier called 'general confusion', with the morale of commanders and troops alike badly affected.[20]

Surprise may apply at all three levels of war. Strategic surprise occurs when a nation does not know when, where or how an opponent will attack. Evidence of impending attack may be ignored as decision-makers draw back from irrevocable action until the evidence is overwhelming. Stalin refused to take steps to meet Operation Barbarossa in 1941 despite no less than 84 separate warnings of its imminence, and Chinese entry into the Korean War in 1950 was a surprise, although specific warnings had been given.[21] Operational surprise is also frequent, and senior military commanders, who are often not privy to the full gamut of intelligence (and especially to its source) are no less reluctant to shelve hard decisions than their political masters. Tactical surprise is often generated by an opponent's

Concentrated Essence of Infantry

9   A German '08/15 Spandau on the Western Front, 1915.

10   A US Army M-60 during Operation *Whitewing*, January 1966.

Armoured Obsolescence?

11   Armour for man and horse in the German 'Gothic' style, late 15th century – slender, elongated and spiky.

12   US M1 *Abrams* main battle tank, late 20th century – squat, sloped and menacing.

In Rank and File

13   Shaka trains Chief Dingiswayo's *iziCwe* regiment in the use of the stabbing spear, enabling Zulu triumph over superior British firepower at Isandalwana, 1879.

14   Men of the Sheffield City Battalion drilling. On 1 July 1916. they fell in their ranks while crossing the first two hundred yards of No Man's Land on the Somme.

Blurring the Dimensions

15   Soviet army: T-55 crews mount up while troop-carrying Mi-4 *Hounds* fly overhead.

16   Vietnam: US Marine *Hueys* touch down at firebase Cunningham. Mobility was an essential ingredient of the American war effort.

speed and shock action, and spins off into the continuous surprise that characterises a force trapped on the outer curve of the Boyd cycle.

Technical and doctrinal surprise may occur at any level, although their effect tends to be most marked in tactical and operational spheres. The sudden appearance of a new or unfamiliar weapons system produces technical surprise. The tank in 1916 and the atomic bomb in 1945 were both totally new, and thus immensely surprising, weapons. The needle-gun in 1866, and the 88mm gun and the *Stuka* dive-bomber in 1940 were also surprising although all had been in use for some years: surprise arose because those who encountered them found them unexpected, difficult to match, and thus deeply shocking. Doctrinal surprise (so often coupled with technical surprise) arises when a new doctrine is unveiled. Blitzkrieg is the paradigm, but there are many other examples, notably the impact of the French *corps d'armée* system on the armies of old Europe, and the effect of Moltke's *aufmarschen* in 1866–70. In all, surprise affects an army's will to fight as well as its ability to do so. It strikes at the bonds of confidence which link military organizations, and persuades soldiers and commanders alike that they are going to lose. In a deeper psychological sense, it has powerful elements of shamanism and magic: it makes the earth shake, the heavens darken, and unrolls a carpet of thunder under which mere mortals are helpless.[22]

The human component forms the third element of the trinity of fighting power. We must approach it with caution, because it is the component most easily misunderstood: overlooked at times and dangerously over-emphasised at others. The US Army's high regard for technology in the Vietnam War contributed to de-emphasis of moral factors which reduced its effectiveness, while, as Colonel W.D. Henderson's work on the Viet Cong shows, its opponents took moral factors very seriously indeed.[23] French military thought before the First World War placed excessive emphasis on moral factors, and in 1914 undoubted élan was not backed by adequate combat power. The quick-firing 75mm field gun, so suitable for offensive operations, was hailed as 'God the Father, God the Son and God the Holy Ghost'. It would have been nice, remarked a more practical officer, to see it surrounded by a few saints. Excessive emphasis on moral qualities may be deeply ingrained within an army's *Weltanschauung*; spring from doctrinal reluctance to grasp fundamental problems; or result from a failure (individual or collective) to understand the impact of new technology, giving rise to demands to meet uncertainty with dash.

I sound this note of caution not because of doubt of the importance of moral factors, but because their very intangibility encourages imprecision. The moral dimension has two main facets, the first concerned with the leader's ability to persuade his subordinates to do what he wants them to when all their instincts suggest a safer course of action, and the second concerned with the bonds that enable soldiers to remain cohesive under stress. The former is closely connected to the technical element of military command, for leaders who are personally inspirational but professionally out of their depth tend not to fare well. Field Marshal Sir John French, commander of the BEF in 1914–15, was a man of unquestioned personal valour, rightly described as the most distinguished English cavalry leader since Cromwell. He was deeply fond of his soldiers (so much so that over-identification with his men was clearly a problem), and spent some time on the first morning of the Battle of Loos in September 1916 at an advanced dressing station, talking to the wounded. One eyewitness saw him 'riding quite alone through the shattered villages behind the line and thanking all he met . . . wearing his familiar khaki stock around his neck and his soft gor' blimey general's hat'.[24] When the reserve corps was to be committed, he drove to its headquarters to issue orders personally. Good inspirational stuff, and as a man I commend him; but his absence from his headquarters meant that vital decisions were late in being taken, and speed was more important than personal briefing where launching the reserve was concerned. It went forward a day late, when the German defences had been reorganised, and its twelve attacking battalions lost over 8,000 officers and men in under four hours.[25] For the converse, far greater professional competence but no human touch, we have only to look at French's successor, Sir Douglas Haig. Lord Chetwode thought that French 'was a lucky general, and inspired the greatest confidence in his troops. Haig never got anywhere near his troops or officers during the war, with the exception of his immediate and personal entourage . . .'[26]

It is fitting that Chetwode, himself an experienced commander, should mention luck, for although luck is unlikely to figure in any official manual it is none the less another of the factors which upsets the run of combat power. 'War is a special province of chance,' wrote an American analyst, 'and the gods of luck rise to full stature on the field of battle.'[27] He was echoing both Frederick the Great, who genuflected to 'His Sacred Majesty Chance' and Hannah Arendt, who observed that 'nowhere else does Fortune, good or ill, play a more fateful role in human affairs than on the battlefield'.[28] Battles are rarely decided by a single throw of fortune's die, although a single accident is sometimes enormously influential. Sir Ralph Hopton was blown up by the accidental explosion of a powder wagon after the battle of Lansdown in 1643 (a prisoner, sitting in the wagon, seems to have been smoking . . .) and the Royalist army lost the initiative which it had so brilliantly seized.[29] Cyrus's army was winning the battle of Cunaxa in 401BC when its commander, pursuing his beaten opponent, was killed. As Cyrus was pretender to the Persian throne, the point at issue in the war, his death left his army purposeless and its collapse followed.[30] The French plan for the Nivelle offensive of 1917 was rashly taken on patrol by a company commander. Believing himself in danger of capture, he gave it to his sergeant-major for safe keeping. The captain escaped but the sergeant-major was taken prisoner and the plan (already widely discussed in Paris) was fatally compromised.

It is usually successive strokes of bad luck that do the damage. Clausewitz described how a battle is rarely won or lost by a single blow, but slips away by degrees. As we look at lost battles, 'the terrible "ifs" accumulate'. All the brilliance of Wellington and the steadiness of his infantry would not have won Waterloo if Napoleon had been on better form, if Count Drouet D'Erlon had behaved purposefully at Ligny or Quatre Bras on 16 June, if Grouchy had pressed the Prussians hard, if one of the shots which hit almost all Wellington's staff had hit the field marshal instead, if Lieutenant-Colonel James Macdonell and his Coldstreamers had not managed to close the gates of Hougoumont, if Berthier had been there . . . Most of these ifs were matters of pure chance. After all, Jerome's and Foy's divisions should have taken Hougoumont: how was Napoleon to know that the defenders, good soldiers in a fine regiment, would be led with particular panache by first-rate officers and NCOs? If Macdonell had been a poltroon, had a head-cold, or had been shot early in the fighting, how different things would have been: Wellington certainly took the view that the closing of the gates of Hougoumont was the battle's decisive act.[31]

The great Moltke argued that there was no such thing as real chance: 'Luck in the long run is given only to the efficient.'[32] He is right inasmuch as an efficient army is better placed to capitalise on good and withstand bad luck than an inefficient one. A well-balanced commander is also likely to seize the fleeting opportunity when it arises, even if it did not form part of his plan. Once again the difference of emphasis between manoeuvre and attrition emerges clearly, for an attritional plan (and the mindset that comes with it) is unlikely to be flexible enough to snatch the good cards shuffled by fate. The capture of Messines Ridge by Plumer's Second Army in June 1917 has been described as exhibiting 'perfect harmoniousness between preparation and performance', and it does indeed bear witness to the close partnership between Plumer and his Chief of Staff, Harington, as well as to the Second Army's justly acclaimed planning. Yet for all its excellence, the operation produced avoidable casualties, for the attacking infantry, following the plan, paused on the ridge although there was little opposition before them.33 Conversely, on 14 May 1940 Guderian (not without some anxious reflection) decided to push the majority of his force across the fortuitously intact bridges over the Bar, running north-south across his route to the Channel coast, and to take the risk (justified by events) that a powerful French counter-attack would plough into his left flank. The trick is to take chances when they are offered, but neither to be mesmerised by consistent runs of good luck, and thus to count on their continuance, nor to be dejected by repeated bouts of bad.

Private soldiers, not generals, are most acutely aware of the influence of luck in war, for in their dangerous world life, death or disablement is a matter of a minute or an inch here or there. Lord Moran recalled that a medical officer in the Durhams, who had survived the fierce fighting at Hooge in August 1915, had his head taken off by a stray shell in a quiet wood near Poperinghe – the only shell to fall there at that time.34 William Manchester, a US Marine sergeant in the Pacific in the Second World War, tripped and fell while running back to his squad – at the very moment that a Japanese shell hit it.35 Some of fate's blows are especially cruel. Soldiers have long fallen victim to their own or their comrades' weapons. The accidental killing of friends, described by Charles R. Shrader's newly minted word 'amicicide', is a consistent feature of war. Rear-rank men in the Greek phalanx were stabbed by the front rank's sharpened spear-butts; Napoleonic infantrymen were accidentally shot by their comrades behind them; the impartial effects of artillery caused grief in the Falklands and Vietnam alike, and aircraft (sophisticated identification systems notwithstanding) are regularly clawed from the sky by 'friendly' guns or missiles. Such accidents are an inseparable part of war, and they echo with the hollow cackle of caprice.

The factors that make men fight are numerous, and before examining how traditional means of maintaining cohesion fit the pattern of war discussed in the last chapter, we should first evaluate the relative importance of the moral, conceptual and physical components of fighting power. The latter are decisive less often than we might expect, and will probably remain so. However, a clear technological lead in a key area will produce so heavy an imbalance of combat power as to enable it to outweigh the other components. At present the impenetrability of Soviet tank armour by many NATO anti-tank weapons must cause concern, and any uneven development of directed energy weapons (lasers, high-powered microwaves, and charged particle beams) would similarly be dangerous. Electronic Warfare is even more likely to produce a decisive imbalance. Long procurement times and even longer in-service runs for major weapons systems mean that the shape of war is already largely predetermined for the next twenty years, but Electronic Warfare changes rapidly, and it is difficult for each side to perceive just where the advantage lies. The success of Israeli Electronic Warfare in the Lebanon in 1982 shows just how significant a previously undetected lead can actually be. In the present state of the art, the three aspects of Electronic Warfare – Electronic Support Measures, Electronic Counter Measures, and Electronic Counter Counter Measures – will in turn enable units to locate opponents more accurately, jam their communications and missile radars, and reduce the chances of the enemy interfering with friendly communications and guidance systems. If there is a single potentially decisive area for the expansion of combat power, it is Electronic Warfare.[36]

The conceptual component remains fundamentally important, for in the past it has often provided the conclusive ingredient of victory. Maintaining doctrinal consistency in an era of reducing risk of war between the superpower alliances, diminishing human resources and threatened military budgets will be both more important and more difficult. There is a danger that the lack of visible threat will combine with shortage of funds and manpower to produce a situation analogous to that in the inter-war years, when lack of clear operational and strategic thought in the West made its own contribution to an unsafe world.

157

The moral component causes most concern. Its importance is no smaller now than it was on the battlefields of history. Xenophon identified the primacy of the moral as ten thousand Greeks marched across Asia Minor after Cunaxa. 'You know, I am sure,' he wrote, 'that no numbers or strength bring victory in war; but whichever army goes into battle stronger in soul, their enemies generally cannot withstand them.' Napoleon argued that the moral is to the physical as three is to one; Montgomery believed that the morale of the soldier was 'the greatest single factor' in war; Clausewitz wrote that study of the 'often incredible effect' of moral forces was 'the noblest and most solid nourishment that the mind of a general may draw from a study of the past'.[37] More recently, General Edward C. Meyer, US Army Chief of Staff, warned that 'The most modern equipment in the world is useless without motivated individuals, willingly drilled into cohesive unit organizations by sound leadership at all levels.'[38]

The World of Mortal Danger

War has not always been a high-risk activity. Some of the battles fought by Italian *condottieri* in the fifteenth century were almost bloodless. Machiavelli complained that at the Battle of Zagonara in 1423, 'famous throughout all Italy, none was killed except Lodovico degli Obizzi and he, together with two of his men, was thrown from his horse and suffocated in the mud'.[39] In some New Guinea tribes combat is highly ritualised, and after much stamping and boasting arrows are exchanged in such a manner that participants are rarely killed. Such instances are comparatively uncommon. Machiavelli was overstating his case even when mocking the *condottieri*, for in his own age battles had become notably bloody, as Cerignola (1503), Agnadello (1509) and Ravenna (1512) demonstrate. For every tribe which ritualises war, there is another which fights with merciless ferocity, and there is little agreement among scholars as to the place of violence in primitive societies.

Yet examples of ritualised combat and almost bloodless engagements are valuable, for they make two important points about the character of battle. First, they tell us much about the nature of hostility. *Condottieri* were professional soldiers who might as often find themselves fighting on the same side as against one another: it is not surprising that they had more interests in common than with the princes or town councils who employed them. Tribal groups which share common beliefs and values are aware that their enemies are members of the same species, men just like themselves.

Hostility is sharpened when a species is subdivided into societies which are recognisably different from their members. Konrad Lorenz observed this in the animal world.

> In their behaviour towards members of their own community the animals here to be described are models of social virtue; but they change into horrible brutes as soon as they encounter members of any other society of their own species.[40]

Lorenz went on to observe that discriminatory aggression towards strangers and the bond between members of a group enhance each other: 'The opposition of "we" and "they" can unite some widely contrasting units.'[41] I am reminded of the Bedouin proverb:

> I against my brother
> I and my brother against our cousin
> I, my brother and my cousin against the neighbours
> All of us against the foreigner.

The distinction between 'we' and 'they' lies at the heart of hostility. 'This side of our wire,' wrote Charles Carrington, an infantry officer in the First World War:

> everything is familiar and every man a friend; over there, beyond their wire, is the unknown, the uncanny; there are people about whom one can accumulate scraps of irrelevant information, but whose real life you can never penetrate, the people who will shoot you dead if they catch a glimpse of you.[42]

Much of the military bonding process, with its distinctive forms of language, dress and behaviour, is devoted to the creation of introspective tribal groups, sensitive to threats (real or imagined) from outsiders. The concrete image of the enemy as an individual, thrust by the fortune of war into a different uniform, is replaced by an abstract image of a hateful, evil enemy, whose beliefs and behaviour may well deny him the right to be treated like a human being. J. Glenn Gray thought that: 'The basic aim of a nation at war in establishing an image of the enemy is to distinguish as sharply as possible the

159

act of killing from the act of murder by making the former into one deserving all honor and praise.'43 This task is easier if the enemy is racially different in the first place; radical political or, perhaps even more crucially in the wake of *The Satanic Verses*, religious differences also assist the process. One of the salient features of military history is the way in which abstract images of a hateful enemy are often eroded by contact with him in battle. To quote Glenn Gray again, battle is marked by: 'The recognition of a common humanity, sinful and pathetic . . . Soldiers of opposite sides, dying in the same shell hole, have frequently transcended their hatred and ended their war in reconciliation.'

These factors must be considered in the context of the political developments of the past few years. The easing of reporting restrictions in the Soviet Union has enabled Western journalists to show a sympathetic concrete image of the Soviet population and its leadership. For all the well-documented reports of Soviet atrocities in Afghanistan, television interviews with nervous conscripts make it difficult for stereotypes of the wicked tartar-Russian to persist. The converse is also true, and the spread, however slow, of real knowledge about the West can scarcely fail to alter the image of the capitalist-imperialist warmonger.

The second major point to emerge from our reflection on ritualised combat is the close connection between war and sport. This strikes chords at many levels, from respect for the adversary as 'the most dangerous game' in a stylised hunt (perhaps with a body-count to reckon up the day's bag); language which applies the terminology of the sports field to battle, and the 'him or me' sense of duelling which mechanised war has not entirely abolished. Captain W.P. Nevill's company of 8th East Surreys went over the top on 1 July 1916 behind platoon footballs, drop-kicked into no-man's-land, with the inscription 'The Great European Cup – The Final – East Surreys v Bavarians – Kick-off at Zero'. 'In this next fight,' Patton told the US 45th Infantry Division on 27 June 1943, 'you are entering the greatest sporting competition of all time.'44 Irenäus Eibl-Eibesfeldt declared that: 'Warlike cultures actually practice more combative sports than unwarlike cultures', and many armies have noted the close connection between good team sportsmen and good soldiers, like the contribution made by 'the lions of the football field' in Vietnam.45

The bold recklessness of British cavalry owed not a little to the stout hedges and rough stone walls of the hunting field. 'Old Will was a foxhunter before he became a cavalryman,' said Sir Henry Havelock of his brother William, killed in the scrambling affair at Rahmaduggur in 1846 when the 14th Hussars charged down a dry river-bed, with guns on either flank, in a vain effort to reach an enemy they could not see. 'Should there be a barracks in the neighbourhood,' R.S. Surtees's sporting character Mr Jorrocks announced, 'some soger officers will most likely mix up and ride at the 'ardest rider amongst them. The dragon soger officer is the most dangerous and may be known by the viskers under his nose.'[46]

We must not exaggerate the sporting component of war. As the damage done to the English nobility by the Wars of the Roses demonstrates, even knightly battle often looked very unlike the tournaments which replicated it, and what an eighteenth-century cavalry officer regarded as the hunting field writ large seemed decidedly unsporting to the infantryman who plied his musket in rank and file amidst the powder-smoke and canister-shot. Nevertheless, a thread of sport is woven into the tapestry of war, and the advent of the computer has lent new strength to it. The close connection between computer games and computer displays in large headquarters has not escaped the attention of film makers. Distance makes the act of killing infinitely easier and assists the dehumanisation of the enemy: to reduce him to a glowing spot on a VDU is the ultimate in depersonalisation. Moreover, the familiarity of so much Western youth with the computer game makes many modern systems both easier to operate and less recognisable as weapons with disagreeable effects at the target end.

The impact of war has been softened by the tendency of hostile soldiers to recognise one another as fellow human beings sharing common perils, and by a sporting ingredient which enables at least some of its participants to gain comfort from playing the game as best they can, but for most combatants the stressors loom large. Fear – of death, wounds or, especially to professional soldiers, failure – is never far away. It may be pushed to the back of the mind by sheer willpower – 'throw the mind over and the body follows' – or masked by palliatives. Hard work and responsibility have helped many leaders to cope with their fear. Lieutenant John Glubb wrote during the Battle of Arras in 1917 that 'one's mind is filled day and night with thoughts of the welfare of one's men and horses. There is very little time to think of oneself'.[47] Fatalism also plays its part. Convinced that he can do little to help himself in the violent and capricious world in which he must live, many a soldier responds by becoming resigned to accepting what fate has to offer. In 1918 an Australian officer wrote: 'a few years of this & one treats life very cheaply really . . . lately some of our officers have been killed who landed with the Battn on 25 April [1915] so that apparently it is only a matter of time . . . one must look at this game from a philosophic stand point.'[48]

Denial helps soldiers to cope. Many believe that the worst will never happen to them. 'War is the business of youth,' wrote Lord Moran, an experienced First World War Regimental Medical Officer, 'and no young man thinks he can ever die.' Most combat soldiers of the twentieth century have been in their twenties. An analysis of 1 million British First World War battle casualties showed 80 per cent to be under thirty. Other evidence supports this: Norman Gladden wrote that a soldier in his thirties 'seemed old to us'; George Orwell thought that the average age in the Spanish Republican militias was under twenty; Roger Little found that 90 per cent of the platoon he observed in Korea were twenty-three or under, and the average age of B Company 2 Para in the Falklands was nineteen.[49] Soldiers have tended to get younger as the century has gone on, in part because limited wars like Korea, Vietnam and the Falklands have not compelled combatant nations to widen the recruiting net to envelop those middle-aged soldiers who rest in First World War cemeteries – a random glance along a line of headstones revealed a major of 26, a lieutenant of 36, a captain of 21, a second-lieutenant of 28, a private of 22 and a private of 37. The youngest British First World War army casualty appears to have been Private J. Condon of the Royal Irish, killed at Second Ypres at the age of 14, and the oldest Lieutenant Henry Webber of the South Lancashires, killed on the Somme at the age of 68.

If we were able to analyse Iraqi and Iranian casualty statistics from the Gulf War we might expect to find a similar spread – not, perhaps, as wide at its upper end, but even more appalling at its lower. The soldiers of the Ugandan National Resistance Army were certainly very young. 'Of a force of over 10,000 soldiers,' wrote an observer, 'almost half are under 15 years old. The rest are mostly under 20, and even the commanders are still in their early twenties.'[50]

Sometimes denial lasts a man throughout his experience of battle, and he never seriously thinks of death or a wound. No less than 42 per cent of John Dollard's sample of Spanish Civil War veterans believed that they were lucky and would never be hit: they were volunteers in a well-motivated unit, which might go some way towards explaining this high proportion.[51] Towards the end of the Italian campaign a group of American soldiers were asked if they thought that it was only a matter of time until they got hit: 21 per cent replied that they occasionally thought this, and 15 per cent almost never thought it. Given the attritional character of the fighting and the US policy of keeping divisions in the line and topping them up with replacements it is surprising that so many soldiers remained so optimistic in the light of evidence to the contrary.[52] Often it is the death of a member of the combat primary group (rifle squad or section, gun detachment or crew of an armoured fighting vehicle) that cracks the shell of denial and whispers to the soldier that he, too, is mortal.

Men use talismans or ritualistic behaviour to strengthen their luck. Lieutenant Edward Campion Vaughan, an infantry officer on the Western Front, had an 'ever-increasing bunch' of holy medals fixed to a ring on his waist, and Lieutenant Raleigh Trevelyan went into battle in Italy in 1943 wearing a St Christopher medal and repeating *Saint Christophe te protège* to himself. Talismans were rife in Vietnam and the Falklands, from the charms and mementoes stuffed in pockets to the parrot on the ammunition ship *Elk* in the South Atlantic.[53]

Fatalism, denial and talismans are refuges from the uncertainty of war. Much of military training and organisation is geared to the reduction of uncertainty, towards the building of rafts of security to weather the gusts and eddies of battle. Ritual plays an important part as an armour against disorder. Sometimes, as with drill, ritual is obvious enough, but on other occasions, as with major exercises, it is more heavily veiled. Charles Grant believed that the parades of the Roman army were intended both to deepen soldiers' feeling of superiority by fostering pride in appearance, and in encouraging an affirmative identification of the army with the gods.[54] Christopher Duffy suggested that Frederick the Great's massive reviews had only limited military value: 'Where their true importance resided was in the ceremonial aspect, in the execution of the tribal ritual which bound the Prussian army to its king.'[55] A modern major exercise has a purely practical dimension – it may be intended to test the reinforcement of Germany in time of crisis, for example – but it also has a ritualistic function, giving the participants a sense of the power of the apparatus of which they form part, and showing their mastery of the rain-dance to potential opponents. It is easy for exercises to become excessively ritualistic almost despite the wishes of those who plan them. A natural desire not to deliberately confuse or inconvenience soldiers, coupled with an equally natural but less creditable reluctance among senior officers to subject themselves to stress and uncertainty in a way that may prove career-damaging, encourages a predictable and well-worn format into which genuine uncertainty seldom intrudes.

I am far from perfect: too many of my battalion exercises were heavily stylised. Deployment, recce patrols, fighting patrols, and a move up into the assembly area under cover of darkness were followed by an attack at dawn. Tac headquarters tramped on to the position behind the assaulting companies in the billowing smoke of trip flares and a furore of blank cartridge fire, its warlike appearance – faces blackened, weapons at the ready – as much of a ceremonial as the periodic crown-wearing of a medieval monarch. It brought the strengthening feel of a battalion on the move, under loads and across terrain that linked us, regardless of rank or function, and proved that the small-hours orders group in a dimly lit barn, amidst the mingled smells of cigarette smoke, paraffin and wet clothing, could produce the magic, four hours later, of companies sliding across the start line at H-Hour. But there was rarely enough uncertainty: one of my few attempts to create it produced such realism (wrong helicopter landing site, Holmes pinned down in impotent fury, leading company shot to pieces, communications gone) that I drew back from the brink thereafter. Brigadier Andrew Whitehead is right to maintain that 'confusion and chaos are an essential characteristic of war, and by no means the result of someone's cock-up. Our training should reflect this, by introducing, at every level, a generous measure of confusion'.[56]

Uncertainty grows more stressful as soldiers expect more from life. The armies of histories were packed with men whose expectations were low. Their existence was close to the Hobbesian cliché of 'nasty, brutish and short'. Life expectancy at birth in Europe at the turn of the century was 45: by the beginning of the next century it is likely to be almost twice as long. Death was familiar – in childbirth, infancy, childhood, by epidemic or accident in adult life, by rope or blade in executions (public until the late nineteenth century), and, of course, in war where 'sacrifice' was expected as a matter of course. It was confronted directly, with deathbeds more often at home than in hospital, and corpses laid out in the front room. Much serious illness

brought pain with no refuge save laudanum, and cuts – so frequent
in stable-yard or factory – often brought death in the 'septic ward'
of a hospital. Natural disaster may have been no more frequent in
our grandfathers' time than it is today, but its effects were often
paralysing and served to emphasise the impotence of man in the
face of nature. 'A world in which even a cold could prove fatal
was indeed a precarious one,' writes Peter Ackroyd. 'That is no
doubt why religious beliefs remained such a natural and instinctive
part of life . . . it may be possible to connect the decline of faith in
Christianity with the progress of medicine.'57

Late twentieth-century Western man has asserted control over
much of his environment. True, he has done it so roughly, and
without full understanding of the long-term effects of his actions,
that we must still be concerned for the fate of the earth even if it
is spared nuclear catastrophe. None the less, this growth of control,
marked by spectacular advances in so many spheres from medicine
to civil engineering, has reduced the effect of the random misfortunes
to which our ancestors were prey. One of the factors that makes Aids
particularly shocking is the way in which it has emerged, quickly and
awfully, as a problem which outstrips our ability to solve it, and some
natural disasters manage to strike a chord of shock even through the
blurring medium of television, where truth and fiction become so
curiously compounded. Where we cannot dull the capricious edge
of nature, and rogue cell, blood clot, icy road or faulty jet engine
projects the uncontrollable or unexpected, we do our best to smooth
over the damage as soon and as softly as we can. Death is ushered
into hospital rooms and funeral parlours and the world rushes on.
We expect to be better paid each year, for our children's lot to be
easier than our own, and for hard work to produce results. Above
all, we expect experts to get things right. Unemployment should
be reversed by the application of proper economic policy. Cancer
should be detected early and treated after sensitive and informed
discussion. International aid should efface the scars left by natural
disasters. War should be the very last resort of balanced and humane
statesmen. Battle, if it comes, should be precise, surgical, and inflict
no unnecessary casualties.

Battle is the realm of uncertainty. Its quirks and jests mock
our expectations of controllability, and its growing depth transmits
chance and caprice over a wider area than ever before. This is
most marked in the case of high-intensity combat, but among the

characteristics of terrorism (which must be regarded as endemic in the twentieth-century world just as smallpox was in the nineteenth) are its uncontrollable and unpredictable nature; and its intermittent outrages – from Belfast to Bologna, from San Diego to Saragossa – flout our desire to eliminate randomness.

Many, but by no means all, of those engaged in terrorism come from societies where randomness – through starvation, disease, disaster or political whim – is firmly entrenched. Ritual and fatalism – often reliance on the will of Allah – help make life tolerable. We cannot expect that our own comfortable and increasingly optimistic world-view will be shared in the Middle East, Africa or Latin America. Western man's growing need for certainty will not be matched elsewhere, and Western armies, reflecting as they must the societies that produce them, may find that this mismatch between their own psychological needs and the lesser demands made by Third World opponents imposes severe strains. The experience of both Vietnam and Korea underlines this point.[58]

Closely associated with the psychological demands of soldiers from developed societies are their physical requirements. Many of the soldiers who fought in the great battles of history would not have passed the medical examination for entry into a modern army. G.H. Berenhorst watched Frederick's Prussians at drill, and noted that: 'None of the higher commanders ever took into account the exhaustion of the younger men, who might be suffering from turberculosis and spitting blood, any more than they did the limping or stiff soldiers of fifty years or so.'[59] In the French army of the Second Empire, records of recruits who had been enlisted but had not found favour with the regiments they joined give some feel for the wide mesh of the medical net. In 1855 the 60th Regiment of the Line received a soldier who had a finger missing, and the 23rd Light Infantry one who could walk only with the aid of a stick. Two years earlier the Cavalry Committee had complained that many cavalry recruits were simply unfit for service.[60] The ranks of nineteenth-century armies were filled with the pockmarked faces, turbercular chests and rickety limbs of post-industrial society. C.E. Montague painted a grim picture of British troops in the First World War: 'battalions of colourless, stunted, half toothless lads from hot, humid Lancashire mills; battalions of slow, staring faces, gargoyles out of the tragical-comical-historical-pastoral edifice of English rural life.'[61]

We would be wrong to see the armies of history as little more than collections of diseased cripples. Montague was overstating his case as he lambasted the social and economic circumstances which had produced what he saw as an underclass, misunderstood by its own officers and looked down upon 'with the half-curious, half-pitying look of a higher, happier caste at a lower' by Dominion battalions of 'men startlingly taller, stronger, handsomer, prouder . . .' Yet his argument was well founded. Physique was generally related to occupation: even now the manual worker is still, on average, shorter than the non-manual worker, though both are taller than their fathers were.[62] Pliny the Elder had argued that countrymen produced a better class of citizen 'the least given of all to evil designs', and there was a deep-seated suspicion of what Moran called 'weak creatures from the towns'. On the eve of the First World War military men, with depressing medical selection statistics at their elbows, feared that degeneracy was overtaking the race which, in terms of the Social Darwinism then fashionable, would lose its right to exist. Lieutenant-General Sir Robert Baden-Powell, founder of the Scout movement, was worried by the spread of cigarette-smoking, loafing, hooliganism, watching (rather than playing) soccer, drinking and gambling.

Whatever British and German officers might disagree about, they were sure of one thing: the urban working class posed particular problems. Its menfolk were weedy, unsoldierly and politically unreliable. The Germans tried to reduce the urban content in their army by ensuring that conscription bore most heavily upon the countryside. The British, depending as they did upon voluntary enlistment, had to accept what the recruiting-sergeant brought in, but at least the 'county' style of most infantry regiments could put the gloss of the shires on the products of the alley.[63] The French army, its ranks filled with young peasants for so much of its history (52 per cent of its dead in the First War were peasants), also looked askance at the urban soldier.[64] When units voted on the reforms of the Liberal Empire in the plebiscite of May 1870, their commanders usually blamed a 'bad' vote on workmen on whom soldiers were billeted, working-class agitators in the area around the barracks, or 'bad types, Parisian in origin' who led honest country boys astray.[65]

Not all would agree that military service was a socially useful and morally strengthening experience, but there is widespread agreement that British soldiers of the Victorian and Edwardian armies ate better in the army than they had in civilian life. Men filled out during their training, and became stocky and fit. George Ashurst, who joined the Lancashire Fusiliers as a special reservist in 1912, recalled that: 'I felt really fit, too, with the cross-country running and gym exercises we had daily . . .'[66] John Baynes cites, as an index of the fitness of a regular battalion before 1914, the fact that 2nd Scottish Rifles marched the just over twenty miles from Harwich to Colchester in 1911 at a steady four miles an hour and not a man fell out.[67]

A balanced view would suggest that, while many soldiers of previous generations were indeed unfit and marked by disease when they joined the army, the rations they ate and the training they received helped to produce robust specimens, especially in an era when they could be physically hardened to some of the stresses of campaign by frequent long route marches in full kit. There were, of course, exceptions: friend and foe alike were struck by the poor quality of some of the conscripts combed out of civilian life into the army in the last year or so of the First World War. Thomas Penrose Marks wrote of one of his comrades, B——, who wet his bed every night: 'He is sloppy – just a large hunk of flesh. He cannot throw a hand-grenade any distance. He is a menace to everybody near him when he picks up a loaded rifle.'[68]

Much more important than physical fitness, or the lack of it, was endurance. Social attitudes which encouraged gentlemanly 'bottom' among officers and uncomplaining stoicism among soldiers formed its foundation. Low expectations, allied to frequent experience of privation and discomfort in peacetime, made their contribution. The immensely strong bonds produced within cohesive combat units encouraged men to endure almost unimaginable stresses, and to return to battle even though honourable avenues of escape were open. In January 1916, when Sergeant-Major Ernest Shephard reviewed his first year on active service, he asked himself: 'Am I tired of the war? Yes, utterly tired, but none the less, my greatest wish is to be here, or in the fighting area as long as the war continues, and my Bn takes an active part.' He greatly admired his fellow company sergeant-major and 'dearest chum', Sam Shapton, mortally wounded after taking his company into the line although he was ill. 'I asked him', wrote Shephard, 'to study his health, and stop back with the Transport for this tour in the trenches (as the Medical Officer said he could). He said, "No, I'm no quitter. I'll go with my boys."'[69] Charles Carrington wrote how: 'We were bonded together by a unity of experience that had shaken off every kind of illusion, and which was utterly unpretentious. The battalion was my home and my job, the only career I knew.'[70] In the Pacific in 1944 William Manchester went AWOL from hospital, where he had been taken with a light wound, to join his squad – and be severely wounded. 'It was an act of love,' he recalled. 'Those men on the line were my family, my home. They were closer to me than I can say, closer than any friends had been or ever would be. They had never let me down, and I couldn't do it to them . . .'[71]

Endurance, then, has its physical and psychological component, and the evidence of the past shows how crucial the latter is. Mere physical fitness is not enough, just as simple combat power does not decide battles. A glance at much modern military equipment might even suggest that physical fitness and bodily endurance are of declining importance. Small arms are lighter and have little appreciable recoil: gone are the days when the infantry soldier's shoulder was 'black as coal' from his rifle's kick. Combat uniform is practical, helmets well-lined and comfortable. Breatheable waterproof clothing keeps rain out and allows condensation to escape, and even the British army, persistently unlucky with its boot design, seems at last to have perfected the wetproof boot. Personal load-carrying equipment distributes weight evenly and does not demand the 'pipe-claying and starching' of yesteryear. The marching, rifle-carrying infantryman of our fathers' generation is a disappearing breed: he may now expect to ride to battle in truck, personnel carrier or helicopter, or even through it in a Mechanised Infantry Combat Vehicle. Moreover, in many operational circumstances the requirement for him seems to have shrunk. Once the mortars and anti-armour weapons in a battalion were 'support weapons' in the literal sense, their purpose to give intimate fire support to infantrymen. The roles are now reversed, and the infantry soldier provides close protection to the heavy weapons in his unit, helps prepare their positions and carry their ammunition. A growing proportion of soldiers are servants of machinery, maintaining and repairing it, acquiring its targets, directing its fire, and sating its appetite for ammunition.

This engaging mirage shimmers as we look at it, for it is at best part-true. While there are undoubtedly some circumstances in which battle is technology-intensive, these lie towards the high-intensity/general war end of the spectrum of conflict, and as such are relatively infrequent. Even then the soldier is much more than a machine-minder with clean finger-nails. The physical environment of battle imposes strains which modern equipment can mitigate but not abolish. Life in the field, even out of contact with the enemy, is increasingly foreign to Westen soldiers. If their ability to sustain it is enhanced by developments in clothing and equipment, it is diminished by their unfamiliarity with privation and discomfort. We should beware of easy assumptions that each generation is less robust than the last, but it is certain that the improvements in living conditions and expectations across much of the West will make the hard old world of foxholes and dugouts, cellars and farmyards a more alien environment to our children than it was to our fathers. The question of expectations is a demanding one, for if *glasnost* persists and the former expectation of war continues to be replaced by a more peaceful prognosis, armies will find it hard to stand aloof, and the expectations of their soldiers may all too easily be dislocated by the fact that war has come at all.

Battle adds it own burdens to those imposed by terrain and climate. The stressors which bore down on men across history – fear of death, wounds and failure, physical discomfort, loss of comrades, lack of privacy, boredom, lack of a sense of individual importance, concern about family and friends – will all continue to apply. Technical and doctrinal change will, however, modify their emphasis, just as changes in social organisation and individual values will alter soldiers' ability to tolerate them.

It has been argued, most recently by Richard A. Gabriel in *No More Heroes*, that 'man has evolved to a point where his implements of war, even conventional war, have become so lethal that his mind cannot endure the fighting'.[72] This argument focuses first upon the high lethality of many modern weapons systems, noting that some conventional munitions are so destructive that their effects exceed those of low-yield nuclear weapons. In 1985 US Army Chief of Staff General John A. Wickham told the House of Representatives Armed Services Committee that: 'The yield of the weapons, the lethality of the weapons, the accuracy of the weapons means that we can build in the next four to five years, conventional weapons which approximate nuclear weapons in lethality, and we are moving in that direction.'[73]

This is a process which has been in train for some time: in 1944 the German defenders of Monte Cassino were subjected to an air and artillery bombardment whose explosive effect exceeded that of nuclear weapons in the kiloton range, and similar effects were doubtless produced by Soviet artillery concentrations on the Eastern Front.[74] High concentrations of conventional explosive can be delivered by tube artillery, multi-launch rocket systems, missiles or aircraft. Fuel-air explosives pose a particular threat, and within the foreseeable future directed energy systems will add to the battlefield's lethality.

The proliferation of smart munitions and the improvement of target acquisition systems between them mean that targets have a much greater chance than before of being seen, and those that are seen are likely to be effectively engaged. This state of affairs was foreseen by General William C. Westmoreland, when Chief of Staff of the US Army, in 1964 'On the battlefield of the future,' he declared:

> enemy forces will be located, tracked and targeted almost instantaneously through the use of data-links, computer assisted intelligence evaluation and automated fire control. With first-shot kill probabilities approaching certainty, and with surveillance devices that can continuously track the enemy, the need for large forces to fix the opposition physically will be less important.[75]

What is, perhaps, surprising is not the essential truth of Westmoreland's prediction, but that it has taken a quarter of a century (at a time of rapid technical change and high defence expenditure) for his prophecy to bear fruit, and even then its effects have been limited.

High lethality enhances battlefield stress. Yet it does so obliquely, for history shows that the weapons that soldiers feel most stressed by are not necessarily those that are most deadly. In the Second World War the dive-bomber was perceived to be particularly frightening by British and American troops alike, but it actually killed far less of them than tanks or snipers, both of which were far less alarming. Weapons which are blind and impersonal are more horrific than those which are operated by another recognisable human being. Many of the veterans I interviewed for *Firing Line* made the point that there were several graduations of being under fire. Being shot at with small arms was one thing – being shelled by guns, especially heavy guns, was quite another. This is partly because of the savage physical effects of shellfire and partly because of its literally inhuman characteristics: 'something as inescapable and unconditionally fated as a catastrophe of nature,' wrote Ernst Jünger.[76] 'If it's a sniper or machine-gunner it's just another man and your training tells you what to do,' observed an NCO in 2nd Battalion The Parachute Regiment of his Falklands experience. 'But what do you do about some fucker four miles away?'

Indirect fire strikes deep into the soldier's psyche. Under it he becomes not a combatant but a target, as passive a victim as the executioner's. This was precisely the analogy drawn by a French soldier who looked at his comrades under shellfire in August 1914.

> The ones I could see, from under my own haversack, were shaking and twitching, their mouths contracted in a hideous spasm, their teeth chattering. They looked, with their heads down, as if they were offering themselves to an executioner.[77]

The phrase 'the ones I could see' is telling, for loneliness is a characteristic of the empty battlefield. Ardant du Picq warned long ago that cohesion was no longer ensured by mutual observation, and the increase of weapon lethality has encouraged the distribution of soldiers in ever-smaller tactical units. The growing number of radio sets may make it easier to communicate with isolated groups of soldiers, but persuading them to do the right thing at a time of acute personal crisis is another matter altogether. It is not axiomatic that isolated groups of soldiers will fail in battle, but their continuing effectiveness needs a powerful mainspring. German defence on the Western Front in 1916-17 depended increasingly upon the small groups of machine-gunners who formed the outer edge of the defensive framework, and their performance, out of the sight of their officers, was usually nothing less than exemplary. When the 30th Division attacked Montauban on 1 July 1916 the single surviving German machine-gun hit every company commander in the three assaulting battalions, and kept at its work until a Lewis-gun team from 1st Manchester Pals killed its crew. Whatever other factors helped sustain German fighting morale, the fact that machine-gunners were grouped around a weapon of proven efficacy undoubtedly helped sustain them. They gained comfort from close proximity, from the damage that their weapon was visibly doing, and from their knowledge that their personal contribution to the battle was valuable to comrades and cause alike. Isolated groups of men will fight more effectively on the battlefields of the future if these strands are woven into their own tapestry of morale: confidence in their weapon's performance is indispensable.

Weapons determine the manner in which death comes. Death in battle rarely comforms to the well-ordered depictions of military artists, and the sight of the dismembered and the disembowelled is genuinely shocking to even the toughest. It shook Ernest Shephard:

> We found two machine gunners belonging to our company who had been blown from the trench and over the railway bank into a deep pool of water collected there, a distance of 70 yards. One man, Pte Woods, was found in 8 pieces, while others were ghastly sights, stomachs blown open, some headless, limbs off, etc. Up to the present we have found 17 and buried them.[78]

It does not follow that increasingly lethal weapons are necessarily more demoralising in their effects than the less scientific projectiles of yesteryear. Frank Barnaby suggests that wounds will tend to be multiple, and more serious than in the past. We may doubt, however, whether being hit by a 120mm flechette round is qualitatively worse than being caught in the blast of chopped-up horseshoes with which the defenders of the Alamo loaded their cannon, and whether the flash of fuel-air explosives is markedly more unpleasant than the jets of 'Greek fire' used in Mediterranean galley warfare. Much will depend upon the speed and efficacy of medical aid (even of the simplest painkilling and life-saving sort). If credible medical support is not available, Western soldiers, with their expectations of expertise and controllability, are likely to have their resolve shaken far more seriously than soldiers from more primitive environments, where medical intervention is uncommon at the best of times.

Nuclear, bacteriological and chemical weapons pose very serious problems. First, because they enhance uncertainty. The soldier in high-intensity war is never sure whether such weapons will be used against him (or, indeed, against his home and family). Even if the prospect of nuclear use can be safely ruled out, the risk of chemical attack heightens sensations of danger. The NBC threat is the ultimate in impersonality: no human enemy, but insidious vapours, microbes or radiation that kill in unexpected and unclean ways. Richard Simpkin reckoned that the sight of a gas casualty would have a far more serious effect on morale than that of a gunshot wound casualty, and wondered 'whether morale can in fact be sustained in the face of even the minimum practical casualty level'.79

In peacetime exercises it is often difficult to persuade soldiers to take NBC protection seriously. Protective suits – even the well-designed and relatively comfortable British version – tend to be hot and uncomfortable, and working in full protection drastically reduces the soldier's efficiency. It also weakens the bonds of cohesion within the unit by making recognition and communication difficult, and depriving leaders of the shorthand of motivation – eye contact here, a gesture there – which adds so much to the bald process of giving orders. Experience of training methods in the British army persuaded Major Keith Dann that it was:

> in philosophy, doctrine and practice unready for war . . . Present thinking within the Army on operations in a chemical environment does not go far enough towards realism . . . We continue to view the chemically contaminated battlefield as a special environment – like the desert, jungle and arctic – despite the fact that, unlike these a chemical environment can be imposed and controlled at will by the enemy.80

In war the problem is unlikely to consist of getting soldiers to don their protective clothing – it will be in persuading them to remove it if there is even the least chemical threat. It is not hard to envisage smoke or mist setting off an over-reaction like the 'gas hysteria' which sometimes occurred in the First World War, with soldiers frenziedly masking up and, confusing the symptoms of their own panic with those of nerve-agent attack, using their atropine autojects prematurely. Yet chemicals are not super-weapons. Charles Carrington, with practical experience of gas attacks in the First World War, wrote that: 'With proper discipline and effective gas-masks good soldiers could defy a gas attack, which merely added another unpleasantness to their comfortless way of life.'81

It is well to note the factors mentioned by Carrington. First, proper discipline – drills which are so well understood that they become second nature. Second, effective gas-masks: NBC warfare is an attractive area for the achievement of technological surprise, for instance by the production of an agent which penetrates the enemy's respirator. Chemical detection devices – like the British Nerve Agent Immobilised Enzyme and Detector and Chemical Agent Monitor

– both of which help obviate the need to don protective clothing before it becomes essential, are a vital part of the panoply. Finally, good soldiers. No cliché, this: the strains imposed by NBC warfare are so great that only the best-trained and most cohesive units can hope to survive without suffering catastrophically high physical and psychiatric casualties.

The arguments in favour of total abolition of chemical and bacteriological weapons are impressive but not one-sided. As Brigadier John Hemsley has argued, chemical and bacteriological warfare is:

> very much more cheap, humane and less destructive than other forms of warfare . . . Military chemical and biological agents are designed to kill quickly or to incapacitate. In the latter case the survivors normally recover completely after a period of time. The image of lingering disability caused by exposure to chemical agents is a misconception stemming from the First World War.[82]

Hemsley goes on to observe that advances in bio-technical engineering have made chemical weapons far more precise in their effects and less greatly affected by weather and terrain. Moreover, legal and moral considerations would, in his opinion, support retaliatory use.

The formidable Soviet chemical warfare capability has long concerned NATO armies, prompting demands for both fully effective protection, detection and decontamination equipment, and a retaliatory capability which would enable the West to respond in kind to a Soviet chemical attack without fighting at a fatal disadvantage on the one hand or escalating to nuclear weapons on the other. Sovietologists are unsure of the likelihood of the Russians using chemical weapons: Chris Donnelly believes, on balance, that 'the Soviet Army would prefer any war in Europe to be restricted to conventional weapons alone', and John Hemsley emphasises that the decision whether or not to use chemical weapons would be a carefully considered political one, 'based upon the risks attendant upon NATO retaliation'. Improvements in East–West relations in general, and discussions of chemical weapons at Paris in 1989 in particular both seem to have reduced the likelihood of the Russians using chemical weapons, but as long as the capability exists the intention may change, and the West should not drop its guard until the Soviet army's chemical capability has been dismantled.

Even then it is unlikely that the chemical threat will disappear. The large-scale use of chemical weapons by Iraq in the Gulf War (including attacks on the Kurdish civilian population) let 'the genie out of the bottle', as George Shultz put it. Chemical weapons are relatively cheap and easy to produce and deliver, and the number of nations in possession of them has risen, according to a Pentagon estimate, from seven in 1970 to twenty-two today. They are an attractive option to a state unable to develop its own nuclear capability, and a Third World nation may well find unreasonable the demands of nuclear powers that it should give up its chemical capability. The success of the Paris conference should not blind us to the wide stocking of chemical weapons in the Middle East. American concern over the Libyan chemical plant at Rabta meant that Robert M. Gates, deputy director of the CIA, was not speaking in a political vacuum when he declared: 'The most immediate threat to world peace may well come from the proliferation of chemical and biological warfare capabilities in the Third World.' His was a timely warning, and the prospect of soldiers braving 'the Devil's breath' on the battlefields of the future remains a grim one.[83]

Not only is the high-intensity battlefield more lethal: it is ever deeper, with ground- and air-launched systems reaching out into the rear, and distinctions between front line and rear area becoming increasingly blurred. Both US and Soviet military doctrine foresee that, in the words of FM 100-5, 'modern warfare is likely to be fluid and nonlinear'.[84] Ground forces push on the exploit weaknesses, and air-delivered and special forces operate from the contact right through to the depth battle.

'Night operations', warned Clausewitz, 'are not only risky: they are also difficult to execute.'[85] As night fell over the battlefield of Mons in August 1914 the British were surprised to hear German bugles sounding the cease-fire, and large-scale night operations were rare throughout the First World War. The reason was partly, as Clausewitz had affirmed, that in the dark an attacker seldom knew enough about the defence to make up for his lack of visual observation. Even if the general outline of the position was familiar he was still at a disadvantage, picking his way over strange ground to face a defender who knew it far better. Control was as serious a problem, for the light signals upon which so much depended were liable to be misunderstood or duplicated. But the blanket of the dark hid movement from artillery observers, encouraging combatants to carry out resupply and relief during the night. Soldiers in forward units might find themselves busier at night than they were in the daylight, for there were trench-mortar ammunition, barbed wire, wire pickets, duckboards, revetting material and a plethora of other 'trench stores' to be brought forward, and work to be carried out on wire and trenches.

Night operations were more frequent in the Second World War. Radio made it easier for commanders to retain control, and the improvement of illuminants, occasional use of searchlights reflected off low cloud, and tracer fired on fixed lines to give direction, made it possible for night to be turned into day at selected times and in selected places. Night still screened movement, and it was often an attractive tactical option to move, under cover of darkness, to a position where an attack could be launched at first light: Rommel's night move around the southern flank of the Gazala line in May 1942 is a good case in point.

Sleep deprivation was a fog through which combat soldiers of the two world wars groped. C.E. Montague wrote of the First World War soldier that:

> For most of his time the average private was tired. Fairly often he was so tired as no man at home ever is in the common run of his work . . . most of the privates were tired the whole of the time; sometimes to the point of collapse, sometimes much less, but always more or less tired.[86]

During the Second World War the soldier in the line was likely to be just as tired. An American survey of troops in Italy revealed that 28 per cent of soldiers got 2–4 hours sleep a night, and an unlucky 3 per cent got less than 2.[87]

The amount of sleep required in order to remain fully effective varies with individuals, but ranges from about six to about eight hours per day. Units can remain militarily effective if their members receive as little as 4 hours in 24. An experiment at the British Army Personnel Research Establishment put three platoons through a nine-day exercise in inhospitable terrain and poor weather. One platoon was allowed no sleep, and became militarily ineffective after the third night. The second was allowed $1\frac{1}{2}$ hours' sleep: 39 per cent of its members voluntarily withdrew after five nights and, though the remainder soldiered on throughout the exercise, they too were militarily ineffective after the third night. The third platoon, with three hours' sleep, remained effective throughout. Its members' mental ability and mood were affected, but the physical effect was much less.[88]

Two riders must be added. The first is that the body's diurnal clock reduces efficiency between 0300 and 0600, making this the most logical period in which to take sleep if operational circumstances permit – and conversely the most vulnerable time for tired men. The second is that although many traditional military tasks – digging, marching, shooting – may be only marginally impaired by sleep loss, specialist tasks suffer more severely. In 1988 a report to the RAF Institute of Aviation Medicine disclosed that a tired civil airliner crew had tried to land on the M56 motorway, mistaking it for Manchester airport. The captain, under commercial pressure to return to England, had persuaded his co-pilot to lie about the time they reported for duty, and both had been on duty for longer than the $12\frac{1}{2}$ hours authorised by law.[89] In a military situation, not only pilots, but numerous skilled personnel from commanders and staff officers through to fire control computer operators will find that lack of sleep reduces their efficiency.

Sleep loss is likely to become more frequent. Since the end of the Second World War night-fighting aids have improved beyond all measure. First came active infra-red devices like the Sniperscope and infra-red headlights. These enabled their users to see at night but imposed a penalty because they were easily detected. Passive image intensifiers (like the British army's Individual Weapon Sight and Night Observation Device) have been in widespread use since the 1960s, and the Yom Kippur and Falklands wars showed the importance of such devices being widely available. Lance-Sergeant Tam McGuinness described how 13 Platoon 2nd Scots Guards fought for Tumbledown Mountain in June 1982: 'We had only six night sights. I was picking my targets with the sight, putting it down, then firing the "66" [66 LAW, a recoilless anti-armour and bunker-busting weapon] and telling the men without sights to fire where the "66" hit.'[90] Thermal imagers, able to penetrate darkness, fog and smoke, have now replaced image intensifiers in many tanks and direct fire weapons. I recently watched through the TI sight on a *Leopard II* while a line of infantry emerged stealthily from a village just south of the Mittelland canal near Minden. They were 1,500 metres away and the night was pitch black, but the dark offered them no cover at all: they were far more obvious than they would have been to the naked eye in broad daylight.

Ability to sweep back the curtain of darkness does not merely have tactical effects. The US OV-1D *Mohawk* aircraft, with its sideways looking airborne radar and infra-red photographic sensors is now old technology. Moving target indicator radars (with Joint Service Target Attack Radar System as the most prominent example) carried by aircraft flying 100 to 200km on the friendly side of the Forward Line of Own Troops provide real-time intelligence through night or cloud. The French *Orchidée* helicopter-borne radar will be able to track moving targets 100km behind the Forward Line of Own Troops, and British experiments suggest that a Synthetic Aperture Radar in a Canberra can stand off 100km from the FLOT and look 200km the other side of it. The ability to see so far into an enemy's deployment confers enormous operational benefits, making it easier to see where main thrusts are likely to develop.[91]

The transparent battlefield is no technocrat's dream: it is already reality, but opaque patches will spread quickly. High-value systems will become the targets of specific attack, with ground, air and Electronic Warfare resources concentrated on the blinding of surveillance in key areas. As mechanical and human casualties mount, and effective command and control diminishes, the tasking of surveillance sources and the response to the information produced by them will deteriorate. Stealth technology, spoofing, tactical smoke generators (making smoke that blinds thermal imagers) and Electronic Counter-Measures will combine with bad weather (and bad luck) to darken the transparent battlefield.

It is dangerous to be dogmatic about the human consequences of improved night-fighting devices and surveillance. Received wisdom suggests that they increase stress, depriving soldiers of sleep and showing that there is nowhere safe to hide on the deep and dangerous battlefield. Yet unless developments in night fighting equipment are markedly asymmetrical, with one side obtaining a clear technical lead, their benefits and burdens will be shared more or less evenly by both sides. Battle will not stop at nightfall, to be sure: but neither will it continue to the point where all combatants find it intolerable in the short term. It will become self-regulating, with the pace of operations slowing because of the tiredness of participants. The Soviet army places great emphasis on ensuring that units have enforced rest on their way to the front. This policy is unlikely to survive intact in the face of long-range conventional attack, but it does indicate a proper appreciation of the need for sleep even in high-tempo operations.

Physical fatigue, increased by the effects of fear on the metabolism, has always been a component of battle. For centuries the soldier, even if he was as well-prepared by long practice as a Roman legionary or medieval knight, could only ply his sword or spear for a limited time until he became ineffective through sheer exhaustion. Marching long distances under a leaden and often badly designed pack, and fighting girt about with encumbrances – weapons, perhaps shield or body armour, and latterly a heavy load of ammunition – has long been the the infantryman's stock-in-trade. Long marches may not be a feature of high-intensity battle, but the ability to cover difficult terrain on foot remains indispensable for at least a proportion of the infantry.

It is tempting to identify this proportion in advance by making infantry role-specific, with armoured infantry, trained to fight from MICVs as part of an armoured battle, at one extreme, and 'light' infantry, designed for operations outside NATO's Central Region, at the other. The arguments for and against institutionalising infantry in this fashion, rather than simply rotating battalions through different roles in successive postings which is in essence what the British army does at present, are too complex to be explored here. Nevertheless, we should recognise that whatever option is adopted, the infantryman will sometimes need to dismount from his vehicle to carry his weapon, ammunition, and possibly much else besides, on foot. Even the *Bundeswehr*, which understands armoured warfare so well, is short of conventional infantry to fight in that 40 per cent of West Germany which is wooded or populated. 'My troops sit in their vehicles, are trained to fight from vehicles, and their weapons are specially suited to fighting a mobile enemy in open country,' said a German general. 'I don't have the manpower, the training, the equipment for city fighting.'[92] In short, the infantryman of the late twentieth century will not find that the demands on his physical fitness or endurance are much lighter than those imposed on his grandfathers. They are likely to be different, with the sprint from the back door of the MICV and the long and dangerous crawl on to the enemy position more frequent than the solid fifteen miles a day pounding down the *pavé*. As armoured warfare in the Central Region becomes less probable, and major powers feel the need to project military force into other areas, the physical demands on the infantryman will increase, not diminish, for it is in precisely those areas that terrain and climate will add to his discomfort.

Digging is another of those uncomfortable archaic practices which will not go away. As the port flows late at night and the advocates of manoeuvre warfare grow more animated, it is easy to imagine a battlefield which is so mobile that nobody is anywhere long enough to dig in. After all, argue the more extreme proponents of mobility, if something can be seen it can be hit; if it can be hit it can be killed, and if you are dug in you can scarcely avoid being seen: ergo . . .

Defensive positions have lately received short shrift before the bench of military judgment. The mud of the First World War still clings to them, and the Maginot Line does not encourage confidence. The threats posed by modern weapons systems, culminating in Ken Brower's warnings on the potential of Fuel-Air Explosives, have further diminished their appeal. Finally, at a time when manoeuvre, focusing on the enemy not on the ground, has gained status at the expense of attrition, defensive positions, attritional by nature, seem less attractive than ever.

This verdict is unjustly harsh. Even the Maginot Line, despite the abuse heaped upon it, actually did what it was intended to do – it prevented the Germans from attacking in strength across the Franco-German border, and only one small fort – the *ouvrage* at La Ferté, a subaltern's command – was actually taken by assault. Thus, while we can quite rightly criticise the Maginot mentality, or observe that the line only made operational sense if combined with a mobile armoured reserve, we should not assume that French collapse in 1940 in itself 'proves' the impotence of fortifications.[93] At the operational level there is a case, well put by John Keegan, for basing the defence of the Central Region at least in part on fortifications, a policy which would meet some of the demands of the proponents of non-provocative defence. Tactically, fortifications have an impressive track-record, and even armies with a penchant for manoeuvre warfare, notably the German, Soviet and Israeli, see no problem in reconciling a mobile doctrine with fortifications.[94]

Improvised field fortifications, like the open-topped two-man slit trench which was standard in the British army for many years, are of diminishing value. They offer no protection against airburst rounds, and, if combined with covered sleeping bays, risk encouraging their occupants to remain in the shelter of the bays rather than fight from the trench. Currently, overhead cover is added to the trench itself, but if the sides are left open the roof serves to funnel the blast of nearby explosions into the trench.95 There a strong case for bunkers that house several men, a group better able to withstand isolation and bombardment. The construction of such a position is voracious in man-hours and stores (angle-iron pickets and revetting material), and if carried out badly brings the risk of deaths from cave-ins – a casualty-producer in both world wars, Korea and Vietnam. Successful experiments have been carried out with pre-formed overhead cover made of Makrolon (the material used to make anti-riot shields and visors), with angled embrasures which would inhibit the entry of blast. Digging in is often done badly in peacetime. Troops are more preoccupied, in the words of a French officer, with 'the rain that soaks rather than the fire that kills', and many of the 'defences' dug on exercise would be mocked by the savagery of artillery fire.

A number of authorities (by no means all of them supporters of non-provovative defence) have argued the case for pre-sited defensive positions. After all, however well-kept one's military secrets may be, it is impossible to pretend that certain key features (natural or man-made) do not have military value. If the troops who must inevitably be sent to defend them would be better placed in prepared positions than in ones they dug on arrival: since key terrain is highly likely to be occupied in any case, security is scarcely compromised by the construction of positions in peacetime. For some time I was very much preoccupied with a bridge over the River Weser. As I was going there in any event (and my opponent did not need the genius of Clausewitz to predict that someone or other would have to hold it) I would far rather have found fortifications awaiting my arrival rather than be obliged to spend the hours before the enemy's arrival digging furiously.

It has been argued that a web of such positions would compound the enemy's intelligence-gathering problem, as he would have to decide which were held and which were not: using valuable Precision-Guided Minitions to destroy every single bunker is neither rapid nor cost-effective. Pre-prepared ammunition shelters would be particularly useful, and, since the defence of a fort requires a lower standard of training, and certainly a lesser degree of fitness, than mobile operations, reservists could be used to hold defensive positions while better-trained regulars provided an armoured manoeuvre force. Chris Bellamy describes 'the Dragon Variation', of a web defence based on such positions in which a Soviet attacker becomes enmeshed. The case for fortification as an adjunct to a manoeuvre-based defence is impressive indeed. The judicious Lieutenant-Colonel John English can hardly be gainsaid when he argues that:

> According to recently completed Canadian Army wargames, the greatest threat to the infantry is from Soviet artillery, which must be expected to destroy all unprotected troops on identified battle positions – and most of their IFVs if the troops are located with them. To dig-in properly while continuing their patrol and sentry tasks, however, calls for far more troops than most armored infantry organizations currently dispose.[96]

It is not only the infantry which will find itself engaged in hard physical labour. The increased mechanisation of ammunition-handling, with automatic loaders and auxiliary cranes on some self-propelled guns, and specialised ammunition vehicles like the British DROPS, has not yet taken broad shoulders and bulging biceps off the gun position – nor will it for some time. The same argument applies to many logistic functions. The logistic appetite of the fighting man has continued to grow. In the First World War a division consumed some 65 tons of material per day. This had risen to 675 tons by the Second World War; 1,000 tons by Vietnam, and 2,000 tons by the Yom Kippur War.[97] Despite a legion of improvements, from computerised accounting to helicopters and fork-lift trucks, there is much back-breaking work along the line of communications in all but the most low-intensity operations.

So far we have seen that the stresses that bear upon the soldiers who fight the battles of the next two decades will be ancient ones enhanced by modern technology and falling, in many cases, upon shoulders less suited to bear them than was the case when men expected less and tolerated more. It is beyond question that many will break under the strain. As an American study based on Second World War experience declared: 'Each moment of combat imposes a strain so great that men will break down in direct relation to the intensity and duration of their exposure. Thus psychiatric casualties are as inevitable as gunshot and shrapnel wounds in warfare.'[98] There are abundant historical examples of the psychiatric casualty long before the condition was properly identified. Captain Cavalié Mercer, a British artillery officer at Waterloo, spoke of men who had fled 'not bodily, to be sure, but spiritually, because their senses seemed to have left them', and the Union surgeon-general in the American Civil War identified a disabling condition which he termed 'nostalgia' but today's psychiatrists would probably term acute depression, one of the ways in which psychiatric breakdown can present.[99] Others are panic states which result in headlong flight; acute anxiety, with extreme restlessness and agitation; exhaustion states, with troops showing abnormal fatigue; and hysterical reactions, including hysterical blindness and paralysis.[100]

It is therefore not true to speak of psychiatric battle casualties as a phenomenon new to twentieth-century warfare, but more correct to observe that it is only in this century that the psychiatric casualty has been accurately diagnosed. During the First World War, when the British army was forced to come to terms with the psychiatric casualty, it was, as an officially sponsored history admits, almost a matter of chance whether a man suffering from psychoneurotic breakdown was considered to be ill from 'shell shock', a malingerer or even a deserter.[101] The term shell shock came into use because the condition was believed to result from concussion resulting from the nearby explosion of a shell. Western doctors have long since abandoned this concept: in the British army the term shell shock was virtually abolished by June 1917 once advanced psychiatric centres had been set up in France. Soviet military psychiatry, however, with its very different traditions and precepts, tends to look for a physiological cause for psychiatric problems, and the Soviet army identifies at least some of what Western medical officers would diagnose as psychiatric casualties as soldiers who have failed in battle through their own fault.[102]

The sheer volume of psychiatric casualties is daunting. In the First World War, nearly 2 million American soldiers served overseas. 116,516 of them were killed and 204,002 wounded. No less than 106,000 were admitted to medical facilities for psychiatric reasons, and 69,394 of them were evacuated.[103] The British army suffered 573,507 killed and 1,643,469 wounded during the war. It is impossible to assess the proportion of psychiatric casulties, but in March 1939 120,000 former servicemen were still in receipt of pensions awarded for primary psychiatric disability.[104] During the Second World War, 1,393,000 American servicemen suffered psychiatric symptoms serious enough to debilitate them for some period. US Army ground forces alone permanently lost 504,000 men for psychiatric reasons; 596,000 were kept out of action for some time, and another 464,500 were treated briefly.[105] Given that the ratio of combat to support troops in the US Army was about 1:12, and that the overwhelming majority of psychiatric problems occurred among the former units, the incidence of psychiatric casualties among combat soldiers is most striking.

Experience of the First World War persuaded the US Army that the psychiatric casualty occurred when an individual who had a predisposition to breakdown was subjected to stress, and that its numbers could be greatly reduced by effective screening to ensure that only the most robust were selected for service. In the Second World War the US military examined 18 million men for military service, rejecting 5,250,000 as unfit for physical reasons – and 970,000 because of emotional and neuropsychiatric problems. As Gabriel pointed out, 'Whatever the psychiatric screening of conscripts accomplished, it had certainly not reduced the rate of psychiatric problems on the battlefield.'[106]

American soldiers who served in Korea ran a very considerable risk of becoming psychiatric casualties. Of the 1,587,040 Americans who served there, 33,629 were killed by enemy action and 103,284 wounded: no less than 48,000 were admitted to hospital for psychiatric treatment.[107] Of the 2.8 million men who served in Vietnam during the ten-year war, 45,735 were killed in action and another 35,200 admitted to military medical facilities for psychiatric reasons: these figures, again, must be seen in the context of the small proportion of US troops in Vietnam who actually did the fighting.[108]

The Israeli army was shocked at the incidence of psychiatric casualties in the Yom Kippur War of 1973, when 30 per cent of all non-fatal casualties were psychiatric. The subject was extensively studied and some organisational changes made to ensure more efficient treatment, and in Operation 'Peace for Galilee' in 1982 the Israelis suffered 465 killed, 2,600 wounded and 600 psychiatric casualties, 23 per cent of non-fatal casualties.[109] There were 250 British military dead and 777 wounded in the Falklands, and no open source gives an accurate indication of the number of psychiatric casualties. In 1983 the World Congress of Psychiatry heard that 21 of the British wounded suffered from psychiatric illness, 7 from a combat reaction, 8 from depression, and 3 from alcoholism, stress-induced dizziness and extreme pain reaction. Yet a Parliamentary question in December 1982 had established that 30 servicemen were still undergoing psychiatric treatment as a result of their experiences.[110]

These raw figures only sketch out the parameters of the problem. Closer examination enables us to make several deductions. First, the term psychiatric casualty is itself a general one, covering battle shock (emotional reaction to the stress of battle), battle fatigue (resulting from long-term exposure) and delayed battle-shock (sudden breakdown after the fighting). Second, such casualties are, as one might expect, related to the nature and duration of fighting. The Second World War American assessment that 200 to 240 aggregate combat days were all a man could stand reflected a policy which kept divisions in the line longer than the British army, which reckoned that about 400 combat days was a man's limit.[111] Periods of intense pressure (May–July 1942 in the desert, Malta during the siege, and Normandy in 1944) wore men out more quickly. Before 1973 it was believed that most men would be unlikely to crack with less than 25–30 days of combat, but in 1973 the Israeli experience suggested that breakdown could occur with as little as 24 hours of really intense fighting. In most cases the individual's performance followed a bell-like curve, with a period of adjustment to combat lasting perhaps ten days in Normandy, giving way to a period of maximum efficiency (perhaps twenty days), a period of over-confidence and finally emotional exhaustion. This profile is strikingly similar to the curve of Selye's General Adaptation Syndrome, and also parallels the 'four ages of man' in the evaluation of a pilot: initial thrill – hot pilot with swagger – airplane driver – fear of flying.[112]

Much depends on the circumstances of combat. The high Israeli figure of psychiatric casualties and relatively rapid breakdown in 1973 is indicative of the surprise and violence of the attack, especially the heavy bombardment on the Suez front. A veteran attributed the high rate of British breakdown in the desert in mid-1942 to the fact that:

The men got tired of fighting, became somewhat apprehensive of German power and leadership, and were 'fed up' with the desert, the rough conditions of living, the flies, and sand storms, the disappointing movements in the wrong direction, and the chronic shortage of effective arms and equipment.[113]

In Vietnam, where the one-year tour and the small number of

American soldiers actually engaged in battle helped keep the overall figure of stress casualties low, there was a rapid rise during the winding-down period, reflecting a deep-seated desire not to be the last man killed in a lost war.[114]

Other factors tend to be associated with a high incidence of psychiatric casualties. In cold climates, units which produce numerous stress casualties are also likely to reveal more than average frostbite casualties, while in a malaria-infested area they will display poor medical discipline and thus suffer a high proportion of malaria casualties. This underlines the importance of cohesion and morale within the unit, and it is not surprising that different units manifest different psychiatric casualty rates under similar circumstances. The US 34th Division suffered psychiatric casualties at the rate of 13 per cent of non-fatal wounds in thirty-six days of heavy fighting on the Gustav Line in 1944, while the 91st Division, in a lighter battle on the Cecina River, had only one-third as many wounded but psychiatric casualties running at 33 per cent of the wounded. Elite units tend to suffer notably fewer psychiatric casualties. The US 442nd Regimental Combat Team, the most decorated unit in the US Army, had almost no psychiatric casualties in the Italian campaign, and the relatively low numbers of British psychiatric casualties in the Falklands may reflect the high morale of the all-regular units engaged. In 1973 the Israelis reported almost no psychiatric casualties among airborne and other elite units, regardless of the intensity of combat. Conversely, the breakdown rate in logistic units was unexpectedly high, reflecting the shock of the deepening battlefield upon men who saw themselves as suppliers rather than warriors.[115]

The varied ways in which psychiatric breakdown presents mirror men's perception of an acceptable way out of combat. In Vietnam, for instance, American and Vietnamese soldiers manifested radically different responses to similar pressure, leading Peter Bourne to conclude that 'Whether [a man] presents with a hysterical paralysis or a self-inflicted gunshot wound may be largely socially or culturally determined.'[116] The difficulties that armies have faced with psychiatric casualties reflect the changing nature of the problem and the manner in which different wars tend to show its different facets. Post-Traumatic Stress Disorder (PTSD) was particularly widespread after the Vietnam War (from 500,000 to 1.5 million cases, depending on whose figures one believes). There is no real agreement over the reasons for its widespread appearance, although the character of the war and the degree of social support received on return from it feature prominently in the copious literature. It is clear that there is also large-scale PTSD arising from the Falklands War. Surgeon-Commander Morgan O'Connell, consultant psychiatrist at the Royal Naval Hospital, Haslar, has helped treat over seventy cases among naval personnel, and PTSD courses are now held regularly at Haslar.[117] Nor is PTSD confined to combat veterans: the recent spate of disasters, including the fire at King's Cross station, the Piper Alpha explosion, the Zeebrugge ferry sinking and the Clapham rail crash have revealed PTSD among survivors, with survivor guilt – 'why did I survive when all those around me died' – as a common ingredient.[118]

It is not easy to relate our knowledge about psychiatric casualties to future war. Richard Gabriel argues that the high incidence of psychiatric casualties will make future combat impossible. Modern war will prove intolerable to its combatants, while the use of drugs to alleviate stress will, he warns, create the inhuman 'chemical soldier', who fights without hope or fear. Lawrence Ingraham and Frederick Manning are more sanguine, though they warn that such optimism as there is must be tempered with extreme caution.[119] We may at least be confident that the principles of treating psychiatric casualties are widely understood, with proximity, immediacy and expectancy as the key ingredients, and that training aids on both sides of the Atlantic have gone a long way towards demythologising psychiatric breakdown.

Gabriel's extreme view is correct only in the most extreme circumstances. High-intensity deep battle, with the likelihood of chemical and nuclear strikes, will impose unbearable stress on most combatants, and will do so rapidly. Lieutenant-Colonel Brian Chermol's assessment of psychiatric to physical casualties in such a war as 1:3 to 1:2 for the first 30 days, with higher proportions thereafter until 'most unit personnel may be psychologically ineffective after 60 days of continued, high-intensity combat' is, if anything, unduly optimistic.[120] A British medical officer observed casualties – real and simulated – on exercise LIONHEART in 1984, noting how sizable batches of real casualties with 'frankly dubious organic pathology' arrived at critical phases in the battle; many real casualties were escorted by fit colleagues, and dressing stations became filled with rumours of unstoppable enemy armour led by the redoubtable Orange Force commander, universally known as

Herman the German, who attained a Rommel-like mystique.[121] One should not read too much into an exercise, but the phenomena described are likely to be typical of many found in a dressing station in war, with the added complications created by air, artillery, and possibly chemical attack, and a tide of casualties which threatens to swamp the facilities available.

However, Gabriel does not seriously address other forms of modern battle, and we have already seen how high-intensity battle has a declining probability. In medium- and low-intensity operations all the signs suggest that, while psychiatric casualties will continue to erode the fighting efficiency of units, they will in no sense make combat unsustainable. The traditional motivators will continue to support men. Mates were, and will remain, the strongest prop: conversely, potential for collapse will increase as physical casualties unravel the fabric of the unit. Competent and courageous leaders will play their own irreplaceable part, though their loss, too, will spread destructive rings of sorrow through their commands.

Understanding the nature of combat, so as to mitigate its savage shock, is fundamentally important. Here the armies of the northern hemisphere face one of their most serious challenges. The political events of recent years are likely to make combat appear decreasingly likely, and will quite properly encourage armies to seek other, less directly combative, functions: these tendencies will prove all but irreversible save in the case of a few units whose technical speciality – like parachuting or amphibious assault – fosters a resolutely martial mindset. Whatever our observations on the utility of battle or the infrequency of combat, fighting will inescapably remain part of the soldier's job-description. Obsessive emphasis on this fact is likely to appeal neither to potential recruits nor to governments, but an army forgets it at its peril.

Armies which perform well in combat must not merely have effective doctrine and weaponry. Their internal structures and corporate beliefs must reflect the fact that the profession of arms, with its contract of unlimited liability which commits a soldier to risk his life on demand, is like no other: and it is to these structures and beliefs that we now turn our attention.

189

5

The Nation's Mirror

What a society gets in its armed forces is exactly what it asks for, no more and no less. What it asks for tends to be a reflection of what it is. When a country looks at its fighting forces it is looking at a mirror: if the mirror is a true one the face that it sees will be its own.

General Sir John Hackett, *The Profession of Arms*

'The army is a state within the state; it is a vice of our time,' lamented Alfred de Vigny in 1835. 'Things were different in antiquity,' he wrote; 'every citizen was a warrior, and every warrior was a citizen . . .'[1] His view was a narrow one, for he wrote when a soldier of twenty years' service had not seen a pitched battle, and the selective conscription law prevailing in France made the army essentially a closed corporation of poor men. Yet he was right to single out the relationship between the soldier and the state, a relationship which remains fundamental as we consider soldiers and combat in the next two decades. Battle, despite its centrality, has long been only the tip of the military iceberg: indeed, it is a tip which will grow smaller (though no less jagged) in the foreseeable future. Beneath its sharp peak lies a pyramid of military structure, its edges constantly washed by cultural, social, political and economic currents. In some states the faces of the pyramid have been sheer and impermeable, resistant to outside pressures: in others, a porous surface and deep internal fissures ensure that external forces are quickly felt. The balance between them changes constantly, and no assessment of soldiers at the close of the twentieth century can neglect the social organism of which they form part.

Modern armies have their origins in the Europe of the seventeenth and early eighteenth centuries, though some of their characteristics, such as organisational patterns which have often resembled those of classical Rome, are much older. Armies are a blend of at least four distinct elements, feudal, mercenary, conscript and volunteer. They are part cause and part effect of the growth of the nation-state. Centralised authority demanded centralised military power, and royal armies replaced the unstable old mixture of feudal levy and foreign mercenary. The process was more gradual than it may seem in retrospect. A visible feudal streak still permeates a few European armies, with strong personal bonds between monarchs and their officers, ties once deliberately strengthened by an ideography which dressed the officer in the king's coat, put the king's cypher on his buttons and the king's signature on his commission.

Today the British recruit swears on attestation to 'be faithful and bear true allegiance to Her Majesty Queen Elizabeth the Second, her heirs and successors . . .' The personal relationship between the British soldier and his sovereign is strongest in the Household Division, with its royal colonels and duties which bring it into frequent contact with the royal family, but we should not underestimate the benefits that accrue to the army as a whole from a profound sense of being the queen's rather than the government's. Cynics might claim that this is mere constitutional fiction, which appeals more strongly to officers and senior NCOs than to private soldiers whose concerns are more mundane. Yet at the very least it reduces the need to find any other national abstraction. A French company commander recognised the problem when he told one of his sergeants in the 1840s that he kept his political opinions to himself so that he could loyally serve all governments: 'I am not a soldier of Peter or of Paul, I am a soldier of France.'[2] It also avoids the difficulty, not unknown to United States soldiers, of serving a commander-in-chief to whom one is politically opposed.[3]

The importance of a personal link between the head of state and his soldiers was not lost on Hitler, who modified the *Reichswehr*'s oath 'to the Reich constitution, the Reich and its lawful institutions', first to an oath 'to the people and Fatherland' and finally, in August 1934, to an oath promising 'unconditional obedience to Adolf Hitler as Führer of the Reich and of the German people, Supreme Commander of the *Wehrmacht* . . .' As Sir John Wheeler Bennett was to write:

Henceforth such opposition as the Army wished to offer to the

191

Nazi regime was no longer in the nature of a struggle with an unscrupulous partner, but of a conspiracy against legitimate and constituted authority, a fact which was to sow the seeds of a harvest of doubt and moral conflict at all levels of the military hierarchy.[4]

Here we cannot ignore the legalistic element and the concept of 'soldierly honour' in German culture. Edward Shils and Morris Janowitz observed that German deserters in 1944–5 were concerned that they had violated soldierly honour by breaking their oath, and 'attempted to appease their consciences by ingenious arguments to the effect that the oaths they took were signed with pencil, or that the sergeant who administered the oath turned his back on them . . .'[5]

The feudal tradition survives most prominently in the household troops of the the armies of the old monarchies. Its less obvious consequences are visible across much of Africa and Latin America, where heads of state often surround themselves with praetorians who serve the president, not the state. In the African context the relationship may be strengthened by genuine tribalism. The term palace revolution is anything but figurative, and contenders for power must defeat or subvert the guard – or, as is sometimes the case, rise from its ranks. When the Russians took the Presidential Palace in Kabul in December 1979, the president's guard died at its post in housecarl style.

Even in armies which lack an obviously feudal tradition, the ties of loyalty linking junior to senior are often personal bonds, not administrative requirements: the little baronies of field formations and the larger earldoms of arms groupings say as much about war-band kinship as about organisational logic or shared technical expertise; and well they might, for the feudal tradition contributes to the characteristics of corporateness, expertise and responsibility which are now recognised as defining the military officer's profession. Corporateness, for the feudal warrior – in medieval Europe or in the Japan of the shōgunate – was acutely aware of his status, and bore its outward symbols, like the knight's spurred heels and blazoned shield, or the samurai's topknot and pair of swords. Expertise, because a warrior class existed chiefly to fight and spent much of its time training to do so. Responsibility, because knight and samurai alike owed obedience not only to his lord, but also to generally accepted standards of behaviour, in battle and out if it.

The mercenary tradition, too, remains alive and well. Mercenaries, so prominent in warfare in late medieval and early modern Europe, formed part of national armies even in the eighteenth century. Frederick the Great relied heavily on what Christopher Duffy calls 'foreign cannon fodder'; the redoubtable Irish brigade in French service bore the heat of the day when Maurice de Saxe beat the Duke of Cumberland at Fontenoy in 1745; and on 10 August 1792 the Swiss Guard (acting out its own scene in a long and bloody Swiss mercenary history) perished defending the Tuileries. Despite international disapproval of the 'dogs of war' who have contributed to so many post-1945 conflicts, the mercenary continues to soldier on, sometimes in eminently respectable guises. British officers serving 'on contract' in the Gulf, and the Gurkhas who still form part of the British army (and long may they continue to do so) are mercenaries in no dishonourable sense. Moreover, the connection between military service and pay lies at the very bedrock of the soldier's relationship with his employer, even in national armies. The word soldier stems from the Latin *solidus* and the old French *soude*, meaning pay, and de Vigny drew the comparison more precisely in modern French, writing of '*L'homme soldé, le Soldat . . .*' [6]

Peacetime recruiting literature tends to make two appeals: one to the potential recruit's manly instincts and yen to see the world ('It's a man's life in the Regular Army' and 'Take the Army's European Tour'), and the other to his desire to receive a regular income and learn a trade. Young men are persuaded to enlist by empty pockets and a bleak future more often than patriotic literature or official history admits. In 1854 Eugene Bandel found himself penniless in St Louis, and signed on: 'This was my only resort if I did not wish to steal or beg.'[7] The future General Count Fleury enlisted into the spahis in 1837 after squandering his inheritance and being faced with the choice of 'jumping in the Seine or joining some regiment'.[8] Henry Giles, in 1939 tired of the depression 'and the commodity [lines] and no jobs but the WPA', thought that 'the army meant security and pride and something fine and good'.[9] In 1960 a sample of young Americans rated 'opportunities for training' and 'choice of career field' as among the most important reasons for embarking on a military career.[10] In a study of American enlisted men in the late 1960s, Charles Moskos suggested that self-advancement was a major inducement for enlistment among those with lower educational levels

– better-educated men tended to enlist so as to beat the draft by choosing their own time of entry or branch of service.[11]

The mercenary element should not be exaggerated, but it is a thread woven into the pattern of military motivation. The sense of financial contract linking soldiers and sailors with their employers has usually been strong. Caesar faced mutinies at Piacenza in 49BC and Rome in 47BC because his soldiers felt that they were insufficiently rewarded; 'constant pay' was a much-reiterated plea by troops in the English Civil War; British naval mutineers at Spithead in 1797 made an increase in pay one of their main demands, and a reduction in pay was the prime reason for the Royal Navy's Invergordon mutiny in 1931.[12] Mutiny in general has many causes, brutal or unpopular leaders, exposure to heavy and repeated stress, and lack of low-level support for the war among them. A common element is often a sense of unfairness, a conviction that the army is not honouring its part of the unwritten contract. Tinkering with pay and allowances in the cause of rationalisation or economy, especially when the well-being of dependents seems threatened, produces disproportionate resentment among soldiers who might face physical danger without complaint.

Alongside the feudal and mercenary element in modern armies marches a tradition which is every bit as old. De Vigny had looked back to the age when the connection between civic right and military duty was simple and direct: every citizen fought in defence of his *polis*, and the hoplite phalanx of the Greek city-state was the political nation under arms. Such was also the case in the early days of the Roman Republic, when a citizen's income determined his equipment and thus his military role. The free men of Anglo-Saxon England turned out for duty in the *fyrd*, so many of whose battles against the Vikings in the ninth century typified the disadvantage faced by the citizen-soldier contending with a seasoned professional.[13] The arrival of the professional household warrior, the housecarl, after the Danish conquest, added a strong central core about which the *fyrd* could coalesce. This 'great gathering of vilanaille . . . of men in everyday clothes' fighting 'shield to shield, and shoulder to shoulder', barking its war-cries 'Holy Cross', 'God Almighty' and 'Out, Out', could not withstand attack by a combined-arms force of cavalry and archers at Hastings in 1066. Nevertheless, if the *fyrd* emphasises the weakness of the amateur facing the professional, I cannot pass without pausing in admiration for those axemen who stood firm around their dragon banner after a forced march of nearly thirty miles a day down from their victory at Stamford Bridge near York: for them King and Country were no vague abstraction.[14]

The principle of obligatory military service continued into the Elizabethan militia, and in 1573 it was decreed that a convenient number of able-bodied men should be selected from the general levy, 'to be sorted in bands, and to be trained and exercised in such sort as may reasonably be borne by a common charge of the whole county'.[15] Expeditionary forces of dubious quality were raised from volunteers and pressed men, and experienced soldiers blanched at the militia's prospects if faced by serious invasion. It was as well that fleet and weather combined to thwart the Armada in 1588, for however misty-eyed Englishmen were to become at remembrance of the Queen's great review at Tilbury, the militia would have cut a poor figure against Spanish tercios.

The English experience was markedly different from that of continental states, which faced invasion more frequently and thus took both the recruitment of mercenaries and the conscription of natives more seriously. The standing armies of continental Europe in the eighteenth century were filled with conscripts, leavened with foreign mercenaries. In the Prussian system, inaugurated by Frederick William I between 1727 and 1735, each regiment had a catchment area round its garrison town, whence it drew recruits for life-long service. Generous exemptions were accorded both to specific areas and trades.[16] Similar policies applied elsewhere, as the regional titles of so many European regiments bear witness, from *Picardie*, first regiment of the French line, raised in Picardy in 1580, to the 3rd Saxon Hussars, raised around Bautzen in 1910.

The weight with which conscription bore down upon the citizen varied. In all but the most exceptional circumstances – such as France after the *levée en masse* of 1793 or Prussia in 1813–14 – it was possible for the well-to-do to avoid or alleviate military service. In Wilhelmine Germany young men who had attained the requisite academic standard could serve for one year instead of two or three, choose their regiment and, within limits, their time of entry into it, and live out of barracks. These *Einjahrige* rapidly attained NCO rank and most went on to become reserve officers. For much of the nineteenth century a young Frenchman who drew a bad number in the conscription lottery might, if he could afford it, hire a substitute to serve on his behalf.

Popular and political attitudes to military service were influenced by numerous factors. The French military service law of 1868 was attacked by the extreme right, alarmed that it would produce an army which would not take on workers in the streets, and the extreme left, which feared that it would subject a growing number of young Frenchmen to the brutalising effects of barrack life. After the Franco-Prussian war there was a short-lived 'Golden Age' when left and right agreed on the need for universal military service. By the late 1880s, with the war a distant memory, there was less unanimity, and popular novels like Abel Hermant's *Le Cavalier Miserey* and Lucien Descaves's *Les Sous-offs* painted a discouraging picture of military life. Universal conscription had been better accepted in Germany. A French observer, writing before the Franco-Prussian war, suggested that if a French soldier was asked why he was serving he would reply 'because I drew a bad number'. His Prussian counterpart, however, would respond: 'To serve my king and country.'[17] Yet even in Germany there were dissident voices, from Social Democrat politicians at one extreme to merciless cartoonists in *Simplicissimus* and *Ulk* at the other.

In Britain, in contrast, there was no conscription into the army until the passing of the Military Service Act of 1916. Seamen had been in danger of being pressed into the Royal Navy, and adult males were liable for home defence duties in the militia. It took nearly two years of major war to convince Englishmen of the legitimacy of compulsory service, which is an index of deep-seated resistance to the concept. Victorian England felt decidedly ambivalent about its army. Its achievements overseas were applauded, but its presence at home was less welcome. Young Wully Robertson's mother told him that she would rather bury him than see him in a red coat – she might have thought better of the bargain had she known he would rise from private to field marshal. When the middle classes flocked to arms in response to the French invasion scare of the 1860s, the Volunteer units they joined, with their grey or green uniforms, looked – and behaved – quite unlike the regulars with whom they had so little in common.

Conscription in peacetime never became entrenched in the way that it had in Europe. Although the traditional basis of Britain's defence policy shifted when she took on a long-standing continental commitment after 1945, conscription ended in 1962. Memories of it remain mixed. Although many look back on the experience with pride and satisfaction, there are others who would agree with the author Auberon Waugh, who found the Guards Depot 'a Buchenwald horror scene', or with the novelist Leslie Thomas, who thought the whole business a waste of time.[18] Reintroducing it to meet the manpower demands of the 1990s has many attractions, but such a step would require enormous political courage and would arouse at best lukewarm support from a military establishment which prefers not to view itself as a conscript-training machine.

The United States' tradition was more British than European. As Allan Millett and Peter Maslowski have written: 'The British military heritage, the all-pervasive sense of military insecurity, and the inability of the economically poor colonies to maintain an expensive professional army all combined to guarantee that the Elizabethan militia would be transplanted to the North American wilderness.'[19] The Indian threat meant that militiamen took their duties more seriously than their Elizabethan or Stuart counterparts, but as the threat receded exemptions increased and training declined. The militia as a whole was not called out for expeditionary service against the Indians or the French, but local quotas were filled with volunteers, draftees, hirelings and substitutes: the well-to-do usually managed to escape. The British tradition of civilian authority over the military was also duplicated, as eighteenth-century colonial legislatures gradually asserted a control assumed by the British Parliament over its army a century before.

True conscription came with the Civil War. The Confederacy, short of manpower as of much else, introduced conscription in April 1862, making all white men of military age (eventually defined as seventeen to fifty) members of the army. At first conscripts were allowed to hire substitutes, and even when substitution was abolished a growing list of exemptions permitted about half potential conscripts to avoid service. After toying with drafting men into the militia, in March 1863 the North too brought in conscription. Northerners who wished to avoid the draft could either hire a subsitute or pay a commutation fee. Commutation was abolished in July 1864, and although the list of exemptions was rather shorter than in the South, it nevertheless permitted about half the draftees to escape. While the South's legislation was genuinely intended to sweep men into the army, the North's was designed as much to prompt volunteering by men who wished to avoid the stigma of being drafted. The payment of bounties to volunteers also encouraged enlistment, but a growing number of 'bounty jumpers' – men who enlisted, took the bounty, and then re-enlisted only to desert again – became a national scandal.[20]

There was substantial opposition to conscription in both North and South. This stemmed from the Whig tradition, inherited from England, which supported a 'dual army' of a small standing force backed by a large militia, but opposed compulsory regular service as an assault on individual liberty; from states' rights adherents, North and South, who saw conscription as an unconstitutional imposition by central government, and from dislike of centrally appointed enrolment officers and provost marshals. The natural desire of individuals to avoid the disruption, discomfort and physical risk posed by military service inevitably fostered resistance. Finally, the generally low regard in which the regular soldier was held before and after the war further diminished the attraction of compulsory service. The social standing of the nineteenth-century American soldier in peacetime was remarkably similar to that of his British counterpart. In 1890 General George Crook warned that:

> The moment a citizen dons the uniform of a private, no matter what his previous social position might have been, he is instantly ostracised by the public . . . A man loses his pride and self-respect when he finds he is despised by the people he meets, that he is shunned by former associates and is no longer regarded as their social equal.[21]

The experience of the Civil War proved invaluable when the United States again introduced conscription in 1917. Local boards played the principal role in the selection process, ensuring that the army received the men it wanted and those society could best spare: most were unmarried, and nearly three-quarters were farm hands or manual workers. During the Second World War, no less than 36 million males registered with the Selective Service System, and 10 million were inducted: in all 16.3 million Americans wore uniform. Conscription bore less heavily upon the American population than it did in most other combatant countries. Men were exempted from service for medical defects which would not have allowed them to escape elsewhere, and industrial deferments were also relatively generous.[22] The sensible operation of the Selective Service System helped reduce anti-war feeling, and the manner in which the United States had been attacked helped quell doubts about the legitimacy of the war. Indeed, there have been suggestions that it was precisely because of his desire to ensure a *casus belli* which would guarantee popular support that President Roosevelt deliberately witheld information of imminent Japanese attack on Pearl Harbor from Admiral Kimmel and General Short, his commanders in Hawaii.[23]

The draft was retained after the war's end, and the outbreak of war in Korea in 1950 saw both conscripts and reservists sent to the Far East. Attempts to create universal military service based on a short period of active duty followed by compulsory reserve service failed, and neither the Universal Military Training and Service Act of 1951 nor the Armed Forces Reserve Act of 1952 introduced genuine universal military training, leaving the draft – its implementation still in the hands of local boards – as the basis of compulsory service. The boards were able to grant deferments and exemptions on a generous scale, which helped cushion the draft's impact, and although there was a widespread and growing belief in the war's futility, there was nothing approaching the surge of anti-war feeling that was to occur fifteen years later.

The Vietnam War, in contrast, provoked immense opposition. As United States force levels in Vietnam grew, from 23,000 in December 1964 to 536,100 in December 1968, the draft bit deeper into the fabric of American society. In 1969 male students in their last year at High School saw the draft as the factor most likely to interfere with their future career plans.[24] Deferments became harder to obtain and young men lived under the shadow of receiving a notification that they were I-A – liable for immediate drafting. The National Guard was a refuge for some who wished to avoid service with the regular army. Others volunteered for another service, or what they saw as a 'safe' branch of the army to avoid becoming a 'grunt' – one of the minority which felt the rough edge of the war in the jungles and paddy fields. Many were deferred on medical grounds – genuine or otherwise – and it is beyond question that draft boards were not immune to local political pressures. Student deferments generally enabled a man to obtain a first degree: it was especially risky to lack the education or resources to attend university, leading to complaints that background and race helped weigh the scales of fate. It was certainly true that a man's chance of finishing up in a combat arm were inversely related to his educational qualifications. A 1968 survey established a close correlation between low education, low income – and service in Vietnam.[25] One commentator maintained (inaccurately) that half the infantry in Vietnam were black – it was 'a white man's war, a black man's fight'.[26]

The war posed the hardest of questions to thousands of young men. John Parrish, facing conscription as a medical officer, assessed his choices as Canada for life, three years in prison, or a year in Vietnam. 'My free country was forcing me to leave home for an undeclared war in a distant country,' he mused. 'To what lengths was I in honour bound to serve my country . . . Where was my freedom of choice? Where were my rights as an enlightened citizen in an enlightened society?'[27] For Stanley Goff, a black man from a blue-collar background, there was no real alternative. 'I got my draft greetings,' he said. 'I just succumbed. What else could I do?'[28] Tim O'Brien thought about going to Canada, but, like so many of his countrymen, decided that he was morally obliged to serve.

> I owed the prairie something. For twenty-one years I'd lived under its laws, accepted its education, eaten its food, wasted and guzzled its water, slept well at night, driven across its highways, dirtied and breathed its air, wallowed in its luxuries.[29]

For every man who left for Canada (a decision requiring no little moral courage) there was another who agreed with Winston Groom's character Lieutenant Kahn: 'Every man owes a debt. It must be paid, After that you are free to enjoy what this country has to offer.'[30]

The choice was rarely a simple one. Social pressures from family, friends and community were often ambivalent. As the war went on some of these, especially on university campuses, favoured resistance rather than acceptance of the draft. The intellectual currents of the 1960s, themselves both a cause of resistance to the war and a reflection of feelings aroused by the conflict, helped lend respectability and internationalism to protest. And the reasons for fighting were not compelling. The 'domino theory' – that Communist victory in Vietnam would lead to the fall of the rest of South-East Asia – lacked widespread credibility, and the character of the South Vietnamese regime led many Americans to wonder if it legitimately merited their support. The lack of immediate threat to the United States was telling, and Allen Morgan summed up the opinion of many draft resisters: 'I sure am going to wait until they get a lot closer

Rehearsals and Drills

17   Soldiers of Plumer's Second Army study a large-scale model of Messines Ridge, 1917. Meticulous preparation and rigid phase lines meant that the British, though successful, failed to capitalise on fleeting opportunity.

18   BTR-60s of a Soviet Motor Rifle Division advance, supported by tanks and ground attack aircraft. In the Soviet view, tactical flexibility is founded on battle drills.

Shelter from the Devil's Breath

19   Men of the Argyll and Sutherland Highlanders wearing the primitive anti-gas protection of goggles and mouthpads, spring 1915.

20   An American soldier in full NBC protective outfit. Morale and efficiency slump during long periods spent shrouded in such clothing.

The Spirit and the Sword

21   *Boy's Own Paper*, 1918.

22   Mass in the field, Indo-China, 1954.

For School
and
Country

Deadlier Than the Male?

23   The part-legendary exploits of Agostina, who took her lover's place on the ramparts of Saragossa during its siege by the French in 1808-9.

24   Galina Boordina, a Soviet night fighter pilot, was credited with three kills. The limited use of women in combat was promoted by the scale of the threat and by German behaviour in occupied areas.

than Vietnam. Maybe when they're in New Jersey . . .'[31] Guenther
Lewy puts feeling about the Vietnam War in a wider context.

> Every war causes large-scale death and suffering, to the soldiers
> fighting it as well as to the civilian population on whose territory
> it is fought. But the moral outrages inherent in war are often
> ignored when the fighting is crowned with success and the moral
> justification of the conflict is sufficiently strong.[32]

Vietnam remains an immensely contentious topic, though analysis
is now more balanced than it was in the war's immediate aftermath,
when the prevailing anti-war attitude in the United States, strengthened by atrocity scandals, coloured much of the historiography.
Many of the problems faced by the US Army were exaggerated,
and the undoubted lapses of discipline – atrocities and fragging alike
– were not seen in the context of a large army fighting a long and
difficult war.

Fragging – the killing of unpopular officers or NCOs by their
subordinates – is a well-polished facet of military history. A British
battalion commander was mysteriously shot at the close of the
battle of Blenheim in 1704, despite having taken the unusual step
of addressing the regiment, promising to mend his ways, before
the battle began. One account suggests that Colonel Cameron of
Fassfern of the 92nd Highlanders was shot by one of his own
men at Quatre Bras in 1815, and the redoubtable Tom Plunkett
of the Rifle Brigade (an admirable soldier when sober) determined,
in a black mood, to shoot his own company commander, but was
eventually persuaded to give up his rifle – to be reduced to the ranks
and given 300 lashes for his pains.[33] The Napoleonic French army
was hard on unpopular officers: one general was fired on by his
own brigade, and another, sent to enlist three companies of Paris
students into the National Guard, was murdered by them.[34] During
the First World War, Australian cameliers made it known that they
shot bad officers, and during the French 1917 mutinies General Emile
Taufflieb of XXXVIII Corps was shot at several times in the streets
of Soissons.[35]

Fragging in Vietnam was a matter of widely repeated anecdote ('a
friend of mine put sixteen rounds in a staff-sergeant's back' – 'an
officer knew that if he messed with you in the field, in a fire fight
you could shoot him in the head') and hard statistics.[36] The

problem with the statistics, alas, is whose one should believe. In *Military Incompetence* Richard Gabriel maintains that 'in the US Army alone, over one thousand officers and NCOs were assassinated by their own men'. A footnote refers to his influential earlier book *Crisis in Command*, where a table indicates that there were up to 1,016 actual and possible assaults in Vietnam in 1969–72, resulting in 86 deaths. Even a generous assumption of under-reporting hardly justifies the suggestion that one thousand officers and NCOs were killed, and the figure of 86 deaths (alarming though it must be to those with the US Army's well-being at heart) is not exorbitant considering 2.7 million young men were armed and sent to a war zone. Some were predisposed to commit violent crime against authority in any case, and, as Gabriel himself observes, six times more Americans were killed by gunshot wounds in the USA during the period of the Vietnam War than were actually killed in Vietnam.[37] There, officers and NCOs were undoubtedly murdered by their own men, as they were in two world wars and across the battlefields of history. Similar things will undoubtedly happen in future war, and will reflect dissatisfaction and indiscipline among the led just as much as incompetence or brutality among leaders. 1989 saw an epidemic of 'fragging' in the Soviet army, largely as a consequence of nationalist tensions. Two officers had been murdered in 1988, but a widely accepted figure suggests that no less than 59 perished in 1989.

Resistance to conscription for the Vietnam War was also not an isolated phenomenon. While some of those who resisted undoubtedly did so for the strongest motives of self-interest, others had genuine conscientious objections either to war in general or to the specific involvement in Vietnam. It is impossible to assess the proportion of convenience resisters to legitimate objectors, and the issue has particular poignancy for the relatives of those who refused to feign a moral objection they did not feel, went to Vietnam and paid the supreme price. Conscientious objection to fighting has a long and honourable history. There were some 16,500 conscientious objectors in First World War Britain, some of whom endured violent public disapproval and harsh penal conditions. The Second World War saw far more – 51,000 in Britain by the end of 1940 – and they were generally better treated. The question of conscientious objection in both wars still arouses sharp feelings, but it is difficult not to admire those objectors who would share the soldier's risks, but not take life:

for instance, the Quakers who served with the Friends' Ambulance Unit or the objectors in the Parachute Field Ambulance who were among the first troops dropped into Normandy on D-Day.[38]

A question often asked by First World War tribunals assessing the legimacy of an individual's objection to war was: 'What would you do if a German soldier was about to rape your mother?' An answer which suggested a violent response undermined the claim for conscientious objection. Yet attitudes to war cannot always be seen in such simple terms. No army encourages its soldiers to make their own moral judgment on the wars they fight, but it is unrealistic to expect late twentieth-century man not to be more questioning than previous generations who might more easily smother individual conscience beneath the collective will.

Colonel Eli Gever, commanding an Israeli brigade at the early age of thirty-two in the Lebanon in 1982, was an officer of proven valour and integrity, but he resigned his command rather than participate in a battle he believed to be morally wrong. The fighting in the Lebanon and the *intifada* in the occupied territories have presented the Israeli army with an unfamiliar moral challenge. General Rafael Eitan, its former Chief of Staff, maintained that: '. . . we cannot indulge in letting individuals decide what kind of military mission to conduct'. However, a growing number of soldiers in the 'Soldiers against Silence' and 'There Is a Limit' movements have protested against what they see as unjust wars. At the court-martial of four soldiers accused of beating an Arab so badly that he died of his injuries, General Dan Shomron, the Chief of Staff, said such beatings were 'a grey area'. His remarks highlighted the judgmental gulf yawning in front of many of his soldiers.[39]

'Supposing they gave a war and nobody came?' was one of the student quips of the Vietnam era. A survey carried out in Britain in 1988 suggested that although 54 per cent of those interviewed would be prepared to fight for their country and 20 per cent would not, 15 per cent would make a judgment based on the *casus belli*. Young, working-class men were more eager to heed the call to arms than the middle classes: 'As on the football terraces, we found the pattern was: the younger, the fiercer.'[40] One should not read too much into such things: after all, shortly before the Second World War the Oxford Union declared that it would not fight for King and Country, but most of its members proceeded to do exactly that. Nevertheless, judgments on the legitimacy of a particular war will become increasingly objective, and inspiring and sustaining conscript support for wars not widely perceived as legitimate will become more difficult.

A survey of four US combat battalions in 1975 detected a similar variation of attitude, with willing obedience to orders dependent on the *casus belli*. Most were prepared to fight if the USA was invaded by a foreign enemy (97.8 per cent of Rangers and 81.4 per cent of infantry agreed to this). Defending West Germany was almost as popular with the Rangers (92.9 per cent) but far less so with the infantry (59.4), while intervening in an overseas civil war where the government asked for American help had the lowest support of all: only 84.5 per cent of the Rangers and 52.8 of the infantry would willingly go into combat in such a situation. Hypothetical questions do not get the best out of soldiers, whose answers may reflect, among other things, a recent disagreement with the company commander or simply a bad meal in the cookhouse. Nevertheless, the survey, dated though it now is, does emphasise the connection between preparedness to do one's duty willingly and the reasons for the war. It also shows the effect of elitism in narrowing the soldier's vision. Major Tom Bridges described the cavalry motto of 1914 as 'We'll do it: what is it?' When I interviewed members of the two parachute battalions on their return from the South Atlantic in 1982 I was struck by a similar professional concern to do a good job. Of course it was useful that the Argentinians were demonstrably the aggressors, but that mattered less than proving that the 'maroon machine' had a right to the respect of friend and foe alike. 'My section was going to take Darwin Hill even if we were the only fuckers left alive,' a corporal in 2 Para told me with unmistakable emphasis.[41]

Vietnam introduces, against the run of popular mythology, the fourth element in the blend that makes up modern armies – the tradition of volunteering for military service. Two-thirds of the men who fought in Vietnam were volunteers, and three-quarters of those who died were volunteers. The latter figure underlines the fact that officers and senior NCOs, many of them regulars, bore a disproportionate share of the burden of death in Vietnam, as in so many other wars. More officers were killed and wounded than might have been expected from their overall percentage in units in both world wars: in the British Second World War infantry, for instance, officers, between 4 and 5 per cent of a unit's strength, made up 10 per cent of killed and 7.7 per cent of wounded in Sicily and 8.5 per cent and 7.7 per cent, respectively, in Tunisia. There were times when the pressure was even heavier. The Commando Brigade in Normandy lost 77 of its 146 officers and 890 out of its 2,452 men, and 19 out of the original 24 US Marine battalion commanders who landed on Iwo Jima became casualties.[42] Warrant officers had a casualty rate 30 times higher in Vietnam than in World War Two, largely because most helicopter pilots were warrant officers, and, with the exception of second lieutenants, army officers had a higher casualty rate than in World War Two up to and including the rank of lieutenant-colonel. The low casualty rate among colonels and generals was a function of the nature of the war, not necessarily an index of lack of courage or dedication.[43]

Nevertheless, the myth of low officer casualties in Vietnam remains particularly obdurate, and the anonymous author of *Self-Destruction* averred: 'Seeing few casualties amongst their own officers, grunts perceived that they were being led by men who lacked dedication.'[44] That there were morale problems among the grunts is beyond question, but it is unreasonable to attribute these to low officer casualties. Attitudes to the war in America itself, the sporadic character of combat, the presence of civilians in the battle area, the frequent and unsettling juxtaposition of soldiers who were at risk and those who were comparatively safe, the one-year tour, and a military structure which did not encourage cohesion all played their part in undermining morale. The latter proved particularly destructive, for the rapid rotation of personnel (notably officers, who did only a six-month command tour during their year in Vietnam) impeded the building of effective fighting units.

What prompted men to volunteer for service in the US Army during the Vietnam era? The same factors that have encouraged men to volunteer across the centuries. The mere existence of conscription encourages men to enlist in the hope of choosing terms of service which suit them best: In October 1964 a US Department of Defense survey found that an average of 38 per cent of enlisted volunteers and 41 per cent of junior officers on their first tour had volunteered because of the draft.[45] Much the same thing had happened in both North and South during the Civil War.

If a proportion of volunteers is impelled into service by a desire to avoid the draft, in time of war or national emergency patriotism plays its part in encouraging men to enlist. It reflects a sense of nationalism which itself influences the way that armies behave in and out of battle.

A nation's culture – its history, mythology, customs, geographical character and position, climate, pattern of land-use, language, racial composition and religion – helps determine the way its soldiers view military service, accept discipline, face hardship, and regard enemies and allies.

In his persuasive book *The Explanation of Ideology*, Emmanuel Todd argued that a nation's political structure is determined less by pure ideology than by the cultural conditioning of its population. The family, maintained Todd, 'acts as the infrastructure: it determines the temperament and ideological system' of human societies. He identified four major family types in Europe, the egalitarian nuclear family in France, the absolute nuclear family in England, the authoritarian family in Germany and the community family in Russia. There is a striking congruence between these family types and their respective armies. For instance, the German army, for much of its history, may be said to have embodied the very qualities of inequality and authority which Todd attributes to the German family, while the French army often displayed the opposite qualities, equality and liberty.[46] General F.C. du Barail, a notable *beau sabreur* of the army of the Second Empire would certainly have agreed. At the peace negotiations at Villafranca in 1859 Franz Josef's cavalry escort remained absolutely immobile. Napoleon III's *Guides*, however, jockeyed for position in the ranks, trying to get a good view of the two Emperors. Du Barail thought that this was no bad thing, for it was a sign of the effervescent French temperament.[47] Another French officer believed that for the Frenchman 'battle is above all an individual action, the presence of dash, agility and the offensive spirit . . . for the German, it is the fusillade, individualism drowned in the mass, passive courage and the defensive'.[48]

While Todd's analysis must be applied to armies with caution, we may be altogether more confident about the influence of the environment upon military attitudes. John Baynes observed that climate, type of soil and the general position of a country dictate the sort of life that is led there, and from that spring certain characteristics which harden into unmistakable ways of doing things. The Lowland Scot, about whom Baynes wrote so feelingly, came from a cold and barren area with sea coasts on both sides, a hard land which bred dour, serious men whose affections were not easily touched. One of the many strengths of the British regimental system is that it brings together like-minded men from the same area. However, this local identity has often been more apparent than real. Baynes admitted that many of his Cameronians were 'outsiders', and the Royal Welch Fusiliers, a line regiment with a superb fighting record, was not nicknamed the Brummagem [Birmingham] Fusiliers for nothing.[49] Christopher Donnelly argues that 'geography is probably the single most important factor in determining a nation's concepts of war', and points to the importance of 'national, historical, cultural and environmental conditioning' upon the Soviet soldier.[50] Improvements in the quality of life through such things as the reduction of working hours, the mechanisation of agriculture and the increasing safety of factory work will, as we have seen in the previous chapter, inevitably change the temperament of armies.

So much for those factors which stem from the shape of the land and the character of its people. But what of the effect of ideology? Most post-1945 studies have tended to devalue the impact of patriotism on military motivation, and there is widespread agreement that other factors, arguably with confidence in leadership at company level as the most important, dominate combat performance.[51] Nevertheless, even though it is true that patriotism, nationalism and political ideology are less significant than many of their propagandists might admit, they are by no means unimportant. In the first place, whatever their value in combat, they are often the mainspring which propels a man into uniform. The mobilisation of August 1914 is an extreme case, for it was the last flare of popular enthusiasm in a Europe that was soon to be changed beyond recognition. Reservists reported for duty with an efficiency which surprised armies expecting a substantial refractory minority, and in Britain, where there was as yet no conscription, some 300,000 men enlisted in August and another 700,000 by the end of the year. There was a rush to enlist among the best-paid manual and non-manual workers. Miners, then relatively well-paid, joined up in huge numbers, and men from Glamorgan, Durham, Northumberland, and some Scottish coalfields – all areas where pre-war industrial militancy had been pronounced – were prominent in their enthusiasm. 'The compatibility of class consciousness and patriotism could have no better illustration,' wrote J.M. Winter.[52]

In more moderate circumstances ideology in its widest sense helps both to persuade men to enlist and then to keep them in the line. We have already seen how national beliefs on the merit of military service colour attitudes to conscription; and what Charles Moskos called 'latent ideology', belief in broad cultural and ideological values, plays its part even when flag-waving patriotism or hard ideology is shunned.

The evidence on the part played by the latter is inconclusive. The German army of the Second World War, with its solid combat performance and professed ideological commitment, is a fascinating case study. On the one hand, Shils and Janowitz believed:

> that the unity of the German army was . . . sustained only to a very slight extent by the National Socialist political convictions of its members, and that more important in the motivation of the determined resistance of the German soldier was the steady satisfaction of certain *primary* personality demands afforded by the social organisation of the army.[53]

However, Omer Bartov, in his work on the German army on the Eastern Front, points out that primary groups were constantly fragmented by casualties, and that losses of leaders upon whom cohesion purportedly depends were especially heavy. In July and August 1943 18th Panzer Division, one of his sample formations, lost a regimental commander, ten battalion commanders, 83 company commanders, 85 officer platoon commanders and ordnance officers, and 15 other officers. Bartov wonders how strong primary groups could possibly survive in such circumstances, and makes a convincing case for the contribution made by propaganda to German fighting morale:

> whatever the men thought of the Nazi party, they were mostly firm believers, almost in a religious sense, in their Führer and, by extension, in many of the ideological and political goals quoted in his name.[54]

Special virulence was reserved for commissars, the enemy's high priests. 'We would be insulting the animals,' brayed the bi-weekly *Mitteilungen für die Truppe*, 'if we were to describe these men, who are mostly Jewish, as beasts.'[55]

Bartov's comparison with religion is an apt one, for even if the minutiae of Nazi theology had limited relevance to soldiers at the front, the broad theme of the struggle between good and evil could scarcely fail to strike a chord. The part played by religion itself in forging and sustaining fighting morale is a complex one. Jokes about 'fire insurance' are common enough, and numerous previously religious men have testified that the squalor and waste of war have destroyed their belief, but both statistic and anecdote bear witness to men's enhanced spiritual needs in time of crisis. Soldiers often find sustenance in prayer, and fervently wish to believe that death is not the end. Proper and reverent disposal of the dead is immensely important: the US Army considered developing a corpse-disintegrating foam which might have had numerous practical advantages but would have struck a telling blow at the morale of soldiers. The need for proper and reverent disposal of the dead is a fundamental tenet of many cultures: being shrivelled by an aerosol scarcely meets the requirement. For all the decline of organised religion in so much of the Western world, there is still a latent spirituality which parallels latent ideology, and meeting the spiritual need of men under stress is scarcely less important than fulfilling their physical demands for food and ammunition. Gerald Kersh encapsulated this fundamental need in his *A Soldier, His Prayer*, which ends:

> I'm but the son my mother bore
> A simple man and nothing more
> But – God of strength and gentleness
> Be pleased to make me nothing else!
>
> Help me again when death is near
> To mock the haggard face of fear.
> That if I fall, if fall I must,
> My soul may triumph in the dust!

For that huge and growing portion of the world which follows Islam, spiritual support is strong, and religion not only provides sustenance to the combatant but helps mobilise popular support for war.

Bartov is right to stress that the conditions, moral and material, of war on the Eastern Front made it 'a unique phenomenon in human history'. One of the dark strengths of Nazism was its ability to feed on German culture, and it brought to the fighting on the Eastern Front a blend of history and mythology, geopolitics and philosophy, which helped sustain soldiers in surroundings of almost unimaginable barbarity. German and Russian culture alike made possible draconian discipline which kept soldiers on both sides at their task. The death penalty was company level punishment in the Soviet army, and one reputable estimate puts German military executions at 11,753.[56] In May 1943 seven soldiers were executed for desertion or self-mutilation in 12th Infantry Division alone, and a divisional order warned that those executed would be buried in graves marked differently from those of men killed in action.[57] Even if Bartov is correct in his assessment of the importance of ideology – and his case is well made and soundly supported – it would be reasonable to conclude that ideology played an unusually prominent role because of the war's particular circumstances.

This conclusion is reinforced by reference to the Soviet army. After the Russian attack on Finland in 1939 and the German invasion in 1941 revealed serious shortcomings in Soviet morale the thrust of propaganda and ideography shifted. Posters exhorted soldiers to emulate pre-Soviet Russian heroes like A.V. Suvorov and Alexander Nevsky, and emphasised the defence of the motherland against a merciless invader; officer ranks were not only revived, but shown on shoulder boards almost exactly the same as their tsarist predecessors. Stalin, with his acute survival instinct, recognised that ideology alone was not enough to win the war: it had to be linked to an appeal to patriotism, and both the fact and nature of the invasion lent weight to this. We may doubt whether unassisted Communist ideology would have nerved the Soviet army for the Great Patriotic War, and there remains room for questioning that army's enthusiasm for fighting outside its own territory except to pursue a repulsed attacker. It is no accident that Soviet military exercises were frequently scripted, however implausibly in Western eyes, with an initial NATO provocation followed by a vigorous Soviet counter-offensive.

Although it is still too early to judge the effects of the war in Afghanistan upon the Soviet army and society, all the signs suggest that ideology, unsupported by appeals to patriotism, was less than satisfactory in buttressing fighting spirit. One conscript called the war 'a crude political mistake', and the father of a dead soldier complained: 'Nobody needed that war in Afghanistan. It is a useless war. Let's get our kids out as soon as possible.'[58] Comparisons with the American experience in Vietnam may be superficial, but they are heightened by the fact that veterans of the fighting – probably more than 200,000 by 1987 – have found it difficult to adjust to civilian life. Mary Dejevosky wrote of how:

> they crave recognition and reassurance that the war they were fighting is justified, that their sacrifice and that of their comrades has not been in vain. That reassurance is not forthcoming. They encounter instead official indifference, euphemisms about 'internationalist duty', and a myth about the Second World War which bears no relation to their experience of combat.[59]

The generation of Soviet officials too young to have fought in the Second World War but using vicarious heroics to strengthen its position has lost ground, and the returning veterans pose one of the many challenges to the Soviet system.

The Soviet army has devoted immense efforts to political education. The Main Political Directorate (GlavPU) of the armed forces maintains representatives at all levels down to company or its equivalent, advising, reporting, and teaching. The political officer (*zampolit*) is no longer the commissar of yesteryear, keeping an eye on a potentially politically unsound commander. Nor is the relationship between *zampolit* and commander necessarily one of mutual suspicion, because the *zampolit* frees the commander from much tedious political instruction and carries out duties designed to bolster the unit's morale. Moreover, the military education of political officers has been taken increasingly seriously, and they were given their own four-year military academies in the 1970s.[60]

Conscripts receive some fifteen minutes of political education each morning and two afternoon lecture periods each week, while officers attend about fifty hours of political education each year. The *zampolit* also organises various other morale-building activities from museum tours to visits by distinguished veterans.

The evidence, such as it is, suggests that much of this effort is wasted. Richard Gabriel's survey of the attitudes of Soviet ex-soldiers in the West revealed an average of 8.6 hours of political indoctrination each week, and no less than 66.76 per cent of his respondents agreed that it was 'almost totally unimportant'. A mere 16.7 per cent found it very important.[61] The former Soviet officer who writes under the name of Viktor Suvorov tells of widespread political cynicism, and describes the arrival of *stukachi* (KGB agents) to stiffen his unit as it prepared for the invasion of Czechoslovakia.[62] Both findings should be treated with some caution, for the very fact that an ex-soldier has left the Soviet Union implies that he was less than enthusiastic about its regime in the first place, and therefore less susceptible to political education than his comrades. Nevertheless, no *zampolit* could gain much comfort from such sources, and the widespread decline of the Communist party's authority in the recent past can hardly have helped.

Yet we should not dismiss the *zampolit*. Even if his earnest exposition of Marxism-Leninism often falls on deaf ears, his function as a political invigilator is probably of enhanced importance at a time of change, when a divergence of interests threatens the relationship between party leadership and army. Interestingly, the Chinese army strengthened the authority of its political officers following the bloody repression of the democracy movement in 1989. The government recognised that its very life depended on military support, and feared (with good reason, for some 3,500 officers are under suspicion of failing to oppose the democracy movement, and the commander of the 38th Army was court-martialled) that the rot had crept into the armed forces. It remains to be seen whether the considerable effort devoted to ensuring the political reliability of the Chinese army bears fruit, or whether the army is more profoundly shocked by what it did in Tienanmen Square than its impassive face suggests.[63]

Many young men, Russian or American, British or German, have required little in the way of patriotic urging to persuade them to enlist. To thousands of the volunteers who flocked to the recruiting offices in August 1914 the war was a great adventure, an opportunity to escape, albeit temporarily, from a humdrum existence, and a challenge to manhood. Their education had prepared the way by stressing the merits of nationalism and the virtues of abnegation and sacrifice. The English middle classes, nurtured in the public schools with generally authoritarian values and emphasis upon physical achievement, responded enthusiastically to the challenge. Between 1914 and 1916, 41.7 per cent of professional men volunteered, compared with an average 29.4 per cent across all occupations: of the 1913 Oxford University matriculants, an awful 31 per cent of those who served were killed.[64] Bartov emphasises the contribution made to German fighting morale by officers who were Nazi party members: they tended to come from middle-class backgrounds, to be far better educated than their comrades, and to have been at university when the tide of Nazism was running strong.[65]

We should also note the influence of pre-service military training upon Soviet youth. The Pioneers, joined by most children at the age of nine, offer preliminary military training, while in the Komsomol, joined at fourteen, 'orienteering and grenade throwing, drill and the stripping and shooting of the Kalashnikov assault rifle are as much a part of the training as erecting a tent or lighting a camp fire.'[66] If we compare the conditioning effect of such environments with the pervasive anti-military sentiments among the teaching staff of American universities in the 1960s, we might be less surprised at the intensity of opposition to the Vietnam War.

The process of conditioning starts long before school. De Vigny traced his own 'uncontrollable longing for military glory' to his father's stories. 'He showed me war in his wounds,' he wrote, 'in the patents of nobility and the heraldic blazons of his ancestors, in their great armoured portraits which hung in an old castle in the Beauce.'[67] D.M. Mantell, in his comparison of Green Berets and war resisters, identified marked differences in the family backgrounds of his subjects. The families which produced Green Berets tended to have one dominant parent, to emphasise material possessions, order and discipline, and to apply threats and punishments, in contrast to the more liberal values in the families of conscientious objectors.[68]

The moulding effect of parental attitudes is also suggested by the frequency with which the sons of serving officers and soldiers themselves join the army. Twenty-one per cent of the candidates for commissions in the British army between 1973 and 1977 were the sons of officers (19 per cent) or soldiers (2 per cent). They enjoyed a high chance of passing the Regular Commissions Board: 100 per cent of the soldiers' sons and 45 per cent of officers' sons were successful. In contrast, although 35 per cent of the sample came from civilian professional or managerial backgrounds, only 36 per cent of them passed the board.[69] No less than 42.87 per cent of German *Kriegsakademie* entrants in the period 1921–34 were the sons of officers or NCOs, and over roughly the same period some 28 per cent of all German officers came from officer families.[70] The American figure is somewhat lower, with 8–12 per cent of each West Point class composed of the sons and daughters of career military personnel, rising to 20 per cent at the Air Force Academy.[71] As far as Russia is concerned, Christopher Donnelly observes that 'one of the most

interesting trends of the last two decades has been the development
. . . of an officer corps which is not only an elite, but an hereditary
elite'.[72]

Art and literature also help to shape attitudes. The military artists
of the late nineteenth century, from Detaille and de Neuville to
Lady Butler and Caton Woodville, had a fondness for the heroic,
with wild-eyed defenders firing their last cartridges, or the line of
Scots Greys thundering out of the smoke. Photography took some
time to displace the war artist, and even then technical limitations,
euphemistic convention, official censorship and sometimes plain
deceit combined to limit its impact. Some of the best-known shots of
dead in the American Civil War had been artistically arranged by the
photographer, with bodies thoughtfully deployed to best advantage,
and even Robert Capa's famous 'Death in Action' from the Spanish
Civil War is now suspect. Combat photography came of age in the
Second World War, and grew to vigorous maturity in post-1945
conflicts, with Tim Page's work from Vietnam as its paradigm.

Feature films made early attempts to portray the hard edge of war,
and an honourable tradition runs from *The Big Parade* through *All
Quiet on the Western Front* to *Full Metal Jacket*. Just as strong a chain
connects romanticised war films, with John Ford's majestic US
cavalry pieces forming perhaps its strongest links and John Wayne
as its classic heroic role model. A growing appetite for designer
violence is demonstrated by the colossal success of *Rambo* at one
extreme and *Top Gun* at another. It would be attractive to conclude
that the romantic and realistic balance one another out, and that for
every young man enthralled by *Rambo* there is another shocked
by *Hamburger Hill*. We should be less confident. Oliver Stone's
Oscar-winning *Platoon*, undoubtedly one of the most important
of the Vietnam films, is unashamedly realistic, and its emphasis
on racial tension, drug abuse and sheer violence persuaded the US
Army to have nothing to do with it. Some of its audience, however,
found a dark beauty in its savagery, leading Peter Biskind, editor of
American Film, to claim that: 'A lot of kids go to the film dressed in
fatigues and combat gear. They get off on the violence and atrocities.
I hope they come out chastened but I'm not sure.'[73] *The Deer Hunter*
was watched enthusiastically by troops on their way to the Falklands,
another indication that realism is anything but repellent.

For the young men who make up the bulk of armies, film and video
have elbowed popular literature from the centre of the stage, and it

has less influence upon them than on their fathers or grandfathers. The generation-moulding appeal once exercised by authors, with Rudyard Kipling as the classic case in point, now comes from the moving image rather than the written word. Nevertheless, military literature is not only copious but widely read, and a glance at almost any bookstore suggests that publishers agree with Thomas Hardy that: 'War makes rattling good history but peace is poor reading.' The effects of war literature parallel those of film. Even those books which take an uncompromisingly realistic stance are read avidly by men who might themselves become involved in battle, and show no signs of having their stomachs turned by strong meat. *The Deer Hunter* was popular on the way down to the Falklands: but so too were war books. It is difficult to reach a balanced verdict even upon something as apparently clear-cut as the effect of the First World War's literature upon the generation which was to fight the Second. If Aldington, Barbusse or Remarque inspired men to believe that there could be no more war, then Jünger, doyen of the 'patriotic realist' school, trickled the addictive tang of test and sacrifice into inter-war German youth.

The changing political situation of the 1990s will inevitably affect the composition of armies. As they shrink with the reduction of perceived threat, so conscription will become at once less necessary and more difficult to justify politically. Professional armies will seem increasingly attractive, although the early evidence suggests that the improvement in superpower relations is dissuading young men from entering what they see as an increasingly pointless profession. The military response to recruitment and retention difficulties will be to press for improvements in pay and conditions of service – in other words, to increase the mercenary component of motivation – citing worsening personnel shortfalls as the justification for spending serious money on packages designed specifically to retain trained manpower. It should also embody a deliberate appeal to the volunteer spirit, by making military training genuinely challenging and exciting, and by including a much-increased emphasis on combating environmental problems or natural disasters.[74]

But what of the conscript component of military service? Although armies will become smaller, the recruiting pool shallower, and the public justification for conscription thinner, the arguments against it are by no means one-sided. The narrowly military case rests on the need to retain a large-scale mobilisation capability for the sort of major conflict which would be beyond the capability of a small largely professional force. The moral case is, I believe, far stronger. If the army de Vigny described was a closed corporation of poor men, well-paid professional armies risk becoming introspective groups of comfortably-off ones. Defence becomes walled up in the ghetto of professional self-interest and public ignorance: the defence of the state becomes a task gratefully entrusted to the few by the many. There is thus a strong case for retaining (or reintroducing) conscription. Not the soulless servitude of bulled boots and snoring barrack-rooms, but a genuinely national service, with a substantial non-military element, which emphasises that defence, be it against flood or foe, is a collective responsibility.

Soldier Boys

Twenty years ago the statement that combat is the business of young men would have been unexceptionable. That it is largely fought by the young remains unassailably true, but we can be less confident about the combatant's gender. The outlines of this particular battlefield, for such it has become, cannot be sketched out quickly, for they comprehend much of what goes on in military units. Wars have been fought by young men organised in groups, their tribal markings of berets, arm patches or jump boots as distinctive as the war-paint of the Plains Indian or the head-dress of the Zulu warrior, often mirroring the ritual dress of an urban gang (studded jackets here, shoulder-chains there) or the supporters of an English soccer club (red and white scarves here, blue and white there). The comparison is more than merely superficial, for there are striking parallels between the behaviour of young men in tribes, gangs and armies. The concept of initiation into the male group exists in all three – what Bruce Chatwin in *The Songlines* called 'a symbolic battle' in which the young man proves his virility. Tests – from ritual circumcision to completion of basic training – alcohol, and combat itself may all have a part to play in the process. The behaviour of English soccer supporters is currently a cause of much soul-searching. However much we may disapprove of the phenomenon, these uniformed figures often display bravery and cunning, as well as a good deal of naked savagery, which we might commend if only the uniform and the cause were different. There may be an element of truth in suggestions that such behaviour is the result of deprivation – of job, money, parental guidance or school discipline: but the fundamental motive is the need to hunt with the pack, to gain status in the tribe.

Sociologists and practical soldiers alike have focused on the function of small-unit cohesion in persuading soldiers to fight, and this point richly merits emphasis. S.L.A. Marshall, for all his lack of academic rigour, is unquestionably right to affirm that 'one of the simplest truths in war [is] that the thing which enables an infantry soldier to keep going with his weapon is the presence or presumed presence of a comrade'.[75] Alexander George wrote of Korea that: 'The most significant persons for the combat soldier are the men who fight by his side and share with him the ordeal of trying to survive.'[76]

The cohesion of these groups is forged in training which gives their members not merely relevant technical expertise but, no less significantly, a sense of community and shared identity – what Marshall called 'the habit of working with the group' – at once increasingly important and difficult to attain as Western society becomes more individualistic. Effective training is rarely painless, nor should it be: Marshall observed that the quickest way of losing a battle was to do so because the troops were not physically hard enough.[77] There is also an identifiable relationship between the toughness of training and the cohesion of the group that emerges from it, and slogans like 'Sweat Saves Blood' and 'Train Hard – Fight Easy' point to an essential truth.

There is a hard side to this. Brutality in training was long a feature of armies, and even after the Second World War a minority of instructors at training depots in both Britain and America lent weight to their lessons by a cuff round the head – or worse. Training in the Soviet army is notably harsh. One Russian writer opined that 'training that does not involve tactical pressures and dangers of warfare is not adequate', and it is clear that some of these stresses are imposed by instructors' fists as well as comrades' boots.[78]

Excesses committed during training have recently attracted publicity on both sides of the Atlantic. They fall into two broad categories. The first consists of pressure applied by instructors who in some cases mean well but lose their sense of proportion or are inadequately supervised, and in others behave with gratuitous violence. The second comprises a variety of 'initiation tests' or 'punishments', often inflicted on the soldier by his own comrades. We may understand, if not always justify, the former, for those training soldiers exercise a heavy responsibility and it is not easy to find the right balance between stick and carrot, a point often overlooked by investigative journalists in their haste to make copy at the army's expense. However, no army which properly calls itself civilised can tolerate the physical maltreatment of recruits by instructors. In an early draft of this book I speculated what effect the increasing openness of Soviet society has upon the way that the military machine conducts its business. The result has been predictable. A report of November 1989 spoke of 'nepotism, abysmal living conditions, and unpunished rapes'. Dissatisfaction with what goes on within the Soviet army has joined the pressures of nationalism (Georgian and Lithuanian conscripts are failing to report for service in growing numbers) in reducing the army's popular support.[79]

The training and bonding process does not end when a recruit leaves the depot to join his unit. Martin van Creveld rightly draws attention to the need to integrate the soldier into his unit, comparing the Second World War German practice of using march battalions and field replacement battalions to cushion the new soldier's arrival with the demoralising American habit of posting men in haphazardly from replacement depots.[80] The one-year tour in Vietnam had a logical basis, given Second World War experience of psychiatric casualties, but it had a baneful effect on unit cohesion as FNGs (fuckin' new guys) rubbed shoulders with men with 'short-timers' fever'. High-intensity combat which results in a heavy drain of casualties will make heavy demands on any replacement system, and simply to earmark 'Battle Casualty Replacements' (in the British army's endearing phrase) to units as required is likely to produce early demoralisation and battleshock. From 1916 British battalions in France maintained a '10% battle reserve', under the second-in-command, to serve as a nucleus for reconstitution, and an army which contemplates fighting a long high-intensity battle might do worse than to study this or the Second World War German example.

Collective training is also vital. As Major Vernon Humphrey, an experienced US Army trainer, has observed, most units preparing to go to Vietnam had less than ten days' total operating as a unit and not more than three consecutive days' predeployment training. Errors in personnel administration resulted in replacements arriving after planned predeployment training, so that units never had a chance to experience long-term operations under realistic conditions prior to combat itself. Moreover, the physical rigours of combat are very different from the sort of training prescribed by physical training experts. He concluded that:

> in analysing combat operations, about 80% of the outcome is attributable to proficiency in 'hard skills' – positioning weapons, accurate shooting, maneuvering, resupplying, and so on. These things can be trained. Of the remaining 20% (cohesion, determination, courage and so on) at least three quarters is a *byproduct* of training.[81]

For much of history military groups, well trained or not, were largely male. Some women disguised themselves as men, like Polly Oliver of the folk song, who determined to ' 'list for a soldier and follow my love'. Others, like Annie Etheridge in the American Civil War or Geneviève de Galard-Terraube at Dien Bien Phu, had an almost mascot-like function, their presence making men behave in a more manly fashion. There were also some notable individual female warriors – from Semiramis to Boadicea and Joan of Arc. But with rare exceptions, like the King of Dahomey's Amazon warriors, women were not generally admitted to a combat role except in armies undergoing revolutionary change, or guerrilla forces which had not yet adopted a stratified military organisation. They thus appear as combatants in the Red Army and in the Republican militias and the Spanish Foreign Legion in the Spanish Civil War. And, as Jillian Becker of the Institute for the Study of Terrorism observed: 'There are a lot of equal opportunities in terrorism.'[82] But as soon as the revolutionary ferment has died away, so women tend to occupy more conventional supporting roles. There were three all-women squadrons in the Second World War Red Air Force, and a few tank crew members and several snipers in the army, but the majority of women served as doctors, medical orderlies, clerks, cooks, typists and traffic police.[83] Samuel Rolbant emphasises that women in the Israeli army 'are not employed in combat duties', and Christopher Donnelly notes that: 'Women in the Soviet Armed Forces play a much smaller role in peacetime than is generally realised' – about 0.25 per cent of the army's strength as opposed to 4 per cent in the British armed forces. Their functions are largely administrative, and only the medical staff are usually found forward of regimental headquarters.[84]

This state of affairs is certain to change, though whether by evolution or revolution remains to be seen. There are, in the first place, serious demographic pressures which are currently reducing the male population of military age. The *Bundeswehr* faced the challenge by increasing conscript service from 15 to 18 months and reducing some units to cadre strength, but even so it expects an overall drop in manpower. Britain, which relies upon volunteers for its regular and reserve forces alike, must face statistics that show the male age group 16–19 will be 28 per cent smaller in 1994 than it was in 1985. This reduction in the recruiting pool will cause difficulties in itself, and these will be magnified by the efforts of other potential employers (and, indeed, the other services) to attract recruits. In December 1988, even before the demographic downturn had really begun to bite, the British armed forces as a whole were 4,000 below strength, and the situation in the infantry was especially serious.[85] Reduction in available manpower is one of the reasons behind President Gorbachev's desire to reduce the size of the Soviet army, and a similar, though less pronounced, manning shortfall will afflict the US Army.

One of the many possible solutions to the problem is to increase the proportion of women in the armed forces, and perhaps to permit them to occupy combat roles hitherto reserved to men. It is already evident that women carry out several military tasks every bit as well as male soldiers, and are better at some of them. In particular, their long attention span makes them well-suited to act as radio operators. Most of the signallers in my battalion headquarters were women. They remained alert at times when the martial zeal of their male counterparts was decidedly ragged, coped well with the rigours of living in the field, and, despite all my apprehensive cynicism, what one female officer called 'the hanky-panky factor' rarely created difficulties. The fact remained, however, that they, and their female colleagues who drove trucks or cooked, were not primarily combat soldiers. Though they carried weapons, they did so in self-defence.

There are already women soldiers with a combat role in Western armies. In an experimental measure in 1986, Denmark, caught by the demographic downturn, admitted about eighty women to combat roles – as armoured infantry soldiers, tank crew members, and gunners in artillery and air defence batteries. The experiment was judged a success, and women are now admitted to combat roles, though they have to pass precisely the same entrance tests as men. In

1989 the Canadian Armed Forces followed suit as their first woman infantry soldier joined the ranks of Princess Patricia's Canadian Light Infantry. Although legislative barriers obstruct the employment of women in the United States armed forces, the boundaries have already been fudged, since both navy and air force train women pilots and women have been allowed to participate in armoured warfare schools and general combat infantry training.[86] In 1989–90 the British armed forces expanded the role of women: the Royal Air Force is to train female transport pilots, and the Royal Navy to allow female personnel to go to sea. In neither of these cases will the tasks of these female personnel be primarily combat, but it is difficult to envisage a crew member on a warship not being in combat if the ship itself went into battle. The navy's experiment was greeted with strong criticism from sailors' wives, who feared that their husbands' long absences from home, the cramped conditions aboard a warship, and the allegedly promiscuous behaviour of female personnel would combine to wreck marriages.

Even a technical insistence that women are deployed in a combat support rather than an outright combat role makes little practical sense in view of the nature of modern war. During the invasion of Panama in 1989, US military policewomen were involved in combat, and many of the female soldiers deployed to the Gulf in 1990 have tasks which will inevitably place them at great personal risk. The prospect of young mothers coming home in body bags may be an appalling one, but it is an inevitable product of the expansion of women's military role.

The case against the admission of women to the combat role starts with the physical differences between the sexes. Hormonal differences make women less aggressive than men, who are also larger, heavier, faster, stronger and have more endurance. Women's capacity for becoming pregnant introduces an added problem in personnel management: in 1977 14.5 per cent of the US Army's female personnel became pregnant, and in Exercise *Nifty Nugget* the following year over a thousand pregnant soldiers were evacuated from Germany at a time of manpower shortage. The principal obstacle is not physical but psychological. Cohesive combat units are knitted together by male bonding, and the inclusion of women in such groups threatens the bonding process. Thus, runs the argument, even if women were capable of coping physically with battle, their presence in it would reduce the fighting efficiency of

221

their male comrades. Winding up his case, American analyst Jeff Tuten concludes that 'the primary function of the military services is to defend the American society, not to change it'.[87] There is also the as yet unappraised question of the effect of military marriages upon effectiveness in both peace and war, especially in the US Army, where about one quarter of all enlisted women have serving husbands.

The counter-arguments are as strenuously championed. First among them comes the indisputable fact that technological advances have made it easier for women to operate many weapons systems: technical skill is more important than physical stength if one is flying a jet fighter, for instance. The deepening of the battlefield means that female soldiers will be at risk even in non-combatant roles, so it is misleading to imply that while combat roles are dangerous, supporting tasks are safe. And, although little objective evidence exists of the effect of women members on the bonding of male combat units, studies of combat support and service support units suggest that bonding is not impaired.[88]

The lines of tension run deeper still. It is not only feminists who take the view that 'political stratification between the sexes is ultimately based on military considerations', and that men's desire to exclude women from combat therefore represents a wish to retain political power and to preserve a stereoypical ideal of the women as the subordinate housewife and mother.[89] Judith Hicks Stiehm has argued that admitting men and women to the military in equal numbers would so change military organisations that they would 'lose some of the coercive power which such institutions have over men'.[90] From an army's point of view she could scarcely have deployed a more telling argument *against* the cause she champions. While some women believe that the main function of the female soldier is 'to aid, to heal, to insure the survival of others', more militant theorists protest vigorously against what they see as 'this narrowly gendered image of womanhood', which makes the continuation of war more likely precisely because it rewards men who fight. Again, this is an argument which runs squarely at the self-interest of armies.[91]

We should not be surprised that feminist authors are passionately dissatisfied with armies' attitudes to women. For however rational the debate may be at one level, down among the cigarette-butts and beer-cans, male combat soldiers are deeply imbued with notions which feminists are bound to find offensive. Military language is a subject of its own, well described by Lucian Truscott as:

> fuelled by cigar smoke and mess hall coffee, greasy fatigues and scuffed boots, afternoons spent ghosting at the motor pool . . . full of aphorisms and clichés discarded by others, which [take] on new life and meaning in the coarse texture of a sergeant's timing and delivery.[92]

Feminising terms of abuse are common in recruit training – I recall one of my early attempts to unfix bayonets being rewarded by the comment that I looked like a pregnant nun. Similar denial of male status by attributing female characteristics to young men who fail martial tests has been noted in African and Plains Indian warrior societies.[93] The drill sergeant, a powerful mixture of father figure, role model and shaman, often encourages his charges to think of women as an underclass – the generic expression 'Susie Rottencrotch' features prominently at the US Marine Corps depot at Parris Island. Mantell observed that his Green Beret sample tended to be 'unscrupulous and unfeeling' in their relationships with women, and to feel contempt for women who slept with them. He quotes a joke meant to put Special Forces values in perspective: 'There's the key to my house. There's the key to my car. You can have my wife, my clothes, my home. But please don't wear my jump boots. I just spit-shined them.'[94]

Mantell's Green Berets were (or, at least claimed to be) sexually far more active than their conscientious objector counterparts. It is difficult to be objective about the nature of the average of 28.5 sexual contacts per man attributed to the Green Berets, but two tendencies emerge. First, prostitutes were widely used, not merely as a measure of convenience, but because they seemed to conform to the men's concept of woman as the underdog. Second, some women are drawn to macho men. As Rosemary Daniell put it in *Sleeping with Soldiers*, 'the more macho the man, the more traditionally feminine, passive and virtuous I felt'.[95] And yet (once again objectivity is veiled in mist) both the emotional balance and sexual tenderness of macho men has been questioned. 'Most of us', wrote one American woman who was a teenager during the Vietnam War, 'had our hopes set on that silent set of men who would not run away, but did not at all want to go to war; they seemed the best prospect for a reasonable combination of quality and quantity.'[96]

The notion of sexual conquest as male victory (the very term conquest says much) has wider implications. Rape in peacetime is concerned with much more than the release of sexual frustration, and it is no coincidence that the increasing tendency for rape to involve practices deliberately intended to degrade the victim has accompanied the rise of women in many professions once the preserves of men. Rape in wartime has even more primitive origins. It is in part a ritual humilation of the enemy warrior, a demonstration that he has been unable to fulfil that most basic of his duties, defence of his womenfolk. Early Israeli experience with mixed-gender combat groups showed that the groups' fighting effectiveness was reduced by men's anxiety to help women who were wounded, and even more so by their protective instincts if the women were in danger of capture. Such instincts cannot be legislated away or removed by logical argument.

'Soldiers should be young and fit, rough and nasty, not powder-puffs,' proclaimed a corporal in John Hockey's *Squaddies: Portrait of a Subculture*.[97] Much military training undoubtedly exaggerates the raw tribalism of young men, and in the process obscures virtues which have formed part of so many warriors' characters. Beowulf combined honour and gentleness, Chaucer's was 'a very perfect, gentle knight', and Kiowa warriors were often decribed as 'brave and courteous'. The samurai tradition blended physical courage and skill at arms with a refined aesthetic appreciation which enabled a warrior to compose an elegant death poem on the eve of battle. There is no inconsistency in the fact that Wolfe declared he would rather have written Gray's *Elegy* than take Quebec, that Lieutenant-Colonel Alan Hanbury-Sparrow read Francis Bacon's *Essays* while commanding his Royal Berkshire battalion at Passchendaele in 1917, or that Lieutenant Robert Santos found a book of poems in the pack of a North Vietnamese regular.[98] As Kipling wrote, 'single men in barracks don't grow into plaster saints,' and it would be unrealistic to expect training organisations to produce young soldiers with finely tuned artistic appreciation. Nevertheless, there is more to the warrior ethos than rough masculinity.

The reasons for male suspicions of women in the combat role may go beyond the assumption that political power and warrior status are closely linked or the chauvinistic disregard, shared in many working-class communities, for the position of women. Some argue that woman's ability to bear children gives her a gender-defined role which men may envy but not usurp, and perhaps the brittle character of the male orgasm increases tension. As Antonia Fraser wrote of the seventeenth century: 'The relative facts concerning the male and female orgasm being well understood, women were regarded in an uneasy light for being undeniably weaker – yet in certain circumstances insatiably stronger.'[99] Desire to preserve one area of uniqueness therefore encourages men to keep women out of combat. The analogy between battle and childbirth must not be taken too far, but it has an informative aspect. There has been substantial opposition to male midwives, on the grounds that women require the presence of another woman at their time of greatest need. Yet the majority of obstetricians are male, and they have long asssisted at birth without their gender causing disquiet. Might female resistance to male midwives not spring from similar motives to those which inspire male suspicion of female soldiers? The midwife's ability traditionally goes beyond the 'task specialism' of a male doctor: she is the 'wise woman', repository of ancient knowledge – and, in a sense, shaman in a way which mirrors the role of the drill sergeant for young men.

The combination of manpower shortages and female pressure will result in most Western armies accepting a greater proportion of women. There is certainly some room for expansion in the British army, although the US Army, which currently has rather more than twice the proportion of women in the British army (about 10 to 4 per cent), may have reached reasonable limits unless traditional barriers are to be crossed on a large scale. Crossing these barriers is unwise. Not primarily because women are physically or psychologically unable to participate in modern combat, but because their presence there risks destabilising male soldiers and weakening the cohesion of small units. There is also the likelihood that the inclusion of a substantial proportion of women in an army would so alter its character as to make it less attractive to male volunteers, and would thus increase recruiting difficulties. When most of my battalion headquarters radio operators were women, it was difficult to persuade male soldiers to do the job: it had become 'womens' work'.

A female officer recently asked me if I thought it fair that her own employability within the army should be restricted because of male attitudes. I do not: there is nothing fair about it. But then there is little fair or logical in the motives that make men fight. Tinkering with something as complex as combat motivation because of short-term constraints or feminist ideology will create more problems than it solves. In the long term things will change, as mixed-sex education and the advancement of women in other areas of society erode traditional attitudes to the bonding of combat groups. Western armies, in this as in much else, will tend to follow external events slowly. Across much of the world, where the role of women has been scarcely affected by the feminist revolution, change will be slower still.

Warriors and Bureaucrats

In his influential book *The Professional Soldier*, published a quarter of a century ago, Morris Janowitz established five working hypotheses for the evolution of postwar armies. There was a changing organisational authority, shifting from authoritarian domination to reliance on manipulation, persuasion and group consensus. Military and civilian elites were separated by a narrowing skill differential, as armies became more like civilian corporations. There was a shift in officer recruitment as a large peacetime military establishment (certainly something new in American history) demanded growing numbers of trained specialists. Career patterns assumed new significance as unconventional and adaptive careers gained entrance to the elite nucleus. Lastly, trends in political indoctrination were changing as the army became more explicitly political.

Charles Moskos's no less important work echoed some of Janowitz's arguments, and described a profound change in the character of the military, from one which inspired moral commitment and self-sacrifice to one whose relationship with its members was primarily contractual, based on material reward.[100] Although both wrote with particular reference to the US Army, their remarks reflected broadly comparable trends in several other armies, and were evident enough in the French army for one study of its postwar development to be entitled *Warriors to Managers*.[101] As we saw in the first section of the present chapter, the raw ingredients of these changes have long been present in armies, and it is reasonable to expect shifts in attitude to occur; quite rapidly in armies whose structure is easily amenable to external influence, and more slowly in armies which are resistant to such forces.

The passage of influence is certainly not a one-way process, for just as the military use of technology has often pointed the way to its civil application, so military structures and methods have helped shape the way that the civil community goes about its business. On occasion this is by direct interference in the governmental process, which may occur at a variety of levels, with the outright replacement of civil by military authority as its extreme form. The thesis that such usurpation of civil authority occurs most frequently in states with simple technical infrastructures, low level of political culture, and armies whose officer corps lacks a proper professional ethic is generally convincing.[102]

Despite concern that the technological muscle now at armies' disposal – especially in terms of communications, surveillance and automatic data processing – makes interference and control in the manner of George Orwell's *Nineteen Eighty-four* easier, the relatively small size of most national armies in relation to their population, and the interdependence of civil and military, combine with the above factors to restrict military control of government to parts of Africa, Asia and Latin America. For instance, the notion that the British army might mount a *coup d'état* is utterly implausible. Even if its long tradition of civil control, professional ethics and comfortable integration into society suddenly ceased to matter, quite how armed forces of 324,800 impose their will on a population of over 56 million is frankly puzzling. Investigative journalists write eagerly of plans for the imposition of rigid control during the run-up to general war, but from the military point of view it is clear that only the preservation of police primacy and maximum public consent would enable the state to continue its normal functions. You cannot marshal public opinion with barbed wire and bayonets. Those who foresee a 'military backlash' following the fall of Gorbachev might ask themselves whether the Soviet army could make its writ run effectively within the Soviet Union. Fear of being involved in internal security is currently one of the major motives behind the desertion of conscripts from the Soviet army, and there is a widespread feeling among junior and middle-ranking officers that the army exists to defend the people, not the state.

More plausible is Harold D. Lasswell's concept of the 'garrison state'. This envisages the growth of military authority within the state under the pressure of sustained international tension, with the military exercising power directly, or indirectly, with the support of political factions.[103] In one form this involves 'designed militarism', with the destruction or transformation of civilian institutions by the military. The Prussian example is the most striking, and its transmission, through the medium of General Emil Koerner, to Chile, and thence to Argentina and Bolivia, has marked our own times. A less self-willed form, 'unanticipated militarism', occurs because political leaders fail to act effectively and the military are drawn into the power vacuum. Some authorities argue that the Cold War, with the maintenance of large standing armies in peacetime and the continuation of high levels of defence expenditure, has produced a garrison state, with the 'military–industrial complex' – a persuasive phrase coined by President Eisenhower on relinquishing office in 1961 – as its most pervasive agency.[104] Others go further, adding gender dominance to produce male-garrisoned states: one such assessment lists the United States, the Soviet Union, Britain and Israel among societies in which 'militarization is rampant'.[105]

Although some aspects of the military-industrial complex rightly cause concern, and the question of defence expenditure is bound to remain contentious, in most of the developed world armies' demands upon states are subject to checks and balances which, in the main, work well. Indeed, from our present vantage-point it is hard not to see much of the debate on military influence upon the state as heavily outdated. There are several contemporary examples, on both sides of the political divide, of armies which are responding to reductions in size, funding and influence with good discipline, if not always with good grace.

If states are now far less threatened by the armies they control than some academics might have argued twenty years ago, armies themselves are in a less fortunate position. The trends observed by Janowitz have become increasingly marked since he first outlined them, and these, together with financial constraints and a sense of uncertain purpose in a changing world, pose a serious threat to the armies of most developed states.

The 'armies in crisis' thesis is familiar enough. Armies, runs the argument, have moved away from the 'institutional' model of being a profession *sui generis*, composed of warriors who are always on duty, whose task is to fight and win wars. They have instead come to resemble civilian occupations, their members doing jobs which do not differ fundamentally from those in the civilian community. In America, the move towards the occupational model was given a powerful impulsion by the Doolittle Report of May

228

1946, which responded to widespread dissatisfaction with military service during the Second World War by finding against the case for traditional barriers between officers and soldiers, and recommending a greater measure of democratisation. Although by no means all of its recommendations were implemented, the Doolittle Report set the agenda for the next twenty years. The 1970 *Report of the President's Commission on an All-Volunteer Armed Force* (Gates Commission Report) was explicitly occupational, arguing that recruitment would best be determined by the monetary values of the marketplace.

The aftermath of the Vietnam War saw a series of books criticise the United States military establishment for having lost the war by failing to display sufficient of the traditional virtues. Its officer corps, allegedly rotted by careerism, was a particular target of criticism. Some attacks came from the liberal left, which had little use for the military at the best of times; others from journalists or academics who sometimes strove to be even-handed and sometimes did not; and others from within the establishment itself, from officers or ex-officers who wrote in honest anguish.

The ferocity of the attacks, combined with the establishment's vigorous attempts to defend itself, make objective judgment difficult – although no impartial observer could fail to note the success with which the US Army ultimately emerged from the worst of the post-Vietnam blues. Nevertheless, two key trends can be identified amidst the tumult. First is the question of professional attitudes. A widely based study carried out by officers at the US National Defense University, whose objectivity is scarcely in question, affirmed 'that military officers in the Army, Navy and Air Force are approaching ambivalence toward their professional orientation. Moreover, they view their services as being more occupational than they are as individuals'. A serving general officer wisely writing under the *nom-de-plume* of Colonel Yasotay (a Mongol warrior who soldiered on unpromoted) made the same point in less smoothly edged terms: warriors did not get promoted – bureaucrats did.[106]

Next is the problem of attracting personnel of the right quality in an age when the humblest infantryman requires a wide range of skills, and technical requirements grow daily. However good the all-volunteer army has proved at recruiting overall numbers – and Caspar Weinberger hailed it as 'not just a success, but a huge success' – the composition of the post-draft forces causes legitimate concern.[107] Recruitment primarily by monetary inducement has led to the diminution of traditional military virtues, leading Moskos to complain that the volunteer army 'reduces an armed force to a form of consumerism, even hedonism, which is hardly a basis for the kind of commitment required in a military organization'. Although the army attracted a fair share of high school graduates, they tended to leave the service much more quickly than non-graduates. Moreover, 20 per cent of the US military was black, compared with 13 per cent of the young population: blacks formed 22 per cent of the enlisted force but only 6 per cent of officers. [108]

Ardant du Picq, writing prophetically about the declining quality of French officers in the years before the Franco-Prussian war, maintained that in a democratic society without a hereditary military class recruitment was directly related to pay, which in turn helped determine the soldier's social status. [109] The status of the officer in the US services has generally lagged behind that in other professional groups, well behind doctors, lawyers and university professors and just behind teachers, with local exceptions, especially before the Second World War, when the socialite connections of the navy and the army's Southern military family traditions both held sway. [110] Pay trailed behind civilian wages in the sixties, achieved parity in the early seventies, but soon slipped again: in the early 1980s the mismatch between civilian and military pay was marked. Increases since then helped considerably, although moonlighting remained common.

Most serious of all is the difficulty of attracting specialist personnel. General William E. DePuy observed that between 1983 and 1990 combat posts would shrink further at the expense of combat support and combat service support posts, increasing the overall level of technical skills required. 'With the current inventory of personnel,' he wrote, 'the army cannot meet the training prerequisites established by its schools.' He expected the most damaging shortfalls to occur in the air force, and a study published in 1983 lent substance to his fears, noting that over the previous four years 12,000 pilots and 5,000 navigators had left the air force for jobs in commercial aviation. [111] Several other observers have commented on the growing gap between the high-technology weapons entering service and the skills of the men who operate and maintain them, and technical errors under the stress of battle accounted for the shooting down of an Iranian passenger aircraft by the USS *Vincennes* in July 1988. [112]

Britain has had no lost war to arouse public passion and private grief, and there remains a general coincidence of military and civic values. The campaign in Ireland grinds on, but, if some of its characteristics set it apart from the mainstream of British experience of counter-insurgency, its small scale (only six of the army's 53 regular infantry battalions are resident there, although four more may be on temporary duty), relatively low casualties (barring bad luck a battalion might expect to lose as many soldiers from road traffic accidents in Germany as from bomb or bullet in Ireland), together with the army's solid grasp of the operational issues and generally high level of public support in mainland Britain have all helped prevent a long war from having dramatic effects upon the army. Yet the strains of the 1980s are showing. The downturn in recruiting cannot simply be attributed to the demographic trough: growing doubts as to whether the army has a meaningful role, dissatisfaction with pay and allowances, conflict between family life and the frequent moves entailed in military service, all play their part. Increases in voluntary resignations, especially among bright middle-piece officers, are creating a series of 'black holes' which will cause further damage as they work their way up the commissioned and non-commissioned hierarchy. A series of bullying scandals undermined public confidence, and the television film *Tumbledown* portraying the experience of a Scots Guards officer badly wounded in the Falklands, exposed the army to further criticism, much of it ill-informed.

Despite the fact that the Conservative government is as supportive as any government might reasonably be expected to be, the financial constraints under which the army operates cause palpable discomfort. Military pay has improved immeasurably from its lamentable position in the early 1970s, when moonlighting was rife and many military families received Supplementary Benefit from the state. Nevertheless, financial stringency provokes growing dissatisfaction. In 1987 Major Lord Morpeth resigned his commission 'to protest about the present government's defence policy, which is having damaging consequences on the training, equipment, manning and conditions of service of the Regular Army'. His forthright letter to *The Times* complained about shortages of spare parts and ammunition, inadequate pay rises and unfair allowances. A response from Field Marshal Lord Bramall questioned the wisdom of Morpeth's action, but went on to warn that 'year by year more and more servicemen and servicewomen will feel let down'.[113] Changes in the army's internal administration, introduced to give commanders financial responsibility, have produced much extra work and even more uncertainty, and economy-driven attacks on the allegedly dispensable 'tail' to strengthen the 'teeth' have added to the general air of overstretch, with commitments threatening to outstrip resources.

If the US Army still bears scars from the Vietnam War, the *Bundeswehr* shows older wounds. The militarisation of German society before the First World War and in the 1930s, coupled with the army's role in the preparation of two world wars and its involvement in contentious aspects of the Second, produced a fierce debate in West Germany on the nature of armed forces. It was natural that, in their efforts to distance themselves from an unpalatable past, the creators of Germany's new army should strive to create the ultimate in occupational armies. The soldier was a citizen in uniform, doing a job much like any other, his purpose primarily to reinforce deterrence, not to fight a war. He could vote and stand for election, join a professional association, and was not subject to an independent military judiciary. The concept of *Innere Führung* – inner leadership, developed by Count von Baudissin and his colleages in the 1950s, permeated the *Bundeswehr*. There was even a demand that the soldier should have only a single functional uniform – his work clothes – and in the event the *Bundeswehr*'s best uniform, with its squarely cut tunic and plain black shoes, was a deliberate retreat from the sartorial glories of *Kaiserheer* and *Wehrmacht* alike. Ironically, the East German army retained far more of the traditional trappings of German uniform.

Tension inevitably arose between the principles governing Baudissin's new model army and the views of the traditionalists, many of whom reappeared in uniform in the mid-1950s to provide the *Bundeswehr* with its senior and middle-piece officers. There were complaints that Baudissin had created an army that was fundamentally 'unsoldier-like', and it proved singularly difficult to translate some aspects of *Innere Führung* into everyday military reality. A 1970 White Paper went further towards defining the new German soldier, comparing him with workers in civilian services and industries, and a further study was initiated in 1985. This resulted in *Bundeswehr 2000*, which frankly addressed the problems of manpower shortages and financial restraint. Recognising that there was insufficient money available to increase the *Bundeswehr*'s volunteer component, the document proposed a restructured army which made greater use of reservists, and in which some battalions formed cadres for expansion on mobilisation.

Important though government policy documents are, they do not define attitudes, and the *Bundeswehr*'s officers have moved closer to the institutional model than the force's creators would have wished. A 1978 survey suggested that while *Bundeswehr* officers saw themselves as very similar to the members of comparable civilian groups, such as teachers or engineers, they believed that they were more conservative, patriotic and discipline-conscious than their civilian equivalents – and also that they were less careerist and not as concerned about income as members of other professions.

This drift towards a more conservative concept of the professional officer, and the development of a 'pragmatic' view of military service – in essence a compromise between the traditionalist and reformist views – is an uncertain one. Bernhard Fleckenstein identified differences between younger officers, influenced by the civilian-oriented education introduced in 1973, and their older colleagues, who tend to 'maintain their professional self-confidence and self-worth by reverting to conservative values and traditional military virtues'.[114] The lines of fracture are undoubtedly more complex than this, and many officers, not simply from the post-1973 generation, find Green politics and non-provocative defence attractive. The defence debate within German society will grow noisier as perceived threat wanes, and the army will find itself compelled to defend its position with increasing frequency. Some of its officers will do so bewailing the onset of careerism and bureaucracy, and pressing for a more institutional army. Others will respond by meeting the radicals on their own ground, and we may confidently expect that opposition to the modernisation of NATO's theatre nuclear forces, and perhaps to the stationing of allied forces on German soil, will come from within the *Bundeswehr* as well as outside it.

Many armies have witnessed growing tension between the soldier's military role and the demands made by his family. Family pressures have contributed to early resignations by officers and NCOs alike. A US Air Force survey of 1981 had shown that 66 per cent of enlisted wives and 45 per cent of officer wives had gainful employment.[115] I have discovered no comparable British statistics, but Ruth Jolly's admirable *Military Man, Family Man: Crown Property?* confirms that young service wives 'expected to continue in employment . . . until they started a family and most expected to resume working at some point after having children'.[116] Such attitudes have inevitably resulted in wives being less prepared to involve themselves in military activities than they once were. This became a major issue in the

United States in 1987, with widespread media attention. It has not attracted the same publicity in Britain, but it is none the less a widely observed fact. Mrs Sandy Gauvain, wife of a former officer, described life on the 'married patch' as an 'oppressive claustrophobic and anachronistic life led by women who have no status other than that conferred on them by their husband's rank . . . I think there is an increasing number of women who are saying: "That's it. I've had enough."'[117] When a former Regimental Sergeant-Major wrote sternly to *Soldier* magazine to take issue with working wives, a sharp volley of response announced that wives worked not only to make money but also to gratify 'pride and self esteem by pursuing a rewarding career outside the home'.[118]

We saw, earlier in this chapter, that fewer American officers were the sons of service personnel than in pre-war Germany or present-day Britain. The increasing proportion of West Point cadets of working-class origins encouraged Janowitz to declare that such recruitment makes 'the military as open a professional group as any in the United States'.[119] Although one commentator argued in 1974 that officer selection procedures in the British army were class-based and thus biased against candidates from working-class backgrounds, this is impossible to substantiate.[120] What can be demonstrated is that the proportion of officers coming from public (in American parlance private) schools has declined, and that the proportion of university graduates has increased.[121]

On the one hand this must be welcomed as evidence of the broadening social and intellectual breadth of the British officer corps. On the other, however, it is evidence that many of the traditional officer-producing schools are sending their boys elsewhere. A disproportionate number of public school entrants seek short-service commissions to use the army as a 'finishing school' between school and final career, which reinforces the view that the army is seen as a bad lifetime investment by a growing number of young men of the sort who provided it with generally gallant and well-motivated regimental officers for much of its history. R.G.L. von Zugbach has acutely observed the way in which many of the 'newcomers' have gravitated towards 'the less prestigious support arms', while control of the army remains the business of 'senior, policy-making posts . . . which exclude parts of the arm structure from entry. These excluded arms are the very parts of the system into which the newcomers to the system have been admitted'.[122] It is, in short, largely the reverse of the situation so hotly assailed by Colonel Yasotay. Clearly, neither is ideal. A system which disadvantages warriors in favour of bureaucrats meets some of the managerial attractions of a peacetime army, but is unlikely to produce cohesive units or effective combat leaders. One which ensures that traditionally based teeth arms dominate bears not a few of the hallmarks of long-standing British mistrust of technical education.

Such problems are not unique to Western armies. The Soviet army, combining increasingly complex equipment with a largely conscript force, uses officers, of which it has a higher proportion than most other armies, to carry out numerous 'hands on' tasks which would not be officer responsibilities elsewhere. It created, in 1972, the new rank of *praporshchik* (ensign or warrant officer) in an attempt to fill many junior command and technical specialist posts. There is a chronic shortage of officers, and frequent resignations testify that better career opportunities exist outside the military. If previous generations of Soviet officers gained comfort from the armed forces' primacy in terms of the state's resource allocation, today's will scarcely feel as confident, and neither this, nor the results of the war in Afghanistan, is likely to enhance the attraction of a military career.

Much has been done to address the problems in the US forces. The COHORT project recognised the value of training soldiers together and keeping them in the same group throughout their tour of duty. It failed to develop along the lines of the British regimental system, as some of its supporters had hoped it would, but it did point in the right direction. At the same time the US Navy's Operation *Pride* and the USAF's Project *Warrior* emphasised tradition, service pride, and leadership rather than management. An enthusiastic article on 'The Military's New Stars' reported the success achieved by a group of brigadier-generals in a testing programme at the Center for Creative Leadership: on IQ tests they emerged in the top 95th percentile of the nation; all but a handful had advanced degrees; and they were judged to be 'more responsible, dominant, self-assured, achievement oriented and psychologically healthy' than their business counterparts. John Keegan observed that: 'The US has the best-educated officer corps in the world. It has the best-educated officer corps that has ever existed in any country'.[123]

There is undoubtedly much further to go. The authors of the 1984 National Defense University study make judicious recommendations for changing the trends which they see as undermining cohesion, and demand a return to traditional military values at the expense of purely rational management analysis. At a higher level, many commentators agree with Congressman Les Aspin, chairman of the House Armed Service Committee, that the forces' 'cumbersome bureaucratic structure' impedes efficiency. John Keegan points out that, man for man, the US Army generates less combat power than its allies – and he could as well have added its potential opponents too. The *Bundeswehr*, with 340,000 troops, fields 12 divisions: the US Army, with 771,000, only 18. The British army, with 162,000 men, produces 75 infantry and armour battalions: the US Marine Corps, with 196,000 has 33. Keegan acknowledges that comparisons are inexact, but suggests geography and function cannot fully account for the differences.[124] He recommends that the individual service baronies should be subordinated to a strong central authority and organised functionally. Richard Gabriel, one of the military's sternest critics, makes a similar recommendation, arguing that the Joint Chiefs of Staff should be replaced by a muscular single-service general staff. He also presses home the now-familiar attack on the army's structure, arguing that it must become 'a true profession, and not just one more enterprise awash in the sea of a free society'.[125]

This demand for warriors rather than bureaucrats is certain to remain strident in America. In Europe, the effects of the diminishing recruiting base will loom larger, and it is hard to see how a real crisis can be averted in Britain. Other European armies are able to achieve some flexibility by their varying conscription terms, and reducing battalions to cadres does not produce the same military grief or political acrimony as it does in Britain. The regimental system makes the British problem all the more acute. The manpower shortfall is at its worst in the infantry, but disbanding battalions to reflect demographic logic or changes in deployment may weaken a structure which needs all the help it can get. The regiment confers a tribal status of its own, no less useful in peace than in war, and attempts to 'rationalise' that complex and emotional world of cap-badges and collar-dogs will undoubtedly create tensions.

It is symptomatic of the British army's character as 'a collection of regiments in voluntary association' that the regimental system provokes such intense debate. This is no place to follow its detail, but two points deserve emphasis. The first is that the regimental system is far more flexible than its defenders often acknowledge.

It has coped well in the past with amalgamations and with changes of role: infantry battalions became anti-tank or armoured regiments and did their new jobs perfectly well. Young officers and soldiers are usually more adaptable than their seniors assume, and the broad cloak of the regimental system can cover radically new organisations. Conservative military men tend to be preoccupied with form rather than with function, and the case of the regimental system shows it. It would be perfectly possible for 1st Loamshires to cease being a four-company infantry battalion and to consist instead of two tank companies, a mechanised infantry company and a self-propelled artillery battery. It would be equally possible for a proportion of its soldiers to be reservists, buckled on to a permanent cadre.

If it is clear that the regimental system is actually extremely flexible, it is no less clear that it is a great deal more than an amusing historical survival roaming free in the great British theme-park. A French report published in early 1990 concluded that French conscripts were 'fragile, individualistic and little inclined to put up with frustration'. The study looked admiringly at Britain, declaring: 'The system of regiments enables the British to get a higher quality from a force of such small dimensions.'[126] The regimental system confers tangible benefits and is worth preserving, but to survive it must change with the times, all the more so in the 1990s as the regimental mafia in government and Parliament, a residue of the Second World War and National Service, fades away. To march on into the next decade the regimental system will need to justify itself to men with no personal experience of its extraordinary appeal.

The coincidence of reduced threat and demographic trough (in fact no real coincidence, for manpower difficulties undoubtedly influenced Gorbachev) will encourage politicians on both sides of the Atlantic to cut establishments to match resources, and conscription in Europe will grow in unpopularity as the perceived need for it diminishes. Although sociologists and practical soldiers can be brought to uncharacteristic agreement on the need to create and sustain cohesive combat units, bound together by ties of loyalty and comradeship and led by men who view their profession as a calling not a career, it is no easy task to maintain essentially spiritual values in an increasingly materialistic world. Yet maintain them we must, or armies will become mere uniformed corporations. No danger to governments or economies, perhaps, but no use for defence in a world which is far from free of tigers. This chapter opened with a quotation from Alfred de Vigny, struggling to find a context for the military ethos in peacetime. It closes with one which may be no less perceptive as once-sharp certainties fade. 'When a modern army ceases to be at war,' de Vigny wrote, 'it becomes a kind of constabulary . . . It is a body searching high and low for its soul and unable to find it.'[127] The burden of the search will fall most heavily upon senior officers, and we must now consider the way they are responding to the challenges of peace and war alike.

6

Man under Authority

For I am a man set under authority, with soldiers under me: and I say to one 'Go' and he goes; and to another 'Come' and he comes; and to my slave 'Do this' and he does it.

Luke 7.8

A French colonel, runs the story, was seriously wounded, and Napoleon's surgeon, Baron Larrey, removed his brain in a field hospital. At that moment one of Napoleon's aides rushed in with the news that the Emperor had promoted the colonel to general for his outstanding bravery. The new general sat up, saluted, and left the hospital at once. 'Wait a minute,' called Larrey, 'you have forgotten your brain.' 'It doesn't matter,' replied the general, 'I don't need it now that I'm a general.' It takes an uncommonly agile mind to connect a Napoleonic joke to Taoist philosophy but Martin van Creveld does it by pointing to Lao Tsu's dictum that:

> . . . advantage is had
> from whatever there is;
> but usefulness rises
> from whatever is not.

Just as the best government, in Lao Tsu's terms, was that which governed least, and was therefore least perceptible to the governed, so the best military command would be that which commanded least, because all the elements of an ideal army would instinctively know what was to be done.[1]

There are few times when the gulf between the real and the ideal is wider than in war; few organisations that have to contend with

239

more chance and uncertainty than armies. An army's problem is complicated because although success in combat is one of its major objectives, it spends the majority of its time not fighting. Despite all our fondness for comparing armies with commercial companies, we should not lose sight of the fact that firms spend most of their time engaged in their principal function. Banks lend money, trucking companies haul goods, and so on: if they ceased doing so they would go out of business. Modern armies, however, fight infrequently. Even the British army, which has had soldiers killed in action in every post-Second World War year except one, has no recent experience of a broad tract of military operations; the *Bundeswehr*, with its deservedly outstanding reputation, has never fought at all; and the Soviet army, despite its recent experience in Afghanistan, has not deployed a tank division in battle since 1945.

If we were to wander down the corridors of power in the Pentagon or Whitehall (and pretty stark corridors they are too) we would find that most of the officers and officials busy at their desks were occupied with things which have little direct concern with the business of fighting. Some labour in the vineyard of long-term financial planning, pruning projects here and there to allow for the growth of a new Main Battle Tank or medium howitzer. Others plow the lonely furrow of personnel administration, marshalling confidential reports for promotion boards, impelling the fortunate upwards and reminding the less lucky that not everyone has a baton in his knapsack. Public information departments stand ready to deal with storm damage, doctrine branches survey the landscape and plan to beautify the distant view, and the seasonal committees clatter on like combine harvesters – though sometimes their ability to discriminate between wheat and chaff becomes blurred. The most senior officers, whose experience and aptitude fit them for contributing so much, often contribute comparatively little, for their long, diary-driven days rarely allow them to rise above tomorrow's hedgerows to glimpse next year's far crests.

Much of an army's effort is expended on the business of day-to-day existence. The skills required are similar to those in any large corporation, and capacity for marshalling a well-argued case or producing an instant financial saving are more useful than the ability to inspire a tired battalion on the march or to launch an armoured regiment in a counterstroke. Yet most armies habitually expect those who excel at the former to be equally competent at the latter. In civilian organisations an individual's ascent of the hierarchy tends to progressively distance him from what goes on at the coal face, so much so that theorists and managers alike recognise the danger of losing touch with the lower echelons. In armies, in contrast, the dictates of well-rounded career development propel individuals between radically different appointments. This has undeniable advantages, for it is salutary – after serving, say, in a major's appointment in a headquarters – to be posted as second-in-command of a battalion to regain contact with grubby and profane reality. The disadvantages are just as striking, for officers are stretched across a wide band of expertise, wider than some of them can bear.

A British lieutenant-colonel needs to be well reported on in command and on the staff if he is to hope for promotion. First, perhaps, comes command of his infantry battalion in the United Kingdom (its *Saxon* wheeled APCs parked on the square behind an Edwardian redbrick barracks in Bulford or Tidworth) with a five-month emergency tour in Ulster (the terraced houses and gaunt flats of Belfast, or the lush but lethal bandit country of South Armagh). He is monarch of all he surveys, a watchful adjutant at one elbow and the regimental sergeant-major with all the tensile strength of the sergeants' mess at the other. He dispenses summary justice – fine here, confinement there – and has immense and lasting impact on the careers of officers and senior NCOs. His brigade commander – a man of influence, for it is he who writes our colonel's confidential report – recognises that there are regimental recesses into which he should not pry. Paper cannot be ignored, for there are accounts to audit and reports to write, but people matter most, from the normally chatty corporal whose unfamiliar silence betokens the disintegration of marriage, bank-account, or both, to the jovial second-in-command whose loyal bonhomie cannot veil his dwindling hope of appearing on the annual Pink List ('officers provisionally selected for promotion to the substantive rank of lieutenant-colonel'). Tactical theory among the rolling ridges of Salisbury Plain jostles tactics of a different sort as the battalion prepares for Northern Ireland. In all, it is totally absorbing and immensely satisfying, marred only by a battalion programme crammed to bursting point and the uncomfortable realisation that there are more seats in the backs of those *Saxons* than there are soldiers to fill them.

Next, our hero leaps from the fire of command to the frying pan of the staff, a Grade One appointment in the Ministry of Defence

Main Building in Whitehall. Does he leave his wife a rustic retreat and live in London for the week, uproot her to a married quarter in the capital, or commute in from the more distant suburbs? The pinstriped worsted, striped cotton and paisley silk of London replaces the camouflaged uniform of the Plain, and status changes radically in this new world where colonels are commonplace and brigadiers do their own photocopying. People are submerged by paper, and the discipline of drafts, redrafts, the incessant telephone, and a superior who himself arrives early and leaves late, extend the limits of the working day. Mist shrouds the future. The annual confidential report, once such a fruitful source of humour ('I would not breed from this officer.' 'This officer should go far. He should start right away.') is read with pounding heart and bated breath, and the eyes dart to the boxes on page three: even EXCELLENT is no guarantee of success, while VERY GOOD, in an appointment like this, is the professional death-warrant. The tight perimeter of the battalion is a million miles away.

It is a truism to say that our lieutenant-colonel is still the same man. Of course he is: but he is expected to display such a wide range of skills in these two very different appointments – and keep fit and stay married into the bargain – that he might almost not be. Luck, ever-present on the battlefield, is scarcely less prevalent in peacetime careers: old affections, loyalties and enmities cast long ripples, and a well-publicised mishap can have disastrous consequences. Sensitive career management ('friends in high places' to the cynic) can help by ensuring that a highly competent commander is not overfaced by a taxing staff appointment but earns his staff recommendation in an easier-paced post; but if this is overdone there are dark whispers about 'ticket punching'. In the old regimental armies the colour of a button or symbol on a cap-badge matter enormously. The Prussian 3rd Foot Guards was a veritable nursery of generals, and the British Royal Green Jackets is scarcely less.

This example has been British, but there are clear parallels in most major armies. The 1984 US National Defense University study cited in Chapter Five argued that the attempt to produce 'jacks of all trades' had gone too far. It suggested that a specialist General Staff Corps should be created, consisting of officers 'who need not possess the empathic, interpersonal skills of leaders. They would fill staff positions at all levels up to and including the Vice Chief's position and the Joint Chiefs of Staff'.[2] The difference between the

British/American and the Prussian/Soviet general staff traditions has already been alluded to, and the creation of 'blue ribbon' general staffs would go some way towards ending the current attempt to create men for all seasons.

Having criticised the US Army for careerism and mismanagement during the Vietnam War, Richard Gabriel mounted a determined assault on what he regarded as American military failure between 1970 and 1983. He singled out the excessive size of the officer corps for particular criticism, noting that there was 1 officer for 9.4 soldiers in the Second World War, 1 for 8.5 during Vietnam, and 1 for 6.8 in 1985, and went on to point to excessive turbulence, with eighteen-month tours of duty commonplace. Between 1960 and 1980 four-star generals averaged twenty months on station, and brigadier-generals averaged less than two years. Gabriel looked admiringly to Britain and Canada, where he believed that five-year tours were the norm, though in fact the two-year tour is far closer to reality in Britain than he suggests.[3] Between 1975 and 1980 British army officers moved house an average of four times, while soldiers moved an average of three times. These figures do not all imply a change of appointment, for they reflect unit as well as individual moves, but they indicate turbulence which was serious enough to warrant a study with the optimistic title 'Towards a More Stable Army'. This met with a lukewarm response: the unattractiveness of long tours in Germany and the infantry's concerns about loss of flexibility and the weakening of the regimental system played their part in undermining the 'Stable Army' proposals. The British army does, however, have a smaller officer–man ratio than its United States counterpart, with 1 officer to 8.3 soldiers.[4]

General Sir Frank Kitson, whose idiosyncratic humour and prominence in theorising on low-intensity operations made him a distinctive figure in the post-war British army, was alarmed at the impact of turbulence on senior appointments in the British army. 'A series of radical and energetic officers relieving each other in an appointment at short intervals will achieve less than one sensible person who remains in post for a longer period,' he maintained.[5] Kitson also identified what he termed 'rank inflation' but an American would term 'grade creep'. This is a favourite target for military reformers and defence economists, who are fond of demonstrating that while armies shrink the proportion of senior officers grows: Kitson observed that the British army of 1956 was roughly three times bigger than in 1986, but had only one-third more generals. Some armies manage to cope with far fewer senior officers than others. Comparisons, as ever, are inexact, but in 1986 in the fully-mobilised West German army there was one major-general or more senior officer to 25,000 soldiers, one to 13,000 in the United States, one to 8,200 in France and one to 4,500 in Britain.[6] In peacetime, when there are no reservists added to bring armies up to their mobilised strength, the ratio tends to be worse. The 1986 British National Audit Office report suggested that 'The UK might have a higher proportion of officers, particularly of senior rank, than many other countries.' Some of the newspaper articles it inspired demonstrated that was a kindly under-statement. *The Economist* reported that the British proportion of senior officers in all services (including brigadiers) to men was four times the American proportion and nearly three times higher than in France or West Germany. *The Daily Telegraph*, again including brigadiers in its comparison, observed that the British army had 258 generals to 435 US Army generals: one general to 612 peacetime soldiers in Britain, and one to 1,784 in the USA.[7] Further inconsistencies appear when comparing the same nations' three services. In 1985 the British army had 87 generals to 249,000 men, the RAF 56 air marshals to 94,000, and the Royal Navy 51 admirals to 77,000. Kitson sharply pointed out that 'if the ratio of admirals to men was right, then the army should have had 208 generals instead of 87, whereas if the ratio of generals to men was right, the navy should have been able to manage on 22 admirals instead of 51'.

It is easy to attack all this as mere careerism, to pour scorn on a system which produces more generals than regiments, and to observe that some leading figures of military history achieved great results despite relatively low rank. James Wolfe died winning Canada for Britain as a major-general; Moltke's 'demigods' in 1870 were colonels; Ludendorff found it extraordinarily difficult to promote his artillery expert, Georg Bruchmuller, from lieutenant-colonel to colonel; several highly competent Second World War US corps commanders did not outrank their own divisional commanders, and Omar Bradley commanded 12th Army Group as a lieutenant-general, while his British counterpart Montgomery was a field marshal. As John Keegan has reminded us, the British-Indian army of 1936, about the size of the British army today, was commanded by four generals, three lieutenant-generals and twenty major-generals: its thirty-nine brigadiers held the substantive rank of colonel.

There is, though, some genuine basis for rank inflation. When financial constraints prevent an overall rise in military pay, increasing the rank attached to an appointment enables its holder to be better rewarded. Tri-service or international staff appointments encourage upgrading to bring their holders into line with other services or allies, and some nations have more administrative posts in military rather than senior civilian hands. In Britain and elsewhere the need to provide officers with careers to the age of fifty-five encourages the construction of a pyramid which tapers less sharply than utilitarian logic demands. Suggestions that greater stability could be introduced into the US Army by ending the 'up or out' principle and guaranteeing careers to the age of fifty, thereby keeping more experience in the army and reducing the strain imposed on the budget by pensions, might create demands for a similar bulging of the pyramid. Indeed, at exactly the same time that some reformers in the United States support longer careers in the cause of more stability, the contrary argument has been used in Britain, where 'careers to 55', combined with allowances which help keep officers in the service, fuel rank inflation, for instance by enabling some officers to reach brigadier towards the end of their career to exercise a command which would not rate a single star elsewhere.

Enlisted structures have already swollen to become pear-rather than pyramid-shaped. Charles Moskos observed that the US Army's modal enlisted pay grade had been E1 in 1935, E2 in 1945, and was E4 in 1967.[8] The sharp difference in enlisted rank structure between the British and US armies prevents meaningful comparison, but the number of sergeants in the British infantry has shot up over the past two decades, first with the promotion of Mortar Fire Controllers and then, massively, with the creation of rank-rich armoured infantry battalions.

All this may be regarded as more evidence of the swing, explored in the previous chapter, from the military as an institution, with traditional structure and values, to an occupation, reflecting the logic of the marketplace. The frequently reiterated attacks on careerism imply exactly that: individuals are placing their own material benefits above the broader good of the organisation. However, we must guard against the assumption that things have only recently deteriorated, and that there was once a golden age when all officers were knightly figures, untouched by materialistic values and imbued with a fine sense of honour.

That elegant façade has numerous cracks. Edward Coffman wrote of the US Army 1815–60 that:

> Although there may have been the romantic, literary image of officers as chevaliers, patriotic gentleman at arms who dedicated their lives to the country, and perhaps some endeavoured to live that legend, others were attempting to keep in step with a nation caught up in a materialistic whirl as the richness of the land and the effects of the industrial revolution seemed to offer up limitless prospects.[9]

It was not merely that civilian life seemed to offer better prospects, but the utter boredom of garrison life drove many officers to drink or resignation – the future General U.S. Grant among them. Among the West Point graduates who rose to prominence in the Civil War there were as many who had left the army before it as could boast of uninterrupted military service.

West Point graduates stayed in the army longer after the Civil War: pay was better, promotion quicker, the officer's social status had improved – and there was more for him to do; but the race for promotion saw political string-pulling on a massive scale. J.J. 'Black Jack' Pershing was undoubtedly an officer of outstanding merit, but his promotion straight from captain to brigadier-general owed much to political contacts, and his opponents' efforts to thwart the move were less than edifying.

Despite the importance accorded to the French army during the Second Empire, officer morale dwindled as the Franco-Prussian war approached. Low pay made the profession unattractive, and visible poverty helped lower the officers' standing in society: the pay rise announced in 1868 was the first general increase since 1837 and (as is so often the case with 'catching up' pay rises) arrived in stages and lost some of its value.[10] Force reductions announced in 1865 slowed promotion, encouraging many young officers to leave the army in search of more promising careers elsewhere: subsequent re-raising of disbanded units was no answer, because the spate of resignations had unbalanced the age-structure of the officer corps. The haphazard nature of promotion and the importance attached, rightly or wrongly, to influence worsened matters: officers quipped that there were three elements in promotion: seniority, selection and son-in-law.[11] Even in the 1880s, at the height of revanchist enthusiasm, graduates of the elite technical academy the *Ecole Polytechnique* preferred to become mining or civil engineers rather than artillery or engineer officers.

The circles of influence which were a feature of the army of the Second Empire had their counterparts elsewhere. In the British army the Wolseley 'ring' which gathered around Sir Garnet Wolseley on the Ashanti expedition of 1873–4 was a charmed circle, bitterly resented by outsiders. Wolseley justified his selection by declaring that the 'ordinary humdrum men usually told off for special service from a "Horse-Guards Roster"' would have been no use to him.[12] Most of his leading collaborators in the Ashanti war went on to be generals, Redvers Buller, George Colley, Henry Brackenbury, Frederick Maurice, William Butler and Evelyn Wood among them, their prospects in no way hampered by Wolseley's becoming commander-in-chief of the army in 1895. Another ring coalesced around Sir Frederick Roberts, and this spread its ripples, through Roberts's Boer War chief of staff Kitchener, into the British high command of the First World War. Personal connections were enormously influential in the British *Generalität* of the period. Sir John French, not a Roberts man, was, unsurprisingly, not a Kitchener man either, and the roots of his hatred of Kitchener – which did not materially improve their relationship as commander-in-chief of the BEF and secretary of state for war in 1914–15 – can be traced back to antipathy during the Boer War. Sir Douglas Haig, French's successor in command of the BEF, had been French's brigade major and owed promotion to lieutenant-colonel to his efforts. French never forgave Haig for 'usurping' his position, and French's London office speedily became a clearing-house for anti-Haig intrigue and a refreshing watering hole for those who fell foul of the new commander-in-chief.

If the Edwardian army had few equals for political intrigue, Sir Henry Wilson, commandant of the Staff College and then Director of Military Operations in the years before the First World War, had none at all. Two of Wilson's self-imposed tasks were to engineer British military support for France in the event of a Franco-German conflict and to bring down the Asquith government. He succeeded in the former, for the 1914 mobilisation and concentration plan was largely his work, his compelling oratory wafted it through the Committee of Imperial Defence, and he pedalled off to the French frontier to lay a copy of the plan at the feet of the statue of France on the Franco-Prussian war battlefield of Mars-la-Tour. He had less luck in bringing down the government, but it was not for want of trying. During the Curragh crisis of March 1914 he kept the Opposition informed of the progress of events, stung several of the leading figures into action, and eventually, after canvasing army opinion at the Staff College point-to-point, told French, then Chief of the Imperial General Staff, 'that he *must* go'.[13] French duly resigned, but retained a high enough opinion of Wilson to take him off to France later that year as Sub-Chief of the General Staff, a post which became inordinately influential because of the illness of Archie Murray, its Chief.

These instances of low pay driving competent officers out of the army, inequitable promotion systems, and intrigue within the officer corps and in the wider political world are not exceptional. Examples of officer corps which held fast to traditional vitues despite lack of material reward are far rarer, and reflect specific socio-political circumstances which would defy any attempt to duplicate them.

The case of Prussia-Germany is pre-eminent. The hardy *Junker* squirearchy of East Prussia provided the Prussian army with the bulk of its officers. Prince Karl zu Hohenlohe-Ingelfingen, who commanded the Guard Corps artillery with distinction in 1870–1, was delighted that most of them were, 'thank God, as poor as church mice'. If pay was meagre but adequate, the immense social prestige of the officer made the profession attractive. In 1785 a Saxon officer noted, not without a trace of envy, that 'every ensign and cornet thinks he is as important as a minister of state', and seventy years later a French officer wrote that in Prussia 'the epaulette opens all doors'.[14]

A Russian military attaché, reporting on the Prussian army in 1875–6, attributed much of its efficency to its officers. Their excellence, he believed, sprang from careful selection and training, the great degree of initiative allowed to them (he was greatly impressed by the independence of company commanders) and from the strong sense of community that came from dining together in a mess and wearing uniform all the time. He thought that the officer corps achieved 'the most brilliant results' because of 'the pitiless exclusion of all worthless individuals . . . [and] the material advantages and honorific privileges accorded to the most deserving'.[15]

The army's prestige, added to the shortage of socially acceptable alternative employment for minor gentry, ensured that there were sufficient applicants for commissions, and close attention to entry standards (social as well as educational) buttressed the officer corps' sense of exclusiveness. Requirements like dining nightly in the mess, and wearing uniform in all except a few clearly specified circumstances – shooting parties and taking the waters at a spa among them – were acceptable because they were more than counterbalanced by the exceptional prestige enjoyed by the officer. Subjection not merely to military law but also to courts of honour which judged infractions of the honour code was also freely tolerated.

The creation of a military caste in Germany was not achieved without cost. The Frederician officer, for all his elevated opinion of himself, was strictly forbidden to interfere with civilians. By the Wilhelmine era this reserved devotion to duty had a thick veneer of arrogance, and the militarisation of German society had reached such lengths that an elderly professor, offered an honour on retirement, replied that what he wanted most was promotion from lieutenant to captain on the reserve. The army's rigid conservatism helped stunt the nation's political growth, its influence on policy-making in peacetime was distortive and the 'military specialist' figures prominently among the architects of Armageddon in 1914.

The Israeli Defence Forces, with their utilitarian discipline and open promotion structure could scarcely look less like the old Prussian army. Grounds for comparison are more real than apparent, not least because of the officer corps' profound sense of duty, the importance attached to low-level initiative and the soldier's standing in what Reuven Gal called 'a warrior society'. In late 1974 military employment scored highly on a career-prestige scale, with a colonel obtaining 96/100, only just below a university professor; a major 81, equivalent to a pharmacologist, and a captain 76, rather better than an airline pilot.[16] Gal attributes the IDF's institutional characteristics to the fact that it originally 'exemplified a calling, an institution dominated by an ideological conviction and a sense of duty . . . it is a fighting army, a citizen's military, an army that is perceived as a critical shield for the very existence of its country'. Sense of external threat, and thus of the real need for an army, underlines military prestige. It is significant that the statistics for societal regard cited by Gal date from 1974, with the Yom Kippur War a recent memory. We may doubt whether they would be as encouraging in the wake of Operation 'Peace for Galilee' and the *intifada*.

The German and Israeli examples illuminate the current situation in Britain and America. A socially exclusive officer corps was difficult to sustain even in Wilhelmine Germany, as growing numbers of bourgeois gained entry, especially to the technical arms. It would be impossible to create today, although the Soviet army has gone some way down the path towards an hereditary officer corps. Social prestige, similarly, cannot be attached to the military profession by the stroke of a pen. In the German case it sprang from the fact that the terms officer and gentleman were synonymous, was reinforced by the sense of military threat inspired by Prussia's geographical position with potential enemies on two fronts, and was enhanced by consistent military success in the century following Waterloo. There was an identified need for an army, the army did its job well, and its officers did not shirk from hard work in peacetime and self-sacrifice in war. The comparison with Israel, in this context, is an apt one. *Glasnost* has struck a fatal blow at the prestige of the Soviet armed forces. For all his concern about Islam and a united Germany, seeing food on supermarket shelves matters more to the average Russian than expensive defence against a diminishing threat. On a recent visit to Moscow I failed to appreciate just how things had changed, and spoke to a Russian officer of the army's high status in Soviet society. He turned to me with amused disbelief. 'The place of the army in Soviet society', he declared, 'is the dirty corner where you spit.'

The drift towards occupational officer corps is more pronounced in some nations than in others, and is exaggerated by our comparison of present problems with an artificially rosy past. Attempts to halt or reverse the trend are doomed to fail unless they are accompanied by recompense. In an ideal world this would involve enhancing the officers' status, not merely increasing material reward. Such social engineering is beyond all but the most totalitarian of states, as the Soviet army's chronic shortage of officers demonstrates. Moreover, if armies are unable to persuade the populations they serve that there is a real need for their existence – a decided possibility in the age of *glasnost* – the prestige of officer corps is likely to decline further, at a time when the recruiting pool grows smaller and the technical requirements of the profession increase.

It is therefore idle to pretend that status can be separated from pay. Paying officers well does not necessarily undermine their warrior ethos, although doing so at a time when military budgets are shrinking will probably mean having less officers. Kitson's point that 'senior staff officers invariably generate a pyramid of filters below them' is well made – all the more reason for smaller, more expert staffs. His suggestion that retirement ages should be drastically reduced would create difficulties. If officers are to think of the military profession as more than just a job, it cannot jettison them with less than a full career, although Keegan's suggestion of a very substantial gratuity which would provide 'a sound platform for a second career' might go a long way towards solving the problem.[17] Promotion opportunities may not increase, but reducing the size of officer corps should limit the tendency of senior officers to 'overcommand' – that is, to do not only their own job but that of their immediate subordinates, thus reducing the latter's sphere of decision and job satisfaction. Increasing pay and allowances in order to retain high-quality personnel is no answer unless it is accompanied by steps to genuinely increase the commander's initiative and authority.

Overcommanding is a potentially fatal disease. Before the First World War L.S. Amery saw: 'a tradition deeply ingrained in the whole of the Army . . . that the chief task of each rank is not doing the work of that rank, but controlling the work of the ranks below'. 'Chink' Dorman-Smith, whose merits still polarise opinion among senior surviving British veterans of the Second World War, wrote in 1953 that:

> Essentially in a professional army . . . the commander is left to carry out . . . [an order] . . . without wet-nursing. In the British system, on the contrary, no subordinate will do anything until he has the next above breathing down his neck. The result is that everyone is doing the proper job of the next below instead of his own battle job. This is the main cause of the stagnation of the British tactical mind.[18]

General Donn Starry recalls that when he took over the US V Corps in Germany he found that it was customary for the corps commander to monitor the readiness states of all vehicles, telephoning company commanders weekly to find out what they were doing about specific vehicles. Starry removed himself from this particular loop, established goals, and left their attainment up to the chain of command – and vehicle readiness immediately improved.[19] Overcommanding is a dispiriting characteristic of peacetime armies, produced largely by the desire to prevent career-damaging mistakes. It sets a deadly precedent for war, when a senior commander either discovers he has to leave more to his subordinates than he would wish, or, alternatively, becomes absorbed with points of detail when concepts matter more. Subordinates unused to independent action are wrong-footed by the former approach and harassed by the latter. A genuine increase in initiative would knock on into the NCO ranks, allowing them to exercise the responsibility for which their training so often richly qualifies them.

Promotion will inevitably remain contentious. Confidential reports which are seen by their subjects encourage many superiors to depict their geese as swans so as not to impair day-to-day working relationships, and a tendency to over-report is deeply entrenched on both sides of the Atlantic. Reports which are not seen by their subject tend to be more objective, but inject an element of mistrust into the process. Lieutenant-General Gerd Niepold – *Wehrmacht* panzer division chief of staff and *Bundeswehr* corps commander – feared that:

> performance for performance, the clever officer does better these days than the man of character, and I would warrant that the former 'unseen' confidential reports were more honest than those of today, which are seen by the person reported on and are open to challenge under due process of law.[20]

The current British system, where the first reporting officer's comments are seen but his superior reporting officer's are not comes close to a reasonable compromise, although some of the latter find themselves writing on officers about whom, given the realities of military life, they actually know very little.

There are sometimes demands that reports should reflect the subordinate's as well as the superior's view. This would undoubtedly concentrate some officers' minds wonderfully. Von Zugbach records the results of informal interviews with the staffs of four brigadiers belonging to a (wisely unspecified) service corps:

> Recurrent themes were 'humourless'; 'grey'; 'bureaucratic'; 'self-centred'; 'excessive concern for detail'; 'concerned only with things being alright on the surface' . . . 'a thorough shit' . . . In one case the officer concerned occupied an office which had once belonged to a high ranking Nazi. The general consensus amongst the officers was that the 'former incumbent would be infinitely preferable to work for.'[21]

Von Zugbach believed that natural selection in non-regimental arms in the British army led to the predominance of 'careerists' in their upper echelons, and his solidly based research strikes a chord with 'Colonel Yasotay's more visceral assault on a US promotion system which in his view 'bend[s] over backwards to kill off our warriors at a young age and give them less consideration in our promotion process than we do adjutant general paper shufflers'.[22] The comparison cannot be taken too far, however, because the British army remains indisputably combat-arm dominated, to the point where logisticians might fairly argue that their importance is not mirrored by their influence, while the main thrust of Yasotay's accusation is exactly the reverse – 'ours is an army of clerks, not fighters, and they are running the show'.

Military ambition is neither a late twentieth-century invention, nor is it necessarily fatal. Most professionals, whatever their field, expect at least a modest degree of advancement, and it would be unrealistic to expect armies to be different. Ambition becomes corrosive when desire for the next appointment clouds the satisfaction of the present one, and when ascent of the hierarchy becomes a matter of ticking boxes and avoiding trouble. Starry tells how his new commander briefed him at their first meeting.

> I want you to understand why I am here. I am here because it is necessary to command this unit for a year – no more, no less – in order to get to be a general. I am going to be a general. Now, your outfit has a tendency to do things differently, to attract attention. I don't like that. For the year that I am in command, I don't want anything to happen. I don't just mean anything bad – I mean anything that will call the attention of higher headquarters to us being different from anyone else.[23]

No ambitious member of any hierarchy relishes stopping his ascent towards the bottom end of the ladder, but it is in the nature of any military structure (even one with convenient bulges) that there will be disappointed officers and NCOs whose desire for promotion goes unfulfilled.

Success or failure in the military promotion stakes is more visible than in civilian organisations. It was no accident that Frederick's officers wore much the same uniform regardless of rank. As Christopher Duffy wrote:

One of the most striking features of the Prussian service was the virtual absence of any visible distinctions of rank within the officer corps. The general wore exactly the same uniform as the subaltern, with the sole distinction of the hat plume which was introduced in 1742. Here we have an outward manifestation of the sense of corporate unity of the body of officers, and an impressive contrast with the glitter of the French and Austrian generals of the period.[24]

There is something of a parallel with the modern British army here, for it is largely those units which are most exclusive in their officer selection (applying stringent military, educational and, one must add, social criteria) which have the most informal officers' messes – all first names apart from the commanding officer, little deference to rank, rules of behaviour governed by a negotiated process of social learning, and so on. The badges of rank worn by officers in some cavalry regiments are so tiny that while one can easily discern that someone is an officer, it is hard to see whether his epaulette bears a second-lieutenant's single pip or a major's crown. Officers of the Royal Green Jackets take the process a stage further by wearing no badges of rank in mess kit. In such a community the expression 'brother officers' is a very real one, and the colonel himself is more of an elder brother than a father.

The Parachute Regiment is just as selective in the standards it sets for its cadet intake: 'It can afford to do this,' argued von Zugbach, 'because it represents a physical elite into which young men wish to buy.' Its criteria are notably different from those governing entry into, say, the Foot Guards or the cavalry, and von Zugbach discerned 'a middle class/lower middle class centre of gravity for the arm'.[25] This is a relatively recent occurrence, for before the Parachute Regiment had a permanent cadre of officers of its own, and relied on attachments from other regiments, its officers had few equals by whatever criteria might be applied. In one important sense, however – the comradeship of its members across the barriers of rank – its functional elitism brings it close to the intellectual and social elitism of some other regiments. There is a parallel with parachute units in other armies, where the shared risks of parachuting and all the rituals and taboos of jump school mark off insiders from outsiders and help submerge other distinctions. Lieutenant-General Sir Frederick 'Boy' Browning, father of British airborne forces in the Second World War, was from that ancient and most self-assured regiment The Grenadier Guards. General Marcel Bigeard, the very epitome of the French para of the turbulent fifties, was son of a railway signalman and was once a bank clerk.

Uniform and address bear daily witness to an individual's progress, or lack of it, up the military hierarchy, and the time-honoured terminology of rank structure makes it difficult to invent evasive job titles which mask low status. A civilian pay clerk is an accounts executive, a salesman is at worst a sales executive and more probably a sales director, and my local rat-catcher has become a vermin disposal consultant. You are either a captain or you are not, and conjuring up some explanatory description cuts little ice. The American practice of adding (P) after an individual's rank to denote that he is 'promotable' helps spread the available status more widely, at least within the military community where such shorthand is understood.

The inflation of expectation in so many civilian fields has coloured military attitudes. For most British regimental officers command of their battalion as a lieutenant-colonel was once the apogee of reasonable ambition: further promotion was a bonus. NCOs saw the post of regimental sergeant major (in terms of influence and status far more analogous to that of commanding officer than the apparent difference between the two ranks might suggest) as their goal. An officer felt that no stigma attached to retiring as a major: until relatively recently many captains habitually carried their military title into retirement. Now, the expression 'passed-over major' sounds a mournful note. Yet the British major, passed over or not, has a better remuneration package than most university teachers and still enjoys a status which reflects 'the historical alliance between the military and other ruling institutions in society'.[26] Though he can identify Sandhurst contemporaries who left the army early and went into the City to enjoy wealth beyond the dreams of avarice, he may be less quick to note others who tried to make the same leap and sank like stones. His uneasiness stems as much from the decreasingly attractive jobs which fall to him if he soldiers on unpromoted as from genuine financial hardship, as well as from the family pressures discussed in the previous chapter. These ills do not have instant cures, but a reduction in the overall number of career officers and an increase in executive initiative would free meaningful jobs for those who have reached their rank ceiling, and some compression of the pay scale to reduce salaries at the very top would increase financial rewards available to middle-piece officers.

Enhanced ambition among British NCOs bears witness to rising expectations in the civilian sector and the erosion of the social boundaries which traditionally separated officers and NCOs, giving rise to what one observer has called the 'middle classing' of the army. The post of RSM is no longer the peak of expectation, and an increasing number of NCOs regard the sergeants' mess as a stepping-stone to the officers'. The importance the British army accords to the NCO is rooted in the days when commissions were purchased and officers were often absent from their units, and it has flourished in the introspective and cohesive regimental system. It makes for a degree of reluctance to 'erode' the sergeants' mess by gratifying the ambitions of a growing number of its members. The currents of change are, however, running strongly, and the army currently commissions more sergeants' mess members than ever before in peacetime. A reduction in the overall proportion of career officers would open more attractive posts to commissioned NCOs and warrant officers, not just within units but also, as Kitson suggests, in junior posts on formation and district staffs.

There are many, officers and NCOs alike, who believe that their promotion prospects depend upon not offending their superiors, and the nature of the reporting system which prevails in most armies suggests that this belief is not without substance. In its most extreme form the 'offence' is political. Stalin's purges disposed of over 50 per cent of the Red Army's officer corps, and upheavals in Latin American armies – Ibanez purged the Chilean army in 1927–8 and the MNR all but disbanded the Bolivan army in the early 1950s – frequently follow changes of regime.

Less violent, but often as deadly to the career, is the treatment meted out to some of those who champion unpopular views. In 1867 General L.J. Trochu published a work illuminating the many faults of the army of the Second Empire. The book was an immediate bestseller, and its author was rewarded by being removed from the list of important command appointments. When the Franco-Prussian war broke out, he was sent off to command an observation force in the Pyrenees, a posting which was almost a deliberate insult. Generals Billy Mitchell and Guilio Douhet, two of the leading early advocates of air power, were both court-martialled, and Major-General J.F.C. Fuller, an outstanding military thinker of the inter-war years, retired after being offered an appointment which was, in its way, as insulting as Trochu's. The future Field Marshal von Manstein was more fortunate. He advised the successful German operations plan for the 1940 campaign against the wishes of the general staff. For this he was removed from his post as chief of staff to the army group which would play the major part in the offensive, and 'promoted' by being given command of a corps on the Polish frontier. It was, he said, 'due to the desire on the part of OKH to get rid of an importunate nuisance who had ventured to put up an operation plan at variance with its own'.[27] His career survived, and he went on to become one of Germany's ablest practitioners of armoured warfare.

The mere fact of pressing for reform does not always earn its champion a prompt posting to outer darkness. Reformers have not always been the most appropriate advocates for their causes, and sometimes it was the manner of their pleading, rather than the character of their case, that brought the shutters crashing down. As Michael Howard observed, Trochu, even by the loquacious standards of his age, was a long-winded bore. Mitchell and Douhet pushed resolute argument beyond the bounds of discipline. Fuller was not only unfashionably trenchant, but his political and religious opinions were unsettlingly extreme. Nevertheless, Fuller went to the heart of the matter when he warned that the British army of his day contained many who would win a Victoria Cross, the nation's highest award for bravery, but few who would write a truthful minute to a conservative senior officer. The promotion system sapped moral courage, because it took courage to espouse an unfashionable and thus potentially career-stopping view.

Field Marshal Lord Slim believed that there were two distinct types of courage. Physical courage was 'an emotional state which urges a man to risk death or injury'. A man's moral courage, in contrast, was 'a more reasoning attitude which enables him coolly to stake career, happiness, his whole future on his judgement of what he thinks is either right or worthwhile . . .' He concluded that 'moral courage is a higher and rarer virtue than physical courage'.[28] Slim reinforced his point by reference to the Japanese generals he had fought during the Second World War. Their physical courage was beyond question, but they lacked the moral courage to admit when their plans had failed.

A judgmental element refines moral courage. It is entirely possible that the Japanese generals criticised by Slim had concluded that true moral courage lay not in recognising that a plan was unworkable, which might have been a Westerner's conclusion, but in persevering with it regardless. In the spring of 1917, when the operational foundations of Nivelle's offensive had been swept away by German withdrawal to the Hindenburg Line, did moral courage lie in recognising that the plan was no longer feasible and calling it off – military suicide in Nivelle's case – or in pressing on with it? We now conclude that true courage lay in acknowledging that the game was up, but we may doubt whether the picture seemed as clear to Nivelle in his agony amidst the gilt and ormulu of his headquarters in the Palace of Compiègne.

Moral courage in peacetime is even more difficult to gauge. Does it lie in a forceful expression of opinion, even though this may not further the cause and may diminish career prospects in the process? Or does it lie in recognition that frontal assault, in peace as in war, generally offers a less promising avenue than a more subtle approach from the flanks? Where is the line between moral cowardice and honest realism? An individual's conscience is his only real guide, and this – like Slim's moral courage – is learnt 'by precept and example' in youth. When a man consistently 'trims' his attitudes for the sake of safety, he not only betrays himself, although in the short term his epaulettes may grow more splendid, but he does his army a disservice by furnishing his juniors with an example which can only corrode their own moral courage. The concept of 'consent and evade' – enthusiastic compliance to a senior's face, prompt oblivion as soon as he is out of sight – will strike a chord with many readers who work for any large corporation, uniformed or not. In an army, however, its consequences are lethal. It dissolves the bonds of mutal trust and respect that link men of character in good armies. Its peacetime seeds are tiny: its wartime fruits, catastrophic.

Chains of Command

Moshe Dayan, architect of Israeli victory in 1953 and 1967, hankered after the good old days when, in the hour of battle, the general mounted his white horse, the trumpet sounded, and off he charged towards the enemy.[29] Martin van Creveld and John Keegan, who have addressed the subject of command in war with their customary acuity, agree that for much of history the commander physically led his men in battle. Alexander the Great was the epitome of the heroic leader, and formidable personal bravery was a characteristic of his leadership: at the siege of Multan in 325 BC he personally led a storming party, was cut off inside the city and dangerously wounded in the lung. Frederick the Great ran away at his first battle, Mollwitz, but at Kunersdorf in 1759 he had two horses killed under him and his snuff-box was flattened by a bullet as he struggled unavailingly to hold his army together. 'My coat is riddled with bullets,' he wrote that evening: 'My misfortune is that I am still alive.'[30] Wellington, with his simple dress and quiet, 'gentleman-like' behaviour, was not a heroic leader in the conventional sense, but he too hazarded his person without stint. At Waterloo death snatched his staff around him as he rode to each successive *Schwerpunkt*, and as he was dismounting at the close of the day his charger, Copenhagen, came close to succeeding where roundshot and musket ball had failed, and narrowly missed braining him with a vicious kick.

In 1870, on the new battlefield laid bare by the breech-loader, Marshal Bazaine plied his sword among a swirl of Prussian hussars and General Legrand had the rare distinction of being the last general to perish by the sword, run through the chest at the head of his cavalry division.[31] We have already seen how the casualties suffered by British generals on the Western Front in the First World War go some way towards refuting the popular image of safe, château-bound generals. Of the seven infantry divisional commanders who took their commands to France in 1914, three were killed and another wounded within six months. Three divisional commanders fell at Loos in 1915, among them Major-General Tommy Capper (author of the characteristic comment 'this is the sort of day on which no good officer should be alive') who, according to one account, fell rifle and bayonet in hand at the head of a shaky company. John Keegan draws attention to the importance of 'forward' leadership, whose practitioners were 'all driven by an ethic, of which the heroic was a strong element, to share the common soldier's predicament and, if bullet hit or steel scored, to share his fate'.[32] De Vigny had argued that the soldier was both victim and executioner, and it was long a hallmark of the commander's trade that he too shared these qualities.

Forward leadership always had its risks. The death or wounding of the leader could have far-reaching consequences. The death of Cyrus at Cunaxa in 401 BC destroyed his cause, and the fall of John Graham of Claverhouse, 'Bonnie Dundee', in the moment of victory at Killiekrankie in 1689 fatally weakened his army. At Lützen in 1632 both the Swedish king Gustav Adolf and the Imperialist General Pappenheim were killed. The latter's demise threw his excellent cavalry into a panic, while the death of Gustav Adolf sucked the wind from the wings of the Swedish army, which was never quite the same again. Stonewall Jackson's fatal wounding at Chancellorsville in 1863 did enormous harm to the Confederacy, depriving Lee of his most capable independent commander. The death of General Stumme at Alamein (from a heart attack as he was fired upon while he drove up to see the situation for himself) hampered the Axis reaction to the British attack, all the more because his subordinates were unsure what had actually happened to him.

There was good reason for most of these tragedies, personal and public. Despite the existence of long-distance communications of varying efficiency, from mounted couriers to visual telegraphs, smoke signals and beacons, a commander's ability to receive and transmit information was limited. As van Creveld has explained, in 'the Stone Age of Command' communications worked best behind armies and were at their most effective in fixed defensive positions. Tactical command until the late nineteenth century was very much a matter of the commander's personal presence close to the front, in visual contact with the battle, and able to intervene, either personally, or by the use of gallopers or aides-de-camp, in the conduct of the battle.

The salient fact about most battlefields of the horse and musket era is their small size. Waterloo is tiny, and even larger battlefields like Königgrätz or Rezonville can be crossed comfortably in an hours' walk. A force over the horizon was beyond the certain communications reach of the commander-in-chief. He might reach it by galloper from time to time, but he could not hope to control its operations in any detailed sense. It was effectively a detachment, and the best that the commander-in-chief could do was to try to ensure that its commander knew what was in his mind, and would therefore act purposefully in the absence of instructions. Cunning turning movements carried out by detachments as often as not came to grief. When the Parliamentarians attacked the Royalists at Second Newbury in 1644, the outflanking column made good progress, but the holding attack on the other flank miscarried – largely because of the difficulty of distinguishing between signal guns and the general roar of battle. Grouchy's detached force was of little service to Napoleon at Waterloo, not so much because of its commander's errors but because of the spongy orders he received. 'His Majesty

desires that you will head for Wavre in order to draw nearer to us,'
ran the crucial message:

> and to place yourself in touch with our operations, and to keep up
> your communications with us, pushing before you those portions
> of the Prussian army which have taken this direction and which
> have halted at Wavre; this place you ought to reach as soon as
> possible.[33]

We may wonder quite what Grouchy was meant to make of that. In
1866, Moltke went through agonies before Königgrätz, waiting for
the arrival of the Crown Prince's army on the open Austrian right
flank. As late as 1914, Russian disaster at Tannenberg stemmed from
bad communications between two armies which attempted to work
in concert – and atrocious security on the one radio net that did
exist.

Routine reports or specific messages from detachments often failed
to reflect reality, and the 'directed telescope' – *missi dominici* reporting
direct to the commander-in-chief – became an important adjunct to
command. Napoleon, who made wide use of the directed telescope,
kept a group of aides and liaison officers in addition to his formal
staff. They could be sent out to report on the state of units and their
commanders, and the general ADCs could be dispatched to take up
the reins where a commander had failed or been killed. The directed
telescope remains a useful means of monitoring the normal chain of
command: Montgomery's loyal and bright young liaison officers are
its most recent example.[34]

There was also a limit to even the most brilliant general's span
of command. It is possible to control about 3,000 men by word
and gesture, though Keegan, reflecting on Alexander's oratory,
surmises that he might have used natural amphitheatres to make
his voice carry unusually far. Beyond this total, however, command
was achieved by giving orders to senior subordinates, who in turn
passed them on: thus the classical chain of command was created,
and it was a primitive army indeed which did not form up in legions,
phalanxes, tercios, regiments or brigades, as much in response to
the limited span of command as to the demands of weapons and
tactics.

The development of the *corps d'armée* system at the end of the
eighteenth century was an important new departure, for it recognised

that large armies, with their enormous logistic appetites, were difficult to feed if united and impossible to command effectively if separated into *ad hoc* detachments. The corps system institutionalised the detachment, for the corps, an all-arms formation with its own limited logistic element, could survive unsupported for several days. It was the large currency of Napoleon's conduct of operations, and its strengths were nowhere better exemplified than in the vast sweeping deployment for the Austerlitz campaign of 1805, when seven line corps, one reserve cavalry and one general reserve corps wheeled from the channel coast to envelop the unfortunate General Mack at Ulm and go on to defeat the Austro-Russian army in Moravia. This wide span stretched the abilities of Napoleon and his corps commanders to breaking-pont. Joachim Murat, as was his way, soon got out of control, and received a sharp reprimand which highlighted the uneasy relationship between orders and initiative in the Napoleonic army. 'I cannot approve of your manner of march;' snapped the Emperor, 'you go on like a stunned fool, taking not the least notice of my orders. The Russians, instead of covering Vienna, have retreated over the Danube at Krems. This extraordinary circumstance should have made you realise that you could not act without further instructions.'[35]

The term chain is itself misleading, for command structures usually resemble pyramids, with each commander dealing with a small but variable number of juniors: groupings based on three or four have been most common. Extending the span of command to enable commanders to deal with a greater number of subordinates without passing through intermediaries has its attractions, not least because it appears to justify the abolition of expensive headquarters and to enhance flexibility. Yet, as experiments from the US 'Pentomic' division to the British army's Field Forces of the 1970s show, it grows difficult for a single commander to deal meaningfully with more than five senior subordinate commanders, even if communications appear to permit him to do so.

Across over two thousand years of military history, then, there was very little divergence between the technical function of command – the reception of information, the formulation of decision and the transmission of orders – and its spiritual content, the need to see and be seen, kill and risk being killed. The commander shared the risks of the men he led and, if he read the battle right, saw its crucial events for himself. In the final analysis he might throw himself into the battle at the head of his last reserve. On 31 October 1914 Sir John French was not being a romantic ass when he spoke of taking his headquarter guard, the last troops at his disposal, to the crack in his line on the Menin Road: he was behaving like the nineteenth-century general he was. Yet what else could he do? He had learnt of the crisis by going to corps headquarters, two miles behind the crumbling front, to be told: 'They have broken us right in, and are pouring through the gap' by the corps commander. He then set off in person to seek French help. With the communications at his disposal – dispatch rider and land line, the latter of questionable use in a mobile battle – he was no better off than Wellington, ninety-nine years before. Indeed, because the battlefield was much bigger and the weapons on it more lethal, he was probably a good deal worse off. He had abundant firepower at his disposal: what he lacked was communications.[36]

The communication explosion has mushroomed out from the development of the electric telegraph, perfected in 1829, through the radio, scarce in the First World War but commonplace in the Second, to the computer, whose field-hardened keyboards and glowing VDUs now illuminate large headquarters. The wise General Omar Bradley recognised that communications were at the heart of the process of command. 'Congress makes a man a general,' he declared, 'but communications make him a commander.' Yet communications have jammed the commander on to the horns of a dilemma. A New Zealand report published in 1949 summed up the problem.

The good commander must continually reconcile two conflicting requirements – namely, that while much of his control can only be exercised in a headquarters in *rear* of the fighting echelons, he must also visit his *forward* troops in order to make his presence felt by the fighting men. On the one hand, it is the duty of the commander to control the fight, and to make the best use of his reserves and of the supporting fire available, and to be accessible at all critical times to his subordinate commanders. This normally requires an established headquarters or a known location, with all the paraphernalia of command. On the other hand, the moral value – both to the fighting troops and to the commander himself – of forward visits is inestimable. In fact they are the essence of battle leadership.[37]

S.L.A. Marshall was more succinct, asking himself: 'How do I reconcile the fact that my post of duty is at the rear with the need that my presence should be felt by my fighting men?'[38]

Acceleration of the pace of change in communications only makes the dilemma more acute. For the nineteenth century and the early part of the twentieth a senior commander was usually close to his headquarters. It was there that his principal staff officers, the adjutant general, responsible for discipline, appointments and promotions, and the quartermaster general, with his wider concern for movements and quartering, were to be found, and although a general might have a smaller staff cell at his personal disposal – like Napoleon's *Maison Militaire* – he would be unwise to put too much distance between himself and the main staff branches. The small size of battlefields and the poverty of tactical communication put headquarters close enough to the firing line for their countervailing tugs not to impose intolerable strain. Moreover, the limited ranges of weapons meant that headquarters were rarely effectively engaged by gunfire, even though they were often mutually visible. As late as September 1870 the whole of German royal headquarters was drawn up on a hill above Frenois, watching the battle of Sedan spread out in the amphitheatre below it, close enough for the King of Prussia to exclaim 'Ah! The brave fellows' as General Margueritte's *Chasseurs d'Afrique* pounded to destruction down the slopes across the Meuse.

The increase in the size of armies that came with universal conscription, the multiplication of firepower, and the refinement of strategic railway communication tightened the Gordian Knot on the Western Front in the First World War. The failure of communications to keep pace with other developments was the quintessential hardening agent, and formation commanders, driven to nodal points whence they had a reasonable chance of communicating by telephone, lost control of the tactical battle. Their attempts to regain it are especially pertinent to present discussions. The British and French, and, through the osmosis of shared experience, the Americans too, moved towards remote control. Plans were centralised and meticulous, and phased objectives featured prominently among them. Given that communications with the attacking troops were likely to be lost, detailed plans would prevent uncertainty from creeping in.

The German conclusion, based on historical evidence as well as recent experience, was exactly the reverse. Since effective higher control was certain to be the first casualty, the best results would be achieved by decentralising authority, and by ensuring that the general principles of the operational plan were clear in surbordinate commanders' minds. It marked, as we saw in a previous chapter, a clear contrast between *Befehlstaktik*, order-driven tactics, and *Auftragstaktik*, directive control.

The communication explosion that has thundered on since the First World War has destroyed many of the assumptions which underpinned the logic of *Auftragstaktik*. The proliferation of combat net radios enables individual vehicles and fire teams (and even individual soldiers) to be radio-equipped. The increasing reliability of radios, and their improving ability to elude jamming and interception by frequency-hopping theoretically permits the tendrils of command to stretch deep into the military infrastructure. In another dimension, satellite communications make it possible for governments to monitor events at the tactical level, and the evidence of the failed Iranian hostage rescue attempt and the Falklands War suggests that the ability of governments to communicate directly fuels their propensity for doing exactly that. It was an encouraging example of self-denial that the US air raid on Libya was controlled not from Washington, which state of the art communications made possible, but from aboard a warship in the Mediterranean.

Allied to all this is the onrush of information technology. Today over one million components can be put on to one silicone chip: by the mid-1990s this is likely to be five million, and by the year 2000 it could be between ten and 100 million. One leading authority predicts that the number of computers deployed in battle systems over the next ten years will increase by 50 to 100 times, the amount of store per computer will increase from tens of kilobytes to tens of megabytes, and that data transmission will increase between ten and one hundredfold.[39] There are, of course, practical barriers to the realisation of these possibilities in the military sphere. Even if the equipment itself does not prove prohibitively expensive, then the demand for an escalating number of military software specialists (of whom there is already a shortage in the civilian marketplace) will tighten the screw of expert manpower.

Nor has armies' experience of computers been universally encouraging. Many, from fire control computers in the Falklands (which answered the question of what to do when faced by two attacking aircraft by engaging neither) to WAVELL, I British Corps' main Information System (which occasionally rivals the popular song 'I've Been Down So Long It Looks Like Up to Me') produce serious in-service problems. As a British officer with personal experience of WAVELL wrote:

> the transition from theory to practice was as ever a salutory one, mainly because we hit software problems and were forced to learn the hard way what everyone else has had to face up to: namely, that with large software driven systems one can simulate and model as much as one likes in factories and laboratories, but the dynamics and complications of real networks will always produce unexpected and unpredictable conditions which reveal major software flaws.[40]

Clausewitz would have called it friction.

Before drifting to the wilder shores of Ludditism we must sound a cautionary note. It is unrealistic to expect armies not to pursue information technology to the best of their ability, and the consequences of being technically outclassed in radios or computers are just as serious as in tanks or ground attack aircraft. Late twentieth-century communications permit operations of war which our grandfathers could scarcely have dreamt of. They also, we would do well to remember, make possible communications between adversaries in crisis, at the very time when conventional diplomacy lacks speed, authority or simply access. Computers accelerate procedures which once called for plotters and slide rules or simple pen, paper and brainpower. Everything from mortar and artillery fire control, through road movement tables to calculations of logistic stocks, have been made more efficient by the computer. In the broader context of human affairs the significance of the information revolution may be justly compared to that of the development of written language or the printed book, and to pretend that commanders can carry on with business as usual is to ignore an event potentially as far-reaching as the industrial or French revolutions.

Communication and information technology none the less pose serious questions. In a speech delivered in 1977, Major-General J.A. Welch, of the USAF's Research Development and Acquisition branch, defined four important criteria of the perfect C^3I system as 'to preserve the order and cohesiveness of our own forces', 'to avoid blunders and ensure freedom of action', 'to ensure a zero non-effectiveness' and 'ensuring efficiency or optimization'.[41] No historical commander would disagree that these criteria were also functions of command. Indeed, according primacy to the preservation of order (or, to put it another way, the elimination of uncertainty) would gratify the shades of hundreds of order-loving generals from Caesar through Frederick to Haig and Montgomery. How, then, does the machine interface with the man? What functions can be entrusted to the computer – and what remains the responsibility of that most efficient computer of all, the human brain?

Van Creveld concluded that: 'Far from determining the essence of command . . . communications and information processing technology merely constitutes one part of the general environment in which command operates.'[42] The weight of evidence tells irresistibly in his favour. Centralised command which relies on either an inflexible plan or uninterrupted communications has a less creditable track-record than decentralised command, with authority and initiative delegated to subordinates within the context of a generally understood mission. Although the latter style did not apply in most Western armies in two world wars, it is certainly not inherently foreign to them. European empires, after all, were won by men who exercised *Auftragstaktik* in its widest possible sense, and both Grant and Lee, for all their differences, increasingly used decentralised command. Grant's instructions to Sherman are a classic preamble to an operational mission: 'I do not propose to lay down for you a plan of campaign . . . but simply to lay down the work it is desirable to have done and leave you free to execute it in your own way.'[43]

Application of *Auftragstaktik* in the age of the information revolution demands attention in several distinct areas. First is the relationship between authority in peace and command in war. Overcommand in peacetime is, as we saw in the previous section, a common characteristic of peacetime armies, and establishes bad habits for leaders and led alike. It encourages commanders to use the products of the information revolution to strive to preserve in war that authority which they sought to exercise in peace. They are inclined to confuse activity with achievement, and cluster in layers behind the *Schwerpunkt*. General Dave Palmer argued that:

the helicopter's most pernicious contribution to the fighting in Vietnam may have been its undermining of the influence and

267

initiative of small unit commanders. By providing a fast, efficient airborne command post, the helicopter all too often turned supervisors into oversupervisors. Since there was rarely more than one clash in any given area at any given time, the company commander on the ground fighting his battle could usually observe in tiers orbiting above him his battalion commander, brigade commander, assistant division commander, division commander, and even his field force [corps] commander.[44]

Failure to allow initiative in peacetime training and administration encourages just such behaviour.

The commander's natural (and perfectly correct) desire to see things for himself, added to the gnawing need to be involved, and even a measure of soldierly guilt which urges him to hazard his person, accelerates the process. In *Fields of Fire* James Webb describes the bonds linking an officer to his soldiers:

The bald, red hills with their sandbag bunkers, the banter and frolic of the dirt-covered grunts, the fearful intensity of contact . . . Down south his men were on patrol, or digging new perimeters, or dying, and he was nothing if he did not share that misery.[45]

The bonds of mateship do not break when a man acquires starred shoulders or a red-tabbed collar, and it often requires more moral courage for a commander to stay back than it does physical courage for him to go forward. The finest of judgments – at a time of conflicting emotions and grinding fatigue – determines how far forward (and how often) a commander should go. If the bullet or surface-to-air missile strikes home, the commander poking about among the battle with no clear function will have done his men the greatest of disservices by dying without good reason. 'The man who cannot bring himself to trust the judgement and good faith of other men cannot command very long,' wrote Marshall, and his comment is as true along the corridors of ministries as it is on and above the battlefield.

There will undoubtedly be times when the commander feels that his personal presence at a post of danger may be so important as to be worth the dislocation that his loss may so easily provoke. Historical evidence and the lessons of the US Army's National Training Center emphasise just how mortal commanders, so often easily identifiable by the presence of radio-heavy command groups, are at platoon, company and battalion level, and how frequently, in the real world, a unit finds itself commanded by the second team – or even a scratch pack headed by a few third team players. Coaching the second team is enormously important, and General von Senger und Etterlin, the German corps commander at Monte Cassino, wrote:

> An important aspect of the co-ordination system in all aspects was the use of second eleven teams. Throughout the campaign, except at moments of crisis, subordinate officers were put into positions of higher authority under supervision. This meant that when casualties were taken the posts could be filled by personnel with at least some idea of the job.

Brigadier George Taylor, who commanded a battalion in north-west Europe in 1944–5, a brigade in Korea and a brigade in Kenya during the Mau Mau rebellion, thought that the correct position for commanders in the attack was 'in the centre of the danger area and not in front', and this is no bad general rule. As Marshall noted, a commander cannot rally his men by spectacular personal intervention if they have grown accustomed to seeing him run unnecessary risks in the average circumstances of battle.[46] He warns that a commander does his men a mammoth disservice by dying unnecessarily, and both historical evidence and contemporary studies emphasise that staying alive should rank high among the commander's priorities.

Next, we must consider the orders process. Elaborate orders are in the most literal sense characteristic of *Befehlstaktik,* and much emphasis at military academies and arms schools is placed upon their comprehensive framing and confident delivery. Yet, again they seek to eliminate uncertainty by describing exactly what is to happen, smothering chance with precision. Their weaknesses are as obvious as their strengths. They seldom equip their recipients to deal with the unexpected, and their considerable volume makes the writing and giving of full orders a lengthy business. The battalion orders group, company commanders in the front row of the stalls, specialist platoon commanders on the balcony and supporting arms representatives in boxes to either flank can become something of a theatrical performance in itself, with the intelligence officer's prefatory comments warming up the audience for the great man's virtuoso display.

Although there may be occasions when such orchestration is possible, there will be more when it is not. Roy Flint encapsulated the difference between the ideal and the real when recalling his own experience as a battalion commander at Nhi Binh in Vietnam in 1968.

All professional training received up to that time led an officer to believe that, as a battalion commander, he would control his units and a wide variety of combat support while studying a detailed situation map painstakingly updated by a staff of experts. Critical decisions concerning the movement of units and the employment of supporting fires were thought to spring from the calm deliberations of the commander surrounded by his helpful staff. In fact, the battalion commander had to 'calmly deliberate' while stuffed into the left front seat of a three-seat helicopter, clutching his wind-blown maps and trying to juggle command frequencies on a woefully inadequate radio set.[47]

On a deep and dangerous battlefield personal contact with a full house of senior subordinates will be the exception rather than the rule. Short orders will go out by radio, and the current state of the Electronic Counter-Measure art suggests that interference or outright jamming will be frequent. In most forms of war it is rash to count upon anything much resembling the orders group of yesteryear and all the more important to ensure that subordinates understand what their commander wishes to achieve.

They will generally be told this by directives, outlining the commander's concept of operations, specifying the mission, the tasks which must be achieved and resources available for their accomplishment. The concept of operations lies at the heart of the matter. This may not always have the comprehensive simplicity of Hannibal's double envelopment at Cannae in 216 BC or von Manstein's equally classic flanking counterstroke at Kharkov in 1944, but it must be the logical product of a directing will. It will embody one or more forms of manoeuvre, such as envelopment, double envelopment, elastic defence, and so on. This list is short and ageless, with vertical envelopment by air being the only genuine twentieth-century addition. The concept should not wait on events, thereby effectively surrendering initiative to the enemy, although the production of a series of responsive projects (if the enemy does this, we will do that; if that, then the other . . .) is a comfortable refuge for weak wills.

Devising the concept of operations is the essence of senior command – self-evidently a task for brain cells not microchips – and lack of clarity at this, the very kernel of operations, will radiate uncertainty throughout. Formulation of directives is a demanding task, because it involves exhaustive examination of all implications of the commander's mission and, as the *British Military Doctrine* observes, requires more pure thought than listing details in a set-piece plan. Given the possibility that subordinates may react in a number of different ways to fulfil their missions, the fabric of supporting staff work must be very robust, and it is here that the computer can play its most useful part by rapid logistic and movement calculation.[48]

The importance of directive control is recognised by current emphasis on mission analysis. This analytical tool enables a subordinate, when framing his own plan, to define his own mission and any secondary tasks that flow from it, capitalise on an evolving situation in a way that his superior would find useful, and react to changes of which his superior is not aware. In short, it helps him to act purposefully, avoiding that shoulder-shrugging knee-jerk reaction of doing something that he strongly suspects will not work, or doing nothing because he has received no orders. 'Men, it is a mad-brained trick, but it is no fault of mine,' rasped Lord Cardigan after the Charge of the Light Brigade. It was indeed a mad-brained venture, made pointless because neither brigade nor divisional commander understood the commander-in-chief's purpose – something of which his order conveyed no real sense.

Genuine *Auftragstaktik* reflects the view embodied in the opening article of the introduction to the 1936 German *Truppenführung* manual that: 'Leadership in war is an art, a free creative activity resting on scientific foundation. It makes the highest demands on a man's entire personality.' Characteristically, this section of the manual concludes, with emphasis, that:

> decisive action remains the first prerequisite for success in war. Everybody, from the highest commander to the youngest soldiers, must be conscious of the fact that inactivity and lost opportunities weigh heavier than do errors in the choice of means.[49]

Simply grafting mission analysis on to the training programme does not produce *Auftragstaktik*. One penetrating examination of the subject opined that: 'There is plenty of fertile ground for an *Auftragstaktik*-like approach to grow in the US Army. But as long as the centralised command tradition remains alive and respectable, such growth will be uneven, confusing, and occasionally contentious.'[50]

The question of the formulation of directives, which play such an important part in *Auftragstaktik,* leads naturally on to consideration of staff structures and procedures. It is tempting to assume that the proliferation of information arriving at headquarters – real-time intelligence from manned aircraft, drones and sensors, reports from forward units and flanking formations as well as summaries from higher headquarters – makes the commander's life easier. Hungry computers digest it all, and uncertainty is swept away by the surge of pure fact, basing the 'information' pillar of the information-decision-action cycle on the most solid of foundations. The commander's decisions crackle out across secure communication links. Prompt and effective action follows, and the hapless enemy is elbowed out of the Boyd cycle.

An alternative view would compare this pleasing image with the reality of a field headquarters in the 1990s, a contrast as stark as Roy Flint's juxtaposition of expectation and fact in Vietnam twenty years ago. Clausewitz's sand has trickled into some of the systems, and there are some empty screens in evidence as technicians replace major components. Malfunctions combine with enemy action to darken the transparent battlefield. But the dominant characteristic – as dominant as the rattle of tracks or the whap of rotors in the forward battle – is the influx of information. It flashes in on screens, hammers out of printers, surges into the headquarters from a dozen radio nets and telephone links. Despite the proliferation of analysts – young majors, most of them, their early promotion and limited military experience testifying to armies' need to catch them in a shallow civilian pool – the staff are drowning. They snatch at what they can, usually facts which do not conflict with their preconceptions, and present their commander with computerised options. He struggles with the rival needs to stay in his main heaquarters to sip from the information torrent and to get in his helicopter and speak to the commanders fighting the forward battle. He has also to contend with the fatigue his long routineless days have brought upon him, the knowledge that the consequences of his actions are momentous, and the unmanning kick to the belly that comes when he looks at the small blue graphical symbol, now almost swallowed by the surrounding red, that marks the position of his son's platoon. Boyd cycle? He is hard-pressed to keep his headquarters on an even keel, let alone win the battle.

This is not a far-fetched view. Practical experience of computers in large headquarters on exercises raises doubts about their durability. Major-General Sam Cowan, Commandant of the Royal Military College of Science and certainly no Luddite, warned that in war systems will be exposed to 'considerable degradation . . . through both electronic attack and physical destruction'.[51] Even when they work as planned, much of the information they generate is valueless because it is never used: the large-scale dumping of thousands of unread print-outs has already occurred on major exercises. The tendency of commanders and their staff to over-identify with units and individuals was recognised well before the First World War, and Sir Ernest Swinton's cautionary tale 'The Point of View' focuses on a staff officer's horror at seeing his old battalion disappear from the situation map.[52] The accretion of hardware around large formation headquarters reduces their mobility, and yet going for the super-hardened option, with a static headquarters ensconced in a pre-constructed position (but generously inviting attention by its electronic signature) only beckons the enemy to contrive an adequate sledgehammer to crack a high-value nut.

Part of the difficulty stems from simply bolting new technology (in information systems as in weaponry) on to existing structures without sufficient thought. As Stephen Canby has observed,

> innovative technology will need to be properly applied by military institutions which in many instances are composed of elements committed by tradition and instinct to preserving their expertise in familiar experience-proven areas. Without institutional adaptiveness, potential technological superiority can be meaningless.[53]

Simply adding computing power to a headquarters because the technology exists and the information it produces seems likely to be useful is squarely in accord with the machinery-gulping tendency of our age, but it does not in itself make for more effective command. We have seen that a concept of operations is central to successful operational command: a clear concept of what military function information technology is expected to achieve is scarcely less important.

Even the question of intelligence admits of no easy solutions. The growth of reliable strategic intelligence, with satellite photography as one of its most valuable sources, fuels the comfortable assumption that commanders in the field will receive a steady flow of relevant intelligence down the chain of command. However, strategic intelligence is over-stretched even in peacetime, and in war it lacks the flexibility to respond to many of the demands made upon it. Not everything it produces is valuable, and there are still questions it cannot answer, a fact underlined by General Noriega's embarrassing if short-lived evasion of US forces in Panama. There is no escaping the fact that intelligence must be acquired by commanders at all levels, and targeting the intelligence effort is no less crucial a function of operational command than targeting a particular weapon system. While technology can help in acquiring, processing and transmitting intelligence, the task of directing the intelligence effort is essentially one for brain cell rather than microchip.

How, then, should the overall balance between the brain and the microchip be achieved? First, by ensuring that the span of command is realistically narrow. Starry advocates:

> a whole lot of smaller units. Three-tank platoons, three-platoon companies, three-company battalions and three-battalion brigades because we may need more leaders for those who are led. This may mean 15 battalions per division. Small battalions commanded by mean SOBs who have nothing but a microphone and tank to run them. No mains, rears, TACS, staffs . . .[54]

This is in accord with van Creveld's belief that it is wrong to respond to the threat of Precision-Guided Munitions homing in on electronic emissions by dispersing the principle members of headquarters, using modern technology to communicate with one another. Far better, he argues, to study the Israeli solution, of putting all key officers in a single vehicle, thus permitting face-to-face interaction. 'Israeli tactical headquarters at brigade level', he writes, 'are no larger than those of US companies, with the added bonus that they are inconspicuous, leave a smaller electronic signature, and are to this extent better protected also.'[55] The 'all eggs in one basket' counter-argument warns of the fatal consequences of a hit on such a headquarters, but its relatively low cost permits duplication, and the ability of decentralised component parts to function with the temporary loss of their nerve-centre is also encouraging. Small, flexible headquarters are also likely to be of growing utility as the prospect of a clash in the Central Region recedes but other areas of military interest remain alive and well.

Next, it cannot be sufficiently emphasised that command is an affair of the spirit as well as the mind, art based upon science. The qualities of the great commander (qualities which must exist in different proportions at various levels of command – Eisenhower was an admirable alliance manager but would have been less successful as a divisional commander) are human ones: strength of will tempered by flexibility, boldness untainted by needless risk, and instinct illuminated by experience. He must command respect, and if he inspires affection too his hand is all the stronger. Drawing up a long list of other desirable leadership qualities is delusive, for so many of the great commanders of history break the rules that we seek to impose upon them. If their qualities are human, so too are their vices, from Alexander the Great's homicidal rage to Napoleon's fundamental callousness and Montgomery's overweening pride. The commander, warts and all, is a man, and his place is at the centre of the loop, driving technology, not being driven by it.

Being at the centre of the loop does not mean being burnt out by the surges pulsing through it. If the information revolution has re-emphasised the importance of the human element in war, it has also highlighted the need for proper division of responsibilities between commander and chief of staff. Von Manstein reflected on the 'flood of paper' which descended upon his headquarters during the phony war of 1939–40, when he was chief of staff to von Rundstedt's Army Group A. 'Thanks to a very proper unwritten law in the German Army that the general commanding a formation be kept free of all minor detail, however, v. Rundstedt was hardly affected and was able to take a long walk every morning on the Rheinpromenade.'[56] The workaholic habits of peacetime die hard, and persuading commanders to relax in war will prove impossible unless they have learned to do so in peace – and many have not. The great von Moltke spent the 1870 mobilisation lying on a sofa reading a novel – it was *Lady Audley's Secret*. Von Rundstedt had a weakness for detective stories, General Baade for Aristotle or Seneca. Alexander, Allied commander in Italy, whose perfect manners charmed even the prickly Montgomery, kept a novel in the drawer of his desk, closing it when his chief of staff, John Harding, entered. General Pete Quesada, who did so much to smooth the rocky road of Allied ground-air co-operation in Normandy, was a keen amateur cabinet maker. The commander-in-chief in Swinton's 'The Point of View' was an avid fisherman, who devoted himself to a fine trout as the battle developed. 'Then all thoughts of war, battle, envelopment and possibilities left him in a flash,' wrote Swinton, 'and his mind rested while he pitted his skill against the cunning of the fish – an old veteran himself. His present duty was to keep his own mind clear, and not to cloud the minds of his subordinates.'[57]

In modern high-intensity battle there may be little enough time for novels, still less for two-pound trout. Yet the principle remains an important one. Sir Martin Lindsay, who commanded 1st Battalion The Gordon Highlanders in sixteen operations in north-west Europe in 1944–5 (scarcely low-intensity stuff) proposed two maxims for successful command. The first was that it should be 'exercised in a relaxed and happy manner at all levels', the second was 'the importance of delegation so as to give time to think about matters far removed from the immediate urgencies'.[58] Lieutenant-General Sir Peter de la Billière, an officer with much recent experience of special force operations, listed loyalty, decisiveness, judgment and risk-taking among the attributes of command – and added humour. 'I like to think,' he wrote, 'that no commander can truly relax his subordinates unless he possesses a sense of *Humour* – particularly when the battle is thickest and the crisis at a peak.'[59]

I.S. Bloch argued that: 'Many officers whose duty it was to make decisions of the highest importance, suffered from too little sleep, hasty meals, and the lack of a proper routine.'[60] The figure of the exhausted senior officer is a familiar one. Archie Murray, French's chief of staff on the retreat from Mons, fainted at his desk, and one of his divisional chiefs of staff, overstretched beyond tolerance, shot himself. Moltke had a nervous breakdown in 1914, and Ludendorff followed suit in 1918. Lieutenant-General Sir Alan Cunningham, victor in Abyssinia in 1940–1, was already tired when he took the helm of the 8th Army, and his nerve failed him during its *Crusader* offensive.

Sometimes failure is the product of a long accumulation of stress. Lieutenant-Colonel Andrew Thorne of the Grenadier Guards described his feelings after commanding a battalion for a year on the Western Front:

> I wish I were going to get a Brigade shortly as I am badly in need of a change. For some time I have had to have 'my whip out' to keep myself up to the mark and that can not be good for the Battalion . . . it is badly in need of ginger which is just what I can not supply.[61]

The moral responsibilities of command weigh heavily. Von Moltke the younger dreaded giving an account of himself at the last judgment, and French believed that his room at GHQ was full of the spirits of his dead friends, demanding some sort of answer.

On other occasions a physical near-miss, or a psychological blow to a commander's self-esteem produced by an unexpected reverse, has much the same effect. Lord Hopton, arguably the most competent Royalist commander in the English Civil War, was knocked off balance by the death of Colonel Richard Bolle and the destruction of his regiment when Sir William Waller stormed Alton in December 1643. The loss was like 'a wound which bled inwards', and it helped bring Hopton to defeat at Cheriton the following year. Many reasons were advanced for 'Fighting Joe' Hooker's defeat at Chancellorsville. He was unlucky to face Lee and Jackson at the peak of their form, but was still in a position to inflict a substantial defeat on the Confederates even after Jackson's flank attack had ripped into his army. He squandered several golden opportunities, and then fell back. Some said he was drunk, others that he had been concussed when a shell hit the wooden pillar of a mansion as he leaned against it. In later life Fighting Joe was disarmingly honest. 'I was not hurt by the shell and I was not drunk,' he admitted. 'To tell the truth I just lost confidence in Joe Hooker.' 'There had been no courage in him, no life, no spark,' wrote Bruce Catton; 'during most of the battle the army to all intents and purposes had had no commander at all.'[62]

Little can be done to insulate a senior officer from the sustained stress of war, and repeated exposure to it will ultimately break him as surely as it will the the sturdiest rifleman. Yet much can be done to mitigate its effects and delay its advance. An army's peacetime career pyramid will ensure that wartime commanders are the men who have ascended the hierarchy by displaying the qualities demanded in the piping time of peace. Some, it is true, will have combat experience, but it will often be long ago or in irrelevant (even delusive) circumstances. Charles Townshend made his reputation defending the fortress of Chitral on the North-West Frontier in 1895, but the model of a gallant garrison holding out against all odds served him ill at Kut-al-Amara in 1916, where his army was compelled to surrender to the Turks. The deference accorded to rank is not always helpful. John Keegan argued that:

> Generalship is bad for people. As anyone intimate with military society knows only too well, the most reasonable of men suffuse with pomposity when stars touch their shoulders . . . military society, that last surviving model of the courts of heroic war leaders, regularly does them the favour of indulging their fantasies.[63]

The lions of peacetime often fail in the changed climate of war. Examine the command lists of major armies at the start of long wars, and compare them with those a year or two later: many of the peacetime selections, men who promised so well, have disappeared. Joffre ruthlessly purged one-third of French generals in September 1914, cropping them even harder than Hitler did the German *Generalität* in December 1941. In the BEF in 1940 if one corps commander (Brooke) was an unequivocal success, another (Baker) was an unmitigated disaster. Brooke found him 'in a very difficult state to deal with . . . he sees dangers where they don't exist . . . whenever everything is fixed he changes his mind shortly afterwards'. Brooke later regretted the apparent criticism of an old friend: he had not realised that he was suffering from a nervous breakdown.[64] The divisional commanders were similarly patchy, while of the brigadiers, many who so looked the part in the spring of 1940, with their DSOs and MCs from the First World War, found themselves unable to dance to the tempo of mechanised war.

Received wisdom points to the importance of youth among senior officers. 'By Jove!' remarked John Glubb's brigade commander in August 1914, hearing that the young Glubb was only eighteen. 'That's the age to go to war.'[65] After a three-day battle in icy weather on the Lisaine in January 1870 a young officer suggested to General Bourbaki, the army commander, that a night attack would be in order. 'I'm twenty years too old,' said Bourbaki (he was fifty-four). 'Generals should be your age.'[66] The Israeli army, the most consistently successful of recent times, is a byword for the youth of its officers, with company commanders aged 22–3 and battalion commanders 26–8.

It is axiomatic that the age of an army's senior officers drops during war. In 1940 the average age of US Army regular division commanders was 52, while the average age of a sample of combat division commanders was 48, with the actual age spread between 33 and 58.[67] This is still old by comparison with the ages of senior officers at the end of world wars, when battalions, and sometimes brigades, were routinely commanded by officers in their twenties. In the First World War Brigadier-General 'Boy' Bradford was killed commanding his brigade at Bourlon Wood in 1917 at the age of 25, and in the Second the future Field Marshal Lord Carver commanded an independent armoured brigade at 28, and the future General Sir John Hackett a parachute brigade at 32. Von Senger und Etterlin wrote of how the fighting at Cassino was 'the business of twenty-five-year-old battalion commanders'. General Kitson suggests that a corps commander should be 43–5, divisional commanders around 40, and brigade commanders around 37: this is not an unreasonable judgment based on the evidence of command in two world wars.

Yet the evidence is not unequivocal. Historical examples are inevitably selective, designed to prove a point, and the particular does not necessarily illuminate the general. However, we do not have to search hard for examples of old men beating much younger ones. A.V. Suvorov was recalled from retirement at the age of 70 in 1799, and promptly beat Moreau (36), Macdonald (34) and Joubert (45). In 1848–9, at the age of 84, Field Marshal Radetzky thrashed Charles Albert of Sardinia (50) at Custozza and Novara. During the first phase of the Franco-Prussian war French generals were on average younger than their opponents (corps commanders 59 to 61). The great Moltke was 70, and his royal master three years older. Although one of the French deductions from the war was that their high command was too old, it was actually younger in 1870 than in 1914, when it performed rather better.[68] Joffre, to whose sang-froid the French army owed its survival, was 62, and Foch, a corps commander in August that year, but destined for greater things, was a year older. Petain, saviour of Verdun, was on the verge of compulsory retirement when the war broke out. In 1940 the oldest of the British divisional commanders, Major-General Dudley

Johnson, turned in a sounder performance than some many years his junior.

To the riposte that a general's life in the field was once far more comfortable than it is today one might interpose several parries. Travel in a coach along rutted roads or on horseback over open country was no less taxing than jeep, staff-car or helicopter. Although a general might expect to be billeted in private house or inn, he would not always have the luxury of removing his boots: senior officers of the King's Army in Scotland slept fully dressed but for their wigs the night before Culloden. For all the rarity of night operations before 1914, there were sleepless nights in awkward places. Napoleon snatched a few hours on a pile of straw before Austerlitz, Wellingon enjoyed 'nine hours' sleep in ninety' in the Waterloo campaign, and Ducrot passed a restless night at Sedan, wrapped in his cloak, sitting by the bivouac fire of one of his Zouave regiments, watching German campfires creep across the hills round the town.

Command in battle generally meant long days in the saddle. Wellington, an excellent horseman, lived on the snappish Copenhagen, donning a short blue cloak when it rained, and snacking in the saddle: at Salamanca he flung a half-eaten chicken leg in the air in delight as he saw that the French were over-extended. Bazaine was less comfortable on horseback, but he spent the blazing August day of Rezonville bucketing up and down his infantry line, laying a gun here, cheering up an edgy battalion there, under fire the whole time, and in pain from a shell-splinter which had hit him in the shoulder two days before, breaking an epaulette and bruising him badly. Physical danger was never far away: John Keegan notes that the French lost one general killed and 13 wounded at Austerlitz, 8 and 15 at Eylau, 12 and 37 at Borodino, 16 and 50 at Waterloo.

Youth in itself is no recommendation for high command, and age is no bar. Physical and mental robustness are more important than *anno Domini*, and a mania for youth should not be allowed to exclude fit and competent middle-aged men from senior appointments. Health must be monitored carefully, given the tendency of senior officers to die from natural causes at moments of crisis: General Gaujal had a cerebral haemorrhage in his corps commander's office in August 1870; Sir James Grieson was carried off by a heart attack on his way to the concentration area in August 1914, and it was a heart attack, not enemy bullets, that killed General Stumme in the opening minutes of the battle of El Alamain. Dr Hugh L'Etang's pioneering work on the pathology of leadership paints an alarming picture of great men riddled by serious (and often detectable) illness.

Nor should we confine ourselves to physical health. It was quite clear from Sir Horace Smith-Dorrien's track record that his spectacular rages cast doubt over his fitness for high command. About his technical competence there can be no doubt whatever, and his decision to stand and fight at Le Cateau unquestionably saved the BEF. During the battle of Mons, however, he fell into such a temper that his chief of staff left on the spot, with the intention of resigning his commission. Although he was told at GHQ 'not to be an ass' and sent back to his corps at once, the incident reflected no credit on the selection system then prevailing in the British army. It was shortly followed by another spectacular set-to, this time between French and Kitchener, whose mutual antipathy and short fuses were a matter of general knowledge among senior officers. Uncontrollable fury or obsessive worry in peacetime must cast serious doubt over suitability for high command in war, and an army which appoints prima donnas or neurotics to senior appointments deserves what it will undoubtedly get.

Establishing a proper relationship between a commander and his chief of staff is of prime importance. The German principle of having an elitist general staff which provides chiefs of staff has much to recommend it. It helps to promote a sound mutual understanding between chiefs of staff, albeit sometimes at the cost of easing the commander on to the sidelines. 'Chief of Staff,' recorded the G3 log of 12 Panzer Division in August 1944, 'with all respect to the old man, watch what you say on the rear link.'[69] It also gives the commander breathing-space, time to rise above the underbrush of the moment to survey the far horizon. A commander may properly divide his time between a small forward headquarters – sometimes as small as the front seat of his helicopter or back of a single armoured vehicle – and his main headquarters in a proportion that the tempo of battle, nature of air and ground threat, state of communications and, not least, his own temperament, will determine. Operational decisions must be taken in his absence, often without reference to him, and a chief of staff who is in his commander's mind is the man to take them. Battle often follows a discernible pattern, with frequent combat pulses in the day and fewer at night, and by identifying these a chief of staff can create a pattern of routine which helps lighten his commander's burden. Understanding when the commander is to be woken and when he should sleep on undisturbed is the very stuff of the commander–chief of staff relationship.

Command is a lonely business, and the commander needs some way of escaping from the spotlight. He may not be able to relax with his chief of staff or his deputies, but both padres and medical officers – in the army but not of it – provide a useful sounding board and, often, convivial and unambitious company into the bargain. Investigative historians who seek a psychological basis for everything cast suspicious glances at the small intimate groups of young men which have surrounded many commanders. We may suspect not latent homosexuality, but a genuine desire to relax in the congenial company of officers who pose no threat, and whose youthful banter takes the commander's mind off tomorrow's hard decisions. Somewhere in the immediate household there is likely to be a particular private soldier or NCO – Wellington had his German dragoon Beckerman, von Manstein his faithful driver Sergeant Nagel – who is allowed gruff liberties that more senior officers would not dare to take, another source of information and another friend with whom secrets are safe. Lieutenant-Colonel Ian Gardiner, reflecting on his time as a company commander in the Falklands, thought that the loneliness of command pervaded the entire chain, and by understanding this junior commanders could make their superiors' lives easier.

> There were times when I felt I had glimpsed the loneliness, the total isolation, of the widow, I was so lonely. But loneliness is a concomitant of power. Spare a thought for Brigadier Thompson . . . who had the fate of the government as well as his brigade in his hands. Or Admiral Woodward who like his First World War predecessor, Jellicoe, could have lost the war in an afternoon. I dwell on this because if you spare a thought you can do your humble bit to help . . . Expect the unexpected and encourage your men to do so. Don't whinge when your company is ordered to move at short notice just after you have cooked your breakfast. Don't stamp your feet when the stores you demand don't arrive. All these things will happen. But have faith in the goodwill and competence of the staff officers of your higher formations. In their own way, they are under greater strain than you.[70]

National policy on deputy commanders varies. They provide another rung on the peacetime ladder, and thus another useful ticket-punch, and form the nucleus for an alternative headquarters which can take over if disaster strikes. There is also some functional logic in dividing responsibilities at divisional and corps level between a deputy commander (manoeuvre) and a deputy commander (logistics). However, such appointments dilute the authority of the chief of staff, for if they are deputies in any genuine sense they will be senior to him. It may be better to have a powerful chief of staff, senior by both rank and function to other members of the headquarters, and to dispense with deputies altogether.

Commanders need training no less than their subordinates. The training of senior officers is an uncomfortable subject, not least in the British army, where it was long assumed that the experience obtained in a variety of appointments while progressing up the hierarchy provided sufficient training, and until the establishment of the Higher Command and Staff Course in 1988 there was no in-depth preparation for command above battalion level. Major exercises tend to follow clearly prescribed patterns (for reasons of exercise planning and damage control if for no others), and rarely impose much real pressure on commanders at brigade and divisional level – still less upon corps commanders. A *British Army Review* article noted that while Command Post Exercises and Field Training Exercises might usefully train the staff: 'the commander, in order to train his staff, assumes the role of chief umpire. He, himself, is not really trained on these exercises for it is very difficult to run an exercise and at the same time exercise oneself'.[71]

Implementation of the Brigade and Battle Group Trainers at Sennelager and Catterick in 1986 was a notable improvement. Nevertheless, the value obtained from such trainers scarcely begins to approach that gained at the US Army's National Training Center, where commanders at brigade and battalion level have a unique opportunity to exercise against a force which mimics Soviet tactics, and Direct Fire Weapons Effects Simulators ensure that tactics is a great deal more than the opinion of the senior officer present. If we consider fire co-ordination, just one of the preoccupations of a commander and his staff – though among the most important, for twentieth-century conflict repeatedly underlines Foch's sharp truism that fire kills – training at the NTC shows how units which lost:

were unable to kill the opposing force (OPFOR) soldiers fast enough. They had got weapon systems that never got into battle; they failed to cover all avenues of approach; they failed to understand engagement priorities; they failed to integrate and coordinate all their means of fire and fire support; they ignored the need for establishing a base of fire; and often they tried to overcome the OPFOR units with sheer numbers.[72]

Learning on the job in the face of a real enemy is infinitely more painful. Before retiring for his sleepless vigil the night before Sedan, General Ducrot vainly tried to persuade his army commander to make proper preparations to meet the coming storm. When MacMahon refused, saying that he expected to be on the move too quickly for that, Ducrot replied: 'M. le Maréchal, tomorrow the enemy will not give you time.'[73] He rarely does. The previous world wars lasted long enough to permit combatants to recover from mistakes in senior personnel selection. Neither a major superpower clash, nor more probable intervention operations like the Falklands or Grenada, will allow such luxuries.

Still less will they permit a lumpy transition from one form of organisation to another. Peacetime military structures must conform as closely as possible to those required in war. This is an old lesson, clearly taught by German organisational superiority in the Franco-Prussian war and re-emphasised on numerous occasions since. It has not always been well-remembered. Confusion over planning and command responsibility bedevilled the US invasion of Grenada, and the sheer difficulty of mounting an intervention operation, especially on a multi-national basis, points unmistakably to the need for permanently constituted peacetime headquarters, working under commanders who will head them in war.

No army can afford two sets of senior officers, one to manage its bureaucracy in peace, the other to command its formations in war. It can best narrow the gap between them by recognising that, save in the case of a few brilliant exceptions, generalship is not acquired by osmosis, but by a mixture of formal training and the practical exercise of command. There is little reason save self-interest for subjecting a battalion commander to a penetrating test exercise but sparing a divisional commander a similar task. The deference accorded to senior officers in peacetime is not always helpful, and it encourages creeping paralysis as the great man's decision is awaited on a matter well within the competence of his juniors. Running an army demands the copious exercise of initiative: it is fruitless to expect officers to employ *Auftragstaktik* in war unless they have learned to make their own hard decisions, in command and on the staff, in peace. The Napoleonic general in the anecdote which opened this chapter was an officer of proven physical courage: but the virtue most demanded of his successors is moral courage – and that is rarer still.

7

The Seeds of Time

If you can look into the seeds of time,
And tell me which grain will grow and which will not,
Speak then to me, who neither beg nor fear
Your favours nor your hate.

Shakespeare, *Macbeth*

A thousand years ago, towards the end of the first millennium, men feared that the world was about to end. God would blot it out in fire and brimstone; the devil's legions would surge up out of the east, and huge epidemics would destroy the human race. Our own age is no less millennial. The mushroom cloud has done duty for fire and brimstone; the legions of the devil march from Moscow or Peking, and in Aids we have an epidemic which plays on our darkest fears. The great terror of the first millennium passed as the world climbed with relief into the eleventh century, but instead of lifting altogether, the fears of our own age are changing character as we approach the twenty-first century. Global warming is taking over from the nuclear holocaust as the ultimate disaster, the new legions will be terrorists seeping from the Middle East or refugees pouring from poverty-stricken South to comfortable North, while Aids, in fresh and obdurate strains, threatens to settle grimly into the role of pandemic.

Perhaps we have lived so long on the edge of the precipice that we would be uncomfortable elsewhere. Certainly, the idea of the holocaust is too firmly entrenched in popular literature to go away. In *Einstein's Monsters* Martin Amis was transfixed by thermonuclear war: now, in his *London Fields,* a vaguer crisis drops its guillotine blade on the end of the millennium. Novels on future war have never

286

sold better: *Team Yankee* and *Red Army* clutter the bookstalls although the events they describe so well have a reduced chance of happening with every day that passes.

This is indeed a world whose present danger snipes at our attempts to find lasting security, but I cannot share the millennial view, at least as far as its military component is concerned. President Gorbachev's initiatives, and the evolving responses from the West, have greatly reduced the prospects of an armed clash between the superpowers, and the risk of high-intensity battle in NATO's Central Region is more remote today than at any point since 1945. It is not yet impossible, for although Soviet military power has been reduced it still remains awesome, and while capabilities take years to develop, intentions can change overnight. Some will doubtless attribute this reduction of tension to a general outbreak of common sense, and thus justify rapid and thoroughgoing disarmament. However, the very existence of NATO, and the strains imposed on the Soviet Union by military expenditure, have contributed to the new Soviet policy, and in our eagerness to dismember the warrior state we should not ignore this.

Balanced reductions in nuclear weapons are to be applauded, and there is certainly little reason for the mutual overkill which still groans within superpowers' arsenals. The total abolition of nuclear weapons is unrealistic, though they could be safely reduced to the level which would give existing members of the nuclear club the ability to deter nuclear attack. If the nuclear weapons which survived such reductions were too few for their use to trigger a nuclear winter, so much the better. It is impossible to legislate effectively against horizontal nuclear proliferation, and before the ink is dry on these pages news will emerged of the addition of more nuclear weapons to the already unstable mixture in the Middle East. The most potent danger lies not in an exchange between the superpowers or the other long-established nuclear powers, but in the spread of nuclear weapons in areas where emotions run high and logic takes a back seat.

The demise of the Soviet threat will undoubtedly have far-reaching effects upon governments and armies alike. West Germany was displaying a visible reluctance to remain the garrison-town of NATO even before reunification pushed its way to the centre of the stage, and it is hard to predict how a united Germany will fit into the loosening jigsaw of alliances. NATO has been 'an alliance under threat' for so long that latest reports of its demise should be treated with more than a little caution. Nevertheless there is a real danger that the alliance will lose its way as the threat which has cemented it for so long loses its adhesion. Moreover, in the past few years NATO has lost the moral high ground to a Soviet peace offensive: if this was an armed conflict, NATO would be so far outside its adversary's Boyd cycle that it would long since have lost the war. NATO will probably evolve into a primarily political alliance, with less emphasis on its integrated command structure than upon its political links. And just as it was traditionally the 'entangling alliance', designed to ensure an American military commitment to Europe, so it will remain an indispensable link between Europe and North America.

The fact that *glasnost* coincides with the demographic downturn, a US budget deficit and widespread fears about the environment, will provoke large-scale reductions in force levels and military expenditure. Controversial or speculative programmes will suffer, and it will be interesting to see how long Star Wars (even in the apparently effective form of BRILLIANT PEBBLES) survives unscathed. Armies which do not currently employ women widely will be encouraged to do so, mounting an intellectual defence of a line of action warmly encouraged by their growing inability to recruit sufficient young men. Manpower – or, more accurately, personpower – will be a major military issue throughout the nineties.

The reduction of defence funding across most of the developed world will sharply increase the gap between available and affordable technology. This will be a matter of very real concern to professional officers, who will respond by warning of the dangers of being technologically outclassed by potential opponents. They should be induced to match doctrine to strategic purpose, and equipment to doctrine, more precisely than many of them do at present: the age of technology gluttony is over. It will become more and more difficult to replace equipment on a one-for-one basis, and the quest for 'more of the same' will prove increasingly delusive. The disappearance of the single alarming but assuring scenario for conflict will further complicate the process. The fields of surveillance and target acquisition, and electronic counter measures, seem to offer the most fruitful areas for exploitation, but here as elsewhere the hunt for a single 'master-weapon' will be fruitless, and the best of technology will be of little use unless it is happily married to doctrine.

The financial shears which prune procurement programmes will also threaten the rewards offered to soldiers in terms of pay and allowances, and temptations to make budgetary cuts in this quarter should be rigorously avoided. High-quality manpower will grow ever scarcer between now and the end of the century, and it must be offered serious money if the profession of arms is to remain attractive.

Yet manpower problems will not be solved simply by throwing money at them. A genuine increase in the initiative offered to officers and NCOs alike, and the pruning of overcommanding hierarchies, will make the profession a more satisfying one. Profession it is, and profession it should remain: reducing entry standards to meet short-term recruiting difficulties will produce destructive long-term weaknesses. Military education must reflect much more than hands-on specialism, and its corrosive technical emphasis should be corrected by a genuine breadth which places an ancient and honourable profession into its proper context. Most armies could cope with having fewer career officers, enabling entry standards to be kept up, and giving a greater prospect for advancement to NCOs, whose reasonable ambition for late-entry commissioning could be fulfilled.

There must now be serious doubt as to whether general staffs on the British and American pattern have had their day. Smaller, more expert general staffs capable of designing a robust military framework within national strategy, building operational and tactical doctrine to match this blueprint, and making their writ run through the army as a whole, can alone bring the speed and consistency which rapid external change demands. Single-service baronies cannot long survive intact. More power will inevitably accrue to the tri-service centre, and functional command structures, reflecting the mission to be carried out rather than the composition of the forces which may execute it, subsume the triple tribes of yesteryear. In practice soldiers will continue to wear khaki, sailors dark blue and airmen light blue: the Canadian experiment with total synthesis does not encourage general imitation, although there is much to be said for a unified medical corps.

It is self-evident that combat has not abolished itself by becoming intolerable to its participants. Although high-intensity battle, fought without restraint, might indeed impose such stresses that the escalating toll of psychiatric casulaties would make it difficult to sustain, that form of battle is increasingly unlikely. In any case the rugged durability of well-trained combat units has withstood the shock of battle in the past – psychiatric casualties notwithstanding – and its ability to do so in future cannot be easily dismissed. Military units of the developed world are far more likely to find themselves engaged in the war against terrorism – as endemic for our children as smallpox was for our great-grandparents – or in projecting national power into another continent, than they are in a stereotyped superpower conflict. This says much about force structure and weapon procurement. Weapons and organisations which are theatre-specific (main battle tanks and armoured divisions are so in practice if not in theory) will be less use than more agile forces with lighter equipment. The tank's day may not be over in technological terms, but its useful employment will be increasingly circumscribed: the future belongs to rotors, not to tracks. Forces structured for rapid intervention – for instance into the territory of a threatened ally – will prove of greater utility than an armour-heavy force whose functions are limited and whose response time is slow. This does not mean that armour is obsolete. A large land power with powerful or unstable neighbours would be rash not to retain some capacity for fighting armoured war, but it must do its best to ensure that this does not in itself provoke or threaten. Special forces are already a growth industry: their suitability for rapid deployment and ability to apply the scalpel when the bludgeon would be inappropriate will make them an increasingly valuable ingredient of the military instrument.

A recurring theme since 1945 has been the impact of public opinion on military operations. The Vietnam War was lost in Washington, and on dozens of campuses across America, rather than in the theatre of war itself. Although popular support for the Falklands War remained strong, we cannot but speculate on the effect of a failure before Stanley and a war which dragged on into a long South Atlantic winter. It is too early to assess the effects of the *intifada*, but it may well impose greater stresses on the Israeli army than conventional wars ever did, and its effects on world opinion have already been damaging.

If maintaining popular support in wartime is effectively a prerequisite for military success, then securing and retaining such support in peacetime is no less important. Failure to do so will diminish the status of the profession of arms, further imperil funding, and do at least as much damage to recruiting as the demographic downturn. Joining an army with a clearly defined role in the superpower confrontation was one thing: enlisting in a force whose very existence is perceived as irrelevant is quite another.

Current interest in the operational level of war and in mission-oriented orders is to be applauded, though we must hope that both concepts reflect a deep-seated understanding of the nature of war rather than a transient military fashion. In fact, the reduction of force levels and the concomitant decrease in the ratio of troops to space should make both even more important than they are today. Fading budgets, diminishing threat, and changes in German public opinion will all encourage the shrinking of NATO's forces in the Central Region. This seems likely to happen as part of mutual force reduction agreements, though in any event it will require careful stage-managing if the haemorrhage of conventional forces from Germany is not one of the first symptoms of unstructured and potentially destabilising disarmament.

There are two immediately attractive responses to the current military situation in Europe. The first, favoured by some senior officers and conservative politicians, is to emphasise present un-certainty and future unpredictability, and to retain the highest force levels consistent with budgetary constraints and electoral survival. In short, to press on with business as usual for as long as is decently possible. The second, beloved of the political left and some military journalists, is to fasten upon a suitable figure of manpower (which a politician might pitch a good deal lower than a defence commentator) and to argue for restructuring on that basis.

Both solutions are wrong. The former will appear increasingly incredible. First, to an electorate more concerned, rightly or wrongly, with kidney dialysis machines than with main battle tanks, and second, to soldiers themselves, who will be uncomfortably aware that they are holding a line from which the battle has already melted away. The second follows the misleading preoccupation with form rather than function, sketching out organisational structures without fully considering the functions the forces within them are expected to fulfil. Unless armies think deeply about their functions they will trundle round the outer loop of the Boyd cycle, reactive, not pro-active, losing public support, finance and recruits.

There can be no substitute for a throughgoing reappraisal of the function which a nation seeks its armed forces to perform, and for their structuring to be driven by a powerful sense of purpose. Foch's maxim, *de quoi s'agit il* – what is it about – is no bad touchstone. Such a fundamental process might well produce alarmingly radical solutions. For instance, the logic underpinning independent air forces seems weaker today than ever before, and force restructuring based upon functional logic could easily result in the air arm being firmly subordinated to ground forces under most operational circumstances. Similarly, the increasing effectiveness of indirect fire weapons, especially related to improvements in surveillance and target acquisition, may well result in tube or rocket artillery becoming the dominant combat arm in its own right in all but the low-intensity end of the spectrum of conflict.

Such conclusions will doubtless not appeal to those whose careers have been devoted to specialisms which have lost much of their relevance, and there will be cautious voices recommending policies that replace like with like to maintain the mixture as before. It is the tiredest of clichés to maintain that a serious challenge is also an exciting opportunity, but such is undoubtedly the case today. Structuring armed forces, top to bottom, so as to meet a strategic requirement, fit operational logic and make tactical sense, will not only ensure that states receive value for money: it will also give a sense of purpose to armies which will flounder without one.

Considering alternative uses of armies ought to be a major preoccupation of defence ministries. There are many circumstances outside armed conflict where discipline, communications and specialist equipment are valuable. The war against drugs is as serious an issue for the Western world as many a shooting war could be, and, despite the concern expressed in several quarters (not least among the military), it is not unreasonable to apply military power to this strategic purpose. Rescue and relief missions, national and international, are also legitimate military functions. It is frankly puzzling that the British fire officers who went to assist earthquake victims in Armenia in 1988 were unable to borrow some of the equipment they required from British service sources, and flew out in civil aircraft – becoming separated from their equipment and wasting much time in consequence. Moreover, although two army field ambulances (medical battalions to American readers) were readily available neither was sent. The use of military personnel for civil aid and development tasks is anything but revolutionary – one has only to look at the contribution made by engineer officers to road building and official architecture world-wide. Yet it is a function of which armies and their employers must remind themselves, for it provides not only a recognisably useful task for armies, but also gives worthwhile gratification to the tribal instincts of young warriors.

Peacekeeping and observation forces are already much in demand, and the erosion of the world's two greatest alliances will make it easier for multi-national forces to be deployed to trouble-spots. Fighting and peacekeeping are self-evidently dissimilar tasks, but both require disciplined and cohesive forces, and the US Army has already had considerable success with the integration of an observer force – wearing, appropriately, a dove and olive branch beret badge – into its Light Infantry divisions. Fighting to preserve peace rather than to win war is neither irrational nor novel, and it is a task which will become increasingly important.

One does not need to be an historian to be struck by the mutability of human affairs, nor an alarmist to point to the appearance of danger, often from unexpected quarters, in an uncertain world. Armies will unquestionably retain a deterrent function, arguably as their primary role, at least as long as the bipolar world survives. They will be required to support diplomacy by armed force where a nation's vital interests are engaged, and to fight when the occasion demands it. Such demands will not be lightly made by states whose political maturity and recent history alike emphasise the inherent imprecision of the military instrument, but it is foolish to assume a similarity of restraint across the globe.

Armies will play a growing part in activities at the very lowest end of the spectrum of intensity, keeping the peace in multi-national forces, sharing the burden of the war against drugs, and assisting (or, more rarely, supplanting) police forces in the struggle against terrorism. Their non-martial functions will also grow, as they apply themselves, not to combat with their own mirror-images, but to battle against man's mistakes or the vagaries of nature.

We can only guess what lies beyond the misty horizon at the millennium's end. Global risk, undoubtedly: global disaster, less probably, if we work hard at reducing the number of nuclear weapons and restricting their spread, and devote some of the zeal and treasure hitherto poured into weapons to the succour of our fragile environment. Certainly not all of it, for we should be mindful that low-intensity conflict will smoulder on across the world, and bursts of higher-intensity war will flash out in areas untouched by the superpower *rapprochement*. Nuclear weapons are more use for deterring war than for waging it, but Nuclear Warriors – competent soldiers in cohesive units – will remain useful into the next century and beyond it. We owe it to ourselves, their patrons, to help them chart the way ahead, for we would be rash to assume that we will not need them on our journey beyond the millennium.

Notes

Introduction: The Warrior State

1   See the US Department of Commerce annual *Statistical Abstract of the U.S.*; for British figures see the annual *Statement on the Defence Estimates*. The Soviet figure is from the US government's *Soviet Military Power: An Assessment of the Threat* (Washington, 1988), p. 32. It is notoriously difficult to assess defence expenditure: the issue is complicated by official secrecy, currency conversion rates, the real cost to an economy of spending on defence, and so on. Even establishing the cost of a single item of military hardware is far from easy. At one extreme a published figure may include all research and development costs and allow for commercial return on sale: at the other it may reflect the use of arms sales as a diplomatic lever, with arms and equipment being sold cheaply to a friendly (or potentially friendly) power.

2   R.L. Sivgard, *World Military and Social Expenditure 1986* (Washington, 1986), p. 26.

3   Kathleen Burk (ed.), *War and the State: The Transformation of British Government, 1914–1919* (London, 1982), p. 6.

4   Robert O'Neill, 'Limited War in the Nuclear Age', in Noble Frankland (ed.), *The Encyclopadia of 20th Century Warfare* (London, 1989), p. 258.

5   Foreword to Asa A. Clark et al. (eds), *The Defense Reform Debate* (Baltimore, 1984), p. xi. This most useful book contains contributions from several of the major participants in the debate.

6   Victor Davis Hanson, *The Western Way of War: Infantry Battle in Classical Greece* (London, 1989), pp. 227–8. John Keegan's introduction does not overstate the case when it calls this book 'wholly original and deeply important'.

7   *Concise Oxford English Dictionary* (Oxford, 1976), p. 649.

1 Occupation Gone?

1   John F. Guilmartin, 'Military Experience, the Military Historian and

NOTES

the Reality of Battle', paper presented at the Shelby Cullum Davis Center, Princeton, 8 October 1982.

For Lt Showers see J.W. Burrows, *Second Battalion The Essex Regiment* (Southend on Sea, 1937), pp. 166–7; for 2Lt Piggott see the Marquis de Rouvigny, *The Roll of Honour* (London, 1916), Vol. 1, p. 290.

3 J.M. Winter, *The British People and the Great War* (London, 1986), pp. 65–99.

4 Ibid., p. 75.

5 Christopher Donnelly, *Red Banner: The Soviet Military System in Peace and War* (London, 1988), p. 79.

6 Patsy Adam-Smith, *The Anzacs* (London, 1978), p. 350.

7 Tim Travers, *The Killing Ground* (London, 1987), p. 13.

8 Paul Fussell, *The Great War and Modern Memory* (London, 1975), p. 70; William Manchester, *Goodbye, Darkness* (London, 1981), p. 67.

9 Michael Glover (ed.), *A Gentleman Volunteer: The Letters of George Hennell from the Peninsular War 1812–13* (London, 1979), p. 18.

10 Capitaine-Commandant Robert de Wilde, quoted in Guy Chapman, *Vain Glory* (London, 1968), p. 18.

11 John Glubb, *Into Battle: A soldier's diary of the Great War* (London, 1978), p. 48.

12 Michael Herr, *Dispatches* (London, 1978), p. 23.

13 Homer, *The Iliad* (London, 1971), p. 249.

14 Christopher Hibbert (ed.), *A Soldier of the Seventy-First* (London, 1976), p. 61.

15 Terry Norman (ed.), *Armageddon Road: A VC's Diary 1914–16*, (London, 1982), p. 194.

16 Guy Sajer, *The Forgotten Soldier* (London, 1971), pp. 93–4.

17 Harold P. Leinbaugh and John D. Campbell, *The Men of Company K* (New York, 1987), p. 200. Artillery had killed men in previous centuries, to be sure: but in the major wars of the twentieth century artillery was the main casualty-producer, and its unpredictable, violent and capricious effects made it a principal source of battlefield stress.

18 Quoted in Chapman, *Vain Glory* p. 385.

19 C.M. von Clausewitz, *On War*, trans. and ed. by Michael Howard and Peter Paret (Princeton, 1976), p. 115.

20 Ibid., p. 54.

21 Ibid., p. 170.

22 Martin van Creveld, 'The Eternal Clausewitz', in *Journal of Strategic Sudies: Special Issue on Clausewitz and Modern Strategy*, 1986. Edward Luttwak's *Strategy: The Logic of War and Peace* (Cambridge, Mass., 1987) develops the important concept of the paradoxical logic of strategy, and is one of the few recent works on strategy that can be considered in the same breath as Clausewitz.

23 Lawrence Freedman, in Peter Paret (ed.) *Makers of Modern Strategy* (Princeton, 1986), p. 735.

24 Quoted in Gwynne Dyer, *War* (London, 1986), p. 230.
25 Quoted in Gwyn Prins (ed.), *Defended to Death* (London, 1983), pp. 18–19.
26 Peter Mullen, 'Hope Beyond the Apocalypse', *The Times*, 1 March 1986.
27 James Adams, 'Forward march of the military market in the world of books', *The Sunday Times*, 1 June 1986.
28 See 'Glory to the Bomb', *The Times*, 20 April 1987.
29 For the former view see McGeorge Bundy in Gwyn Prins (ed.), *The Choice: Nuclear Weapons versus Security* (London, 1984), p. 47. For the latter, see Neville Brown in Neville Brown and Sir Anthony Farrar-Hockley, *Nuclear First Use* (London, 1985), p. 24.
30 Press Conference, 3 July 1974, reported in *Survival*, September/October 1974.
31 Herman Kahn, *On Thermonuclear War* (Princeton, 1960); *Thinking about the Unthinkable* (New York, 1962), and *On Escalation: Metaphors and Scenarios* (New York, 1965).
32 Thomas Schelling, *Arms and Influence* (New York, 1966), p. 93.
33 Freedman, in *Modern Strategy*, p. 763.
34 Major-General N. Vasendin and Colonel N. Kuznetsov quoted in Derek Leebaert (ed.), *Soviet Military Thinking* (London, 1981), p. 100.
35 Jon Connell, *The New Maginot Line* (London, 1986), pp. 138–42.
36 Ibid., p. 169.
37 Quoted in Prins, *The Choice*, p. 115.
38 Brown and Farrar-Hockley, *Nuclear First Use*, p. 23.
39 Richard Smoke, *War: Controlling Escalation* (Cambridge, Mass., 1977), pp. 30–1.
40 John G. Stoessinger, *Why Nations Go to War* (London, 1985), p. 19. See also Ole R. Holsti, 'The 1914 Case', in *Crisis Escalation War* (Montreal, 1972).
41 McGeorge Bundy, 'To Cap the Volcano', in *Foreign Affairs* No. 48, October 1969.
42 Admiral Noel Gaylor in Prins, *The Choice*, pp. 16–17.
43 General Sir John Hackett, *The Profession of Arms* (London, 1983), p. 167, and quoted in Dyer, *War*, p. 196.
44 Quoted in Brown and Farrar-Hockley, *Nuclear First Use*, p. 100.
45 Michael MccGwire in Prins, *The Choice*, p. 76.
46 See Cardinal Basil Hume, *To Be a Pilgrim: A Spritual Notebook* (London, 1984), pp. 184–5.
47 Brown and Farrar-Hockley, *Nuclear First Use*, p. 14.
48 Quoted in Dyer, *War*, p. 195.
49 See Richard Pipes, 'Why the Soviet Union thinks it could fight and win a nuclear war', in *Commentary*, July 1977.
50 For Soviet Civil Defence see Donnelly, *Red Banner*, pp. 163–70, and L. Goure, *War Survival in Soviet Strategy* (Miami, 1976). Admiral

Gaylor suggests (in Prins, *The Choice*, p. 23) that Soviet Civil Defence is largely *pokuzuka* – shadow without substance.

51 Paul R. Ehrlich, Carl Sagan et al., *The Nuclear Winter* (London, 1985), p. xxi.

52 Ibid., p. xxiii.

53 *The Effects of Nuclear Weapons*, Office of Technology Assessment of the Congress of the United States (Washington, 1979).

54 *Nuclear Weapons: Report of the Secretary-General of the United Nations* (London, 1981), p. 73.

55 *The Effects of Nuclear War on Health and Health Services* (World Health Organization, Geneva, 1984).

56 Robin Clarke, *The Science of War and Peace* (London, 1971), p. 39.

57 Nicholas Humphrey, 'Four Minutes to Midnight', in *The Listener*, 29 October 1981.

58 Dan Smith and Ron Smith, *The Economics of Militarism* (London, 1983), pp. 9, 58. For a rational argument of the contary case, see Michael Seagrim, 'Does Relatively High Defence Spending Necessarily Degenerate an Economy', in *Journal of the Royal United Services Institute*, March 1986.

59 Dr G. de Q. Robin in *The Times*, 3 August 1988.

60 Paul Kennedy, *The Rise and Fall of the Great Powers* (London, 1988).

61 Quoted in Dyer, *War*, p. 233.

62 Nicholas Fotion and Gerard Elfstrom, *Military Ethics* (London, 1986), pp. 37–8.

63 I am grateful to Professor Ray Hobbs, of MacMaster College, Hamilton, Ontario, for his help with this section. See also Elizabeth Anscombe, 'War and Murder', in Malham H. Wakin (ed.), *War, Morality and the Military Profession* (Boulder, Colorado, 1979).

64 Michael Howard, *War and the Liberal Conscience* (London, 1978), p. 13.

65 Quoted in Wakin, *War, Morality*, pp. 247–8.

66 Quoted by General Sir John Hackett in 'The Man at Arms in the Nuclear Age', the Chesney Lecture given at the Royal United Services Institute on 14 November 1985, and printed in the *Journal of the Royal United Services Institute*, March 1986.

67 Donald Wells, 'How much can the "Just War" Justify?', in Wakin, *War, Morality*, p. 270.

68 Telford Taylor, 'Just and Unjust Wars', in Wakin, *War, Morality*, p. 251.

69 Taylor in Wakin, *War, Morality*, p. 257.

70 General Order No. 100, *Instruction for the Government of Armies of the United States in the Field*, 24 April 1863.

71 *Manual of Military Law*, (London, 1914), p. 234.

72 Richard A. Falk (ed.), *Crimes of War* (New York, 1971), p. 153.

73   'Demand for answers on Navy killing of civilians', *The Times*, 9 May 1988.
74   Quoted in Charles de Gaulle, *The Edge of the Sword* (London, 1960), p. 13.
75   Jacques Elleul, *The Technological Society* (New York, 1964), p. xxix.
76   1Lt Stephen L. Dankert, 'Officers Without Chests: Literature and the Education of Army Leaders', *Military Review*, November 1988, p. 76.
77   'German Admiral Faces Discipline', *The Sunday Times*, 1 January 1989.
78   'Z', 'Gorbachev's Forlorn Hope', *The Times*, 11 January 1990.
79   David Selbourne, 'Grass sounds a warning on "German disease"', *The Times*, 10 February 1990.
80   Clausewitz, *On War*, p. 260.
81   Luttwak, *Strategy*, pp. 3–4.
82   Michael Howard, *The Causes of War and Other Essays* (London, 1984), p. 7.
83   E.M.F. Durbin and John Bowlby, *Personal Aggressiveness and War* (London, 1939).
84   See Robert Ardrey, *The Territorial Imperative* (London, 1967) and *The Hunting Hypothesis* (London, 1977); Irenäus Eibl-Eibesfeldt, *The Biology of Peace and War* (London, 1979); Erich Fromm, *The Anatomy of Human Destructiveness* (London, 1977); Konrad Lorenz, *On Aggression* (London, 1966); Desmond Morris, *The Naked Ape* (London, 1967), and Wilfred Trotter, *Instincts of the Herd in Peace and War* (London, 1947).
85   Quoted in Kenneth N. Waltz, *Man, the State and War* (New York, 1959), p. 28.
86   T.C.W. Blanning, 'The Origins of Great Wars', a chapter of his book *The Origins of the French Revolutionary Wars* (London, 1986), p. 14. Dr Blanning's comprehensive and beautifully written chapter would have saved me much labour (and greatly reduced the profits of the Macallan Distillers) had I discovered it sooner.
87   Jack S. Levy, *War in the Modern Great Power System 1495–1975*, (Lexington, Kentucky, 1983), p. 160.
88   Howard, *Causes*, pp. 9–10.
89   Marc Bloch, 'Historical Causation', in *The Historian's Craft* (Manchester, 1976), pp. 192–3, and Bernard Brodie, *War and Politics* (New York, 1973), p. 339. Geoffrey Blainey, *The Causes of War* (London, 1973), and A.J.P. Taylor, *How Wars Begin* (London, 1980), also form part of the required reading on this topic.
90   Howard, *Causes*, p. 236.
91   Ernest Skalski, 'Why Poland must have a say in Germany's future', *The Times*, 17 February 1990.
92   Frank Barnaby, *The Automated Battlefield* (London, 1986), p. 10, and Richard A. Gabriel, *No More Heroes: Madness and Psychiatry in War* (New York, 1987), p. 43.

93   Elleul, *Technological Society*, p. 322.

2 The Nature of War

1   Otto Hoetzsch, *The Evolution of Russia* (London, 1966), p. 37.
2   Richard Muir, *The Lost Villages of Britain* (London, 1985), p. 80. It is impossible to be certain of the casualties inflicted during the Harrying of the North, but it is probable that, in terms of the percentage of the population killed, the Harrying dwarfed even the genocide of our own century.
3   John G. Stoessinger, *Why Nations Go to War* (London, 1985), p. 205.
4   Martin Middlebrook, *Operation Corporate: The Story of the Falklands War, 1982* (London, 1985), pp. 142–3.
5   Field Manual No.100–5 *Operations* (Washington, 1986), pp. 9–11.
6   Quoted in Middlebrook, *Operation Corporate*, p. 151.
7   Edward N. Luttwak, 'The Operational Level of War', in *International Security*, Winter 1980/1, p. 61.
8   Christopher Donnelly, *Red Banner* (London, 1988), p. 199.
9   *Design For Military Operations: The British Military Doctrine* (London, 1989), p. 38.
10   In his *The Race to the Swift: Thoughts on Twenty-First-Century Warfare* (London, 1985), p. 24, Brigadier Richard Simpkin laid down five criteria which a plan, concept or warlike act must meet in order to be considered 'operational'. It must have *mission* lying at one remove only from a strategic aim; be a *dynamic, closed-loop system*, characterised by speed and appropriateness of response; consist of *at least three components*, one of which reflects the opponent's will; be *synergetic*, that is the whole must have a greater effect than that of the sum of its parts; and be *self-contained* within the scope of its mission.
11   Shelford Bidwell and Dominick Graham, *Fire-Power: British Army Weapons and Theories of War* (London, 1982).
12   Luttwak, *Operational Level*, p. 61.
13   Field Manual No. 100–5 *Operations* (Washington, 1976). The transition from the doctrine embodied in the 1976 edition of FM 100–5 to that in the markedly different 1982 version is ably described by John L. Romjue in *From Active Defense to AirLand Battle: The Development of Army Doctrine 1973–1982* (Fort Monroe, Virginia, 1984).
14   André Beaufre, *The Suez Expedition* (London, 1969), p. 142.
15   Quoted in Max Hastings, *The Korean War* (London, 1987), p. 236.
16   Guilio Douhet, *The Command of the Air*, trans. Dino Ferrari (Washington, 1983).
17   For a critical view of the Grenada operation see the relevant chapter in Richard A. Gabriel, *Military Incompetence: Why the American Military Doesn't Win* (New York, 1985).
18   S.L.A. Marshall, *Men Against Fire* (Washington, 1947), p. 27. Recent

research has thrown much doubt upon the methodology used by Marshall in this book. However, although Marshall's research methods were questionable, his overall judgments remain sound.

19   Antoine-Henri Jomini, *Précis de l'Art de Guerre* (2 vols, Paris, 1855), Vol. 2, p. 5. Carl von Clausewitz, *On War*, trans. and ed. by Michael Howard and Peter Paret (Princeton, 1976), p. 227.

20   Charles Ardant du Picq, *Battle Studies: Ancient and Modern Battle*, trans. Col J.W. Greely and Maj. R.C. Cotton (Harrisburg, Pennsylvania, 1958), p. 39.

21   John Keegan, *The Face of Battle* (New York, 1976), p. 29.

22   Ernest Shephard, *A Sergeant Major's War: From Hill 60 to the Somme*, ed. Bruce Rossor (Ramsbury, 1987).

23   A good general account is in W. Baring Pemberton, *Battles of the Crimean War* (London, 1962), pp. 81–3. For a sceptical view see Lieutenant Richard Barter's account of his conversation with Lieutenant McBean of the 93rd in *The Siege of Delhi: Mutiny Memories of an Old Officer* (London, 1984), p. 99. Even this is suspect because, as Barter freely admits, he had no time for Sir Colin Campbell, who had commanded the Highland Brigade in the Crimea, maintaining that he embroidered his despatches in order to gain more credit. John Selby used the episode to entitle his book on the Crimea *The Thin Red Line of Balaklava* (London, 1970).

24   Tim Travers, *The Killing Ground* (London, 1987), p. 203.

25   C.W.C. Oman, *The Art of War in the Middle Ages* (Ithaca, New York, 1963), p. 63. After a gentlemanly discussion it was agreed that Bela should ford the river and draw up his army unhindered. He did so, only to be disastrously defeated at Kressenbrunn.

26   Chrisopher Duffy, *The Army of Frederick the Great* (Newton Abbot, 1974), p. 146.

27   Quoted in Jacques Elleul, *The Technological Society* (New York, 1964), p. 239.

28   James Clavell (ed.), *The Art of War by Sun Tsu* (London, 1982), p. 23.

29   Hew Strachan, *European Armies and the Conduct of War* (London, 1983), p. 15.

30   Ibid., p. 40.

31   David Chandler, *The Campaigns of Napoleon* (London, 1967), p. 47.

32   Ibid., p. 141.

33   Ibid., p. 142.

34   Quoted in Peter Paret (ed.), *Makers of Modern Strategy: From Machiavelli to the Nuclear Age* (Oxford, 1986), p. 267.

35   For Napoleon's staff system see Chandler, *Napoleon*, pp. 367–78 and Martin Van Creveld, *Command in War* (Cambridge, Massachusetts, 1985), pp. 65–78.

36   Jomini was a prolific author, and John I. Alger's *Antoine-Henri Jomini: A Bibliographical Survey* (West Point, New York, 1975) is the best

starting-point. For comment on Jomini see John Shy, 'Jomini', in Paret, *Modern Strategy*, and Strachan, *European Armies*, pp. 60–75.

37   Clausewitz, *On War* p. 77.

38   Ibid., p. 87.

39   Ibid., p. 248.

40   Ibid., p. 259.

41   Ibid., p. 260.

42   Ibid., p. 370.

43   Quoted in Paret, *Modern Strategy*, p. 289.

44   Paret, *Modern Strategy*, p. 298.

45   In May 1870 Moltke set out his views for the benefit of the heads of sections of the General Staff. 'The operation against France', he wrote, 'will simply consist of advancing as concentrated as possible on French soil for several days' march until we meet the enemy's forces, and then giving battle. The general direction of this march is Paris, because it is by marching on this town that we can count most surely on meeting our objective, the enemy army.' Note of 6 May 1870, in Helmuth von Moltke, *Correspondance Militaire du Maréchal de Moltke, Guerre de 1870–71*, (3 Vols, Paris, ND), Vol. 1, p. 171.

46   Fritz Hönig's impartial and analytical *24 Stunden Moltkescher Strategie entwickelt und erlautert an den Schlachten von Gravelotte und St Privat* (Berlin, 1891, translated as *24 Hours of Moltke's Strategy* . . . Woolwich, 1895), exposed many of the weaknesses of the German official account. This led to its author being challenged to a duel, which he, a crippled retired officer, declined to fight: he was then deprived of his officer status by a court of honour.

47   Delbrück (1848–1929) was a German military historian whose controversial *History of the Art of War* put war firmly in the context of political history, and applied logical analysis to the past battles. He discovered that Clausewitz, in a note of 1827, had argued that there were two distinct forms of strategy. Delbrück expanded this argument, calling the forms *Niederwerfungsstrategie* (the strategy of annihilation, aimed at decisive battle) and *Ermattungsstrategie* (the strategy of exhaustion). The former focused upon battle, while the latter concerned both battle and manoeuvre. It is significant that the concept of *Ermattungsstrategie* was rejected by an army schooled in belief in short, decisive war. See Gordon A. Craig, 'Delbrück: The Military Historian', in Paret, *Modern Strategy*.

48   Jehuda L. Wallach, *The Dogma of the Battle of Annihilation* (London, 1986), p. 77.

49   For the plan itself see L.C.F Turner, 'The Schlieffen Plan', in Paul Kennedy (ed.), *The War Plans of the Great Powers 1880–1914* (London, 1979), and G. Ritter, *The Schlieffen Plan* (New York, 1958). The most readable account of its failure remains 'The Tragic Delusion', in Correlli Barnett, *The Swordbearers* (London, 1963).

50   See Michael Howard, 'Men against Fire: The Doctrine of the Offensive
      in 1914', in Paret, *Modern Strategy*, and Douglas Porch, 'Clausewitz and
      the French', in *Journal of Strategic Studies: Special issue on Clausewitz and
      Modern Strategy*, 1986.

51   Memoir by Captain Grenier, 5th Cuirassiers, July 1868, in *Archives
      Historiques de Guerre* MR 2024: emphasis in original. Grenier uses
      reserve cavalry in the French sense: *cuirassiers* and *carabiniers* were, in
      theory, held in reserve until the moment came for them to deliver
      shock action. We should not be surprised that attitudes like Grenier's
      produced fruitless valour. In August 1870 his regiment was cut to
      pieces in an unsuccessful attempt to rescue the French 5th Corps at
      Beaumont, losing its colonel, lieutenant-colonel, five other officers,
      11 sergeants and 90 men in the process. One account speaks of the
      regiment's charge as 'heroic, but badly conducted'.

52   Quoted in Travers, *Killing Ground*, p. 44.

53   Wallach, *Battle of Annihilation*, p. 171.

54   Erich Ludendorff, *My War Memoirs 1914–18* (London, 1919), p. 590.

55   Quoted in John Terraine, *Douglas Haig: The Educated Soldier* (London,
      1963), p. 481.

56   For the pro-Haig view see Terraine, *Douglas Haig* and *The Road to
      Passchendaele: the Flanders Offensive of 1917: a Study in Inevitability*
      (London, 1977). Chapter 8 of Travers's *Killing Ground* effectively
      demolishes the Official History's support for Haig over Third Ypres.

57   B.H. Liddell Hart, *Paris, or the Future of War* (New York, 1925),
      p. 79.

58   See A.J. Trythall, *'Boney' Fuller: The Intellectual General* (London,
      1977), and Brian Holden Reid, *J.F.C. Fuller: Military Thinker* (London, 1988).

59   The best short account is Brian Bond and Martin Alexander, 'Liddell
      Hart and de Gaulle: The Doctrines of Limited Liability', in Paret,
      Modern Strategy. Bond's *Liddell Hart: A Study of his Military Thought*
      (London, 1977) remains the definitive study of Liddell Hart, albeit
      tempered by John J. Mearsheimer's critical view in *Liddell Hart and
      the Weight of History* (New York, 1988).

60   Richard Simpkin, *Deep Battle* (London, 1987), pp. 19–20.

61   Simpkin, *Deep Battle*, p. 35. See also Bruce W. Menning, 'The Deep
      Strike in Russian and Soviet Military History', in *Journal of Soviet Mili-
      tary Studies*, April 1988.

62   Donnelly, *Red Banner* pp. 75, 88.

63   Simpkin, *Deep Battle*, p. 22.

64   See Paret, *Makers of Modern Strategy*, p. 263.

65   Omer Bartov, *The Eastern Front, 1941–45: German Troops and the
      Barbarisation of Warfare* (London, 1985).

66   Lawrence's views on guerrilla warfare are summed up in his *The Seven
      Pillars of Wisdom* (London, 1935), pp. 188–96.

67   The best account of the battle in English remains Bernard B. Fall, *Hell in a Very Small Place* (London, 1967). For analysis of French military thought in this period see Peter Paret, *French Revolutionary Warfare from Indochina to Algeria* (London, 1964).

68   Attributed to Colonel Harry G. Summers.

69   This is a view reflected in a recent substantive contribution to the immense quantity of literature on Vietnam, Lt-Gen. Phillip B. Davidson, *Vietnam at War 1946–1975* (London, 1988). For a pertinent comparison of American and Australian approaches see Bob Breen, *First to Fight* (Sydney, 1988).

70   Richard Holmes, *The Little Field Marshal: Sir John French* (London, 1981), pp. 232–4.

71   Michael Howard, 'The Forgotten Dimensions of Strategy', in *Foreign Affairs*, Summer 1979.

72   Allan R. Millett and Peter Maslowski, *For the Common Defense* (New York, 1984), p. 215–8.

73   Chris Wrigley, 'The Ministry of Munitions: an Innovatory Department', in Kathleen Burke (ed.), *War and the State* (London, 1982).

74   For American production see James A. Hudson, *The Sinews of War: Army Logistics 1775–1955* (Washington, 1966), pp. 455–490, and Constance McLaughlin Green et al., *The US Army in World War II: The Technical Services. The Ordnance Department: Planning Munitions for War* (Washington, 1955). For German and Soviet production see Albert Seaton, *The Russo-German War* (London, 1971), pp. 401–2. In *The Audit of War* (London, 1986), Correlli Barnett makes a convincing case for the dependence of Britain on American war material, suggesting that many of the 'traditional' weaknesses of British industry prevailed during the war.

75   Lisle A. Rose, *Dubious Victory* (New York, 1973), pp. 365–6.

76   Millett and Maslowski, *Common Defense*, p. 554.

77   Chris Bellamy, *The Future of Land Warfare* (London, 1987), p. 282. This admirable study is the best book on the subject to date.

78   For the issue generally, see John U. Nef, *War and Human Progress* (London, 1950), and Clive Trebilcock, 'The British Armaments Industry 1890–1914: False Legend and True Utility', in Geoffrey Best and Andrew Wheatcroft (eds), *War, Economy and the Military Mind* (London, 1976). Maurice Pearton, *The Knowledgeable State* (London, 1982); William H. McNeill, *The Pursuit of Power: Technology, Armed Force and Society since AD 1000* (Oxford, 1983), and Martin van Creveld, *Technology and War* (New York, 1988) are important surveys.

79   Michael Howard, 'War and Technology', *Journal of the Royal United Services Institute*, December 1987, p. 21.

80   Quoted in Elleul, *Technological Society*, pp. 432–3.

81   Paul F. Walker, 'Emerging Technologies and Conventional Defence',

in Frank Barnaby and Marlies ter Borg (eds), *Emerging Technologies and Military Doctrine* (London, 1986), pp. 39–40.

82   Mary Kaldor, *The Baroque Arsenal* (London, 1982), p. 24.
83   Ibid., p. 184.
84   Jon Connell, *The New Maginot Line* (London, 1986), p. 33, quoting Bill Kelly of the *New York Times*.
85   John Foley, *The A7V Sturmpanzerwagen*, Armour in Profile No. 7 (London, 1968), p. 10.
86   Steven L. Canby, 'Military Reform and the Art of War', in *Survival*, May/June 1983, p. 124.

3 *Field of Battle*

1   Quoted in Hew Strachan, *European Armies and the Conduct of War* (London, 1983), p. 128.
2   Tim Travers, *The Killing Ground* (London, 1987), p. 68.
3   Michael Howard, 'War and Technology', in *Journal of the Royal United Services Institute*, December 1987, p. 17.
4   Diary of Maj. R. Stokes, 4 July 1916, Public Record Office WO 158/137. The last two hundred metres of the assault present the twentieth-century infantryman with his greatest challenge, and tactical manuals and battle drills alike are often a hazy guide to action at this moment of supreme crisis. For a good discussion see Maj. T.A. Coutts Britton, 'The Assault', *British Army Review*, April 1974. The best study of infantry remains Lt-Col John English, *A Perspective on Infantry* (New York, 1982).
5   Thomas Pakenham, *The Boer War* (London, 1979), is a good general history. British field artillery did not receive a high-explosive shell until October 1914, just in time to be used at First Ypres. For the artillery see Edward M. Spiers, 'Rearming the Edwardian Artillery', in *Journal of the Society for Army Historical Research*, winter 1979, and Shelford Bidwell and Dominick Graham, *Fire-Power* (London, 1982), pp. 7–21. For the cavalry see Edward M. Spiers, 'The British Cavalry 1902–14', in *Journal of the Society for Army Historical Research*, summer 1979; Brian Bond, 'Doctrine and Training in the British Cavalry', in Michael Howard (ed.), *The Theory and Practice of War* (London, 1965), and a summary in Richard Holmes, *The Little Field Marshal: Sir John French* (London, 1981), Chapter 5. A contrary view, well pressed home, is S.D. Badsey, 'Fire and the Sword', unpublished Cambridge PhD thesis, 1983. The most useful account of British military preparation for 1914 is John Gooch, *The Plans of War: the General Staff and British Military Strategy* (London, 1974).
6   For British neglect of the operational level in South Africa see Charles Townshend, *Britain's Civil Wars* (London, 1986), pp. 179–184. The less than adept performance of GHQ in 1914 is examined in Holmes,

Little Field Marshal, pp. 210–40, and David Ascoli, *The Mons Star* (London, 1981), *passim*.

7   Peter Young, *The Israeli Campaign* (London, 1967), p. 184.

8   For suggestions that the 1973 war ushered in a new era, see Col John T. Burke, 'The Changing Nature of Modern Warfare', in *Army*, March 1974, and Col Edward B. Atkeson, 'Is the Soviet Army Obsolete?', in *Army*, May 1974.

9   Figures from Maj.-Gen. Chaim Herzog's Royal United Services Institute lecture, 6 November 1974: see also his *The War of Atonement* (London, 1975), p. 272. It is no criticism of Herzog's judgment to emphasise that these must be regarded as Israeli figures.

10   The most atmospheric account of Nivelle's failure is Brig.-Gen. E.L. Spears, *Prelude to Victory* (London, 1939).

11   See Capt. Timothy F. Lupfer, *The Dynamics of Doctrine: the Changes in German Tactical Doctrine during the First World War* (Fort Leavenworth, Kansas, 1981).

12   We should note that Soviet doctrine has traditionally claimed to be defensive in strategic purpose but offensive in operational application. As Christopher Donnelly puts it, it is 'aimed at repelling an aggressor and then decisively destroying him' (*Red Banner*, p. 219).

13   My judgments on Soviet doctrine are much influenced by the views of Mr Christopher Donnelly and Colonel David Glantz, notably by the latter's draft paper 'Soviet Military Strategy After CFE: Historical Models and Future Prospects'. See also Jacob W. Kipp, '*Perestroyka* and Order: Alternative Futures and their impact on the Soviet Military', *Military Review*, December 1989, and John Erickson, 'On the March for Tsar Mikhail', *Sunday Times*, 4 March 1990.

14   Gen. Sir Nigel Bagnall, 'Concepts of Land/Air Operations in the Central Region', lecture given at the Royal United Services Institute on 23 May 1984 and printed in the *Journal of the Royal United Services Institute*, September 1984.

15   Quoted in James A. Hudson, *The Sinews of War: Army Logistics 1775–1953* (Washington, 1966), p. 455.

16   James Clavell (ed.), *The Art of War by Sun Tsu* (London, 1982), p. 20.

17   Ibid., p. 23.

18   B.H. Liddell Hart, *Strategy: The Indirect Approach* (London, 1982), p. 164.

19   See William S. Lind, *Maneuver Warfare Handbook* (Boulder, Colorado, 1985), p. 4.

20   Ibid., p. 5.

21   Col Jonathan Alford's *Mobile Defence: The Pervasive Myth* (unpublished thesis, King's College, London, 1977) makes this point with irrefutable logic.

22   FM 100–5 *Operations* (Washington, 1986), p. 78.

23   Christopher Donnelly, *Red Banner* (London, 1988), p. 28.

24   Gen. Erich Ludendorff, *My War Memoirs* (London, 1919), p. 598.
25   Jac Weller, *Wellington at Waterloo* (London, 1967), p. 114. See also Weller's useful comments on the capricious nature of Waterloo mud on p. 110.
26   Chris Bellamy, *The Future of Land Warfare* (London, 1987), p. 283.
27   Tom Wintringham and John Blashford-Snell, *Weapons and Tactics* (London, 1973), p. 22.
28   Ferdinand Lot, *L'art militaire et les armées du Moyen Age* (Paris, 1946), p. 343.
29   Hugh Faringdon, *Confrontation: The Strategic Geography of NATO and the Warsaw Pact* (London, 1986), pp. 59–60.
30   1Lt Peter R. Mansoor, 'The Defense of the Vienna Bridgehead', *Armor*, January–February 1986.
31   Ken Brower, 'Fuel-Air Explosives and Dismounted Infantry', June 1986, p. 8.
32   *Janes Weapons Systems*, 1981–2, pp. 415–16.
33   M.J. Armitage and R.A. Mason, *Air Power in the Nuclear Age* (London, 1986), pp. 139–40.
34   Donnelly, *Red Banner*, p. 252.
35   For an assessmement of Soviet reaction to the Yom Kippur War see Philip A. Karber, 'The Soviet Anti-Tank Debate', *Survival*, May/June 1976.
36   Maj.-Gen. Richard Scholtes, 'Where Have All the Infantrymen Gone?', *Armed Forces Journal*, October 1966.
37   Bellamy, *Land Warfare*, pp. 106–7.
38   Donnelly, *Red Banner*, table on p. 257.
39   Ibid., p. 257.
40   Air Cdre E.S. Williams, '*Perestroika* and the Soviet Air Forces', *Journal of the Royal United Services Institute*, winter 1988.
41   The debate is well summarised in John L. Romjue, *From Active Defense to AirLand Battle: The Development of Army Doctrine 1973–1982* (Fort Monroe, Virginia, 1984).
42   TRADOC pamphlet 525–5, 'AirLand Battle and Corps Operations – 1986', (1981), p. 2.
43   FM 100–5 *Operations* (1982), p. 1–5.
44   Quoted in *New Technology for NATO: Implementing Follow-On Forces Attack* (Congress of the United States: Office of Technology Assessment, 1987), p. 113.
45   Semantic difficulties loom large when we consider current US doctrine. FM 100–5, now in its 1986 edition, embodies the current official US Army AirLand battle doctrine. It is *not* the same as *Air Land Battle 2000*, which looks twenty years ahead, nor *Focus-21*, (a development of the AirLand theme) nor yet *Army-21*, which seeks to provide a conceptual framework for the development of equipment.
46   *New Technology*, p. 111.

47 Lt-Col John E. Peters, 'Evaluating FOFA as a deterrent', *Journal of the Royal United Services Instiutute*, December 1987, p. 43.

48 AVM John Walker, 'The Conundrum of Air-Land Warfare', *Journal of the Royal United Services Institute*, summer 1988, p. 21. See also Steven Canby, 'The Operational Limits of Emerging Technology', *International Defense Review* 6 (1985).

49 *New Technology*, pp. 135–9.

50 Col John R. Landry et al., *Essays on Strategy* (Washington, 1984), p. 246.

51 RPVs are already at an advanced state of development and have been used successfully in combat, notably by the Israelis in 1982. See Steven M. Shaker and Alan R. Wise, *War Without Men* (London, 1988), pp. 87–123. For a survey of deep strike in general, see Rob de Wijk, 'Deep Strike', in Frank Barnaby and Marlies ter Borg, *Emerging Technologies and Military Doctrine* (London, 1986), pp. 73–88.

52 Lt-Gen. H.H. von Sandrart, 'Operational Considerations on the Battle-in-Depth', *The Army Quarterly*, July 1987.

53 Ministry of Defence, Federal German Republic, *The Security of the Federal German Republic* (Bonn, 1983), p. 44.

54 The question of the function of infantry in mid- or high-intensity battle is too complex to be satisfactorily addressed within the parameters of this book. The tendency of infantry to become increasingly weapon-heavy and vehicle-mobile must not obscure the fact that there are roles which demand dismounted infantry – the defence of woods, urban areas and bridges, for instance. It may not be cost-effective to use armoured infantry with MICV for them: mechanised infantry with APC are better fitted for the task. Using infantry with no inherent armoured protection in high-intensity battle places formation commanders on the horns of a cruel dilemma. Should such troops be left behind in the swirl of the armoured battle to stand or fall on their own, or should operations be structured so as to break them out? Yet the need for light, non-mechanised infantry outside Europe (for reasons of strategic mobility as much as anything else) will encourage both Britain and the United States to maintain such forces. The answer lies in recognition that the day of the multi-purpose infantry soldier is past, and that the infantry must now be role-specific, with 'house infantry' for armoured units as one of its elements. Quite apart from considerations of arm and unit identity (which have recently provoked a sharp debate in the British army), the specialisation of infantry calls for hard strategic decisions, for one sort of role-specific infantry may be little use in circumstances intended for another.

55 Faringdon, *Confrontation*, deals with military geography with characteristic brilliance.

56 Gen. Sir Martin Farndale, 'Counter Stroke: Future Requirements', *Journal of the Royal United Services Institute*, December 1985, p. 6.

57 A Camberley team led by Major B.W. Barry, 'Future Airmobile Forces', *Journal of the Royal United Services Institute*, autumn 1988, p. 34. The British 6 Brigade, based in Germany, carried out the airmobile role on a trial basis and has now been re-mechanised. Its airmobile role has been taken over by the UK-based 24 Brigade.

58 This is an Anglocentric view, as my own tribal markings and long association with Major Barry might imply. For a more bullish approach, from an army which takes its attack helicopters very seriously indeed, see the three important articles by Gen. Crosbie E. Saint and Col Walter H. Yates Jr, 'Attack Helicopters in the AirLand Battle . . .', *Military Review*, June, July and October 1988. The military application of the microlight aircraft was provocatively aired in Frederick Hogarth's prizewinning 1986 Royal United Services Institute Trench Gascoigne essay. By the time the counterblasts appeared (Correspondence, *Journal of the Royal United Services Institute* December 1987), microlights had been successfully used to insert saboteurs into an Israeli installation. Their military use really does deserve fuller consideration than it has received to date.

59 Egbert Boeker and Lutz Unterseher, 'Emphasising Defence', in Barnaby and ter Borg, *Emerging Technologies*.

60 See Laszlo Valki, 'Arguments and Counter-Arguments Concerning Defensive Defence'; Unterseher, 'Emphasising Defence', and 'Dialogues on the Military Effectiveness of Non-provocative Defence', all in Barnaby and ter Borg, *Emerging Technologies*.

4 *The Real Weapon*

1 The International Institute of Strategic Studies' annual *The Military Balance*, from whose 1987–8 edition these figures come, remains the brand leader in its field and is scrupulously unpartisan.

2 I follow here the definition in *Design For Military Operations: The British Military Doctrine* (London, 1989), p. 32.

3 This is a rough and ready analysis of the battles described by Maj.-Gen. J.F.C. Fuller in *Decisive Battles: Their Influence upon History and Civilisation* (2 vols, London, 1939–40). In another 13 cases combat power was more or less evenly balanced, or our information is too inaccurate to permit a meaningful comparison to be drawn.

4 Charles E. Heller and William A. Stofft (eds), *America's First Battles* (Lawrence, Kansas, 1986). This very useful book considers twelve battles, but two (San Juan Hill and El Caney) are so closely linked that I have considered them as a single action for the purpose of this survey.

5 Carl von Clausewitz, *On War*, trans. and ed. by Michael Howard and Peter Paret (Princeton, 1976), p. 194.

6 Quoted in Gregory Blaxland, *A Guide to the Queen's Regiment* (Canterbury, ND), p. 42.

7   Christopher Donnelly, *Red Banner* (London, 1988), pp. 225–8.

8   *British Military Doctrine*, p. 32.

9   For a general outline see Alistair Horne, *To Lose a Battle: France 1940* (London, 1969), pp. 291–5, 310–15. More detail is to be found in Le Goyet, 'Contre-attaques manquées: Sedan 13–15 mai 1950', *Revue Historique de l'Armée* No. 4 1962, and Flavigny's evidence in *Les événements survenus en France de 1933 à 1945* . . . (9 vols, Paris, 1947–50), Vol. V, pp. 1253–9.

10 For operational detail see Brig.-Gen. Sir James Edmonds, *History of the Great War: Military Operations, France and Belgium* (14 vols, London, 1922–48), and *The German March Offensive and its Preliminaries*. Tim Travers's *The Killing Ground* (London, 1987), pp. 220–43, puts this work into perspective, and Martin Middlebrook's *The Kaiser's Battle* (London, 1978) gives the view from the trench parapet. See also John Terraine, *To Win a War: 1918, the Year of Victory* (London, 1978).

11 The Austrian case illustrates just how difficult it is to get doctrine right in an era of rapid technical change. Austria modelled her shock tactics on the French in time to use them in 1866 against Prussian infantry armed with the breech-loading needle gun, against which frontal attack was potentially disastrous. It is to the credit of long-suffering Austrian infantry that at Trautenau (27 June 1866) they defeated the Prussians, albeit at immense cost: they were less fortunate on all the other battle-fields of the Austro-Prussian war.

12 For the French tactical debate see Richard Holmes, *The Road to Sedan* (London, 1984), pp. 199–223.

13 Donnelly, *Red Banner*, p. 228. For Soviet artillery see Chris Bellamy, *Red God of War* (London, 1986).

14 For the British general staff see John Gooch, *The Plans of War: The General Staff and British Military Strategy c.1900–1916* (London, 1974). There is no good history of staffs in general: Brig.-Gen. J.D. Hittle, *The Military Staff* (Harrisburg, Pa, 1961), is disappointing.
Martin van Creveld, *Fighting Power: German and US Army Performance 1939–1945* (Westport, Conn., 1982), p. 146–51, and Allan R. Millett and Peter Maslowski, *For the Common Defense: A Military History of the United States of America* (New York, 1984), pp. 310–12.

16 Hans Rosenberg, *Bureaucracy, Aristocracy and Autocracy: The Prussian Experience 1660–1815* (Boston, 1966).

17 Van Creveld, *Fighting Power*, p. 146. Walter Goerlitz, *The German General Staff* (London, 1964), remains useful, although it now shows its age. The best survey is H-G Model, *Der deutsche Generalstabsoffizier* (Frankfurt am Main, 1968).

18 Brig. J.J.G. Mackenzie, 'Surprise: The Neglected Principle', *British Army Review*, April 1988. For a general study see Richard Betts, *Surprise Attack* (Washington, 1984), and for the importance of surprise in Soviet military theory see Donnelly, *Red Banner*, pp. 80–1, and

John Erickson et al., *Soviet Ground Forces: An Operational Assessment* (London, 1986), pp. 53, 202.

19 Arthur Behrend, *As from Kemmel Hill* (London, 1963), p. 53.

20 Account of Brig.-Gen. Sandilands, printed as an appendix to Travers, *Killing Ground*, p. 278.

21 For the case of 1941 see Richard G. Sherwin and Barton Whaley, 'Understanding Strategic Deception . . .', in Donald C. Daniel and Katherine L. Herbig, *Strategic Military Deception* (Oxford, 1972), and for Korea see Max Hastings, *The Korean War* (London, 1987), pp. 153–61.

22 For the magic/surprise comparison see Barton Whaley, 'Towards a General Theory of Deception', in John Gooch and Amos Perlmutter (eds), *Military Deception and Strategic Surprise* (London, 1982).

23 W.D. Henderson, *Why the Vietcong Fought* (Westport, Conn., 1979).

24 Account by Col. T.M.M. Penney, Department of Documents, Imperial War Museum.

25 Richard Holmes, *The Little Field Marshal: Sir John French* (London, 1981), pp. 301–5.

26 Chetwode to Lord Wigram, 29 August 1935, Royal Archives GV P 564/54.

27 S.A. Stouffer et al., *The American Soldier* (2 vols, Princeton, 1965) Vol. II, p. 83.

28 Hannah Arendt, *On Violence* (London, 1970), p. 4.

29 Hopton was temporarily blinded and paralysed, but his retreating army took him with it in a coach. He had recovered sufficiently to give influential advice at a Council of War five days later, and his army went on to assist in the victory of Roundway Down. See Brig. Peter Young and Richard Holmes, *The English Civil War* (London, 1974), pp. 131–2.

30 The Greek mercenaries in Cyrus's army were allowed to withdraw. The epic story of their march home is the subject of Xenophon's *Anabasis*.

31 The best account of the battle for Hougoumont remains Jac Weller's in *Wellington at Waterloo* (London, 1967), pp. 86–94.

32 Quoted in Alfred Vagts, *A History of Militarism* (New York, 1959), p. 469.

33 C.R.M.F. Cruttwell, *A History of the Great War* (Oxford, 1940), p. 437. The counter-argument to my case, of course, is that permitting troops to grasp a fleeting opportunity would have risked disorganisation. The real problem lies in mindset and training, for the Germans were perfectly prepared to run this risk in the spring of 1918, when they succeeded tactically, even if limited resources and defective judgment condemned them to operational failure.

34 Lord Moran, *The Anatomy of Courage* (London, 1966) pp. 69–70.

35 William Manchester, *Goodbye, Darkness* (London, 1981), p. 69.

36 Chris Bellamy, *The Future of Land Warfare* (London, 1987), pp. 218–41.

37 The quotation from Napoleon has various forms: for the most usual see Lt-Col L.H. Ingraham and Maj. F.J. Manning 'Cohesion: Who needs it, what is it?', *Military Review*, June 1981. For the Montgomery quotation see *The Memoirs of Field Marshal the Viscount Montgomery of Alamein* (London, 1958), pp. 83–4, and for Clausewitz see *On War*, p. 185.

38 Gen. Edward C. Meyer, 'Leadership: A Return to Basics', *Military Review*, July 1980, p. 4.

39 Quoted in Felix Gilbert, 'Machiavelli: The Renaissance of the Art of War', in Peter Paret (ed.), *Makers of Modern Strategy* (Princeton, 1986), p. 21.

40 Konrad Lorenz, *On Aggression* (London, 1966), p. 134.

41 Ibid., p. 162.

42 Charles Carrington, *Soldier from the Wars Returning* (London, 1965), p. 87.

43 J. Glenn Gray, *The Warriors: Reflections on Men in Battle* (London, 1970, pp. 132, 141. The soldier's relationship with his enemy is explored more fully in Richard Holmes, *Firing Line* (London, 1985), pp. 360–93.

44 Ladislas Farago, *Patton: Ordeal and Triumph* (London, 1963), p. 231.

45 Irenäus Eibl-Eibesfeldt, *The Biology of Peace and War* (London, 1979), p. 110.

46 Quoted in Leonard Cooper, *British Regular Cavalry* (London, 1965), p. 161.

47 John Glubb, *Into Battle: A Soldier's Diary of the Great War* (London, 1978), pp. 132–3.

48 Quoted in Bill Gammage, *The Broken Years: Australian Soldiers in the Great War* (Canberra, 1974), p. 261.

49 Norman Gladden, *Ypres 1917* (London, 1967), p. 88; George Orwell *Homage to Catalonia* (London, 1951), p. 20; Roger Little in Morris Janowitz (ed.) *The New Military* (New York, 1969), p. 195; interview with OC B Coy 2 Para, November 1982.

50 Peter Godwin, 'The Boys' Own Army', *Sunday Times Magazine*, 27 April 1986.

51 John Dollard, *Fear in Battle* (Westport, Conn., 1977), p. 35.

52 Stouffer, *American Soldier*, Vol. II, p. 88.

53 E.C. Vaughan, *Some Desperate Glory* (London, 1981), p. 3; Raleigh Trevelyan, *The Fortress* (London, 1956), p. 22–3. For talismans in Vietnam see Mark Baker, *Nam* (New York, 1981), p. 106; for *Elk* see *The Daily Telegraph*, 13 July 1982.

54 Charles Grant, *The Army of the Caesars* (London, 1974), p. xxvii.

55 Christopher Duffy, *The Army of Frederick the Great* (Newton Abbot, 1974), p. 149.

56 Brig. A.F. Whitehead, 'Are We Training For the Right War?' *Globe and Laurel*, November/December 1988.

57 Peter Ackroyd, 'Patience under their Sufferings' (review of Roy Porter and Dorothy Porter, *In Sickness and in Health: The British Experience 1650–1850*), *The Times*, 1 December 1988.

58 For Vietnam see Henderson, *Why the Vietcong Fought*: the point about fatalism is made on p. 60. For Korea see Hastings, *Korean War*; Alexander L. George, *The Chinese Communist Army in Action* (London, 1967), and William Bradbury et al., *Mass Behaviour in Battle and Captivity: The Communist Soldier in the Korean War* (Chicago, 1968).

59 Quoted in Duffy, *Army of Frederick the Great*, p. 58.

60 Infantry Committee note of 17 March 1855 in *Archives Historiques de Guerre* (AHG) Xs 67a; Cavalry Committee note of May 1853, ibid. Both refer specifically to the medical standards of replacements, soldiers who voluntarily enlisted (with financial enducement) to replace conscripts who could afford to pay someone else to do their military service.

61 C.E. Montague, *Rough Justice* (London, 1926), p. 98.

62 'Medical Briefing', *The Times*, 27 October 1988.

63 For an atmospheric survey of the regimental system see John Keegan, 'Regimental Ideology', in Geoffrey Best and Andrew Wheatcroft (eds), *War, Economy and the Military Mind* (London, 1976).

64 Marc Ferro, *The Great War 1914–18* (London, 1973), p. 156.

65 Reports on the plebiscite in AHG G^8 204.

66 George Ashurst *My Bit: A Lancashire Fusilier at War 1914–18*, (ed. Richard Holmes (Ramsbury, 1987), p. 25.

67 John Baynes, *Morale* (London, 1967), pp. 155–61.

68 Thomas Penrose Marks, *The Laughter Goes From Life* (London, 1977), p. 79.

69 Ernest Shephard, *A Sergeant-Major's War*, ed. Bruce Rossor (Ramsbury, 1987), pp. 82, 75.

70 Carrington, *Soldier from the Wars Returning*, p. 199.

71 Manchester, *Goodbye, Darkness*, p. 391.

72 Richard A. Gabriel, *No More Heroes: Madness and Psychiatry in War* (New York, 1987), p. 174.

73 Gen. John A. Wickham to House of Representatives Armed Service Committee, 6 February 1986, quoted in Frank Barnaby, *The Automated Battlefield* (London, 1986), pp. 8–9.

74 The best account of Cassino is John Ellis, *Cassino: The Hollow Victory* (London, 1985).

75 Address to the Association of the United States Army, 14 October 1969, quoted in Barnaby, *Automated Battlefield*, p. 1.

76 Ernst Jünger, *Storm of Steel* (London, 1929), p. 96.

77 Galtier-Boissière quoted in Ferro, *Great War*, p. 85. The comparison is very French, because the guillotine's victim died prone.

78 Shephard, *Sergeant-Major's War*, p. 52.
79 Richard Simpkin, *Human Factors in Mechanised Warfare* (London, 1983), p. 42.
80 'Chemical attack – the battlefield norm?' *Soldier*, 21 September 1987.
81 Carrington, *Soldier from the Wars Returning*, p. 64.
82 Brig. John Hemsley, 'The Soviet Bio-Chemical Threat: The Real Issue', *Journal of the Royal United Services Institute*, spring 1988.
83 Andrew Hogg, 'Genie is out of the bottle', *The Sunday Times*, 8 January 1989. For Soviet views see Donnelly, *Red Banner*, pp. 277–82. The most up-to-date general study is now Edward M. Spiers, *Chemical Warfare* (London, 1986).
84 FM 100–5 *Operations* (Washington, 1986), p. 27.
85 Clausewitz, *On War*, p. 275.
86 C.E. Montague, *Disenchantment* (London, 1940), p. 75.
87 Stouffer, *American Soldier*, Vol. II, p. 78.
88 Maj. Henry L. Thompson, 'Sleep Loss and Its Effect in Combat', *Military Review*, September 1983; Lt-Col Brian H. Chermol, 'Psychiatric Casualties in Combat', *Military Review*, July 1983; Peter Watson, *War on the Mind: The Military Uses and Abuses of Psychiatry* (London, 1978), pp. 317–20.
89 'Tired air crew tried to land on M56 in error', *Independent*, 10 August 1988.
90 Quoted in Martin Middlebrook, *Operation Corporate* (London, 1985), p. 364.
91 Brian Wanstall and Ramon Lopez, 'Second-echelon surveillance: Stand-off radars to even battlefield odds', *Interavia* 11/1978.
92 Quoted in Lt-Col John A. English, 'Thinking about Light Infantry', *Infantry*, November–December 1984, p. 24.
93 The best study in English is Anthony Kemp, *The Maginot Line: Myth and Reality* (London, 1981).
94 Bellamy, *Land Warfare*, p. 289.
95 Rodney Cowton, 'The Army changes entrenched ideas', *The Times*, 18 September 1984. See also Maj. J.B.A. Bailey, 'Preplaced Hardened Field Defences', *Journal of the Royal Artillery*, March 1983, and 'The case for preplaced field defences', *International Defense Review* 7/1987.
96 English, 'Light Infantry', p. 26.
97 Lawrence Freedman, 'Logistics and Mobility in Modern Warfare', *Armed Forces* 1986, p. 69.
98 J.W. Appel and G.W. Beebe, 'Preventive psychiatry: an epidemiological approach', *Journal of the American Medical Association*, 18 August 1946.
99 Gabriel, *No More Heroes*, pp. 45–69.
100 Maj.-Gen. T.S. Hart, 'Determination in Battle (paper presented to Director Royal Armoured Corps, conference, 29 November 1978).

101 R.H. Ahrenfeldt, *Psychiatry in the British Army in the Second World War* (London, 1958), p. 7.

102 The only serious study in English is Richard A. Gabriel, *Soviet Military Psychiatry* (Westport, Conn., 1986). See also his chapter, a condensed form of the above, in Richard A. Gabriel (ed.) *Military Psychiatry: A Comparative Perspective* (Westport, Conn., 1986).

103 Gabriel, *No More Heroes*, p. 73.

104 For casualties see 'Army Estimates of effective and non-effective services for the year 1921–22', *Accounts and Papers, Army Pensions,* (25 vols. HMSO, 1921), Vol. 20, pp. 73–4, 539. The pensions figure is from Ahrenfeldt, *Psychiatry*, p. 10.

105 Gabriel, *No More Heroes*, pp. 73–4.

106 Ibid., p. 72.

107 Ibid., p. 75.

108 Ibid., p. 76.

109 G.L. Belenky, 'Military Psychiatry in the Israeli Defence Force', in Gabriel, *Military Psychiatry*, pp. 147–77.

110 Pat Healy, 'Few Falklands troops cracked under strain', *The Times*, 10 September 1983; Parliamentary report in *Daily Telegraph*, 16 December 1982.

111 Ahrenfeldt, *Psychiatry* (using Appel and Beebe as his US source), pp. 172 ff.

112 For the combat effectiveness graph see R.L. Swank and W.E. Marchand, 'Combat Neuroses: Development of Combat Exhaustion', *Archives of Neurology and Psychiatry*, Vol. 55 (1946). Selye's curve is reproduced in Tom Cox, *Stress* (New York, 1979), p. 6. I am grateful to Professor Peter Suedfeld of the University of British Columbia for drawing the similarity to my attention.

113 Brig. James quoted in Swank and Marchand, 'Combat Neuroses', p. 179.

114 Guenther Lewy, *America in Vietnam* (New York, 1978), p. 160.

115 David Marlowe, 'The Human Dimension of Battle and Combat Breakdown', in Gabriel, *Military Psychiatry*, p. 12–13. The Falklands deduction is my own: it is made cautiously in view of possible under-reporting of psychiatric casualties at unit level.

116 Peter G. Bourne (ed.), *The Psychology and Physiology of Stress* (New York, 1969), p. 299.

117 'Falklands men hit by delayed trauma', *Sunday Times*, 5 April 1987; personal communication with Surg.-Cdr O'Connell.

118 Anne McElvoy, 'Survivors are victims too', *The Times*, 13 December 1988.

119 Lawrence Ingraham and Frederick Manning, 'American Military Psychiatry', in Gabriel, *Military Psychiatry*.

120 Chermol, 'Psychiatric Casualties', p. 28.

121 Capt. G. Vincenti, 'Stress Reactions to Simulated Battle Conditions', *British Army Review*, August 1986.

5 *The Nation's Mirror*

1 Alfred de Vigny, *Servitude et Grandeur Militaires* (Paris, 1914), p. 12.
2 S. Commissaire, *Mémoires et Souvenirs* (2 vols, Lyons, 1888), Vol. I, p. 23.
3 The comparison is technically imprecise, for unlike the US Army, the British army has had no commander-in-chief since the post was abolished in 1904, and the Army Board collectively commands the army.
4 J.W. Wheeler-Bennett, *The Nemesis of Power: The German Army in Politics 1918–1945* (New York, 1964), pp. 339–40.
5 Edward A. Shils and Morris Janowitz, 'Cohesion and Disintegration in the Wehrmacht in World War II', *Public Opinion Quarterly*, summer 1948, p. 294.
6 De Vigny, *Servitude et Grandeur*, p. 14.
7 Quoted in Peter Karsten, *Soldiers and Society: The Effects of Military Service and War on American Life* (Westport, Conn., 1978), p. 59.
8 Gen. F.C. du Barail, *Mes Souvenirs 1820–1879* (3 vols, Paris, 1894–96), Vol. I, pp. 76–8.
9 Quoted in Karsten, *Soldiers and Society*, p. 89.
10 Ibid., p. 89.
11 Charles C. Moskos, *The American Enlisted Man* (New York, 1970), pp. 50 1.
12 For the Roman mutinies see Michael Grant, *The Army of the Caesars* (London, 1974), pp. 29–30; for the Civil War see C.H. Firth, *Cromwell's Army* (London, 1967), pp. 195–201.
13 C.W.C. Oman, *The Art of War in the Middle Ages* (Ithaca, NY, 1963), pp. 22–3.
14 From the dramatic but unreliable Robert Wace, *Master Wace His Chronicle of the Norman Conquest, from the Roman de Rou*, trans. Edgar Taylor (London, 1837).
15 Quoted Firth, *Cromwell's Army*, p. 5. For a scholarly survey see Lindsay Boynton, *The Elizabethan Militia* (Toronto, 1967).
16 Christopher Duffy, *The Army of Frederick the Great* (Newton Abbot, 1974), p. 54.
17 Gen. L.J. Trochu, *Oeuvres Posthumes* (2 vols, Tours, 1896), Vol. II., p. 87.
18 'Called Up', BBC 1 Television, 23 November 1983.
19 Allan Millett and Peter Maslowski, *For the Common Defense: A Military History of the United States of America* (New York, 1984), p. 2.
20 Ibid., pp. 196–201.

21 Gen. George Crook, 'Army and Navy Journal', 11 October 1890, quoted in Nancy L. Goldman and David R. Segal, (eds), *The Social Psychology of Military Service* (London, 1976), p. 121).

22 Millett and Masloswki, *Common Defense*, pp. 331–2.

23 See Ronald H. Spector, *Eagle Against the Sun: The American War with Japan* (New York, 1985), pp. 93–100.

24 Karsten, *Soldiers and Society*, p. 106.

25 M. Useem, *Conscription, Protest and Social Conflict* (New York, 1973), p. 141.

26 Stanley Goff and Robert Sanders with Clark Smith, *Brothers: Black Soldiers in the Nam* (Novato, Ca., 1982), p. ix.

27 John Parrish, *Journal of a Plague Year* (London, 1979), p. 12.

28 Goff and Sanders, *Brothers*, p. xvi.

29 Tim O'Brien, *If I Die in a Combat Zone* (London, 1973), p. 18.

30 Winston Groom, *Better Times Than These* (London, 1980), p. 71.

31 Quoted in Karsten, *Soldiers and Society*, p. 115.

32 Guenther Lewy, *America in Vietnam* (New York, 1978), p. 222.

33 Antony Brett-James (ed.), *Edward Costello* (London, 1967), pp. 13–15.

34 Jean Morvan, *Le Soldat Impérial* (2 vols, Paris, 1904), Vol. I, p. 111, Vol. II, p. 7.

35 Richard M. Watt, *Dare Call It Treason* (London, 1964), p. 164.

36 Al Santoli, *Everything We Had* (New York, 1981), p. 95; Mark Baker, *Nam* (New York, 1981), p. 190.

37 James H. Webb, 'Military Competence', speech delivered at the Commonwealth Club of California, 28 August 1986; Richard A. Gabriel, *No More Heroes* (New York, 1987), p. 16.

38 John Rae, *Conscience and Politics* (London, 1970); Dennis Hayes, *The Challenge of Conscience* (London, 1949).

39 Hugh Davies, 'Israeli Colonel on leave after refusal to fight', *Daily Telegraph*, 27 July 1982. 'General tells court beating may have been a mistake', *The Times*, 2 March 1989.

40 Paul Barker, 'Would They Fight?', *Sunday Telegraph Magazine*, 29 May 1988.

41 Quoted in Sam C. Sarkesian, *Beyond the Battlefield: The New Military Professionalism* (London, 1981), p. 121.

42 John Ellis, *The Sharp End of War* (Newton Abbot, 1980) p. 162; Lord Lovat, *March Past* (London, 1978), p. 348; Ronald H. Spector, *Eagle Against the Sun* (New York, 1985), p. 502.

43 Webb, 'Military Competence'.

44 Cincinnatus (pseud. Cecil B. Currey), *Self-Destruction: The Disintegration and Decay of the United States Army during the Vietnam Era* (New York, 1981), p. 153.

45 Karsten, *Soldiers and Society*, p. 92.

46 Emmanuel Todd, *The Explanation of Ideology* (Oxford, 1985), p. 196.

47 Gen. F.C. du Barail, *Mes Souvenirs* (3 vols, Paris, 1984), Vol. II, p. 251.
48 'Tactique allemande . . .' *Spectateur Militaire*, 3rd series No. 4, 1866.
49 John Baynes, *Morale* (London, 1967), pp. 107–8.
50 Christopher Donnelly, *Red Banner: The Soviet Military System in Peace and War* (London, 1988), pp. 17, 23.
51 Reuven Gal, 'Unit Morale: Some Observations on its Israeli Version' (Washington DC, Army Institute of Research, 1983).
52 Winter, *Great War*, p. 35.
53 Edward A. Shils and Morris Janowitz, 'Cohesion and Disintegration in the Wehrmacht in World War II', *Public Opinion Quarterly*, summer 1948, p. 281.
54 Omer Bartov, *The Eastern Front, 1941–45*: German Troops and the Barbarisation of Warfare (London, 1985), p. 149.
55 Quoted in ibid., p. 83.
56 Martin van Creveld, *Fighting Power: German and US Army Combat Performance 1939–1945* (Westport, Conn., 1982), p. 114. This figure includes executions for the broadly defined offence of *Zersetzung der Wehrkraft* (undermining the war effort) and civilian crimes which were punishable by death.
57 Bartov, *Eastern Front*, p. 30.
58 'First Tuesday', Independent Television, 4 October 1989.
59 Mary Dejevesky, 'Back from the war to shatter the Kremlin myth', *The Times*, 18 August 1987.
60 Donnelly, *Red Banner*, p. 193.
61 Richard A. Gabriel, *The New Red Legions: An Attitudinal Portrait of the Soviet Soldier* (Westport, Conn., 1980), pp. 190–2.
62 Viktor Suvorov, *The Liberators* (London, 1981), p. 171.
63 Donnelly, *Red Banner*, p. 193.
64 Winter, *Great War*, pp. 96–8.
65 Bartov, *Eastern Front*, p. 50.
66 Donnelly, *Red Banner*, pp. 173, 175.
67 'China's Army: Strife Torn', *The Economist*, 17–23 February 1990.
68 D.M. Mantell, *True Americanism: Green Berets and War Resisters* (New York, 1974), pp. 206–15.
69 R.G.L. von Zugbach, *Power and Prestige in the British Army* (Aldershot, 1988), pp. 77–9.
70 Van Creveld, *Fighting Power*, pp. 22–3.
71 Webb, 'Military Competence'.
72 Donnelly, *Red Banner*, p. 182.
73 Quoted in Simon Freeman, 'Outgunning the opposition', *Sunday Times*, 5 April 1987.
74 'Army believes Cold War may be hitting recruitment', *The Times*, 18 February 1990.
75 S.L.A. Marshall, *Men Against Fire* (Washington, 1947), p. 42.

76 Alexander L. George, 'Primary Groups, Organization and Military Performance', in *The Study of Leadership* (West Point, 1972).

77 Marshall, *Men Against Fire*, p. 173.

78 Herbert Goldhammer, *The Soviet Soldier* (London, 1975) p. 114.

79 'Soldier attacks army abuses', *The Times*, 27 November 1990.

80 Van Creveld, *Fighting Power*, pp. 75–9.

81 Maj. Vernon Humphrey, personal communication to the author, 12 November 1986.

82 Liz Gill, 'Deadlier than the male?', *The Times*, 26 January 1987.

83 Col Albert Seaton, *The Russo-German War 1941–45* (London, 1971), p. 89.

84 Samuel Rolbant, *The Israeli Soldier* (London, 1970), p. 136; Donnelly, *Red Banner*, pp. 189–90.

85 Peter Evans, 'Professions worried over fewer young people', *The Times*, 5 April 1988; *The Times*, 2 December 1988.

86 George H. Quester, 'The Problem', in Nancy Loring Goldman (ed.), *Female Soldiers – Combatants or Noncombatants?* (Westport, Conn., 1982).

87 Jeff M. Tuten, 'The Argument Against Female Combatants', ibid., p. 261.

88 Mady Wechsler Segal, 'The Argument for Female Combatants', ibid., p. 278.

89 Ali A. Mazrui (ed.), *The Warrior Tradition in Modern Africa* (Leiden, 1977), p. 11.

90 Judith Hicks Stiehm, 'The Effects of Myths about Military Women on the Waging of War', in Eva Isaksson (ed.), *Women and the Military System* (London, 1988), p. 104.

91 Wendy Chapkis, 'Sexuality and Militarism', in ibid., pp. 107–8.

92 Lucian K. Truscott IV, *Dress Gray* (New York, 1978), p. 37.

93 Mazrui, *Warrior Tradition*, p. 153; Evan S. Connell, *Son of the Morning Star* (New York, 1984), p. 266.

94 J.H. Faris, 'The impact of basic training: the role of the drill sergeant', in Nancy L. Goldman and David R. Segal (eds), *The Social Psychology of Military Service* (London, 1976); Mantell, *True Americanism*, p. 132.

95 Rosemary Daniell, *Sleeping with Soldiers* (London, 1986), p. 17.

96 Personal communication to the author, 12 April 1989.

97 John Hockey, *Squaddies: Portrait of a Subculture* (Exeter, 1986), p. 34.

98 A.A. Hanbury-Sparrow, *The Land-Locked Lake* (London, 1932), p. 272; Santoli, *Everything We Had*, p. 197.

99 Antonia Fraser, *The Weaker Vessel: Woman's Lot in Seventeenth-Century England* (London, 1984), p. 4.

100 Charles C. Moskos, 'From institution to occupation: Trends in military organization', *Armed Forces and Society*, autumn 1977.

101 Michel L. Martin, *Warriors to Managers: The French military establishment since 1945* (Chapel Hill, NC., 1981).

102 S.F. Finer, *The Man on Horseback* (London, 1962); Samuel P. Huntington, *The Soldier and the State* (Cambridge, Mass., 1957).

103 Harold D. Lasswell, 'The Garrison State', *American Journal of Sociology*, January 1941.

104 Sidney Lens, *The Military Industrial Complex* (London, 1980).

105 Cynthia H. Enloe, 'Beyond Rambo: Women and the Varieties of Militarized Masculinity', in Isaksson, *Women and the Military System*, p. 73.

106 John H. Johns et al., 'Cohesion in the US Military' (Defense Management Study Group on Military Cohesion, National Defense University, 1984); Colonel Yasotay (pseud.), 'Warriors: An Endangered Species', *Armed Forces Journal*, September 1984.

107 Caspar Weinberger's address to midshipmen at the US Naval Academy, 1983, in William Bowman et al., *The All-Volunteer Force after a Decade* (Washington, 1986), p. 2.

108 Charles C. Moskos, in ibid., pp. 17, 19, 34.

109 C. Ardant du Picq, *Battle Studies: Ancient and Modern Battle* (Harrisburg, Penn., 1956), p. 218.

110 Morris Janowitz, *Military Conflict* (London, 1975), p. 63.

111 Adam Yarmolonsky and Gregory D. Foster, *Paradoxes of Power: The Military Establishment in the Eighties* (Bloomington, Ind., 1983), p. 77.

112 US Department of Defense Investigation Report, 'Formal investigation into the circumstances surrounding the downing of Iran Air Flight 655 on 3 July 1988' (Washington DC, 1989). 'Airbus disaster', *Daily Telegraph*, 6 December 1988.

113 Major Lord Morpeth, *The Times*, 5 March 1987; Field Marshal Lord Bramall, *The Times*, 9 March 1987.

114 Bernhard Fleckenstein, 'Federal Republic of Germany', in Charles C. Moskos and Frank R. Wood (eds), *The Military: More Than Just a Job?* (London, 1988), p. 184.

115 Charles C. Moskos, 'Institutional and Occupational Trends in Armed Forces', in Moskos and Wood, *The Military*, p. 22.

116 Ruth Jolly, *Military Man, Family Man: Crown Property?* (London, 1988), p. 28.

117 Ibid., p. 55.

118 Letters pages, *Soldier*, 22 February, 21 March, 21 April 1988.

119 Morris Janowitz, 'Basic Education and Youth Socialization in the Armed Forces', in R.W. Little (ed.), *A Survey of Military Institutions* (New York, 1969), p. 151.

120 G. Salaman, *Organizations as Constuctors of Social Reality* (Milton Keynes, 1974).

121 Von Zugbach, *Power and Prestige*, pp. 73, 78.

122 Ibid., p. 180.

123 Michael Satchell et al., 'The Military's New Stars', *US News and*

World Report, 18 April 1988; John Keegan, 'Break up the Baronies', ibid.
124 Keegan, ibid.
125 Richard A. Gabriel, *Military Incompetence: Why the American Military Doesn't Win* (New York, 1983), p. 189.
126 Tim Witcher, 'British cope better with war', *Daily Telegraph*, 7 February 1990.
127 De Vigny, *Servitude et Grandeur*, p. 14.

6 Man under Authority

1 Martin van Creveld, *Command in War* (London, 1985), p. 275.
2 John H. Johns et al., 'Cohesion in the US Military' (National Defense University, 1984), p. 65.
3 Richard A. Gabriel, *Military Incompetence: Why the American Military Doesn't Win* (New York, 1983), pp. 9–13.
4 Cathy Downes, 'Great Britain', in Charles C. Moskos and Frank R. Wood (eds), *The Military: More Than Just a Job?* (London, 1988), p. 169.
5 Gen. Sir Frank Kitson, *Warfare as a Whole* (London, 1987), pp. 140, 144.
6 John Keegan, 'Too Many Generals?', *Daily Telegraph*, 16 May 1989.
7 Kitson, *Warfare*, p. 121.
8 Charles C. Moskos, *The American Enlisted Man* (New York, 1970), p. 54.
9 Edward M. Coffman, *The Old Army: A Portrait of the American Army in Peacetime* (Oxford, 1986), p. 84.
10 Pierre Chalmin, *L'Officier français de 1815 à 1870* (Paris, 1957), p. 214.
11 V.D . . . (pseud. Gen. V. Derrecagaix) *Histoire de la guerre de 1870* (Paris, 1871), pp. 66–7.
12 FM Viscount Wolseley, *The Story of a Soldier's Life* (3 vols, London, 1903), p. 284.
13 Diary of Sir Henry Wilson, 28 March 1914, Imperial War Museum.
14 Christopher Duffy, *The Army of Frederick the Great* (Newton Abbot, 1974), p. 25; Capt. E. de la Barre Duparcq, *Etudes historiques et militaires sur la Prusse* (Paris, 1854), p. 215.
15 Col Baron Kaulbars, *Rapport sur l'Armée allemande . . .* , trans. Capt. G. Le Marchand (Paris, 1880), pp. 317–61.
16 Reuven Gal, 'Israel', in Moskos and Wood, *The Military*, p. 272.
17 Keegan, 'Too Many Generals'; Kitson, *Warfare*, pp. 170–2.
18 I owe both these references to Capt. R.A.D. Applegate's trenchant 'Why Armies Lose in Battle: An Organic Approach to Military Analysis', *Journal of the Royal United Services Institute*, December 1987.
19 Gen. Donn A. Starry, 'Running Things', *Parameters*, September 1987, p. 17.

20   Gerd Niepold, *Battle for White Russia* (London, 1987), p. 278.
21   R.G.L. von Zugbach, *Power and Prestige in the British Army* (Aldershot, 1988), pp. 53–4.
22   'Colonel Yasotay', 'Warriors: An Endangered Species', *Armed Forces Journal*, September 1984.
23   Starry, 'Running Things', p. 15.
24   Duffy, *Army of Frederick the Great*, pp. 40–1.
25   Von Zugbach, *Power and Prestige*, p. 142.
26   Downes, 'Great Britain', p. 174.
27   FM Erich von Manstein, *Lost Victories* (London, 1958), p. 120.
28   FM Sir William Slim, *Courage and Other Broadcasts* (London, 1957), pp. 5–6.
29   Van Creveld, *Command*, p. 17.
30   Ludwig Reiners, *Frederick the Great* (London, 1975), p. 191.
31   Henry Wilson was the last general to die sword in hand, shot down by gunmen in 1922 outside his house in Eaton Square as he was returning from a ceremony in full uniform.
32   John Keegan, *The Mask of Command* (London, 1987), p. 122.
33   Quoted in David Chandler, *The Campaigns of Napoleon* (London, 1967), p. 1067.
34   See Maj. Gary B. Griffin, 'The Directed Telescope: A Traditional Element of Effective Command', *Combat Studies Institute Report* (Fort Leavenworth, 1985).
35   Quoted in Chandler, *Napoleon*, p. 406.
36   Richard Holmes, *The Little Field Marshal: Sir John French* (London, 1981), pp. 251–2.
37   'Infantry in Battle' (Army 251/4/242, Wellington, October 1949), para. 58.
38   S.L.A. Marshall, *Men Against Fire* (New York, 1947), p. 103.
39   Brig. Sam Cowan, 'System Integration: The Promised Land?', *Journal of the Royal United Services Institute*, autumn 1988, pp. 47–8.
40   Ibid., p. 48.
41   Maj.-Gen. Jasper A. Welch, 'C3 I Systems: The Efficiency Connection', in John Hwang et al. (eds), *Selected Analytical Concepts in Command and Control* (London, 1982), pp. 4–6.
42   Van Creveld, *Command*, p. 275.
43   Quoted in Marshall, *Men Against Fire*, p. 189.
44   Dave Richard Palmer, *Summons of the Trumpet* (San Rafael, Ca., 1978), p. 142.
45   James Webb, *Fields of Fire* (Englewood Cliffs, NJ, 1978), p. 258.
46   Gen. F. von Senger und Etterlin, *Neither Fear Nor Hope* (London, 1963) p. 228; Brig. George Taylor, 'Further Thoughts in Command in Battle', *British Army Review*, March 1982; Marshall, *Men Against Fire*, p. 189.
47   Roy K. Flint, 'Nhi Binh: A Memoir of an Infantry Campaign in Viet-

nam', paper presented to the British Military History Commission, RMA Sandhurst, 22 July 1979.

48 *British Military Doctrine*, p. 73. See also Gen. William E. DePuy, 'Concepts of Operation: The Heart of Command, The Tool of Doctrine', *Army*, August 1988.

49 Quoted in Martin van Creveld, *Fighting Power: German and US Army Performance, 1939–45* (Westport, Conn., 1982), pp. 28–9.

50 Maj. John T. Nelson '*Auftragstaktik*: A Case for Decentralised Battle', *Parameters*, September 1987, p. 31.

51 Cowan, 'System Integration', p. 51.

52 Ole Luk-Oie (pseud. Sir Ernest Swinton), 'The Point of View', in *The Green Curve and Other Stories* (Edinburgh, 1915).

53 Stephen Canby, 'The Alliance and Europe: Part IV, Military Doctrine and Technology', *Adelphi Paper No. 109* (London, 1975), p. 14.

54 Gen. Donn A. Starry, 'Leadership and Technology', *Armor*, Jan–Feb 1986, p. 47.

55 Van Creveld, *Command*, pp. 273–4.

56 Von Manstein, *Lost Victories*, p. 69.

57 Swinton, 'The Point of View', p. 269.

58 Sir Martin Lindsay et al., 'Thoughts on Command in Battle', *British Army Review*, December 1981, p. 4.

59 Ibid., p. 7.

60 Quoted in Col M.J.H. Hudson, 'Conditioned in Peace', *British Army Review*, April 1986, p. 9.

61 Quoted in Oliver Lindsay (ed.), *A Guards' General: The Memoirs of Major General Sir Allan Adair* (London, 1986), p. 30.

62 Bruce Catton, *Glory Road* (New York, 1964), pp. 222–3.

63 Keegan, *Mask of Command*, p. 233.

64 David Fraser, *Alanbrooke* (London, 1982), p. 154.

65 Sir John Glubb, *Into Battle: A Soldier's Diary of the Great War* (London, 1978), p. 30.

66 Michael Howard, *The Franco-Prussian War* (London, 1961), p. 426.

67 Lt-Col Gary H. Wade, 'World War II Division Commanders', *Military Review*, March 1986, p. 62.

68 Table in *Revue Historique de l'Armée*, 1971 No. 1 *Spécial*, p. 21.

69 Niepold, *White Russia*, p. 106.

70 Maj. Ian Gardiner, 'Some Realities of Command at Company Level in War', talk delivered to 49 Infantry Brigade, 22 November 1986.

71 Brig. I.M. Rose, 'The Training of Commanders and their Staff', *British Army Review*, August 1987, p. 25.

72 Maj. Vernon W. Humphrey, 'Winning at the NTC: Fire Coordination', *Infantry*, May–June 1984, p. 34.

73 Howard, *Franco-Prussian War*, p. 205.

Select Bibliography

No short bibliography can hope to do justice to a topic which has generated literally thousands of books and articles. This select bibliography simply lists books that the author has found particularly useful in writing his own.

Ardrey, Robert, *The Territorial Imperative* (London, 1967).
—— *The Hunting Hypothesis* (London, 1977).
Armitage, M.J., and Mason, R.A., *Air Power in the Nuclear Age* (London, 1986).
Barnaby, Frank, *The Automated Battlefield* (London, 1986).
—— and ter Bord, Marlies (eds), *Emerging Technologies and Military Doctrine* (London, 1986).
Bartov, Omer, *The Eastern Front 1941–45: German Troops and the Barbarisation of Warfare* (London, 1985).
Baynes, John, *Morale* (London, 1967).
Bellamy, Chris, *The Future of Land Warfare* (London, 1987).
Best, Geoffrey, and Wheatcroft, Andrew (eds), *War, Economy and the Military Mind* (London, 1976).
Betts, Richard, *Surprise Attacks* (Washington, 1984).
Bidwell, Shelford, and Graham, Dominick, *Fire-Power: British Army Weapons and Theories of War* (London, 1982).
Blainey, Geoffrey, *The Causes of War* (London, 1973).
Blanning, T.C.W., *The Origins of the French Revolutionary Wars* (London, 1986).
Bloch, Marc, *The Historian's Craft* (Manchester, 1976).
Bond, Brian, *Liddell Hart: A Study of his Military Thought* (London, 1977).
Brodie, Bernard, *War and Politics* (New York, 1973).
Brown, Neville, and Farrar-Hockley, Anthony, *Nuclear First Use* (London, 1985).
Carver, Michael, *War Since 1945* (London, 1980).
Chandler, David, *The Campaigns of Napoleon* (London, 1967).
Clausewitz, C.M. von, *On War*, trans. and ed. by Michael Howard and Peter Paret (Princeton, 1976).

Connell, Jon, *The New Maginot Line* (London, 1986).

Davidson, Phillip B., *Vietnam at War 1946–1975* (London, 1988).

Design For Military Operations: The British Military Doctrine (London, 1989).

Donnelly, Christopher, *Red Banner: The Soviet Military System in Peace and War* (London, 1988).

Dyer, Gwynn, *War* (London, 1986).

Ehrlich, Paul R.; Sagan, Carl, et al., *The Nuclear Winter* (London, 1985).

Eibl-Eibesfeldt, Irenäus, *The Biology of Peace and War* (London, 1979).

Elleul, Jacques, *The Technological Society* (New York, 1964).

Ellis, John, *The Sharp End of War* (Newton Abbot, 1980).

English, John, *A Perspective on Infantry* (New York, 1982).

Faringdon, Hugh, *Confrontation: The Strategic Geography of NATO and the Warsaw Pact* (London, 1986).

Field Manual 100–5 *Operations* (Washington, 1986).

Fotion, Nicholas, and Elfstrom, Gerard, *Military Ethics* (London, 1986).

Fromm, Erich, *The Anatomy of Human Destructiveness* (London, 1977).

Fussell, Paul, *The Great War and Modern Memory* (London, 1975)

—— *Wartime* (London, 1989).

Gabriel, Richard A., *Military Incompetence: Why the American Military Doesn't Win* (New York, 1985).

—— (ed.), *Military Psychiatry: A Comparative Perspective* (Westport, Conn., 1986).

—— *No More Heroes: Madness and Psychiatry in War* (New York, 1987).

—— *Soviet Military Psychiatry*, Westport, Conn., 1986).

Goldman, Nancy L. (ed.), *Female Soldiers – Combatants or Noncombatants?* (Westport, Conn., 1982).

—— and Segal, David R., *The Social Psychology of Military Service* (London, 1976).

Gooch, John, *The Plans of War: The General Staff and British Military Strategy* (London, 1974).

Gray, J. Glenn, *Warriors: Reflections on Men in Battle* (London, 1970).

Hackett, Sir John, *The Profession of Arms* (London, 1983).

Heller, Charles E., and Stofft, William A. (eds), *America's First Battles* (Lawrence, Kansas, 1986).

Henderson, W.D., *Why the Vietcong Fought* (Westport, Conn., 1979).

Herr, Michael, *Dispatches* (London, 1978).

Hockey, John, *Squaddies: Portrait of a Subculture* (Exeter, 1986).

Howard, Michael, *War and the Liberal Conscience* (London, 1978).

—— *The Causes of Wars* (London, 1983).

Isakson, Eva (ed.), *Women and the Military System* (London, 1988).

Janowitz, Morris, *The New Military* (New York, 1969).

Kahn, Herman, *On Thermonuclear War* (Princeton, 1960).

—— *Thinking about the Unthinkable* (New York, 1962).

—— *On Escalation: Metaphors and Scenarios* (New York, 1965).

Kaldor, Mary, *The Baroque Arsenal* (London, 1982).

Karsten, Peter, *Soldiers and Society: The Effects of Military Service and War on American Life* (Westport, Conn., 1978).

Keegan, John, *The Face of Battle* (New York, 1976).

—— *The Mask of Command* (London, 1987).

Kennedy, Paul, *The Rise and Fall of the Great Powers* (London, 1988).

—— *The War Plans of the Great Powers* (London, 1979).

Kitson, Frank, *Warfare as a Whole* (London, 1987).

Lind, William S., *Maneuver Warfare Handbook* (Boulder, Colorado, 1985).

Lorenz, Konrad, *On Aggression* (London, 1966).

Lupfer, Timothy F., *The Dynamics of Doctrine: The Changes in German Tactical Doctrine During the First World War* (Fort Leavenworth, Kansas, 1981).

Luttwak, Edward, *On Strategy: The Logic of War and Peace* (Cambridge, Mass., 1987).

Marshall, S.L.A., *Men Against Fire* (Washington, 1947).

McNeill, William H., *The Pursuit of Power: Technology, Armed Force and Society Since AD 1000* (Oxford, 1983).

Mearsheimer, John J., *Liddell Hart and the Weight of History* (New York, 1988).

Millett, Allan R., and Maslowski, Peter, *For the Common Defense* (New York, 1984).

Morris, Desmond, *The Naked Ape* (London, 1967).

Moskos, Charles, *The American Enlisted Man* (New York, 1970).

—— and Frank R. Woods (eds), *The Military: More Than Just a Job?* (London, 1988).

Middlebrook, Martin, *Operation Corporate* (London, 1985).

Paret, Peter (ed.), *Makers of Modern Strategy: From Machiavelli to the Nuclear Age* (London, 1986).

Pearton, Maurice, *The Knowledgeable State* (London, 1982).

Prins, Gwyn (ed.), *Defended to Death* (London, 1983).

—— *The Choice: Nuclear Weapons versus Security* (London, 1984).

Sajer, Guy, *The Forgotten Soldier* (London, 1971).

Sarkesian, Sam C., *Beyond the Battlefield: The New Military Professionalism* (London, 1981).

Schelling, Thomas, *Arms and Influence* (New York, 1966).

Simpkin, Richard, *Deep Battle* (London, 1987).

—— *Human Factors in Mechanised Warfare*, (London, 1983).

—— *The Race to the Swift: Thoughts on Twenty-First Century Warfare* (London, 1985).

Smith, Dan, and Smith, Ron, *The Economics of Militarism* (London, 1983).

Smoke, Richard, *War: Controlling Escalation* (Cambridge, Mass., 1977).

Spiers, Edward M., *Chemical Warfare* (London, 1986).

Stoeffer, S.A. et al., *The American Soldier* (2 vols, Princeton, 1965).

Stoessinger, John G., *Why Nations Go to War* (London, 1985).

Strachan, Hew, *European Armies and the Conduct of War* (London, 1983).

Travers, Tim, *The Killing Ground* (London, 1987).

Van Creveld, Martin, *Command in War* (Cambridge, Mass., 1985).
—— *Fighting Power: German and US Army Performance 1939–1945* (Westport, Conn., 1982).
—— *Supplying War: Logistics from Wallenstein to Patton* (Oxford, 1977).
—— *Technology and War* (New York, 1988).
Vigny, Alfred de, *Servitude et Grandeur Militaires* (Paris, 1914).
Wakin, Malham H. (ed.), *War, Morality and the Military Profession* (Boulder, Colorado, 1979).
Wallach, Jehuda L., *The Dogma of the Battle of Annihilation* (London, 1986).
Winter, J.M., *The British People and the Great War* (London, 1986).
Zugbach, R.G.L. von, *Power and Prestige in the British Army* (Aldershot, 1988).

Acknowledgments

This has not been an easy book to write, and the task would have been beyond me without the generous help freely given by so many friends. I owe an enormous debt to Mr John Keegan and Mr Keith Simpson. Without the former's kindness I would never have ventured into serious print at all, and without the latter's encouragement I would have sought an easier way of making a living. My other former colleagues at the Royal Military Academy Sandhurst have also been most tolerant, and I am especially grateful for the wisdom of Dr Christopher Duffy. Mr Chris Donnelly and Mr Michael Orr of the Soviet Studies Research Centre gave useful guidance, though I seldom emerged from their hospitable clutches without a sore head. I have greatly valued the advice of Professor Ray Hobbs of McMaster University.

My associates on the Higher Command and Staff Course at the Army Staff College have proved remarkably tolerant of my idiosyncracies – worsened, as they have been of late, by the imminence of literary deadlines. General Sir John Waters, Lieutenant-General Sir John Learmont, Major-General Jeremy Mackenzie, Major-General Rupert Smith, Brigadier Rob McAfee, Brigadier Gage Williams and my learned friend Dr Brian Holden Reid all deserve my thanks. The students deserve my apologies; first, for going on at length whenever offered the opportunity to do so, and second, for shamelessly looting all their best ideas: Brigadier Mike Jackson, Brigadier Dair Farrar-Hockley, and Brigadier Tim Granville-Chapman may well discern their influence upon some of what precedes. The Staff College Librarian, Mr Mike Sims, has been immensely supportive, and I extend my thanks to his staff and to their hard-pressed colleagues at the library of the Royal Military Academy Sandhurst.

My own 'military family' gave me tremendous support when I was commanding 2nd Battalion The Wessex Regiment, and Major Gerald Blight, Major Colin Bulleid, Captain Ian Blewitt, Captain Tony Thornell and Corporal Ian Allcock all know the debt I owe them. My real family has been acutely aware that dual commitment to pen and sword has left precious little time for them. My daughters Jessica and Corinna, and my dear wife Lizie, deserve more thanks than mere words can express.

I must make it clear that, despite all this help, I have undoubtedly made errors, and these are mine alone. It is, moreover, entirely possible that my views will not be shared by some of those whose support I acknowledge. Their assistance in no way implies their approval, although I hope they will not be too affronted by the finished product. Finally, any similarity between my opinions and those of the Ministry of Defence is pure coincidence, and this book is in no sense an embodiment of official views. But that much, I am sure, will have become speedily apparent.

Richard Holmes
Ropley
November 1990

Index

accidents in battle 155, 156–7
Ackroyd, Peter 165
Active Defense 60, 131–2
Adams, James 23–4
Afghanistan, Soviet invasion of 52–3,
  108, 148, 160, 192, 210, 235, 240
Afheldt, Horst 139
Africa, role of army in 192
age: of battle casualties 162; of combat
  soldiers 162; of commanders 278–80;
  retirement age of officers 251
Agnadello, battle of (1509) 158
Aids (Acquired Immune Deficiency
  Syndrome) 165, 286
air assault units 91
air forces: Israeli 102; and the operational
  level of war 62–3; recruitment 230–1;
  restructuring 292; Soviet 131; United
  States 230–1; women in 221;
air-defence systems 125–6
aircraft 94; accidents in war 156–7; in
  the Korean war 113; and night fighting
  179; in the Second World War 89, 90;
  technological developments 90; in the
  Vietnam War 90; in the Yom Kippur
  War 102, 103
AirLand Battle doctrine 132, 134, 135,
  137, 140
airmobile operations 137–8, 139
Alexander the Great 151, 258–9, 261, 275
America see United States
American Civil War 69, 86, 107, 109,
  246, 260, 277; and conscription 197–8;
  enlisted volunteers 205; photographs of
  214; psychiatric casualties 184
Amery, L.S. 251
amicicide 156
Amis, Martin 24, 286
ammunition 91, 182, 183
Andropov, Yuri 28–9
Anglo-Saxon England 194–5
animals, groups of 159
anthropologists: and the causes of war 48–9

anti-tank mines 125
anti-tank weapons 124, 129, 138
Aquinas, St Thomas 39
Arab-Israeli wars 80–1
Ardant du Picq, Colonel Charles
  64, 75, 172, 230
Arendt, Hannah 155
Armenian earthquake (1988) 32, 292
'armies in crisis' thesis 228–9
armoured corps 96
armoured knights 119–20
armoured vehicles 121, 127
Arras, Battle of (1917) 161
artificial intelligence 141
artillery 124, 148, 152
artillery units 91
artists, military 65, 214
Ashurst, George 168
Aspin, Les 236
Asquith, H.H. 48
atomic bomb 100, 153
attitudes to war 57, 202–16
attrition warfare 109–11, 112, 115, 128,
  156; and defensive positions 181–2; and
  military doctrine 131, 132, 137
Auftragstaktik 265, 267, 271–2, 285
Augustine of Hippo, Saint 39

Bacon, Francis 224
bacteriological warfare (NBC) 173–6
Baden-Powell, Sir Robert 167
Bagnall, Field Marshal Sir Nigel 108–9
Balaklava, battle of 64–5
Bandel, Eugene 193
Barnaby, Frank, 51, 173
Barton, Doris 14
Bartov, Omer 80, 208, 209, 210, 212
Baudissin, Count von 232
Baynes, John 168, 206–7
Bazaine, Marshal 259
Beaufre, General André 62
Beaverbrook, William Maxwell Aitken,
  1st Baron 88–9

331

Becker, Jillian 219
Befehlstaktik 265, 269
Behrend, Arthur 152
Beirut, fighting in 81–2, 119
Bellamy, Chris 91, 118, 121, 129, 182
Bennett, Sir John Wheeler 191–2
Beowulf 224
Berenhorst, G.H. 166
Beresford, Marshal 145
Bergson, Henri 75
Berthier, Alexandre 69, 155
Bidwell, Shelford 60–1
Bigeard, General Marcel 255
Biskind, Peter 214–15
Bismarck, Otto von 74
blacks, United States Army 230
Blainey, Geoffrey 50
Blanning, T.C.W. 49
Blenheim, battle of (1704) 201
Bloch, I.S. 98, 99, 276
Bloch, Marc 50
'blue ribbon' general staffs 148–9, 243
Boer War 76, 82, 88, 101–2
Bolivia 84
Bolle, Colonel Richard 277
bombing 42, 62–3
Borodino, battle of (1812) 69, 110
Bourne, Peter 187
Boyd, John 113
Boyd cycle 153, 272, 273, 288, 291
Bradford, Brigadier-General 'Boy'
    279
Bradley, Omar 244, 263
Bramall, Field Marshal Lord 232
Bridges, Major Tom 204
bridges, 116, 135
Britain: attitudes to war 23, 203–4; defence
    expenditure 1, 36; state intervention,
    and the two world wars 2–3; *Trident*
    programme 7
British army: Battle Casualty
    Replacements 218; circles of influence
    247–8; combat power 236; conscription
    196–7; fitness of troops 167–8; infantry
    180; infantry combat vehicles 127; length
    of tours of duty 243; and the Malayan
    campaign (1948–60) 82; manpower
    shortages 220; mercenary tradition 193;
    military doctrine 108–9, 136–7; officers
    213, 234–5, 244, 254–6; at operational
    level 60–1; Parachute Regiment 254;
    present day 231–2, 240; promotion
    system 252, 253, 255–6, 257; psychiatric
    casualties 184, 185, 187, 188; rank
    inflation 245; regimental system 206–7,
    236–7; service wives 234; short service
    commissions 234–5; size of logistic corps
    91; staff systems 148–9; and state control

227; tank development 98, 123; women
    in 225; *see also* Falklands War; First
    World War; Second World War
Broadwood, Lieutenant-General R.G. 15
Brodie, Bernard 21, 50
Brower, Ken 125, 181
Brown, Neville 29, 31
Browning, Lieutenant-General Sir
    Frederick 'Boy' 254–5
Bruchmuller, Georg 244
brutality in training 217–18
Bundeswehr (West German army) 136,
    139, 180, 220, 232–3, 236, 240
Bundy, McGeorge 30
bunkers 182
Burk, Kathleen 2

Caesar, Julius 100, 194, 267
Cameron of Fassfern, Colonel 201
Canadian Armed Forces 221
Canby, Steven 96, 132, 273
Cannae, Hannibal's victory of 73, 270
'capital tanks' 123
Capper, Major-General Tommy 259
career structure 226; senior officers 240–58
Carnot, Lazare 67
Carrington, Charles 159, 168–9, 174
Carthage, Rome's victory over 54
casualties 2, 173, 218; age of 162; officers
    204–5; disposal of dead 209; infantry,
    in conventional warfare 127; NBC
    warfare 173–4; in Northern Ireland 231;
    psychiatric 183–9, 218, 276–7, 289
Catton, Bruce 277
cavalry 75–6, 102, 161, 166
Cawley family (Berrington Hall,
    Herefordshire) 14–15
Cerignola, battle of (1503) 158
Chamberlain, Neville 48
chance, in battle 154–7
Chassepot rifle 121, 147
Chatwin, Bruce 216
Chaucer, Geoffrey 224
chemical energy weapons 124, 126–7
chemical weapons 53, 173–6
Chermol, Lieutenant-Colonel Brian 188
Chernobyl disaster 32
Chetwode, Lord 154
Chieftain (tank) 123, 137
childbirth 225
Chinese army 212
Christianity 38–9, 165
Church of England: and nuclear weapons
    31
civil aid, use of military for 292–3
Civil Defence 32–3
civilian occupations 229
Clancy, Tom 96

class *see* social class
Clausewitz, C.M. von 19, 21–2, 50–1, 59, 143, 155, 176, 182, 266, 272; on the function of battle 63–4, 69, 71–2, 74, 86; importance of numbers in battle 145; on moral forces 158
Claverhouse, John Graham of 'Bonnie Dundee' 259
clothing 169; NBC protection 174–5; *see also* uniforms
Coffman, Edward 246
cold climates 187
Cold War 52, 141, 228
combat, ritualised 158–61
combat power 236; imbalance in 157; and luck 154; and moral factors 153; and victory in war 144–6
command, control and communication (C3) systems 135
commanders 258–85; chain of command 261–2; and chiefs of staff 281–2; and communication 263–7; concept of operations 270–1; deputy 283; killed in battle 258–9; leadership in battle 189, 258–64, 268–9; leisure activities 275–6; orders 269–70; overcommand 251–2, 267–8; in peacetime and war 277–8; personal qualities 275; skills of 151; stress 276–8
communication: on the battlefield 263–7
computer games 161
computers 263, 265–7, 271, 272–4
conceptual component: of fighting power 157
Condon, Private J. 162
Congreve, Major Billy 17
Connell, Jon 28, 95
conscientious objectors 202–4
conscription 167, 168, 190, 194–201, 205, 207, 215, 216, 237; in the Soviet Union 107–8
Conventional Deterrence (Mearsheimer) 35
conventional weapons 35–7, 125, 170–3
cost-gain analysis: and the causes of war 50–1
courage, moral and physical 257–8, 268, 285
Cowan, Major-General Sam 273
Crécy, battle of 65, 116–17
Creveld, Martin van 21–2, 150, 122, 218, 239, 258, 267, 274
Crimean War 64–5
Crisis in Command (Gabriel) 202
Crombie, Captain J.E. 18
Crook, General George 198
Cuban missile crisis (1962) 12, 26
culture, and military attitudes 206–7
Cunaxa, battle of (401 BC) 155, 259

Cuneo, Terence 65
Cunningham, Lieutenant-General Sir Alan 276

d'Alenson, Colonel 104
D'Erlon, Count Drouet 155
de Gaulle, Charles 78
de la Billière, Lieutenant-General, Sir Peter 276
du Barail, General F.C. 206
danger, denial of 162–3
Daniell, Rosemary 223
Dann, Major Keith 174
Day After, The 23
Dayan, Moshe 258
death: attitudes to 164, 165; fear of 161–2; killing of officers (fragging) 201–2; military executions 210; numbers of war-related 2; *see also* casualties
Decisive Battles: Their Influence upon History and Civilisation (Fuller) 144
Deer Hunter, The (film) 215
defence: British army, First World War 146–7; Clausewitz's views on 72; defensive positions 181–3; and manoeuvre warfare 112; non-provocative 139–40
defence expenditure 93–5; economic costs of 1–2; and the garrison state 228; redeployment of money involved in 6, 36–8; reduction in 140, 288; Soviet Union 105–6
defensive warfare 72, 77
Dejevsky, Mary 211
Delbrück, Hans 67, 73
denial of danger 162–3
Denmark: women soldiers 220–1
DePuy, General William 230
Descaves, Lucien 196
deterrence: as function of armies 293; and FOFA 133
digging in (troops in battle) 181–2
Direct Fire Weapons Effects Simulators 283
doctrinal surprise 153
doctrine, military 145–8; NATO 133–6; *see also* under individual countries, e.g. Soviet army
Dollard, John 162–3
Donnelly, Christopher 32, 59, 95, 117, 175, 207, 214, 219–20
Doolittle Report (1946) 229
Dorman-Smith, 'Chink' 251
Douhet, Guilio 62, 256, 257
Dragomirov, General 76
drills: in manoeuvre warfare 113
drugs, war against 292, 293
Ducrot, General 280, 284

Duffy, Christopher 163, 193, 253–4
Dupuy, Colonel T.N. 122
Durkheim, Emile 49

Eastern Europe 45
education, military 150, 289
Egypt, 102
Ehrlich, Paul R. 33
Einstein's Monsters (Amis) 24, 286
Eisenhower, Dwight D. 228, 275
Eitan, General Rafael 203
electromagnetic guns 127, 141
Electronic Warfare 157, 179
electrothermal guns 127
Elfstrom, Gerard 38
Elizabethan militia 195, 197
Elleul, Jacques 44, 52
employment: service wives 233–4
'End of History, The' (Fukuyama) 45
endurance among soldiers 168–70
Engels, F. 68, 80
English, Lieutenant-Colonel John 183
English Civil War 155, 194, 260, 277
environment: influence on military
    attitudes 206–7; problems of, and
    military training 215
Erickson, John 81
Esher Committee (1903–4) 148–9
Etheridge, Annie 219
ethologists: and the causes of war 48–9
European land battle: as outdated
    concept 141
Explanation of Ideology, The (Todd) 206
Explosive Reactive Armour 126

Face of Battle, The (Keegan) 51
FAESHED (Fuel Air Explosives Helicopter
    Delivered) 125
Falkenhayn, Erich von 76
Falklands war 43, 51, 53, 56, 59, 80, 84,
    231; age of combat soldiers 162;
    accidental killings 156; attitude of
    troops 204; Battle of Goose Green 145;
    commanders 282; communications 265;
    military technology 94; night-fighting
    aids 178; psychiatric casualties
    185, 187, 188; and talismans 163;
    and war films 215
families of servicemen 233–4
family types 206
Farrar-Hockley, General Sir Anthony 31
fatalism 161–2, 163, 166
Fate of the Earth, The 24
Ferguson, A.K. 62
feudal armies 191, 192
Fieldhouse, Admiral Sir John 59
films, and military attitudes 214–15
firepower 110, 118–20; and Active Defense

61; and death in battle 16–18; and the
    function of battle 75–6; and the infantry
    100–1
First World War: ammunition 88; Anglo-
    French alliance 85; attrition warfare
    110; British defence structure 146–7;
    British infantry and gunners 101; British
    Official History of 65; British
    staff officers 149; casualties 2, 13–18,
    33–4, 44, 162, 184, 218; divisional
    commanders 259; psychiatric 184, 185;
    commanders 263, 278, 279, 281;
    Commission on Responsibilities 40;
    communications 264; conscientious
    objectors 202; and conscription 196, 198;
    deaths *see* casualties; effects of shellfire
    172; endurance of soldiers 168–9;
    fatalism 162; fitness of troops 167–8;
    fragging 201; and the function of battle
    77–8; gas attacks 174, 175; German
    defence 172; hard physical labour 183;
    impact of technology 92; isolated groups
    of soldiers 172; lack of military
    judgment 29–30; leadership of BEF 154;
    literature 215; memories of veterans
    63–4; military doctrine 104–5, 146–7;
    moral factors 153; night operations
    176–7; Nivelle's offensive 258; numbers
    enlisting 207; personal attitudes to
    11–12; role of luck 156; settlement 55;
    sleep loss 177; and state intervention 2–3;
    surprise attacks 152; tactical stalemate
    during 99; volunteers 212
Flavigny, General Jean 146
Fleckenstein, Bernhard 233
Fleury, Count 193
Flint, Roy 270, 272
Foch, Marshal 279, 283, 291–2
FOFA (Follow-On Forces Attack) 130,
    133, 134, 135
Ford, John 214
fortifications 181–2
forward defence 115–16, 136
Fotion, Nicholas 38
fragging 201–2
France: and Clausewitz's ideas on battle
    75; and the Indo-China war 82–3; *see also*
    French Army
Franco-Prussian war (1870–1) 72–3, 74,
    75, 196, 246, 248, 256, 259, 264, 284
Fraser, Antonia 225
Frederick II, King of Prussia (the Great)
    67, 112, 155, 163, 166, 193, 259
Freedman, Lawrence 22, 26
French, Sir John 84, 154, 247, 248, 263,
    276, 277, 281
French army: conditions of service
    246–7; conscription 190, 195–6, 237;

corps d'armée system 153, 261–2; and the French family 206; military doctrine 147; officer-soldier ratio 244; peasants and urban soldiers 167; Revolutionary army 3, 66–8; Second Empire 246, 256; health of soldiers 166
French Revolution: and the Swiss guard 193
Fuel Air Explosives 125, 171, 181
Fukuyama, Francis 45
Fuller, J.F.C. 78–9, 119, 144, 256–7
Fussell, Paul 15

Gabriel, Richard A. 52, 170, 185, 188, 189, 202, 211, 236, 243
Gal, Reuven 249
Gardiner, Lieutenant-Colonel Ian 282
garrison state concept 228
Gates, Robert M. 176
Gates Commission Report (1970) 229
Gaujal, General 280
Gaylor, Admiral Noel 30
General Belgrano, sinking of 58
Geneva Convention (1864) 41
geography: and manoeuvre warfare 115–17
George, Alexander 217
German army: commanders 275; communication and control 264–5; conscription 167, 196; First World War 104–5, 172; general staff system 73, 150; and the German family 206; infantry combat vehicles 127; military executions 210; and Nazism 122, 191–2, 209–10; officers, social background 213–14; Second World War 78–9, 150, 218, 257; traditional versus reformist views 232–3; *see also* Prussian army
Germany: changing attitudes to military occupation 6; and Clausewitz's ideas on battle 74–5; military doctrine 136, 146; unification of 47, 51, 136, 287
Gever, Colonel Eli 203
Gibb, Robert 65
Giles, Henry 193
Gladden, Norman 162
Glantz, Colonel David 128
Glubb, Lieutenant John 16, 161, 278
Goff, Stanley 200
Gorbachev, Mikhail 24, 46, 92, 105–6, 131, 220, 227, 287
Gort, John, 6th Viscount 84
Graham, Dominick 60
grand strategy 58–60
grand tactics 60
Grant, Charles 163
Grass, Günter 47
Gray, J. Glenn 159, 160
Greece, ancient 194

'Greek fire' 173
Green Berets 213, 223
Green politics 6–7, 233
Grenada, US invasion of 59, 63, 86, 284
Grieson, Sir James 280
Groom, Winston 200
Grotius, Hugo 40
Grouchy, Emmanuel, Marquis de 155, 260–1
groups 49; bonding process 158–9, 217–19, 222, 226; isolated groups of soldiers 172–3; young men in 216–17
Guderian, Heinz 78, 156
Guedalla, Philip 13
guerrilla warfare 5, 82–4
Guesclin, Bertrand du 66
Guevara, Ché 84
Guibert, Comte de 69
Guilmartin, John 11
Gulf Crisis 5, 6, 221
Gulf War (Iran-Iraq War) 2, 51, 85, 162, 176
guns 153; anti-tank 90, 124; effects of shellfire 171–2; electromagnetic 141; recoilless 124
Gurkhas 193

Hackett, General Sir John 23, 30–1, 98, 190, 279
Haig, Sir Douglas 78, 154, 247, 267
Haldane, General Sir Aylmer 99
Haldane, R.B. 101
Halleck, Henry Wager ('Old Brains') 70
Hamburg firestorm (1944) 33
Hamilton, Sir Ian 76
Hamley, Sir Edward 70–1
Hanbury-Sparrow, Colonel Alan 224
Hannig, Norbert 139
Hanson, Victor Davis 8
Harding, John 276
Hardy, Thomas 215
Hastings, battle of (1066) 194–5
health: of senior officers 280–1; of soldiers 166–8
helicopters 90, 91, 94, 96, 125, 138, 183; in Vietnam 267–8
Hemsley, Brigadier John 175
Henderson, W.D. 153
Hennell, George 15–16
Hermant, Abel 196
Herr, Michael 16
Havelock, Sir Henry 161
high-intensity operations 57–8
Hindenburg, P. von 76
Hitler, Adolf 80, 122, 191–2
Hobbes, Thomas 54, 97
Hobbs, T.R. 38–9

Hockey, John 49, 224
Hoetzsch, Otto 55
Hohenlohe-Ingelfingen, Prince Karl zu 248
Homans, George 49
Homer: descriptions of death 16–17
Hooker, 'Fighting Joe' 277
Hopton, Sir Ralph 155, 277
Howard, Michael 21, 39, 44–5, 47, 72, 87,
    93, 100, 257; on the causes of war 48,
    50–51
Hrzywarn, Pfc John 15
Hume, Basil, Cardinal-Archbishop of
    Westminster 31
Humphrey, Major Vernon 218–19
Humphrey, Nicholas 34
Huntington, Samuel P. 7
Hutchinson Committee (1905) 149
hysterical reactions among soldiers 184

ideology 45, 207–12
Indo-China wars 82–4; see also Vietnam
    war
infantry: battalions 90–1, 93; combat
    vehicles 127; defensive positions 181–3;
    French 147; modern role of 169; physical
    fatigue 181–2; role-specific 180; weapons
    100–1; women in 221
information technology 265–7, 272–4
infra-red night fighting aids 178
Ingraham, Lawrence 188
initiation tests 216, 218
intelligence, strategic 274
intervention, military 86–7
Iraq 2, 81, 176
Islamic fundamentalism 45–6, 47
Israeli army: Arab-Israeli wars 51,
    81–3; headquarters organisation 274–5;
    and the intifada 290; numbers killed and
    wounded 185; officers 249, 250, 278–9;
    psychiatric casualties 185, 186, 187; and
    surprise attacks 151–2; tank development
    124; women in, 224; see also Lebanon
    war; Yom Kippur war

Janowitz, Morris 192, 208, 226, 228, 234
Japan 192; Russo-Japanese war 75;
    samurai tradition 224; Second World
    War generals 257–8
Jena, battle of (1806) 69, 150
Joffre, J.J.C. 278, 279
Johnson, Major-General Dudley 279–80
Johnson, Samuel 103
Joint Service Target Attack Radar
    System 179
Jolly, Ruth 233–4
Jomini, General Henri 63–4, 69–71, 131
Jones, John 88
Jünger, Ernst 172, 215

Kahn, Herman 25–6
Kaldor, Mary 94–5
Keegan, John 52, 64, 181, 236, 244,
    251, 258, 259, 261, 280
Kellogg-Briand Pact (1928) 39
Kennedy, John F. 30
Kennedy, Paul 37
Kersh, Gerald 209
Khomeini, Ayatollah Ruholla 39–40
Khrushchev, Nikita 26
Killiekrankie, battle of (1689) 259
killing see casualties; death
kinetic energy weapons 124
Kiowa warriors 224
Kipling, Rudyard 4, 215, 224
Kissinger, Henry 25
Kitchener, H.H., 1st Earl, 84, 85,
    102, 247, 281
Kitson, General Sir Frank 61, 243, 244,
    250–1, 256
Koerner, General Emil 228
Kohl, Helmut 51
Königgrätz, battle of 260, 261
Korean War, 12, 25, 61, 62, 122; age of
    combat soldiers 162; Chinese entry into
    152; and conscription 199; differing
    psychological attitudes 166; and group
    cohesion 217; numbers killed and
    wounded 185; psychiatric casualties 185

L'Etang, Dr Hugh 280–1
Laffargue, Captain André 102
language, military 223
Lansdown, battle of (1643) 155
Lao Tsu 239
Larrey, Baron 239
Lasswell, Harold D. 228
latent ideology 208, 209
Latin America 82, 192, 227, 228, 256
Lawrence, T.E. 14, 82
Lawson, Major Algy 149
leadership 151, 154, 232; see also
    commanders
League of Nations 40, 42–3
Lebanon war (1982) 124, 125–6, 157, 203
Lenin, V.I. 124
Leopard (West German tank) 124, 136
Leviathan (Hobbes) 54
Lewis, C.S. 44
Lewy, Guenther 201
Libya, US air raid on 265
Liddell Hart, Basil 48, 72, 78–9, 111
Lieber, Francis 40, 41
life expectancy 164
limited war 55–6
Lind, William 113
Lindsay, Sir Martin 276
literature 44, 215

Little, Roger 162
Lloyd George, David 89
logistics of war 86–91
long wars 56
Loos, Battle of (1916) 154, 259
Lorenz, Konrad 159
Lot, Ferdinand 119
Low Intensity Operations (Kitson) 61
low-intensity operations 56–7, 293
luck, role of: in battle 154–7; in
    peacetime careers 242
Ludendorff, Erich von 77, 105, 276
Luttwak, Edward 47, 58, 59, 60
Lützen, battle of (1632) 259–60
Lyndon, Barry 67

MacArthur, General Douglas 61, 62,
    93, 117
Macdonell, Colonel James 155
Machiavelli, Niccolò 48, 158
machine guns 88
macho men 223–4
Mackenzie, Brigadier Jeremy 151
MacMahon, Marshal 284
malaria casualties 187
Malayan campaign (1948–60) 83–4
Malplaquet, battle of 3, 67
Manchester, William 15, 156, 169
Manning, Frederick 188
manoeuvre warfare 111–22, 128, 141;
    and attrition 156; and British military
    doctrine 137; criticisms of 138–9;
    and defensive positions 181, 182–3;
    importance of leadership 151; and US
    military doctrine 131, 132; and the Yom
    Kippur war 126
manpower shortages 7, 220, 289;
    present-day military services 220
Manstein, Field Marshal Erich von
    116, 257, 270, 275, 282
Mantell, D.M. 213, 223
Mao Tse-tung 82
Marks, Thomas Penrose 168
Marlborough, John Churchill, Duke of 67
marriages, military 222
Marshall, S.L.A. 35, 63, 217, 264, 268,
    269
Marx, Karl, 69, 80
Maslowski, Peter 197
McDonald, Dwight 37
McGuinness, Lance-Sergeant Tam 178
MccGwire, Michael 31
McNamara, Robert S. 26–7, 31
Mearsheimer, John J. 35
Mechanised Infantry Combat Vehicles
    (MICVs) 91, 127, 169, 181
medieval Europe 192
mercenaries 193, 194, 215

Mercer, Captain Cavalié 183
Metternich, Prince 69
Meyer, General Edward C. 132, 158
mid-intensity operations 57–8
Middle Ages 65–6, 119
Middle East: and chemical weapons 176
midwives 225
Military Incompetence (Gabriel) 202
military service *see* conscription
military strategy 59
Millett, Allan 197
mines 125
mission analysis 271–2
Mitchell, Billy 256, 257
Moltke, Helmuth 29, 75, 277
Moltke, Helmuth, Count von 72–4, 80,
    130, 153, 155, 244, 261, 275, 276
Montague, C.E. 166, 177
Montgomery, Bernard Law, 1st Viscount
    111, 123, 158, 244, 261, 267, 275, 276
moral component: of fighting power
    158
Moran, Lord 156
Morgan, Allen 200–1
Morpeth, Major Lord 231–2
Moskos, Charles 193–4, 207–8, 226, 230,
    245
motor rifle divisions, Soviet 107
mud, impact of: in manoeuvre warfare 118
Muir, Richard 55
Multan, siege of (325 BC) 259
Multi-Launch Rocket Systems 124
Mumford, Lewis 66
Murat, Joachim, 262
Murray, Archie 248, 276
mutual assured destruction (MAD) 27

Napoleon Bonaparte, Emperor 130, 151,
    155, 158, 239, 261, 262, 264, 275, 280
Napoleon III, Emperor 73, 206
Napoleonic wars 156, 201, 262
National Guard (United States) 199
'Nationalist Revival' movement 75
NATO (North Atlantic Treaty
    Organisation): and chemical warfare 175;
    command at operational level 59; future
    of 287–8, 291; and imbalances in combat
    power 157; military doctrine 133–6;
    modernisation of nuclear forces 233; and
    non-provocative defence 139;
    and Soviet military doctrine 130, 131;
    and surprise attacks 151
natural disasters 165, 188, 215
NBC warfare (nuclear, bacteriological
    and chemical weapons) 173–6
NCOs (non-commissioned officers) 252,
    255, 256
needle-guns 153

Neubach, Ernst 17
Nevill, Captain W.P. 160
Nevsky, Alexander 210
New Guinea 158
Neznamov, A.A. 76
Niepold, Lieutenant-General Gerd 252
night operations 176–9
night-fighting aids 178
Nivelle, General Robert 104, 258
No More Heroes (Gabriel) 170
Northern Ireland 231
novelists, and future war 96, 286–7
nuclear war/weapons 22–36, 293–4;
    anti-nuclear movement 52; balanced
    reductions in 287; and the causes of war
    50–1; estimates of casualties 33–4; and
    Fuel Air Explosives 125; and highly
    lethal conventional weapons 170–1; and
    non-provocative defence 139; public
    attitudes to 4, 23; Soviet 106; and
    Soviet military doctrine 130, 131; and
    US military doctrine 133; and the
    Vietnam war 56; and the Yom Kippur
    war 126
'Nuclear Winter' theory 33, 287
number of forces: and combat power 145
Nuremberg trials 40–1

O'Brien, Tim 200
O'Connell, Morgan 188
O'Neill, Robert 5
Obizzi, Lodovico degli 158
observation forces 293
officers: British army 213, 234–5, 244,
    254–6; in the *Bundeswehr* 232, 233;
    career structure of senior officers 240–58;
    casualties 204–5; Chinese army 212;
    fragging of 201–2; length of tours of
    duty 243; German army 213–14; Nazi
    party members 212–13; officer-soldier
    ratios 243; rank inflation 243–5; Second
    World War 204–5; Soviet army 107–8,
    211, 235; staff systems 148–50, 242–3;
    training of senior officers 283–4; United
    States Army 229, 230, 234, 235–6;
    Vietnam war 204, 205; with unpopular
    views 256–7; *see also* commanders
Old Testament: teachings on war and
    killing 38–9
Oliver, Polly 219
Oman, Sir Charles 65–6
OMGs (Operational Manoeuvre Groups),
    Soviet 129–30
operational surprise 152
opinion polls: on German unification 51;
    on nuclear war 23
Orwell, George 44, 162, 227
Othello (Shakespeare) 11

pacifism 37–8
Page, Tim 214
Palmer, General Dave 267–8
Panama, US invasion of 86, 221, 274
Parachute Field Ambulance 203
parachute units 254–5
parental attitudes 213–14
Paret, Peter 21, 72
Parrish, John 200
Pascal, Blaise 42
patriotism 207, 210
Patton, George Smith 15, 61, 117, 131,
    160
pay 194, 215, 246, 288–9; in the British
    army 231; of officers 250–1, 255–6; in
    the United States Army 230
peace settlements: negotiated versus
    imposed 55
peacekeeping forces 293
Pearl Harbor, Japanese attack on 199
Pershing, J.J. 'Black Jack' 246
Petain, Marshal 279
Peters, Lieutenant-Colonel John E. 134
photography 214, 274
physical component: of fighting power
    157, 169, 183, 219; women soldiers
    221
physical fatigue: in battle 181–2;
    senior officers 276
Piggott, Second Lieutenant Gerald
    Wellesley 14
Platoon (film) 214
Pliny the Elder 167
Plumer, Herbert Charles Onslow,
    1st Baron 156
Plunkett, Tom 201
Poland: and German unification 51
political education: in the Soviet
    army 211–12
pregancies: among women soldiers
    221
promotion: British army 255–6; senior
    officers 241–7, 252–3
prostitutes 223
Prussian army: bureaucratic absolutism
    in 150; conscription 195, 196; health of
    soldiers 166; officer corps 248–9; tribal
    ritual 163; uniforms 253–4; *see also*
    German army
psychiatric casualties 183–9, 218, 276–7,
    289
psychology: barriers to women soldiers
    222; explanations of war 48–9
PTSD (Post-Traumatic Stress Disorder)
    187–8
public attitudes: to military operations
    290–1; to nuclear weapons 4; to soldiers
    4

INDEX

Quakers 203
Quesada, General Pete 276

radar systems 179
radio operators, women as 220, 225–6
radios 91, 270
RAF (Royal Air Force) 221, 244
railways, adaptation to military use 89
Rambo (film) 214
rape 224
Ravenna, battle of (1512) 158
Reagan, Ronald 28
recoilless guns 124
recruitment: reasons for enlisting 193–4;
    United States Army 229–31; volunteers
    197–8, 204–5; and women soldiers
    225–6; *see also* conscription
religion 165; and military attitudes 208–9
reports 252
Retz, Cardinal de 42
revolutionary wars 56–7
rifles, automatic 90
ritual 166; military 163–4; ritualised
    combat 158–61
Roberts, Sir Frederick 247
Robertson, Field Marshal Sir William
    100
robotic battlefields 141
robotic mines 125
Rogers, General Bernard 32
Rolbant, Samuel 219
Roman Catholic Church: and nuclear
    weapons 31
Rome, ancient 55, 194
Roosevelt, Franklin D. 199
Root, Elihu 149
Rosenberg, Hans 150
Roskill, Captain Stephen 100
Royal Air Force (RAF) 221, 244
Royal Armoured Corps 100
Royal Navy 196, 221, 244
Royal Tank Regiment 96
royalty, and the army 191
Russell, W.H. 66–5
Russo–Japanese War 76, 102

Sagan, Carl 33
Sajer, Guy, 17
salaries *see* pay
Sandrart, General Hans-Henning von 136
Santos, Lieutenant Robert 224
Satanic Verses, The (Rushdie) 160
Saxe, Maurice de 67, 193
Schall, James 44
Schelling, Thomas 26
Schlieffen, Count Alfred von 74–5, 89,
    99, 115, 130
Schmaling, Admiral Elmar 46

Scholtes, Major-General Richard 128
Second World War: Anglo-French alliance
    85; attrition warfare 109–11;
    commanders 278, 279–80; conscientious
    objectors 202–3; and conscription 198–9;
    deaths 15, 204–5; endurance of soldiers
    169; German army officers 257; and
    the German General Staff 150; German
    invasion of Russia 80–1; hard physical
    labour 183; importance of ideology
    209–10; Italian campaign, denial of
    danger 163; lethal weapons used 170–1;
    logistics 88–9; Maginot Line 181; and
    military doctrine 146; night operations
    177; Normandy landings 186; number of
    combat days 186; psychiatric casualties
    183, 184, 185, 186, 218; role of ideology
    209–10; role of luck 156; settlement 54;
    sleep loss 177; and Soviet military
    doctrine 148; surprise attacks 151; and
    underfunded defence 20; and the United
    States Army 230; war crimes trials 41–2;
    women soldiers 219
Selective Service System (United States)
    198–9
sexuality among soldiers 223–5
Seyle's General Adaptation Syndrome 186
Shakespeare, William: *Macbeth* 286;
    Othello 11
Shapton, Sam 168
shell shock 184
Shephard, Sergeant-Major Ernest 64, 168,
    173
Sherman, William 267
Shils, Edward 192, 208
Shomron, General Dan 203
short wars 56
Showers, Lieutenant St George Swaine
    13–14
Shultz, George 176
Sickengen, Franz von 119
signallers, women as 220
Simonyan, Soviet General Rair 32
Simpkin, Richard 79–80, 173–4
Singapore 143
Singer, David 50
sleep loss 177–8, 179, 280
Sleeping with Soldiers (Daniell) 223
Slim, Field Marshal Lord 257–8
Small, Melvin 50
Smith-Dorrien, Sir Horace 281
Smoke, Richard 29
Sobczynski, Sergeant 18
soccer supporters, behaviour of 216–17
social class: and attitudes to war 203,
    207; and volunteers 212–13
Soldier, His Prayer, A (Kersh) 209
soldiers: age of combat soldiers 162;

339

soldiers (Cont.)
  endurance 168–70; and moral choice
  43; origin of word 193; physical
  requirements 166–8; psychological
  demands 164–6
Somervell, Major-General Brehon B. 110
Soult, Marshal 145
South America *see* Latin America
Soviet army: artillery 183; combat
  power 145; drills 111–12; fragging 202;
  general staff system 148; and glasnost
  250; impenetrability of tank armour 157;
  inexperience of present-day 240; infantry
  combat vehicles 127; and manoeuvre
  warfare 126; and mechanisation 79–80;
  military doctrine 95, 105–8, 128–31,
  140, 148; military executions 210;
  officers 214, 235, 250; political education
  211–12; psychiatric casualties 184; role
  of ideology 210; in the Second World
  War 15, 80–1, 89, 122; and state
  control 227; surprise attacks 151, 153;
  tank development 123; training 217, 218;
  women in 219–20
Soviet Union: changing Western attitudes
  to 160; chemical warfare capability
  175; and Civil Defence 32–3; deaths in
  the Second World War 15; defence
  expenditure 1–2, 92; defence policy 140;
  and *glasnost* 46–7; influence of pre-service
  military training 213; nationalism and
  Islam 46
Spanish Armada 195
Spanish Civil War 162–3, 214, 219
sport, and war 160–1
staff officer systems 148–50, 242–3
Stalin, Joseph 79, 80, 152, 210, 256
Starry, General Donn 132, 251, 253, 274
Steinmetz, General von 73
Stiehm, Judith Hicks 222
Stockhausen, Karlheinz 23
Stoessinger, John G. 29–30, 55, 81
Stone, Norman 47
Stone, Oliver 214
Strategic Arms Limitation Talks 27
Strategic Defense Initiative (Star Wars)
  28–9, 288
strategic intelligence 274
strategic surprise 152
strategic 58–9, 60–3, 70
stress 170–3; commanders 276–8; and night
  operations 179; psychiatric casualties
  183–9, 218, 276–7
Stumme, General 260, 280
Suarez, Francisco 40
Sun Tsu 66, 111
*Supplying War: Logistics from Wallenstein
  to Patton* (van Creveld) 86

surprise attacks 151–3; NBC warfare 174
Surtees, R.S. 161
Surveillance and Target Acquisition
  Systems 125
Suvorov, A.V. 210, 279
Suvorov, Viktor 211
Swinton, Sir Ernest 273

tactical command 260
tactical surprise 152
tactics 59–60
talismans 163
tanks 78–9, 91, 96, 100, 122–4, 153;
  Soviet 107; in the Yom Kippur War 103
target acquisition systems 171
Taufflieb, General Emile 201
Taylor, A.J.P. 50
Taylor, Brigadier George 269
Taylor, Telford 40–1
technology, military 92–7, 141, 153–4,
  157, 227; and women soldiers 222
telescopes, directed 261
television 165
Terminally-Guided Sub-Munitions 124–5
terrain, importance of: in manoeuvre
  warfare 115–17
terrorism 57, 166, 219, 286, 290
Thirty Years War (1618–48) 3, 57, 259–60
Thomas, Leslie 197
Thorne, Lieutenant-Colonel Andrew
  276–7
Threads 24
tiredness *see* physical fatigue; sleep loss
Todd, Emmanuel 206
Tolkien, John Ronald 12
Tolstoy, Leo 96
'Tommy' (Kipling) 4
Townshend, Charles 278
training, military 217–19, 283–4
transparent battlefield 179
Travers, Tim 64
Trevelyan, Lieutenant Raleigh 163
Triandifillov, V.K. 79
tribalism/tribal ritual 158–9, 163, 192
Trochu, General L.J. 256, 257
Truscott, Lucian 223
M.N. Tuchachevskii, Marshal 79–80
Tumbledown (film) 231
Tuten, Jeff 222
Two Marshals, The (Guedalla) 13

Uccello, Paolo 65
Ugandan National Resistance Army 162
uniforms 289; British army officers 149;
  Bundeswehr 232; Prussian army 249,
  253–4
United States: attitudes to war 23, 204,
  205; and *Auftragstaktik* 272; defence

INDEX

expenditure 1; estimates of nuclear war casualties 33–4; military doctrine 131–5, 140; military reform debate 7; *see also* American Civil War; Korean War; Vietnam War

United States Army: age of commanders 279; Combat Aviation Brigades 138; combat power 236; conditions of service 246; conscription 197–201; and deaths in battle 209; general staff system 149; Joint Surveillance Target Attack Radar System 134; manpower shortages 220; National Training Center 268–9, 283–4; observer force 293; officers 214, 235–6, 244; and the operational level of war 61; overcommanding 251; peacetime careers 242–3; present difficulties 229–31; promotion system 253; psychiatric casualties 184–5, 186–7; rank inflation 245; *Sergeant York* air-defence gun 95; service wives 234; tank development 122–3; women in 221, 222, 225

Unterseher, Lutz 140

Vaughan, Lieutenant Edward Campion 163

Versailles, Treaty of 52, 55, 150

Victorian England: attitude to army 196

Vietnam war 42, 56, 61, 83–4, 123, 224, 232; accidental killings 156; age of combat soldiers 162; attitudes to 166, 213, 290; combat photography 214; commanders 267–8, 270; and conscription 199–201; criticism of US failure 243; films of 214–15; and fragging 201–2; and group cohesion 218; hard physical labour 183; helicopters 88; moral factors 153; numbers killed and wounded 185; psychiatric casualties 185, 186–7, 187–8; and sportsmen 160; and talismans 163; training of troops 219; and US military doctrine 131–2; veterans 210–11; volunteers 204

Vigny, Alfred de 190, 193, 194, 213, 216, 238, 259

Vitalis, Oderic 55

volunteers for military service 204–5

Walker, Air Vice Marshal John 134

Waller, Sir William 277

War and Peace (Tolstoy) 98

war crimes 41–2

War of the Worlds (Wells) 98

Wars of the Roses 161

Waterloo, battle of 118, 120, 155, 260–1, 280

waterways 116

Waugh, Auberon 197

WAVELL (information system) 265–6

Wayne, John 214

weather, impact of: in manoeuvre warfare 118

Webb, James 268

Webber, Lieutenant Henry 162

Weinberger, Caspar 230

Welch, Major-General J.A. 266–7

Wellington, Arthur Wellesley, 1st Duke of 68, 100, 155, 259, 263, 280, 282

Wells, Donald 40

Wells, H.G. 98

West Germany: American attitudes to defending 204; British armoured divisions in 136–7; and non-provocative defence 139; officer-soldier ratio 244; tank development 124; and US military doctrine 133; *see also Bundeswehr*; Germany

Western Way of War, The (Hanson) 8

Westmorland, General William C. 171

When the Wind Blows 24

Whitehead, Brigadier Andrew 164

Wickham, General John A. 170

Wilson, Sir Henry 247–8

Winter, J.M. 14, 207

Wintringham, Tom 119

wives of servicemen 233–4

Wolfe, James 224, 244

Wolff, Christa 23

Wolseley, Sir Garnet 247

women 219–26; wives of servicemen 233–4

World Wars *see* First World War; Second World War

Worner, Manfred 133

Wright, Quincy 50

Xenophon 158

Yamashita, Lieutenant-General Tomokjuki 'Tiger of Malaya' 41

Yasotay, Colonel 235, 253

Yemen Arab Republic 143

Yom Kippur war 102–3, 125, 126–7, 178, 183, 185, 249

Zagonara, battle of (1423) 158

Zhukov, G.K. 106

Zugbach, R.G.L. von 234–5, 252–3, 254

341